PATRIA: Puerto Rican Revolutionary Exiles
in Late Nineteenth Century New York

PATRIA: Puerto Rican Revolutionary Exiles in Late Nineteenth Century New York

Edgardo Meléndez

Centro Press

Library of Congress Cataloging—in-Publication Data
Names: Meléndez, Edgardo, author.
Title: Patria : Puerto Rican revolutionary exiles in late nineteenth century New York / Edgardo Meléndez.
Description: New York, NY : Centro Press, [2019] | Includes bibliographical references and index.
Identifiers: LCCN 2018052581 (print) | LCCN 2018060775 (ebook) | ISBN 9781945662294 (ebook) | ISBN 9781945662287 (pbk. : alk. paper)
Subjects: LCSH: Puerto Ricans--Press coverage--New York (State)--New York--History--19th century--Sources. | Patria (New York, N.Y.) | Exiles--New York (State)--New York--History--19th century--Sources. | Puerto Ricans--Political activity--New York (State)--New York--Sources. | Cuban newspapers--New York (State)--New York--Sources. | Puerto Rico--History--Autonomy and independence movements--Sources. | Revolutionaries--New York (State)--New York--History--19th century--Sources. | Puerto Ricans--New York (State)--New York--Social life and customs--19th century--Sources. | Cubans--New York (State)--New York--Social life and customs--19th century--Sources.
Classification: LCC F128.9.P85 (ebook) | LCC F128.9.P85 M45 2019 (print) | DDC 974.7/03--dc23
LC record available at https://lccn.loc.gov/2018052581
Printed in the United States of America

Centro Press
Center for Puerto Rican Studies
Hunter College, CUNY
695 Park Avenue, E-1429
New York, NY 10065
centrops@hunter.cuny.edu
http://centropr.hunter.cuny.edu

A las aladas almas de las rosas
del almendro de nata te requiero,
que tenemos que hablar de muchas cosas,
compañero del alma, compañero.
Miguel Hernández, *Elegía*

To the memory of my dear friend Jaime Vélez, who loved this book so much.

PREFACE

In 1992 the Cuban people, along with many Puerto Ricans, commemorated the 100th Anniversary of the founding of the Cuban Revolutionary Party (CRP). The CRP, a political organization established by Cuba's national hero José Martí, led the Cuban struggle against Spanish colonialism in the largest of the Greater Antilles. That same year, in order to channel the struggle of Cuban separatists in the United States, Martí founded the newspaper *Patria*, the main organizational force and voice of the exile community. The most memorable writings of Martí are found in the pages of *Patria*. The newspaper also presented important events in Puerto Rico's struggle for independence from Spain, as well as articles on Puerto Rico and writings by some of the most distinguished Puerto Ricans of the time, including Ramón Emeterio Betances, Eugenio María de Hostos, Sotero Figueroa, Pachín Marín, and Lola Rodríguez de Tío, among others.

The presence of Puerto Rico in *Patria* reflected revolutionary Cuba's commitment, especially Martí's, to Puerto Rico's independence. For Martí, the independence of Puerto Rico was an important ideal of the CRP, as it was expressed as part of the party's *Bases* or platform In 1895, the Puerto Rico Section (PRS) of the CRP was created to encourage independence for the smallest of the Greater Antilles. Likewise, the participation and inclusion of Puerto Ricans in *Patria and* the CRP showed their dedication to the Cuban cause. Betances, by Martí's request, represented the CRP in Paris, where there was a large and influential Cuban émigré community. Sotero Figueroa was the director of *Patria* and was one of Martí's chief collaborators within the party and the newspaper. *Patria* and the CRP reflected the vision of Martí, Betances, Hostos and the other great leaders of the independence movement of the 19th century to unite the Caribbean peoples' struggle for liberation, especially Cuba's and Puerto Rico's. The events following the Spanish-American War of 1898 separated the destinies of Spain's last standing colonies in the Americas.

Part II of this book gathers the main writings on Puerto Rico that appear in *Patria*. The majority of them were written by Puerto Ricans of stature such as Betances, Hostos, Figueroa, Marín, and by Martí himself. Most of these writings have not been previously published in Spanish or English and are important documents that help us understand Puerto Rico's history and Puerto Rican political ideologies and politics of the time, specifically that of the separatist movement. By reading these texts, one is able to study a variety of important matters that help us understand the Antillean politics of the late 19th century. These include the role of *Patria* in Cuba and Puerto Rico's fight for independence; the sense of Antillean identity in Cuba and Puerto Rico's revolutionaries; Martí's vertical commitment to the cause of independence for Puerto Rico and how the CRP abandoned this cause after his death; the role of Puerto Ricans in *Patria* and the CRP; the relationship between the CRP and the Puerto Rico Section (PRS); the planning of Puerto Rico's independence in the

19th century; the PRS and the Puerto Rican community in New York; the tensions within the CRP and the PRS between those that fought for an independent republic and those that sought the annexation of Cuba and Puerto Rico to the United States; the role of the PRS and the CRP in the United States' invasion of Cuba and Puerto Rico; and the protection of Martí's legacy by Cubans and Puerto Ricans.

I have chosen to arrange these documents by subject matter (independence of Puerto Rico, the CRP, the Cuban War, patriots, etc.) because it facilitates the presentation and reading of the texts, as well as the historical analysis of the events and debates published throughout the newspaper. The documentary section of the book is divided into five subjects: the CRP, the independence of Puerto Rico, Puerto Rico's place in Martí's thought, the protection of Martí's legacy by Puerto Ricans, the different publications by well-known Puerto Rican figures in the newspaper, and articles and events related to the Cuban war as well as its impact on Puerto Rico and the Puerto Rican separatists.

The first two chapters of Part I of the book seek to provide a historical context and background so that readers can better comprehend the documents section presented in Part II. It analyzes several important topics in this regard like the links between Puerto Rican and Cuban separatists in the nineteenth century; the role of *Patria* and the CRP within the Antillean separatist movement; the presence of a Puerto Rican nationalist discourse in the pages of *Patria* and the attempt to construct a new and counter balancing narrative of Puerto Rico's history in opposition to the dominant version on the island; and the role played by Puerto Ricans in *Patria* and the CRP. Chapter 3 provides a historical background to the formation and evolution of the Cuban and Puerto Rican communities in New York City during the nineteenth century. This chapter should also provide a background to the events, ideas, and writings presented in other parts of the book. Chapter 4 takes a look at the exile community –particularly at the Puerto Rican one-using the news and writings published in *Patria*. The newspaper was not only a means of propaganda and education, it was also used as a means of communication, of sharing news and ads related to the daily lives of Cubans and Puerto Ricans in New York City. It provides a window into the exile community at that time.

.....

The documents presented in Part II of this book do not gather all of the texts on Puerto Rico that appear in *Patria*, although it does gather the majority of them. The articles that are published here are those that reflect the topics and events that I consider the most important in understanding *Patria*'s main purpose, the role of Puerto Ricans in the newspaper, as well as the party. I left out many news items, announcements, and articles of minor relevance to facilitate the presentation. Some of the texts that are presented here had already been published in Spanish. Most of Martí's writings have appeared in several publications, including one that is specifically about his writings on Puerto Rico. Likewise, the writings of Sotero Figueroa "La verdad de la historia" have also already been published.

The overwhelming majority of the texts presented in Part II are published in English here for the first time. This, I think, is a major contribution of this book: to allow English speakers to have access to this voluminous amount of information and primary texts so important for Cuban and Puerto Rican history, as well as for the understanding of the Cuban and Puerto Rican community in New York City by the end of the nineteenth century. Even the majority of Martí's texts presented in this book are for the first time published in the English language. Most of Martí's writings that have been translated into English –and he is by far the best known author presented in this book- are in the area of literature and poetry, with some of this political writings also available in English.

A large part of the initial investigation was carried out in New York City while I served as Visiting Professor at Lehman College (City University of New York) during the 1989-90 academic year. I was then a faculty member of the Department of Political Science at the University of Puerto Rico in Río Piedras. Collecting the texts then was an arduous task. The microfiches were not of the highest quality, and I therefore had to look through several copies. Only one complete copy of the newspaper existed in the United States, at Columbia University's library in New York. I used the Columbia library's microfiches and also a copy belonging to the Center for Puerto Rican Studies. During the summer of 1991, I had the opportunity to compare my copies with the original, which was not in good condition, at Cuba's National Library. The revised microfiches were apparently made from this original, which explains why some of the texts presented in the Spanish book were incomplete, since the original print of *Patria* was illegible. Most of the missing texts in the Spanish version have been included in this book thanks to the publication of the complete edition of *Patria* during the life of José Martí (1892-1895) by the *Centro de Estudios Martianos* (CEM) in Havana, Cuba. My heartfelt thanks to Alberto Hernández, director of Centro's Library and Archives, for allowing me to use his personal copy of this CEM cd. I would like to acknowledge the extraordinary work done by CEM that allows people like me to have not only access to but also a better understanding of the work and thought of José Martí. There are still a couple of instances where small parcels of text could not be reproduced due to illegibility in the original copies of *Patria* after 1895.

.....

My deepest gratitude to the Center for Puerto Rican Studies (Centro) at Hunter College of the City University of New York for publishing this book and allowing English speakers, particularly younger Puerto Ricans and Latinos, to have access to these valuable documents and gaining a new perspective of their presence in New York City. A special acknowledgement must be given to Xavier Totti, Centro's publications di-

rector, who shepherded this project since its inception and provided valuable sugges-
tions throughout. Also crucial to this book was the editorial work of Ryan Morgan, who
cleaned the introduction from my colonial English and also worked in editing the English documents in Part II, as well as on the new format for the book. I also thank Edwin
Meléndez, director of Centro, for supporting the publication of this book. A heartfelt
thanks to Paul Bendernagel and Jennifer Hinojosa at Centro's Data Center for creating
the intricate map featured here. An additional thanks to the New York Public Library
for distributing--under a Creative Commons Universal Public Domain Dedication--
the images used for our map. Xavier was able to get the University of Puerto Rico's
Graduate Program in Translation, then under the directorship of Dr. Aurora Lauzardo
Ugarte, to do the translation of the documents. Three students took upon the ardous
task as part of the M.A. thesis projects. My thanks to Melanie Kinch Pérez, Rebecca
Summer Burgos and Mark Gereghty, who engaged in the unenviable job of translating these wonderful texts from Spanish to English. This was no easy task, as anyone
engaged in translations can attest. The Spanish in these late nineteenth century texts
is quite different from the oral and written Spanish used nowadays, including that of
Cuba and Puerto Rico. Translating the writings of one of the best writers of the Spanish language such as José Martí, and others of similar caliber such as Sotero Figueroa,
requires not only an acute knowledge of both languages, but also the patience, commitment and skill that these translators surely had. All translations of texts not included in
the documents section in Part II were done by the author.

.....

One final word regarding the use of two Spanish words throughout the book: *patria* and *pueblo*. Translation is a hard job and one of the problems faced by the translator is using and applying meaning to a specific word as used over a century ago with
that of today's. Such is the problem we faced when translating the word *patria*. In
its most simple definition, *patria* translates into English as homeland, fatherland, nation, country. I have decided to keep the word *patria* in the English texts to preserve
the closest meaning of what these revolutionaries and thinkers were trying to convey,
to be as faithful as possible to the original text. This is particularly important in texts
by Martí. It is no coincidence that the newspaper was called *Patria,* as he discusses
in the very first issue. In very few occasions these authors used the word nation since
this was not a common notion then. The popular use of "nation-state" was also not in
vogue at the end of the nineteenth century. Of much less use for these revolutionaries
would be the word country, of quite superficial meaning with regards to their use of
patria. As freedom fighters seeking the independence of their two islands from Spanish colonialism, *patria* is very far away from the chauvinistic, male-oriented, and aggressive meaning of fatherland, particularly as used by imperialistic and expansive
nationalistic nation-states like Nazi Germany. Perhaps the closest translation would

be homeland, particularly as this word relates to diasporas hoping the go back to their ancestral land or exiles struggling to achieve the independence of their beloved native land. But again, the meaning of homeland nowadays has transformed into that of fatherland of earlier decades, as in the US Department of Homeland Security. But even in the most comforting meaning of the word, homeland does not really represent the meaning of *patria* for people like Martí and his closest followers: not only the territory and their people, defined by a specific culture, ideals, history and language, but also linked to a specific political project of equality for all and with all.

Similar concerns arise with the translation of *pueblo*. The translation into "people" in English perhaps does not carry all the problems that might arise with translating *patria*. The *pueblo* is the physical manifestation and soul of the *patria*. In the minds of these Cuban and Puerto Rican revolutionaries, it is the *pueblo* who has the inalienable right for independence, the right to construct their own *patria*. In this sense, it is a precursor of the idea of "the right of self-determination of peoples" that will dominate decolonizing discourse in the twentieth century and was introduced into world politics by the League of Nations after World War I. But again, I think that in keeping the original Spanish word *pueblo* we can remain as close as possible to the original meaning of the Spanish text.

Finally, one word that was indeed translated was "*las Antillas*" or the Antilles. But in no instance it was translated as "the Caribbean," since this is a more recent, more Americanized and Westernized notion of the region. The notion of "*el Caribe*" or the Caribbean was never used by these nineteenth century thinkers and revolutionaries. Martí, Betances, and Hostos, for example, proposed the *Confederación de las Antillas* not the Caribbean Confederation.

MAP

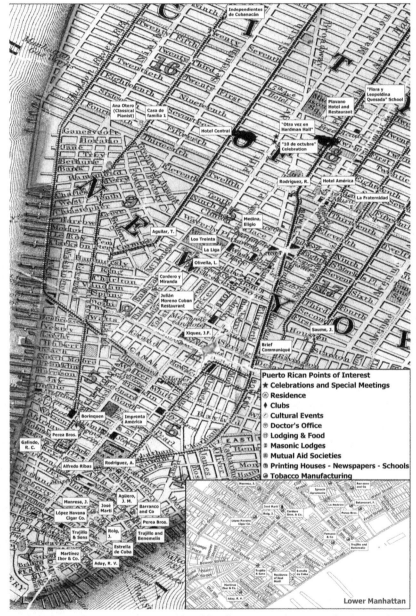

Paul Bendernagel, 2019. Source New York Public Library's Map Warper, under the Creative Commons Universal Public Domain.

PART 1

CHAPTER 1

"CUBA AND PUERTO RICO ARE THE TWO WINGS OF A BIRD...": THE CUBAN REVOLUTIONARY PARTY AND PUERTO RICO

For Cubans and Puerto Ricans, the year 1992 meant something more than just the 500th anniversary of Europe's "discovery" and colonization of America. That year also marked the 100th anniversary of the establishment of two institutions that are an essential part of Cuban and Antillean history: the Cuban Revolutionary Party (CRP) and the newspaper *Patria*. Both played a key role in organizing and leading Cuba's Second War of Independence (1895–1898), which ended for the Cuban people in the so-called "Spanish-American War" and the United States' invasion of Cuba and Puerto Rico. The political party and the newspaper were the brilliant creations of the great Cuban and Antillean patriot José Martí.

This chapter will examine the importance of Martí's work concerning the CRP, the connections between Cuba's and Puerto Rico's independence movements and their ideological basis in the nineteenth century, the creation and development of the Puerto Rico Section and its relationship with the Cuban Revolutionary Party, and the role of *Patria* in struggles against Spanish colonialism in the Caribbean.

José Martí and the CRP

The second War of Independence in Cuba was successful due to the organization and propaganda carried out for many years by the CRP and *Patria*. Through these institutions, Martí was able to achieve what no other leader in the ranks of Cuban separatism could: the unification of various sectors within "separatist Cuba." The internal divisions go back to the first Cuban War of Independence—the Ten Years' War (1868–1878)—and subsequent events like the Pact of Zanjón, the "little war," and the several invasion attempts by ex-military chiefs. Cuban separatism had political, social, and class divisions (Casasus 1953; Foner 1963; Poyo 1983, chs. 1–4).

After the end of the Ten Years' War, the Pact of Zanjón created even more divisions among the different groups of Cuban nationalists. These were divided between those who had made peace with Spain and those who desired to continue the war, and between conservative reformists and revolutionaries (mainly military). There were also differences among civilians and the military: the military accused civilians of subordinating the war to political interests, while the civilians accused the military of doing the opposite. Class and race influenced these divisions. Political leaders catered mostly to the white Cuban elite, while the army welcomed peasants, mulattoes, and blacks. The elite's reluctance to abolish slavery created great distrust among black Cubans. The more conservative groups maintained the ideal of annexing Cuba to the United States and advocated its insertion into the Cuban conflict. The more revolutionary groups were seeking independence by mobilizing the Cuban people in a war against Spain without foreign intervention (Armas 1975, 57–74; Ibarra 1981, ch. 2; Pérez 1983, ch. 1; Poyo 1983, ch. 5).

Scholars of this period insist that Martí's greatest achievement, an indication of his exceptional political and organizational capabilities, was the unification of the various sectors of "Cuba in exile." For him, the CRP represented *el exilio organizado* (the "organized exile community")—the revolutionary organization of all Cuban separatist sectors outside Cuba—with the sole purpose of obtaining independence for Cuba. He was able to convince the military chiefs to allow the party to plan the war. Máximo Gómez and Antonio Maceo's favorable reception of this proposition and of Martí himself is an indication of how effective his political activism was. He knew the war's execution had to be extremely well organized, of short duration, and with perfectly clear objectives. Failed attempts at insurrection in Cuba and poorly planned invasions had already demonstrated their irrelevance to the process of liberation. The party's role was to plan the war in Cuba from the outside, to obtain the support of Cubans in the island and in exile, and to give political direction to the conflict (Martí 1978).

After the Ten Years' War, the Cuban exile community consisted of three specific communities located in Florida, New York, and Paris. Each community represented a distinct social background. The tobacco sector in Florida included businessmen as well as merchants and tobacco workers. Even though there was a clear class demarcation (a tobacco strike in 1894 almost destroyed the CRP in Florida), these sectors were able to settle their differences and abide to a common objective: independence for Cuba. The majority of the Cuban exile's military organizations also settled in Florida.

In New York, there were mainly petty bourgeoisie Cubans, merchants, intellectuals, and a working class community that included a significant number of tobacco workers. Martí's political activity was based in New York. Cuba's bourgeoisie, mainly from the sugar cane industry, mostly settled in Paris and represented the conservative, reformist, and autonomist sector in exile. Martí's great political deed was to unify in a common program the various sectors in Florida and New York. The CRP was founded in Florida, under Martí's own initiative. *Patria*'s headquarters were in New York; Martí guided its publication and editorial content (Estrade 1984; Ibarra 1981, 138–48; Pérez 1978; 1983, 96–7; Poyo 1983, chs. 5–7).

The alliance of the different social and political groups that formed the Cuban exile community was possible thanks to Martí's organizational notion of respecting differences while bringing them together into a common cause. Cuban exiles, mainly in Florida and New York, were scattered into numerous organizations that represented several political, social, and racial groups. However, the organizational structure of the CRP was extremely simple but very effective. It was composed of various Cuban organizations in exile—clubs—that elected a regional structure (the Cuerpo de Consejo): the executive body of the CRP, the Delegate, and the Treasurer. The executive body of the party coordinated all the assignments of all the local organizations and enforced direction for the revolutionary and organizational mission of the party. Martí was overwhelmingly elected as delegate of the CRP.[1]

Several Cuban scholars have debated the nature of the CRP's ideology and program. Some of Martí's followers have indicated that, in its beginnings, the CRP embodied the ideology and program of its founder, and that once Martí died, his successors abandoned and transformed the party's *martiano* character (Quesada 1982). Others point out that Martí also competed with other ideologies and programs within the CRP without necessarily being dominant, and that after Martí died, the conflicts between other ideologies and programs that were fighting for control of the party increased (Llanos 1975, 231). Jorge Ibarra, on the other hand, recognizes that several sectors were competing to define the party's ideology and program, but suggests that Martí's ideology and program prevailed within the party while he was still alive. The main organizational and propaganda instrument of the CRP, the newspaper *Patria*, spread Martí's ideology and program throughout the Cuban exile community (Ibarra 1981, 158).

Martí, without a doubt, was the most illustrious Cuban thinker of his time. His ideas on independence for Cuba stretched beyond Cuba and even the Antilles. He considered the Cuban War of Independence necessary and just; it would free Cubans as well as Spaniards, the oppressed and the oppressors, from the opprobrium of colonialism. The detailed planning and short duration of the war would avoid unnecessary destruction of life and property. But such war could not be limited to gaining independence to later justify the substitution of one oppressing caste by another; it would be devoted instead to creating a more just and democratic society in the future Republic. Although Martí was not socialist, he did share some ideas with the socialist thought of the time. He believed, for example, that the oppression of one class over another and of one race over another was unjust, as was the domination of one nation over another. It was this vision of both social justice and a democratic republic that allowed Martí to attract several social groups into a common political bloc.[2]

Martí's death in Dos Ríos greatly affected the revolution's unity in Cuba. In great measure, it was he who brought about the unity and solidarity of the various groups within Cuban separatism. With his death, the old quarrels and differences reemerged. The three main institutions of Cuba en armas ("Cuba up in arms")—the army, the provisional government, and the CRP—came into conflict over how to lead the war and on political strategies, particularly regarding the United States' intervention in the war against Spain. Old disputes between the army and the provisional government, the "civilians" and the "military," and the white elite and working class were revived. The CRP's leadership had quarrels with the army and the provisional government.

The organizational structure and politics of the CRP suffered great changes after Martí's death. Tomás Estrada Palma, who represented the most conservative sector of the Cuban exile community and had annexationist leanings, replaced Martí as the Delegate of the CRP. During his leadership, autonomist bourgeois sectors, which had belatedly separated from the Spanish government because of the repression they had previously suffered in Cuba, joined the CRP. Estrada Palma, who later became the first president of the Cuban Republic under the US neocolonial regime that came along with the Platt Amendment, aimed to end the war through negotiation by specifically requesting the intervention of the United States, instead of winning it through armed struggle. The US intrusion in the Spanish-Cuban war became a goal to the CRP's efforts under Estrada Palma's leadership. He encouraged what Martí had tried to prevent: US presence in Cuba. By 1898, both the CRP and Patria were a far cry from what they were under Martí's leadership (Armas 1975, 75–83; Pérez 1983, 99–111, 188–93; True 1965, ch. 7; Preece 1976, chs. 3–5).

Many things changed in the CRP's ideology and program after Martí's death. Among them was Martí's commitment to the independence of Puerto Rico, which was not remembered well by many under the heat of the Cuban war in the manigua. Gonzalo de Quesada and Miranda, one of Martí's main followers, recognized Cuba's obligation to help achieve Puerto Rico's independence:

In this way, it is undeniable that the Cuban Revolutionary Party's second stage... presents a very different picture, sometimes even contradicting its first stage. And maybe this is, unfortunately, the best explanation as well as the cause for the noncompliance, in the Republic, of the principles stated by Martí in his famous revolutionary program. Maybe this is also the reason why the fervent desire of the Apostle, the written commitment in the bases of the Party that Puerto Rico equally obtain its freedom, was not fulfilled, and that we are still in debt with our Antillean sister. (Quesada 1982, 21)

Martí's commitment to Puerto Rico's independence was not based on a political opportunism of the moment: it responded to the historical tradition of Antillean revolution and to Martí's notion of the Antilles' role in America.

Cuba and Puerto Rico

The first article in the Bases (platform) of the Cuban Revolutionary Party establishes: "The Cuban Revolutionary Party is created to achieve the absolute independence for the island of Cuba and to aid and encourage that of Puerto Rico" (Bases del Partido Revolucionario Cubano 1892). Thus, the CRP's commitment to the independence of Puerto Rico was formalized in the very creation of the party. This commitment in the principal statutes of the CRP seems to be the work of Martí, although we cannot dismiss the solidarity that many Cuban leaders had with the sister island. Still, no other Cuban at that time stood out in his commitment to Puerto Rico and Puerto Ricans like José Martí. This commitment is deeply rooted in the historic tradition of Antillean solidarity, which was manifested in the idea of an Antillean confederation and in Martí's notion that true Latin American independence resided in the independence of the Antilles, Cuba, and Puerto Rico.

Outstanding Antillean leaders such as Martí, Ramón Emeterio Betances, Eugenio María de Hostos, Gregorio Luperón, and others professed the idea of joining the freedom struggles of the Spanish Antilles together. This plan finally came about formally in 1865, when Cubans and Puerto Ricans in New York established the Republican Society of Cuba and Puerto Rico. Although the Puerto Rican and Cuban uprisings of Lares and Yara in 1868 were not coordinated, when the Puerto Rican exploit failed, many Puerto Ricans went on to support the Cuban War of Independence through different means. Some of them, like General Juan Rius Rivera, fought bravely and became leaders in the Cuban battlefield. The correspondence between prominent Cubans and Puerto Ricans points towards a link between Cuban and Puerto Rican separatism in the last thirty years of the nineteenth century. Later, many Puerto Ricans became leaders within the CRP, among them Betances, Hostos, and Sotero Figueroa. Martí's commitment must have also become stronger because he kept close contact with Puerto Rican revolutionaries. Martí's friendship and ties with prominent Puerto Ricans, some of which were his main collaborators, are reflected in his biography. As shall be discussed later, this Cuban patriot surprised many with his incredible knowledge of Puerto Rico and its history.

The commitment of Cubans and Puerto Ricans to Antillean freedom became evident through the shared idea, held by their most outstanding patriots, of creating an Antillean confederation. Historically speaking, Betances and Hostos were among the first to propose the idea of an Antillean confederation, even before the uprisings in 1868. In 1865, the Republican Society of Cuba and Puerto Rico was already proposing the idea of an Antillean confederation. According to Carlos Rama, the relative weakness of Puerto Rican separatism in the nineteenth century led Puerto Rican leaders to promote the idea of an Antillean confederation (Rama 1980, 18). Once the uprising of Lares failed, and the Ten Years' War moved forward, it seemed logical to propose the idea that the Puerto Rican cause could advance if it was linked to the Cuban struggle and obtained the support of other Caribbean countries, such as the Dominican Republic.

But the idea of a Caribbean confederation entailed something more than a strategic stance in Antillean freedom struggles. It represented the notion that the Antilles formed a separate and distinct entity with its own racial, ethnic, cultural, and historical heritage. For Betances, Hostos, and Martí, the Antilles faced an historical challenge that joined them in a shared destiny: only united would they be able to confront the expansion of European and US imperialism. Betances clearly presented these ideas as early as 1870:

...Let us join together! It will be in vain that Spain tries to crush the insurrection in order to sell Cuba to the United States, which would be the beginning of the absorption of the entire Antilles by the Anglo-American race. Let us unite! Let us build a people, a people of true Freemasons, and we then shall raise a temple over foundations so solid that the forc-es of the Saxon and Spanish races will not shake it. We fight for Independence, and in its shadow we will engrave the inscription, as imperishable as the patria itself, which is dic-tated by our interest and our hearts, the most generous way of acting and the most selfish instinct of self-preservation: "The Antilles for the Antilleans." (Bonafoux 1987, 116)[3]

Only independence for the Antilles could guarantee the cultural, political, and economic self-determination of its people. For these three Antillean patriots, the an-nexation of Cuba and Puerto Rico to the United States would represent not only the subjugation of these two Antillean nations, but also the economic and political ab-sorption of the Antilles—and possibly that of Latin America—by the northern colos-sus. The independence of Puerto Rico and Cuba, and the Antilles in general, repre-sented for them a bulwark against US expansionism and imperialism, not only in the Caribbean and Americas, but also throughout the world. For these great Antilleans, Cuba and Puerto Rico's independence would guarantee political "balance" in the world. That is what Betances stated in 1874:

It is a grave error to appeal to the United States only in the development of the Antilles to serve as an American bastion, as a stronghold for the Union, instead of being, as its geo-graphic position suggests, a general center for relations between all peoples. It is clearly evident that the more interest there is by others in the development of its prosperity, the more powerful it will be and the more its tranquility will be respected. Given the rights to these islands to their own destiny, taking action in its defense would protect for each *pueblo*, American or European, their own interests. Cuba would then be the true pearl, the beloved pearl, caressed by the Caribbean Sea; its independence would be putting a halt to the selfish desires and utilitarian greed of the United States. It would serve as a base for the new Antillean nation, placed between Europe and Asia by the isthmus, almost of equal distance between both poles, as if destined to serve as a pillar for the equilibrium of the world [*destinada a servir de columna a la balanza del mundo*].[4]

In a similar way, Hostos defends Cuba's independence in 1896:

The United States, because of its force and power, is naturally a member of that oligarchy of nations. To be born under its aegis is to be born dependent of it: It is not convenient for Cuba, for the Antilles, for the Americas, for the future of Civilization, that Cuba and the Antilles have their weight on the side that will soon have more power in the world. It is convenient for all and everything that the noble Archipelago, making itself worthy of its destiny, be the true balance of the world [*el fiel de la balanza*]: neither North Ameri-can nor South American, but Antillean. That is our motto, and it shall be our purpose of struggle, for today's independence, as well as for tomorrow's freedom. (Roig de Leuch-senring 1974, 261)[5]

Martí shared Betances' and Hostos' notion that the Antilles should play the role of balance (*balanza*) in Latin American and world politics and contain the already evident expansionist impulses of the United States. He presented it in the extremely significant and transcendental article "El tercer año del Partido Revolucionario Cubano: el alma de la revolución y el deber de Cuba en América" ("The Third Year of the Cuban Revolutionary Party: The Soul of the Revolution and Cuba's Duty to the Americas"), published in *Patria* on April 17, 1894 (document no. 55):

At the center of the Americas [*en el fiel de las Américas*] are the Antilles, which, if enslaved, would merely be a military pontoon of an imperial republic against a jealous and superior world which is already preparing to deny them power—merely a small fort for the American Rome. If free—which they would be worthy of by freedom's just and laborious order—they would guarantee stability in this continent and independence for a yet threatened Spanish America. They would also guarantee honor for the great northern republic that in developing its territory—already having the misfortune of being feudal and distributed in hostile sectors—will find more greatness than with the shameful conquest of his smaller neighbors as well as the inhumane battles which would arise against world powers over the control of the entire world. It is not with a quick hand, but with timeless consciousness that the new life of the redeemed Antilles will be made up of... What we are balancing out is the world: we will not only liberate two islands... With such reverence, with confidence and compassion, the Cuban Revolutionary Party celebrates its third year in existence, convinced that the independence of Cuba and Puerto Rico is not only the means to insure a decent wellbeing for the free man through the just work of both islands' inhabitants, but also an essential historical event that will save the already free Antilles from the threat of losing their independence as well as the dignity of the North American republic. The weak-hearted, respect! The greathearted must go forward! This is a task for the big-hearted. (Martí 1894c)[6]

Martí clearly understood that independence for Puerto Rico was essential in guaranteeing independence for Cuba and, consequently, the independence of these Spanish colonies was crucial in guaranteeing independence for the Antilles. He clearly understood that by the twentieth century, the real danger for the Antilles and Cuba was not Spain, but the "colossus from the north." Only the independence of Cuba and Puerto Rico could stop US expansionism and guarantee independence for the Antilles and the Americas, as well as "equilibrium" of the world.

The reading of *Patria* and other similar documents of the time seems to indicate that not all the Cuban leadership shared the sense of urgency and significance that Martí bestowed upon the cause for Puerto Rico's independence. Even though the first article in the CRP's platform formally established Cuba's commitment to Puerto Rico's independence, not all members of the CRP shared that commitment. The CRP was made up of a multiplicity of Cuban separatist clubs whose political objectives and interests were diverse. However, Martí considered the CRP something more than just the sum of the various revolutionary clubs. He conceived it as an organization with superior principles and objectives, the independence of Puerto Rico among them. Ibrahim Hidalgo Paz, a Cuban historian, discusses this:

...the clubs that joined the Party had to help increase their own active funds and protect those assigned for the war; they had to convince all other revolutionary elements to work towards Cuba's freedom. They also had to "encourage and help achieve independence for Puerto Rico," a duty that bestowed a Latin American-Antillean character to the cause of freedom, but did not explicitly appear in any of the clubs' own regulations. We must point out that the goal of the majority of the associations was to raise funds and do other activities to *aide* and support the battles that would arise in the island, whereas the Party had a specific goal of *arranging* and *preparing* a liberating war and a revolution, which did not imply denying aide and support to whomever needed it. (Hidalgo Paz 1981, 212—emphasis in the original)

It was probably Martí who decided to include Puerto Rico's independence in the Platform as a commitment of the CRP. After all, he was the author of the Platform and Statutes of the CRP. But this commitment to the cause of independence for Puerto Rico was not as strongly shared by Martí's successors in the leadership of the CRP, as Estrada Palma's actions revealed.

The links between Cubans and Puerto Ricans were forged in different ways at the end of the century. Hundreds of Puerto Ricans participated in the wars of independence for Cuba and hundreds of others joined the CRP.[7] The Puerto Rico Section of the CRP was created in 1895 to achieve Martí's commitment to Puerto Rico's independence. But the disputes between Cubans and Puerto Ricans and among Puerto Ricans themselves with different political ideologies prevented Martí's, Hostos's, and Betances's dream of seeing Cuba and Puerto Rico joined hand in hand in independence.

The Puerto Rico Section of the Cuban Revolutionary Party
The Puerto Rico Section of the Cuban Revolutionary Party (PRS-CRP) was founded in New York City on December 22, 1895, once the war in Cuba had begun and after Martí's death. For the most idealist Cuban and Puerto Rican revolutionaries, the PRS was the materialization of the commitment made by the CRP in the first article of its platform. According to the most pragmatic Cubans, the PRS would serve as a spearhead in the war against Spain, and would therefore hasten their victory.[8] Likewise, the PRS represented the closest thing to a Puerto Rican independence party at the time. After the Lares uprising, Puerto Rican separatism was brutally suppressed in Puerto Rico, many former *independentistas* began to support autonomy, and the most devoted to the cause (including its best-known leadership) went into exile. Contrary to Cuba, Puerto Rican independence did not have a deeply rooted tradition in the island (as the Ten Years' War proved in Cuba), nor was it well organized in exile (its

most revered representatives, Betances and Hostos, remained far away in Europe and South America). The Puerto Rican independence movement in the late nineteenth century was relatively weak, both politically and organizationally.

This relative weakness of the Puerto Rican independence movement determined the PRS's political trajectory. Towards the end of the nineteenth century, the main political movement in Puerto Rico was autonomist and reformist, a political movement led by the Creole elite. This was a relatively weak class, which led them to reject more radical movements like independence.[9] Contrary to Cuba, Puerto Rican separatism could not convince the autonomist reformists to join their cause. Just like the Cuban movement, the Puerto Rican separatist movement was divided between those that sought a later annexation of the island to the United States and those that supported an independent republic, although the former did not have as much influence as those in Cuba. Being weakly organized in exile and not having solid support on the island, Puerto Rican separatism required foreign support to achieve its goal of political independence. This was the main factor that led Puerto Rican independentistas to create the PRS within the Cuban Revolutionary Party. [10]

The fact that the PRS was established during Estrada Palma's leadership of the CRP influenced the organization's development, specifically regarding the relationship between Puerto Ricans and Cubans, and also among Puerto Ricans themselves. Estrada Palma agreed with the petition of creating the PRS but suggested vehemently that José Julio Henna be designated as president of the organization (Partido Revolucionario Cubano–Sección Puerto Rico 1898, 4).[11] Henna, a well-known doctor with ties to the elite of New York City, was known for his conservative ideas and annexationist leanings; in other words, he resembled Estrada Palma very much. This decision had immediate repercussions in the organization. Bernardo Vega–the great chronicler of Puerto Rican life in New York City until 1950–recounts how the working class felt marginalized by the organization due to Henna's election and the presence of other conservative members (Vega 1977, 117–8).[12] In fact, the main Puerto Rican clubs in the CRP at the time–Borinquen and Dos Antillas–did not affiliate with the PRS; only some of its members did individually. From its foundation, the PRS reflected the divisions within Puerto Rican separatism by social class and politics (revolutionaries vs. conservatives, independence supporters vs. annexationists).

From its beginnings, the PRS tried unsuccessfully to launch a war in Puerto Rico and raise a second liberation front against Spain. This failure created conflicts between the PRS and the CRP and among Puerto Ricans within the PRS. Between 1896 and 1897, the PRS concentrated all of its organizational efforts in carrying out an invasion in Puerto Rico and beginning a war against Spain on the island. These failed plans, along with changes that took place in Cuba's war, created serious conflicts between PRS and CRP leaders. The frustration of not being able to carry out the invasion led the conservative leaders of the PRS to model themselves on their CRP counterparts and promote US intervention in Puerto Rico by early 1898. This action caused major conflicts with the most radical independentista faction of the PRS.

The PRS was associated with three invasion attempts in Puerto Rico during 1896 and 1897. The first attempt was linked to a plan under the name "Rius Rivera." The renowned Puerto Rican general of the Cuban army was detached by the CRP in March of 1896 to carry out an invasion in Puerto Rico. The general gave up on the plan after becoming aware of the lack of determination and organization for a revolution in Puerto Rico and decided that conditions were not favorable (PRC-SPR 1898, 72–89, 116–25, 195–216, 220). Rius Rivera returned to the manigua, where he succeeded Antonio Maceo, the "Bronze Titan," in the Cuban revolutionary army. This failed mission—under the command of an important Puerto Rican military leader of the time—showed the island's organizational incapacity for an uprising. Furthermore, this made Estrada Palma and other CRP leaders lack confidence in the PRS's ability to extend the war to Puerto Rico, creating more distance between the CRP Delegate and the PRS's objectives.

A second attempt to carry out an invasion in Puerto Rico was the so-called "Plan Morales," devised by the Dominican general Agustín F. Morales. Together with Antonio Mattei Lluveras, a Puerto Rican separatist, he had scrutinized the Spanish military forces in Puerto Rico and prepared a plan detailing the necessary weapons, tactics, and troops to launch an invasion of the island. The PRS leaders approved Morales's plan, but Estrada Palma refused to provide the funds or resources for its execution. The conflicts between the PRS and CRP worsened when the PRS leadership, with the opposition of Sotero Figueroa and Juan de la Matta Terreforte, approved a vote of no confidence against Estrada Palma (PRC-SPR 1898, 72–89, 116–125, 195–216, 220). Estrada Palma's lack of confidence in the PRS increased with the failure of the Yauco uprising, which took place on March 24, 1897 (reported on *Patria*, see documents no. 81 and 82). Even though only a few people related to the PRS participated in this event and the PRS was not officially linked to it, the failed "attempted coup" was seen by the Delegate as one more failure for the PRS and Puerto Rican rebels.

The last attempt to organize an uprising in Puerto Rico was the so-called "Lacret Morlot Plan." On August 13, 1897, the Council of the Republic of Cuba approved an invasion plan, prepared by the Cuban general José Lacret Morlot, which stipulated the assignment of funds and soldiers from the Cuban army. Estrada Palma objected to this plan and refused to offer any funds or support. Factions within the Cuban army, including General Calixto García, who favored independence for Puerto Rico, also opposed the plan. Later on, the provisional government's House of Representatives in Cuba put an end to this project (PRC-SPR 1898, 88–97; Bonafoux 1987, 40–53.). The "Lacret Morlot Plan" was a victim of increasing disputes between the three institutions of "Revolutionary Cuba:" the army, the provisional government, and the CRP. The disputes were based on who would have control over the war. Furthermore, Estrada Palma was already unwilling to take any action in Puerto Rico at that time. The CRP

Delegate had been trying for a long time to resolve the conflict by diplomatic means, specifically by allowing US intervention in the war. To establish a second liberation front in Puerto Rico would complicate the matter by calling into question the desire for intervention by the United States. Furthermore, Estrada Palma paid special attention to Cuba's bourgeoisie, who were crying out for an end to the dispute that was making them lose their wealth and peace of mind; establishing a second liberation front in Puerto Rico would prolong the war (Preece 1976, 51–2; Estrade 1984, 136).[13]

The PRS leadership began entering into negotiations with US government leaders during the first months of 1898, urging them to invade Puerto Rico should they intervene in the Cuban conflict. There are two reasons to explain why the conservative leaders of the PRS took this action. First, during this time, there was already some distance between conservatives and revolutionaries and between annexationists and supporters of the independence movement within the PRS. In view that no action was being taken to open a "second front" in Puerto Rico, many Puerto Rican revolutionaries (Francisco Gonzalo "Pachín" Marín, Modesto Tirado, and Gerardo Forrest, among others) decided to join combat in the Cuban manigua. In addition, the distancing between the PRS and the CRP made others decide to create stronger ties with the Cuban party (e.g., Sotero Figueroa, J. M. Terreforte). As a consequence, the PRS leadership was left in the hands of its most conservative and annexationist leadership (Henna and Roberto H. Todd). The frustration of having failed to start a war in Puerto Rico and their support for US intervention on the island prompted this faction to lobby Washington functionaries.[14] Henna and Todd contacted the "imperialist" sector of President McKinley's administration (Theodore Roosevelt, Henry Cabot Lodge, and Senator John Tyler Morgan) that believed in Manifest Destiny and were interested in intervening in Cuba. Thus, resembling Estrada Palma and the CRP, the PRS linked itself to the most conservative and expansionist sector of the United States to achieve its goal of liberating Puerto Rico from Spain. As expected, the actions taken by the PRS leadership created opposition from the revolutionary factions of the PRS. Under Sotero Figueroa's initiative, they defeated a motion proposed by Henna that sought approval of their negotiations in Washington as well as participation of Puerto Ricans in a US invasion of Puerto Rico (PRC-SPR 1898, 231–2).[15]

The invasion and occupation of Puerto Rico by the United States brought about the disintegration of the PRS. Even the annexationists themselves had contrasting reactions to this event. According to Todd, Henna was "deeply disappointed" with Puerto Rico being transferred as war booty to the United States without allowing Puerto Ricans to exercise their right to self-determination (in his case, choosing annexation.) Todd and other annexationists "that never practiced that blind faith Hostos and Henna had" in the democratic principles of the United States saw the annexation of Puerto Rico to the United States as the culmination of their goals (Todd 1930, 29). On August 2, 1898, members of the PRS gathered in assembly to discuss the disintegration of the organization (Algo de todo 1898—document no. 90). There were no big debates, and everyone accepted the idea (PRC-SPR 1898, 233–6.). In this assembly, Hostos (1898) suggested the creation of a new organization that would fight for Puerto Ricans' right to self-determination. This is how the Liga de Patriotas (Patriots League), headed by Hostos and Henna, was born (the League's Manifesto appears in Patria, document no. 91).

Patria: The Newspaper of Cuban and Puerto Rican Exiles

On March 14, 1892, *Patria* published its first issue. José Martí was the driving force behind the newspaper, as well as the CRP. For Martí, the CRP and *Patria* were institutions that complemented each other: the party was the organization destined to gather all Cuban exiles and join their forces together for the Cuban War of Independence, while the newspaper served as the main tool in spreading the ideology of liberation and to "aunar voluntades" ("gather all forces") of the émigré community. Patria was the instrument used to disseminate the message and work of the party. Even more importantly, *Patria* became a means to disseminate the rising national consciousness among Puerto Rican and Cuban émigrés. For Sotero Figueroa, *Patria*'s goal of "aunar voluntades" was one of the newspaper's and Martí's greatest achievements. This is why Martí refused, in March 1892, the idea of turning *Patria* the official organ for the PRC or any other separatist organization, since the newspaper had to serve as a mouthpiece for all the émigré factions, above all political or ideological differences.

Ibrahim Hidalgo Paz, an expert in Martí's work and *Patria*, summarizes the newspaper's significance in Martí's work:

Even before the Cuban Revolutionary Party had been established, José Martí and his closest collaborators decided to give life to an appropriate means to propagate the principles and foundations of the political structure that was beginning to take shape: a newspaper whose pages would systematically carry a message of strength and combat where letters and speeches were not sufficient anymore; they decided to build ideological trenches, which at the time were more effective than trenches built of stones. (1989, 139)

One of Martí's closest collaborators was Sotero Figueroa, a Puerto Rican journalist and typographer, who was his faithful follower until his death. Antonio Vélez Alvarado and Francisco Gonzalo "Pachín" Marín, whom Martí also trusted and respected, collaborated in the newspaper as well. For several months during 1893 and 1894, *Patria* was published in *La Gaceta del Pueblo*'s printing press, owned by Vélez Alvarado (see Martí 1892k—document no. 10). In March 1894, it began publishing in the Imprenta América printing press, which belonged to Sotero Figueroa. Solidarity and commitment between Cubans and Puerto Ricans were evident in many levels of its production.

Patria's main objective was to promote and spread the cause of freedom for Cuba and Puerto Rico, just as Martí stated in "Nuestras ideas," an article published in the newspaper's first issue: "This newspaper is born from the desire and resources of Cubans and Puerto Ricans in New York who support the cause for independence, in order to contribute, without haste and without rest, towards the organization of Cuba and Puerto Rico's freemen" (Martí 1892a). In another article titled "Patria," in the same issue, Martí explained yet another important purpose of the newspaper: the union of Cubans (and Puerto Ricans) in a common goal. "For all the timeless fighters gathered in the same spirit, those in war and those in exile, those who are newcomers and those who have never rested, those from one region and those from another, those who are young and those who are old, those with whichever occupation, we searched for a slogan for this newspaper that would belong to all—and we named it *Patria*" (1892b).

But above all these objectives, for Martí, *Patria* fulfilled a function that only the newspaper was capable of achieving: to promote and propagate an awareness of a Puerto Rican and Cuban national consciousness. Hence, it is established in the first issue of *Patria,* in which Martí details the newspaper's sections:

We will publish in *Patria* "The Political Situation," which should reflect, both inside and out, what both Cubans and Puerto Ricans need to know of their country; "Heroes," which will describe those who have not tired of being so; "Characters," the personalities of our people, from the poorest to the most fortunate so that the absentminded shall not lose their faith; the "War," or better yet, its reporting, whether in accounts or anecdotes, where we can see glimpses of our power during difficulties and our steadiness in misfortune; the "Revolutionary Primer" will teach everything from shoes to dying in combat, the art of fighting for the independence of our countries: how to dress, wear shoes, heal wounds, make cartridges and gunpowder, and repair weapons. *Patria* will report the works and merits of Puerto Ricans and Cubans, and the social life of the rich and poor. The entire country's strength will be read from its pages. (1892b)s

We can see in this outline that Martí always linked independence for Puerto Rico to the Cuban cause, both in the party's efforts as well as in the pages of *Patria*. To organize the Puerto Rican exile, prepare the forces for the freedom struggle, and encourage a sense of national identity would be the mission that Puerto Rican revolutionaries would profess in the pages of *Patria*.

Patria was published from March 1892 until December 1898, after the end of the Cuban War and US occupation had begun in Puerto Rico. All the experts on *Patria* agree that the newspaper's lifespan can be divided in two major periods: the first being of more significance when Martí managed the newspaper; and the second following the death of Cuba's national hero, when *Patria*, as well as the CRP, was managed by Estrada Palma and the most conservative faction of the émigré community (True 1965, ch. 5).

This periodization is important for our study, since both periods reflect different stands on the Puerto Rican cause. Under Martí, there is an abundance of articles on the island by Puerto Rican authors, including various writings on Puerto Rico by Martí himself; the newspaper's interest in the Puerto Rican cause is very evident. During the second period, the number of articles on Puerto Rico or by Puerto Rican authors noticeably diminished, showing much less interest in the Puerto Rican cause. This coincides with a time when there were plenty of disputes between Cuban and Puerto Rican leaders of the party. By 1898, *Patria*'s attitude toward Puerto Rico reached the point of supporting the US invasion and annexation of the island in its articles.

The Cuban historian Ibrahim Hidalgo Paz proposes dividing the first period that *Patria* went through under Martí into more specific stages (1989, 139–61). In the first stage, from March to October of 1892, there is emphasis on the organization of the party and propaganda of its objectives. During this stage, *Patria* also "pays special attention to Puerto Rico, which is reflected in its first issue with the publication of the manifesto 'Al pueblo puertorriqueño' from the Club Borinquen; in the following issues, articles, commentaries, news, historical analysis, and accounts by various authors from the Antillean Island were published" (Hidalgo Paz 1989, 146). There were also constant topics discussed by Martí: the fight against autonomism and annexationism.

During the second stage, from November 1892 to December 1893, the campaign against Cuban autonomism and against the attempt of a premature uprising in Cuba without the rebel forces being prepared for an "organized war" was emphasized. Even though Martí already discussed these topics constantly, he further emphasized the need to unite all Cuban factions above any class, racial, ideological, and political differences. In this stage, Martí also began to highlight the Americanist and anti-imperialist nature of the Cuban war. The latter was the main topic in the third stage, from January 1894 to January 1895. It was then that Martí (1894c) published the transcendental article "El tercer año del Partido Revolucionario Cubano" (document 55), where he eminently stated both purposes as the driving force behind the revolutionary efforts of the Cuban and Puerto Rican exiles. During this stage, there are also more critical essays by Martí on US society and government; he also began to develop his plan on Cuba's constitution as a future republic, giving special importance to the revolution's populist nature. By the end of this stage, imminent concrete actions for the uprising in Cuba were being highlighted in the newspaper.

The fourth stage, from February to June 1895, began with the war and lasted until Martí's death in Dos Ríos. Once the Cuban insurrection broke out, *Patria* offered its unquestionable support to the war, and it served as the most efficient propaganda instrument for the War of Independence led by the CRP. The newspaper informed the Cuban and Puerto Rican exiles of the war issues and was an essential instrument in obtaining support from Latin America and the United States in favor of the Cuban and Antillean cause. This stage ends with rumors of Martí's death published in *Patria* during the month of June, an event that at the time was not believed to be true by many separatists. On June 25, *Patria* acknowledged the death of Cuba's national hero in an issue dedicated entirely to him; the headline on the first page was titled "Immortal," written by Martí's close collaborator, the Puerto Rican Sotero Figueroa.

CHAPTER 2

THE PRESENCE OF PUERTO RICO IN *PATRIA*

Puerto Rico was present in the pages of *Patria* throughout its publication from 1892 to 1898. Puerto Rican presence in the newspaper took different forms, and, as mentioned in the first section, was apparent to varying extents. If we classify the articles on Puerto Rico as well as the essays written by Puerto Ricans which appear in Patria by subject matter, we would obtain the following outline: the development of a political discourse of independence and the appeal to developing a sense of Puerto Rican national consciousness; articles on Puerto Rico and Puerto Ricans written by Martí; the praise of Puerto Rican patriots, in which Betances stands out; the protection of Martí's legacy; and news on the political situation in Puerto Rico, including an emphasis during 1898 of the war in the smallest of the Greater Antilles.

Puerto Rican national consciousness and the political discourse of independence

One of the most noticeable elements in the articles written by Puerto Ricans was an attempt to instill a sense of Puerto Rican national consciousness by developing an ideology that highlighted historical elements defining Puerto Ricans as a people, the history and heroes of the independence movement, and the radical criticism of political, economic, and ideological structures of the Spanish regime in the island. All of these elements coincide in the development of a political discourse of independence that serves as an axis to a sense of national consciousness that Puerto Rican separatists were seeking to encourage.

The political discourse of independence that appears in *Patria* is very important for the history of the independence movement and of nationalism in Puerto Rico, since it is one of the first systematic and concrete attempts in developing the general outlines of a nationalist discourse, an effort that would later be made by the independence movement of the twentieth century. The outlines of this political discourse of independence at the end of the nineteenth century were defined by the attack on the Spanish colonial regime, autonomism, and annexationism; validating absolute independence in political, economic, and moral aspects; and looking back at the independence movement's history, in particular the Lares uprising. This discourse was presented concretely in the writings of Sotero Figueroa, Antonio Vélez Alvarado, and Francisco Gonzalo "Pachín" Marín.

These Puerto Ricans understood, as Martí did, that to develop a sense of Puerto Rican national consciousness, the independence ideology had to be validated next to the two main political-ideological alternatives in Puerto Rico at the time: autonomism with Spain or annexationism with the United States. In the first issue of *Patria*, Figueroa, Vélez Alvarado and Marín (1892a- document no. 30) published their well-known manifesto for Puerto Ricans "To the people of Puerto Rico" on behalf of Club

Borinquen, the most renowned of the CPR's Puerto Rican clubs. In it, they attack the subjection and ideological hesitation of the Puerto Rican autonomist leadership of the time. They also respond to criticism by the autonomist leaders who stated that those (like the three authors themselves) who were once autonomists in Puerto Rico become separatists once they leave the island and are in exile. Figueroa, Vélez Alvarado, and Marín respond to this accusation:

Those here, who belong to the expatriate community in New York and hail from the Puerto Rican Autonomist camp, have no reason to be apologetic. They had affiliated themselves with the most progressive party—considering the existing colonial situation—and their attitude was proper and disciplined while they were members. After the tempestuous period of 1887, the unforgettable year when they resigned themselves to suffer the same fate as those of similar beliefs, they refused to engage any longer in dealings with evil and, while by no means meek, agreed to live under an artificially imposed moral peace that undermines public prosperity, diminishes character, and demands continuous declarations of loyalty in order to tolerate the political actions of a tame liberalism, all without ending repression... (Figueroa, Vélez Alvarado and Marín 1892a)

As the authors would mention in another essay, separatists in exile "prefer to live freely in a foreign land than to be slaves in the beloved motherland" (Figueroa, Vélez Alvarado and Marín 1892d). Thus, they respond to the accusation that on the island, the only political alternative is autonomism, while separatism is something for exiles that are disconnected from the reality in Puerto Rico.

While it is true that the authors were bitter opponents of autonomism (a topic discussed further on), they also vehemently opposed annexing Puerto Rico to the United States, an alternative favored by some within Puerto Rican separatism. The authors established that "there are two groups in the American Union that are trying through diametrically opposing paths to open new horizons for the only two remaining enslaved territories in America. One aspires for absolute emancipation, the other for annexing the Spanish Antilles to the Northern Giant." Figueroa, Vélez Alvarado, and Marín reject Puerto Rico's annexation to the United States:

[F]or we must not aspire to surrender ourselves to the absolute absorption of our race by another, one that does not seduce us to the point of wanting to forsake our language, customs, traditions, sentiments... everything that constitutes our physiognomy as a Latin American people, nor do we wish to do so.

One must have lived in this country a few years to understand that this race does not have a propensity to perfect or improve, simply through contact, those it believes inferior and has no other reason to abandon this proud belief—save for material advancement—as if man, in fact, does live by bread alone. For this reason it exterminates, in its victorious march, elements that pose resistance by refusing to be absorbed. (1892a)

Annexation to the United States would represent the destruction of a Puerto Rican national identity, since it would convey assimilation to another race and culture. The authors support absolute independence for a more important reason: independence is the inevitable culmination in the development of nationalities. Here they compare the development of nationalities with that of individuals:

If we favor emancipation, it is because it is the natural law from which neither peoples (*pueblos*) nor individuals can escape. And, just as the son wants to establish a separate home for himself upon reaching the fullness of reason—regardless of how good he is to his parents, for he cannot pursue his heart's desires or invest his own energies in sowing healthy young crops; similarly, colonies, which are nothing else but embryo nationalities, a people under guardianship while they cannot yet rule themselves—react against all pressure, against any yoke—as mild as it may be... Happy are the parents—happy are the nations—who teach prudence and prepare their children—prepare the colonies—to fulfill their eminent duties in agreement with collective life. (1892a)

According to the authors, colonialism is the process by which—under the protection of the colonial power—a specific people (*pueblo*) becomes a nationality. Once a sense of nationality has flourished and the people reach their maximum development, colonial tutelage is therefore unnecessary and independence is inevitable.

If it is to be, if it is the law of history—as has been acknowledged by more than a few shrewd Spanish politicians—that emancipation is to come inevitably (a triumphant day, which is not far away), it is patriotic and prudent to channel this redemptive movement in the high spirit of justice, without defamation and without hate. Let us find that magnificent formula that leads to a free *patria* for all, where the process of ensuring the common good is not at the mercy of those who have set out to dominate the Spanish Antilles, but is rather tied to those who have been born there. Let us not strive for a false autonomy that will forever be subordinated to the conquerors—becoming slavery in disguise—but move toward the absolute emancipation of those nations that reach maturity and demand their rights—rights that have been accorded to them by nature, reason, and history. (1892a)[1]

Independence of peoples is therefore the result of the historic evolution of mankind, consisting of a wide variety of nationalities; it is the inevitable result of history. To support autonomy in Puerto Rico is to go against history and not carry out the patriotic obligation that a nationality conveys. We can already see here some of the elements that would characterize the twentieth century's political discourse of independence, such as Pedro Albizu Campos's thoughts on nationalism.

In the series of articles "La dominación y la independencia," Figueroa, Vélez Alvarado and Marín (1892b, 1892c, 1892d, 1892e, 1892f—documents no. 40, 41, 42, 43, 44) further elaborate their concept of a political discourse of independence.

These articles are written in reaction to several essays published in *El Criterio,* a newspaper in Puerto Rico that defended autonomy and rejected independence. These articles present a sharp and intelligent critique of Puerto Rican autonomist ideology, while arguing the validity of independence as an option. According to the autonomist newspaper, autonomy is the most convenient option for Puerto Rico, a position that the authors criticize and attack. For them, Spanish colonialism not only financially exploits Puerto Ricans, but also politically subordinates and morally degrades them:

We do not understand how this is opportune when it systematically—and for almost four centuries—has borne bad fruit. We do not understand how this is opportune when it keeps the colonial subject under perpetual servitude, constricts his freedom, and overwhelms him with countless tax burdens that only serve to support an extravagant administration imported from the dominating metropolis. And, since he has no emotional attachments or deeply rooted assets in the land where he has arrived as a privileged gentleman, little does it matter to him that the country is drowning in bankruptcy, if from the administrative disorder he can withdraw intact his lavish allowances, which he will later enjoy far away from the wretched and ruined colony. We do not understand how this is opportune when it denies Puerto Rico institutions of higher learning; does not guarantee the waning rights which were granted by the generous acts of better times, rather than the good will of the metropolis; and imprisons and inflicts unspeakable torture upon *campesinos* for their conspiratorial daydreams, and later bestows generous rewards on the instruments of violence, leaving the victims without their due redress, so that all those who suffered torture may realize that they are mere serfs with no personhood, although they may naively believe that they are citizens of the Spanish nation. We do not understand how this is opportune when it heavily taxes colonial products in the metropolis, while it permits all manner of favorable terms for the introduction of peninsular goods into the colony, thus proving that there are two weights and two measures... (Figueroa, Vélez Alvarado and Marín 1892b)

The authors question the so-called reforms made to the colonial regime in Puerto Rico, indicating that nothing significant has been achieved, while Puerto Ricans continue to be repressed—including the autonomists—and the press is being silenced. If autonomy should be granted to Puerto Rico, this would be a futile and senseless option. Why? "Because we are not thought to be *essentially* Spaniards, no matter how many flowery protestations of *españolismo* we make. Because, within our fits of loyal adherence, beat the hearts of the children of America who long for freedom; because the desire to break the bonds that limit or pervert our sphere of action grows; and because it is considered dangerous to hand over provincial administration to the children of a subjugated land" (Figueroa, Vélez Alvarado and Marín 1892b).

Another argument against independence given by the autonomist newspaper is that Puerto Rico, a small territory with a supposedly limited productive capacity, does not have the qualities nor is it in the right conditions to become independent. According to the authors, the autonomists present

[T]he immoral principle that peoples [*pueblos*] of limited size cannot be the arbiters of their own destinies... As if the right to national sovereignty had gradations according to territorial expanse, geographical area, or material prosperity! If we were to follow this complacent solution, Switzerland would not be independent because it is small next to the great European nations; Portugal would not exist as a kingdom nestled in the southwest corner of Europe; nor would Denmark or Holland or any of the independent European states that are relatively small compared to the great world powers. (1892e)

The authors compare Puerto Rico's population and volume of exports to those of Central and South American countries to point out how the island's figures exceed those of these countries; they come to the conclusion that if we follow the logic of this argument, Puerto Rico is much more prepared for independence than the majority of its Latin American neighboring republics (1892f).

Figueroa, Vélez Alvarado, and Marín also refute the autonomists' argument that given the island's small territorial size, an independent Puerto Rico would be at the mercy of the great powers, specifically the United States. The authors respond to this argument:

In other words, that shameful guardianship must be accepted to avoid the offenses that a covetous neighbor might perhaps inflict on us. The little bird must remain in its cage for fear that the hawk might perhaps snatch it with its talons. The longing for freedom, which is innate to the human heart, must not be satisfied for it might perhaps be ridden roughshod by the brutal omnipotence of despotism. But this does not take into account that there are laws regulating international relations, and that it is not easy to openly violate them without incurring the wrath of other nations which might equally feel ridiculed, since respect shown toward smaller nations is a guarantee of security, recognition, and fond respect for the powerful ones. (1892c)

That is, the supposed protection that Spain offers to Puerto Ricans against the northern neighbor's greed is false (later proven in 1898). International laws and systems provide the means for small powers to survive without fear of being dominated or annexed by the great powers.

El Criterio also argues that independence has not produced favorable results in Latin American republics, where there is poverty as well as despotic political systems. This is, that independence for Puerto Rico would carry the same consequences as for its fellow nations. Figueroa, Vélez Alvarado, and Marín brilliantly respond to this argument: if political despotism exists in Latin American republics, it is because of the colonial heritage left by Spain after centuries of colonialism in the continent.

Indeed, if these independent nations have not yet been able to erase the footprint of individual predominance and despotic servitude, whose fault is it if not the conquerors, who carried to the virgin soil of the Americas their own power struggles, their mortal hatred for territorial domination, and their unquenchable thirst for control? Did Spain teach the peoples of the Americas to live the life of free citizens or, perhaps, to be the eternal slaves of money-hungry heads-of-state who come to the subjugated land only to seek prosperity? (1892c)

But the authors further extend their argument against autonomism. They indicate it is twice as incorrect, since, in addition, remaining with Spain does not guarantee Puerto Ricans the democratic regime to which they aspire. It is so since Spain is not a democracy. Paraphrasing Betances's well-known statement that 'Spain cannot give what it does not have," they establish their opinion:

Although it is *true that no one can give what he does not have*, and if Spain has continuously fought to expel administrative centralization and religious fanaticism as far away as possible, but has not succeeded in doing so (nor will succeed for a long time), it would be naïve to believe that Spain would grant her possessions in the Americas what she herself does not enjoy. Hence, Cubans and Puerto Ricans have learned, through sorrowful experience, that to ask the metropolis for a form of government that broadly ensures their freedom and allows them to manage their own interests is to dream the impossible dream. And so they have set out on their own initiative to seize what nature and history have accorded, namely, democratic institutions within a Free State. (Figueroa, Vélez Alvarado and Marín 1892d—emphasis in the original)

Figueroa, Vélez Alvarado, and Marín refute in this way the autonomist argument of the impossibility of independence for Puerto Rico and the so-called dependency on Spain. The development of a political discourse of independence—like that of the authors—was an important element in encouraging an incipient sense of national consciousness.

"The Truth about History"
An extremely important element in the attempt of encouraging a sense of national consciousness was to understand the need for developing a historical memory that would rescue a "forgotten" history, hidden so by "official history." This was even more essential when dealing with the history of a liberation and independence movement that was repressed and persecuted relentlessly by the colonial regime as well as by autonomists and annexationists. *Patria* played an important role in disclosing this hidden history, and Sotero Figueroa's work was crucial in achieving this goal. He dedicated a large part of his journalist work to rescuing the history of the liberation movement in his two "homelands," Cuba and Puerto Rico, as well as their patriots' deeds.

Perhaps the series of articles by Sotero Figueroa titled "La verdad de la historia" (The Truth about History) (1892a, 1892c, 1892d, 1892f, 1892g, 1892h— documents no.

31, 32, 33, 34, 35, 36) is the most accomplished attempt in *Patria* to present a nationalist discourse based on a reinterpretation of Puerto Rico's history. In taking an inventory of Puerto Rican national history, Figueroa starts with the premise that every
community of people that has attained nationhood has the inalienable right to independence (as discussed earlier).

Subjugated peoples [*pueblos subyugados*] always have the tendency to regain their independence, the same way a caged bird struggles to recover the sky as its dominion...

Freedom is such a precious gift that we cannot accept it secondhand. It is an imprescriptible
and inalienable right that is born with us, and, just as we cannot be deprived of our life or our
land without committing a crime or a monstrous usurpation, there ought to be no attempts on
our freedom, for we shall unflinchingly rise up until we succeed, either peacefully or by force.

Therefore, judge for yourself how odious tyranny can be when exercised not against an
individual, but against an entire people [*pueblo*]. Hence, just and sacred are the revolutions
that tend to bring independence to the homeland (*suelo patrio*). And these, according to
irrefutable law, always triumph. It is of no consequence that oppressive regimes might win
partial victories...

Hence, conquered peoples [*pueblos conquistados*] never passively accept the yoke of their
conquerors, but always fight to break the chains of slavery until they ultimately succeed.
(Figueroa 1892a)

If a nation's independence is an "inalienable and imprescriptible" right, the actions of those who struggle for independence, the patriots, therefore comply with
the rulings of history. But history's records are reported by those who are in power,
which in Puerto Rico would be the colonial regime and its followers. They present
a distorted—and on occasion, even false—view of history, especially concerning the
deeds of those who supported the independence movement:

...but they have sung and repeated the chorus of the Puerto Rican liberal faction: that in the
smallest of the Spanish Antilles there are no separatists, nor have there ever been any. As the
popular saying goes, this is to block out the sun with two fingers, for this absolute negation
tends to deny historic truth and make of Puerto Ricans—who are conscientious about their
future destiny and who have consistently fought for their freedom—faithless and debased
helots without regional aspirations who tolerate insult, seek no redress with pride, and accept
their punishment by submissively kissing the hand of their abuser. (Figueroa 1892a)

As a journalist, writer, and faithful follower of Martí, Figueroa understands that the
fight against the colonial regime should be taking place at all levels, and the ideological

aspect should not be neglected. The struggle to establish history's content and characters along with the consequences of their actions was necessary to avoid a situation wherein it could only be interpreted by the regime and its collaborators. This is why Figueroa dedicated a huge effort as well as many pages to clarify the historical accounts of the island, specifically achievements in the liberation movement and its patriots.

In "La verdad de la historia," he presents Puerto Rico's history from a revolutionary perspective, making this text one of the first historical accounts of the island's struggle for independence. In this series of articles, Figueroa pays special attention to the Lares uprising in 1868, which since the late nineteenth century has remained one of the most outstanding heroic deeds for independence. The Lares revolt had been organized by illustrious Puerto Rican separatists, many of them still living at the time of Figueroa's writing, but its account was slandered and distorted by the official history of the regime and its autonomist collaborators. It was necessary to rescue the Lares uprising from obscurity in order to reestablish the "historical truth" and recognize the heroic deeds of those who sacrificed their lives for the building of the Puerto Rican patria.

Therefore, for the glory of the patriotic efforts that were demonstrated at Lares, we come to vindicate the respect for Puerto Ricans who do not traffic in the shame of the homeland, who do not abdicate their rights, and who do not scorn or forget the saviors of yesteryear or curse their revolutionary work. Abandon at once the urge to strip all consequence and grandeur from one of the most significant political events ever recorded in the annals of Puerto Rican history and in which those who distinguished themselves in this enterprise will exult as a badge of honor, if they are still alive—or their descendants, if they themselves have passed away—when Puerto Rican nationhood has been proclaimed; and when, by its freest will, the patria of Betances and Ruiz Belvis, of Baldorioty and Corchado, of Padial and Vizcarrondo, becomes part of that Antillean Confederation we can now see outlined on the horizon of our hopes... (Figueroa 1892c)

Figueroa seeks to rescue Lares's history not only to establish "the historical truth," but also to establish the uprising as a glorious deed of the Puerto Rican people in their struggle for independence:

The Lares revolution was not a pitiable and miserable pronouncement by a few disgruntled men, nor was it a disorganized skirmish led by a wretched and ignorant mob seeking not the procurement of the noblest ideal, but the satisfaction of their instinct for greed and extermination.

The liars who attempt to disseminate such statements apparently know little about the people of Puerto Rico. No, the Lares revolution... was an eloquent demonstration of a proud people [pueblo altivo] wanting to break the yoke of enslavement: It was the culmination of the people's regionalist sentiment which materialized and laid the foundations for a free homeland [*una patria libre*]; it was the reassuring result of the emancipatory ideology that started to be felt in 1821 and that today can and will restrict overpowering force, which will not succeed in annihilating this passion—even if the persecution persists and spreads—for there are eternal laws of the physical and moral order from which neither nature nor societies can escape. (1892c)

For Figueroa, the Lares revolt was the realization of the inevitable movement in history, and of the efforts by the Puerto Rican people to obtain their ineludible independence. But, even more, independence for Cuba and Puerto Rico would be the final goal of the early nineteenth century project to achieve independence for Latin America. For Figueroa, Lares was:

...the transcendent work of Bolívar which lent itself to completion. It was the irresistible expansion of freedom, which is innate to all peoples, that eloquently expressed itself... But if the structure collapsed, it was not due to the incompetence of the one who directed the project, but to an unforeseeable and fortuitous event. However, the wreckage has resisted the sands of time and from it the lasting structure of Antillean independence will be erected, one that is even more solid than before... (1892c)

For Figueroa, to raise the historical importance of the heroic deed in Lares was essential to create the historical consciousness of Puerto Ricans as an independent nationality and a Latin American people. Lares allowed Puerto Rico to take its place in Latin American history, which began with Bolívar's quest for continental freedom and would finish with the project for Antillean independence proposed by Puerto Ricans and Cubans led by Martí, Hostos, and Betances.

Betances and Puerto Rican patriots

As previously established, to rescue the heroic deeds of Puerto Rican patriots from ignorance and opprobrium was essential in developing a sense of national identity that was required by the separatist movement in the late nineteenth century. The writings published in *Patria* by Figueroa, Vélez Alvarado, Marín, Terreforte and Martí himself that praised the work of illustrious Puerto Ricans and outstanding patriots of the independence movement were of great significance in this task. Among the Puerto Rican patriots, none was featured more in the pages of *Patria* than "the memorable Betances," who was without a doubt the highest figure of Puerto Rican patriots in the late nineteenth century.

During the first years of *Patria*'s publication under Martí's leadership, a large number of articles on Puerto Rico, especially important figures of Puerto Rican history, appear in the newspaper. Even though the majority of these biographical notes appear with no authorship, the style of writing points unmistakably towards Sotero Figueroa, a tireless contributor to *Patria* while it was under Martí's management.

In the article "Revolucionarios puertorriqueños" (1894—document no 70)), the author (possibly Figueroa) explains the purpose of a series of essays on Puerto Rican patriots that are compatible with his purpose of establishing "the historical truth": "What of the immortality of history if in its pages the most prestigious, outstanding defenders of an oppressed people are overlooked? Justice must be made complete if we truly profess the ennobling veneration of memories, and PATRIA is called to do just that at every opportunity." The historical figure of Betances stands out among Puerto Rican patriots, "the one who has the highest ranks in the praising memory of his fellow countrymen" (Revolucionarios puertorriqueños 1894).

When reading through the pages of *Patria*, it is no surprise then to find Betances mentioned countless times, as well as several messages in support of the separatist struggle from Betances, who was exiled in Paris. "La voz de un patriota" published excerpts of a letter sent by Betances to members of the Club Borinquen, where he thanked them for electing him honorary president. In the letter, Betances also remembers the fallen heroes in the fight for independence and reiterates his unshakable commitment to independence. In his mission, he recognizes Martí as a wonderful figure:

This tremendous battle that irreversibly penetrates great souls, like that of Martí, is worthy of all of you, with Martí as your leader... Tell Martí to take full advantage of my name, if he so wishes, for the country's benefit, and, if necessary, to expose my name to the infamy of posterity to help save our patria. To such extremes would I go! (Betances 1892—document no. 64)

Betances, as accustomed in all his messages, whether official, personal or propaganda, finishes with a call on all Puerto Ricans and Cubans for unity and an Antillean Confederation:

With an indivisible union between Cubans and Puerto Ricans, triumph is ours! The Puerto Rican proclaims, "¡Viva Cuba!" The Cuban exclaims, "¡Viva Borinquen!" Both sing out together, "¡Vivan las Antillas!" By your deeds a glorious nation awaits you, one that is free, happy, and independent! (1892)

Betances reasserts his commitment to the cause of Puerto Rican independence in "Con la revolución," an article published on September 23, 1893 (the 25th anniversary of the Grito de Lares):

Today, after twenty-six years of expatriation, battles, disappointments, and all manner of pain, and without my companions who have nobly fallen, I can repeat while invoking their memory: No, a thousand times no! Spain cannot give what it does not have, and there is nothing for Cuba and Puerto Rico, save one true and unique opportunity for salvation: REVOLUTION... (1893—document no. 67)

In "La verdad de la historia," Sotero Figueroa underscores the significant role played by Betances in Puerto Rico's struggle for independence. He describes the island patriot as follows:

Still standing, firm and lively, without succumbing to blandishments or threats, was the incorruptible Betances. His name would command the respect of his bloodiest enemies. The people would see in him the spokesman for their freedom. The needy would see him as their providence. The sick, as destitute as they were, would never seek his medical assistance in vain, so much so that he was known as "the poor man's doctor." A well-deserved chorus of praise followed him wherever he went, and he took pleasure in the lavishing of good deeds. (1892c)

"Revolucionarios puertorriqueños," a series that unfortunately did not continue, begins with the most distinguished Puerto Rican revolutionary, Betances. The article presents a letter written by him, where, among other things, the venerable Puerto Rican patriot stresses the importance of the Lares revolt in Puerto Rican history:

Those who judge our revolution in Lares with disdain do not know of the dangers that stemmed from that uprising, all that it accomplished; the results it achieved; the pains, the suffering, the deaths, and the vigils that were held; nor are they at all aware of what the exiles themselves suffered or the recognition they deserve. For the world is plagued by ungratefulness, and the arrogant forget that this revolutionary act is nothing less than the greatest demonstration of dignity that Puerto Rico has achieved in four centuries of egregious slavery, stamping the abolition of slavery and independence for the island into her very flag. (Revolucionarios puertorriqueños 1894—document no. 70)

The intellectual and personal greatness of Betances allows him to rightfully judge the revolt's value in the historical development of Puerto Rico, although, always faithfully humble, he downplayed his leading role in the heroic deed.

The figure of Betances cannot be underestimated in the history of the late nineteenth century independence movement. Even though he remained distant from Puerto Rico, Betances was without a doubt the most adored and respected symbol of nineteenth-century separatism.[2] This view is confirmed by the opinion of the most distinguished Puerto Rican revolutionary exiles of the time (Figueroa, Henna, Terreforte, Vélez Alvarado, Schomburg, Lola Rodríguez, and many others), as well as those of Cubans (Martí, Máximo Gómez, Juan Gualberto Gómez, Gonzalo de Quesada, José Varona).[3] Even though he was expatriated in Paris, Betances's determination never ceased in his fight to achieve independence for Puerto Rico and Cuba, as his biographies clearly show. Even though Betances at the time was physically and emotionally overwhelmed by many years of struggle, he never diminished his work for the cause of the Antillean islands. In Paris, he was in charge of the CRP's affairs in

France, a task that he accepted at Martí's request even though the foremost members of the Cuban exile (bourgeoisie from the sugar cane industry) were located in the French capital; he was also a delegate for the Cuban provisional government. Betances's diplomatic correspondence during the war shows how important he was in the European front during the fight for Cuban independence.[4] Hence, the great respect and admiration by Cubans in general for the eminent figure of Betances (Betances 1983, 1985; de la Luz León 1947; Estrade 1984).

Once the Cuban war against Spain began, Puerto Rican rebels saw the possibility of taking advantage of this event to expand the war to Puerto Rico. As discussed earlier, the Puerto Rico Section elaborated several invasion plans to ignite a war on the island. While drafting the war plans for Puerto Rico, one of the first decisions Puerto Rican separatists in New York made was to offer Betances command of the insurrection. He politely declined, since his health would not have even allowed him to travel overseas.[5] But Betances sent a message to *Patria* calling on all Puerto Ricans to rebel against Spain:

Onward! Onward! What are you waiting for? I am at a loss. I feel compelled to repeat this to everyone I meet: sacred Liberty never descends from heaven like a virgin of peace, and she does indeed demand that all those worthy of her be willing to spill their blood for their homeland... And what do they ask of Spain? For almost thirty years, the unforgettable patriots Ruiz and Basora—and later Hostos and Rius, along with many others—have joined my voice in proclaiming the defense for the Antillean revolution—'Spain cannot give what it does not have'—and today's Spain is the same Spain that has always been... (1885—document no. 72)

Betances died a few weeks after the US invasion of Puerto Rico. He spent the last months of his life suffering with illnesses and the frustration of not having his life's dream fulfilled: independence for his country. His letters during this time reflect his fear that the conservative Cuban leaders would abandon Puerto Rico in this essential phase of the war and that the United States would annex the island permanently (see PRC 1943–1946 vol: III, 126–47; letter to Henna in Betances 2013 vol: V, 479–80). His fears came true. Those who knew Betances during his last days testify that he could not recover from the blow of seeing his country annexed by the United States. His death was modestly reported in *Patria* by reprinting an article by a Spanish journalist. This lack of attention to the death of such a distinguished Puerto Rican was comprehensible in the context of the time: *Patria* reflected the lack of organization of Cuban rebels in exile when confronting Cuba's occupation by US troops. Furthermore, not a single Puerto Rican remained on the newspaper's staff. Even so, an elegy was published for Betances, which as a last resort emphasizes the respect that even the Spanish had for the Puerto Rican patriot.

He was a man of handsome features: tall, dressed in black with a white tie. He cut an artist's profile like few others—white, naturally curly hair in abundance as well as a full, white beard at an age when other men, who had yet to know true work or suffering, still wore theirs black... He resembled an apostle with his sweet appearance and tender eyes. He always spoke in soft tones and was never seen upset. Anger never furrowed his brow. Everything about him was evangelical and distinguished. His integrity was never questioned. He made a career and a name for himself in Paris as he worked and waited for his ideals to become a reality. He resembled a dreamer, a tenacious sectarian who never, at any moment, stopped conspiring to win independence for Puerto Rico. (Blasco 1898—document no. 77)

Concerning Betances's work towards revolution during his final years of life, the author says:

As the war began, Dr. Betances was the leader, director, and representative of these filibustering organizations in Paris. All eyes followed him, including those of the embassy and its futile surveillance. This did not change his demeanor, life, or habits. He never raised his voice over a level pitch, and he directed everything without anyone perceiving it. "He would slip in like a shadow," Hebrard said, "but that shadow dealt out orders to everyone." (Blasco 1898)

Even those who did not agree with Betances had to recognize his greatness, the foremost figure of the Puerto Rican independence movement in the nineteenth century.

Other Puerto Rican patriots

Another article of unknown authorship that seems to come from Sotero Figueroa by its style and content is "José de Celis Aguilera" (1894—document no. 68). This writing is important because it reviews the historical role of certain figures in Puerto Rican autonomism by a recognized independentista. At this point, no one could deny Figueroa's credentials as an intimate collaborator of Martí and confidant of Betances. But Figueroa had an autonomist background in Puerto Rico. He had been part of the Creole leadership that founded the Autonomist Party in 1887 and was a close collaborator of the most important representative of creole autonomism in the late nineteenth century, Román Baldorioty de Castro. But the repression carried out against the Autonomist leadership by Spanish colonial functionaries and loyalists in what became known as the "terrible year of '87," as well as disappointment with the reformism and passivity of autonomist leaders, led him to abandon the country and autonomism forever. Figueroa never returned to Puerto Rico; after the annexation of the island by the United States, he refused to live in a US colony just as he had refused to live in a Spanish colony. He went to live in the free country of Cuba, where he died.

Figueroa was one of the most honorable Puerto Rican revolutionaries of the time. It seems interesting that an independentista like him would have words of acknowledgment for autonomist leaders like Aguilera and Baldorioty de Castro. In the article on Aguilera, the author (presumably Figueroa) emphasizes the abolitionist and reformist work of this Creole leader and concludes as follows:

He never joined the Antillean independence camp, like Ruiz Belvis, Betances, and Hostos, but why should that matter? He led Puerto Ricans as they took their first steps toward freedom, and he was one of the many who cleared our path, fraught with thorns and thistles. We march onward, and if we advance more and more resolutely, it is because we have traversed the most fatiguing part of the journey upon the shoulders of our forefathers. (José Celis Aguilera 1894—document no. 68)

Figueroa states that the path towards nationhood and patriotic freedom is very diverse, and it includes any Puerto Rican that follows it regardless of their political stance. Taking his political experience into account, the fact that Figueroa was once an active member of the autonomist party allowed him to see the limitations of this political ideology in Puerto Rico.

Another distinguished Puerto Rican who wrote for *Patria* was the acclaimed journalist and poet from Arecibo, Francisco Gonzalo "Pachín" Marín. Distinguished in the genres of prose and verse, Pachín was highly praised by Martí. Along with Sotero Figueroa and Antonio Vélez Alvarado, he made a well-aimed attack on Puerto Rican autonomism and defended the cause of independence. Marín became part of Martí's select workgroup in *Patria*. His last article in *Patria* is very personal and intimate. It is an elegy for his brother Wenceslao Tomás Marín, who died in the Cuban manigua. Like many other patriots, Wenceslao Marín underwent exile in New York City, where he worked as a modest tobacco destemmer, unbeknownst to his brother. In the article, Pachín recounts the surprising encounter with his brother in New York and how he, like many other Puerto Ricans who were part of the liberating army, left to the Cuban manigua to fight against Spanish dominion. The poet from Arecibo was profoundly dismayed by his brother's death; the pain and respect for a brother fallen in combat is expressed in Marín's exquisite prose:

My brother has died. He died defending those ideals that I planted in his heart; he died without ever turning his back on his patria, offering her all the wages he earned in his final months in New York; he died never doubting the future of Cuba and Puerto Rico; Oh! maybe even cherishing in his heart that far-off day when he would return to his enslaved country as a famous warrior to offer his own mother—my mother as well—a patria worthy of our grandparents' honor. He died confronting the enemy I taught him to hate with my articles and my verses; he died at the very forefront of the fight, where the brave battled; in the end, he died elevated from blacksmith to patriot, from man to hero, from fighter to martyr. (1896—document no. 75)

Facing the memory of his lost brother, full of remorse for having instigated in him a sense of patriotism that lead him to his death, Pachín swears to follow his brother's footsteps to rescue his country's honor, as well as his own:

I cannot—woe is me!—aspire to call myself his brother while I do not give myself up in sacrifice to his executioners or fail to avenge his death by contributing to the salvation of these two wretched islands.

The early years of our adolescence were spent in a blacksmith's shop and a printing press: he forged iron and I pressed lead.

Today I will shed no tears in his memory. What good are tears?

The only offerings that I believe to be worthy of him are those of iron and lead. (Marín 1896)

Pachín did not make an empty promise. Shortly after, the Puerto Rican journalist and poet sailed off to Cuba, where he came to be part Máximo Gómez's general staff and later, just like his brother, died in the manigua.

The unity between Cubans and Puerto Ricans in their struggle for independence was not only materialized with a newspaper's publication or the work of revolutionary clubs. It was also achieved in the actual practice of war. We have already pointed out how outstanding Cuban revolutionaries tried to fulfill the dream of achieving independence for the Antilles by establishing a war front in Puerto Rico. Likewise, hundreds of Puerto Ricans participated in the second liberation war in Cuba, as they also did in the first (the Ten Years' War). These Puerto Ricans performed multiple duties and reached various ranks in the liberation army. No other Puerto Rican reached higher distinction in the Cuban army of the manigua than General Juan Rius Rivera. Rius Rivera had fought in the first liberation war, reaching the rank of general. He participated with Maceo and other distinguished Cuban soldiers in the Protest of Baraguá, rejecting the Pact of Zanjón that declared the end of the Ten Years' War. The Puerto Rican general went into exile in Honduras until Cuban leaders summoned him once the war of '95 began. As already pointed out, Rius Rivera led the first plan for invasion in Puerto Rico in 1896, which he dismissed after not finding support on the island. After a while, the general led an expedition to Cuba, where he joined combat in the manigua under the command of Antonio Maceo, "the Bronze Titan." After Maceo's death, the huge task of replacing the Cuban hero fell on his shoulders. Rius Rivera was eventually wounded in battle and taken prisoner by the Spaniards; he spent the rest of the war incarcerated in Spain. Patria announced this unfortunate event in its pages:

Since the death of the heroic MACEO, a heavy burden had fallen upon Rius's shoulders. He handled this arduous responsibility with imperturbable stability and commendable modesty, and without yielding an inch or losing any ground in a province teeming with enemy soldiers. From the beginning, he demonstrated that he was worthy of the rank and confidence granted

him by that shrewd leader, who was ever appreciative of his compatriot's military strengths... General Rius Rivera has fully lived up to the demands of the extremely difficult position in which he found himself. His expertise, bravery, and leadership qualities have been clearly displayed after four months of unquestionable trials. What is more, his unrelenting support for our independence was clearly evident when the enemy tested his resolve with offerings of peace and reforms. (Rius Rivera 1897—document no. 76)[6]

After the war, *Patria* reported (in what would be the last issue) on the celebration held in the general's honor upon his return to the United States, courtesy of Figueroa and his spouse, Inocencia Martínez. The most highly regarded individuals of the Cuban and Puerto Rican exile community in New York at the time attended the meeting, including Estrada Palma, Emilio Agramonte, Hostos, Manuel Zeno Gandía, and Lola Rodríguez de Tió (En honor del general Rius Rivera 1898—document no. 79).

Martí and Puerto Rico

Since the newspaper's first issue, up to the day of his death, *Patria* was Martí's instrument in spreading the cause for Cuban independence and his own ideas. The cause for Puerto Rico was an essential part of Martí's liberation project for the Antilles. But Puerto Rico also represented the background for some of his experiences as a Cuban exile in New York City. There is no doubt that his exile in New York brought him closer to Puerto Ricans as well as to their cause for independence. This explains why *Patria*, under Martí's leadership, clearly espoused the Cubans' support for and their ties to Puerto Ricans and Puerto Rico's independence. During this time, there were plenty of articles on Puerto Rico and written by Puerto Ricans in the newspaper. At the same time, Martí himself prolifically wrote about issues occurring in the smallest of the Spanish Antilles and its historical as well as popular characters. Martí's writings on Puerto Rico vary from political strategies to patriotic figures to daily life to enhancing the everyday work of Puerto Ricans who are committed to the struggle.

Martí understood that independence for Cuba and Puerto Rico would serve as an experiment for the Americas in providing a new sense of democracy, equality, and justice in the new continent. In the already mentioned "El tercer año del Partido Revolucionario Cubano" (document no. 55), Martí (1894c) explains how he conceived Cuban and Puerto Rican independence as part of a process to maintain the political balance of the Americas while guaranteeing independence for Latin America and stopping US expansionism. Another essential article on Martí's thought is "'¡Vengo a darte patria!': Puerto Rico y Cuba" (1893a—document no. 51), in which he uses a meeting among fellow Cubans and Puerto Ricans as an opportunity to explain the historical links and principles that joined Cubans and Puerto Ricans in their struggle for freedom and to present his ideas on what patriotism and the future republic should be like. Martí believed patriotism should be an individual's total and unselfish dedication to the cause of his country: "The foremost quality of patriotism is the relinquishing of one's self, the disappearance of personal passions and preferences before public life, and the need to accommodate its structures to the ideal of justice" (1893a). Martí thought that patria is not an empty concept to be defined by each person individually; our homeland should represent justice, solidarity, and equality for all. Our patria—"the place on Earth where the beauty of the world was first seen, as well as the sorrow and affection that keeps tying us to it"—is not a toy for us to be used as we wish, but a cause we must serve.

A pueblo is not an endless banquet set out for our enjoyment, with fireworks as the first course. Rather, hope and suffering must first be combined with triumph over injustice and a virtue worthy of defense to make the daily bread, which must also include impassioned ignorance and enlightenment, as well as the strength of character to rescue and guide it. Men must be ministered to and served, as the doctor serves the sick patient who bites his hand. To serve the homeland, one stands naked; the wind strips away the flesh; and savage beasts suck out the marrow until there is nothing left of that voluntary immolation, except for the light that guides and incites its assassins. La patria is not a pretext that rings true or false as we wish; nor is the republic a new form to keep lazy and arrogant men in the lap of luxury and protected under the shield—men who, with depraved selfishness, believe themselves to be the natural burdens and inevitable masters of their inferior people. *La patria*, in both Cuba and Puerto Rico, is the valiant will of a people ready for the triumph of their emancipation—a triumph which is incontestable because of the unified and powerful attack that independence launches against the immoral soul and ruined fortune of its oppressors. (Martí 1893a)[7]

Independence is achieved to serve the patria, not to serve specific purposes of individuals, groups or social classes. The republic—the result of independence of our patria—is therefore an instrument at the service of the nation and its significance:

The republic, in Puerto Rico as in Cuba, will not be the unjust dominance of one class of people over the rest; rather it is the open and sincere balance between all the country's genuine forces and the liberated hopes and ideals of all Cubans. We do not want to emancipate ourselves from one tyranny only to enter into another. We do not want to escape from one lie to fall for another. We love freedom because, in it, we see the truth. We are willing to die for true freedom, but not for the kind of freedom that functions as a pretext for maintaining some men in extravagant affluence and others in unnecessary suffering. We will die for the republic later, when the time comes, as we will first die for independence. From the very outset of the war for independence, which must be as sharp and direct as lightning, there will be those who die—let us say, from this day onward!—to reconcile the spirit behind our actions with the virtue of the republic. (Martí 1893a)

These passages reflect Martí's thought on the future republic: it must personify the basic ideals of the patria—justice, freedom, and equality. Martí believed that these ideals had to be fought for to guarantee achievement of the future republic and had to be espoused from the earliest stages of the independence movement, including within the CRP.

The idea of a political and cultural union of the Antilles was a concept that motivated several Caribbean leaders, such as Betances, Hostos, and Martí. In "Las Antillas y Baldorioty de Castro," Martí used a reception in the Dominican Republic honoring this distinguished figure as an opportunity to present his concept of the Antilles as one big family. In Martí's opinion, uniting Cuba, Puerto Rico, and the Dominican Republic represented more than the union of three fellow nations; it symbolized the realization of his ideal for the Antilles. Martí speaks of

...the three islands, which—at the heart of independence and their aspirations for the future—extend their arms across the sea and face the world together, as three wounds of the same bleeding heart; three sisters guarding the true and righteous America that will ultimately triumph over the venal America.

...the three Antilles, which must save themselves together or together must perish; those three sentinels of an open and enduring America; those three sisters who have been exchanging progeny and delivering emancipators for centuries; the three embracing islands of Cuba, Puerto Rico, and Santo Domingo. (1892j—document no. 50)

According to Martí, the unity among the three Antillean islands would be possible because of their common historical culture and background and because of the historical duties that they must accomplish together: the achievement of independence for the three sister islands and the end of US imperialism. Martí considered this as a project of the people, which went above any political ups and downs of any historic situation: "The alliances forged between the souls of a people and signed by its purest sons before an altar where women and children offered flowers to a man whose only power was derived from his intellect and goodness are more lasting and desirable than pacts that favor political pursuits and wealth" (1892j)

Martí stated that "appreciation towards the righteous patriots is the republic's most fertile seed;" to honor your patriots (in the literal sense of the word, those who dedicate themselves to their patria) is a way of building a nation. The fact that Baldorioty de Castro was once an autonomist did not matter; this praised and eminent Puerto Rican figure had to be honored by the people of the three Antilles for setting an example and showing patriotic devotion:

America needs sincere and innovative men, poisoned as it is already by so much corruption. The Spanish colonies of the Americas need pure and honest men to purge themselves of despotism and bureaucratic vices through independence. And the world needs compassionate and visionary men who will heal the wounds that their axes must carve in the uncharted forest with the soothing balm of their love. The three sister nations—the three islands that must save themselves together or together must perish—have done well at Azúa to crown with flowers that wise and righteous rebel, that founding father, that American, Román Baldorioty de Castro. (Martí 1892j)

Thus Martí honors one of the most distinguished Puerto Ricans of the nineteenth century, who was a fellow party member as well as close collaborator of Sotero Figueroa in the Puerto Rican Autonomist Party.

Martí's connection to Puerto Ricans was not out of political convenience, but out of personal ties and sincere friendship with those he valued. His frequent commentaries on figures and events related to the exile community as a journalist for *Patria* and Delegate of the party reflect this view. These commentaries emphasized Martí's admiration for well-known Puerto Ricans in New York City who would later reach fame in Puerto Rico's cultural history; among them, a tribute to one of our most beloved nineteenth-century poets, Pachín Marín, one of the most honorable figures of the Puerto Rican exile at the time.

One cannot speak lightly of the poet Marín because he infuses in his easy and elegant—albeit at times flowery—style the pains and contradictions of his agitated existence with fire and artistic modesty. In Puerto Rico, he loved freedom; in his ongoing exile, he continues incorrigibly to love romance. With one blow, any of us could be toppled like a house of cards for the grievous sins of our burning youth. But what this blow does not create in us is such elegant and swift style, such strong and firm verse, and such personal and natural treatment of the subjects in his dramatic poetry. He is enamored of compassion, through which all pain is consumed; compassion, the aristocracy of the soul (Martí 1892i—document no. 62)

Acquaintances and biographers of the Arecibo poet agree with Martí's characterization of Marín.

One of the most praised Puerto Rican figures by Martí in *Patria* is the famous pianist Ana Otero. Martí announced her concerts on many occasions. In an extensive article in August 1892, Martí describes the Puerto Rican pianist with a beautiful prose that appeals not only with its style, but also with its emotion:

She has not taken theatrics or jealousy from her profession, or the mercenary desire that consumes the wings of music; rather, she beautifully adorns herself with simplicity, without letting the art which gives her life—much like a chosen soul—freeze, from pure servitude, the poetry that spills out from an innocent heart and that goes through the world wrapped in a white veil. She is faithful to the truth, to friendship, and to her homeland.

From this—as well as from her pious and sincere soul—comes the gift of understanding and interpreting the most varied and sought-after composers, just as music is born of real emotion or the desire to extract a painting from nature...

They say that the generous hand that wrote her country's heroic danza for PATRIA —the danza that moves the Puerto Rican, like an order from his conscience, to battle and honor—weaves subtle lace upon the keys, and through whose threads emerge sparks of starlight, heroic cavalcades, and glimmers of dawn. (1892m—document no. 63)

In the last sentence, Martí refers to "La Borinqueña," the beloved Puerto Rican hymn to which Otero wrote the music that appeared in the pages of *Patria* on September 3, 1892 (Vélez Alvarado 1892—document no. 45).

Another popular figure among Puerto Rican exiles in New York City, and not very well known in Puerto Rican historical accounts, to whom Martí gives a heartfelt tribute is Demetria Betances, sister of the patriot in exile. Although she was not as distinguished as her brother, she was, as Martí indicated in his beautiful elegy, a well-loved member of the Cuban and Puerto Rican exile community in New York.

Only goodness knew the way to her doorstep. She, who was unacquainted with pompous ways, knew all too well where unhappiness dwelled. She did not want to live in her enslaved land, or in any land of suffering, even if it masquerades under the name of liberty. She embroidered our flag—procuring its gold trim through her own toil—placed her own bouquet of flowers on the orator's podium and on the hero's tomb, and encouraged those who looked exhausted or bewildered with her principled counsel and her passion for freedom. Work was her pleasure; her trade, mercy; her honored brother, her idol; Borinquen, her heart. Fire consumed her because in life she was a pure flame that no storm could cause to tremble or extinguish, and she wished to die like that flame. (1894a—document no. 69)

Once again, Martí's beautiful prose captured for posterity a great Puerto Rican figure who, although she preferred anonymity, knew how to serve her homeland just like her brother and hundreds of other unknown Puerto Ricans.

Patria's pages are full of stories and descriptions of events related to Cuban and Puerto Rican exiles in the city; they are genuine records of the Antillean revolutionary exiles' daily life at the time. No other figure at the newspaper paid higher tribute to the exile community, to its daily life, to its political as well as daily struggle to maintain itself, to its most outstanding figures such as José Martí and their heroic actions; and, as we have seen, he did this with both Cubans and Puerto Ricans. For Martí, *Patria* was an instrument of struggle itself and an instrument for inspiring others to struggle. Hence, nothing was more important than drawing attention to the revolutionary exiles and their struggle for freedom. Martí therefore constantly recognized the work of the separatist clubs that made up the Cuban Revolutionary Party. (In fact, there was a section dedicated to the clubs while Martí managed the newspaper.) Perhaps no other club received more of Martí's attention than the Puerto Rican Club Borinquen.

The importance of Puerto Rico as well as Puerto Ricans for Martí should not be underestimated. In the newspaper's first issue, Puerto Rico appears as an important topic. One of the two headlines was about Puerto Rico—the manifesto of the Club Borinquen (1892—document no. 30) "Al pueblo puertorriqueño"—; the other was the historic article "Nuestras ideas," by Martí (1892a). Martí writes two other articles dealing with Puerto Ricans: "El convite a Puerto Rico" (1892d) and "La sesión del

Club Borinquen" (1892f–document no. 2) the latter being the first description of a separatist club by the newspaper. Martí praises the club's confirmation on March 11, 1892, as well as its membership in the CRP. Among other things, Martí states the following about the assembly celebrated by the Puerto Rican club:

> They proclaimed as honorary chairmen of the Club three Antilleans who have long been joined in the closest sympathy born of a common desire to see the progeny of their country fully realized in the fruition of their prosperity and dignity: Ramón Emeterio Betances, who, like the ancient Persians, kept the fire of the nation burning in the desert and sheltered in the castle of his heart; Eugenio María de Hostos, who presented the Americas as living proof of the superior strength and order that can be achieved through virtuous deeds; and that Cuban who is devoted to Puerto Rico, José Martí. (1892f)

The Club Borinquen was presided over by Sotero Figueroa; Antonio Vélez was vice president; Pachín Marín was secretary; and Modesto A. Tirado was treasurer. Martí's affection towards this club can be inferred by the number of articles that he dedicated to it throughout the years. The other most highlighted Puerto Rican and Cuban club at the time was "Las Dos Antillas," where Rosendo Rodríguez and Arturo Schomburg (who would later become one of the most prominent figures of the Harlem Renaissance in the United States) were members. It was one of the clubs with the largest amount of members with working-class backgrounds. This club received compliments by Martí in "Banquete patrio del club 'Las Dos Antillas'" (1893f) and "Pobreza y patria" (1893d) (documents no. 17 and 53, respectively). The first women's club of the party, "Mercedes Varona" (Martí 1892n) was made up of Cubans and Puerto Ricans. It was presided over by Inocencia Martínez de Figueroa, Sotero Figueroa's Puerto Rican wife (see documents no. 12 and 27).

Sotero Figueroa and the defense of Martí's legacy

Sotero Figueroa and Martí
Without a doubt, the most highlighted Puerto Rican figure on the pages of *Patria* was Sotero Figueroa. His frequent writings on Puerto Rico expressed a viewpoint of combining Cuba and Puerto Rico's struggle for freedom. Figueroa drew particular attention to a sense of national identity in Puerto Rico, and sought to write a national history free from colonial ties. While in Puerto Rico, he was an editor, journalist, and typographer in the town of Ponce, besides publishing plays and a biography collection of famous Puerto Ricans. He was an active member of the Autonomist Party, where he was a faithful follower of Baldorioty de Castro. Following the cruel repression of 1887 (the "terrible year"), Figueroa migrated to New York, where he established ties with Cuban and Puerto Rican exiles in the city. He later worked for *La Revista Ilustrada,* the leading Latin American magazine in the country.[8]

Perhaps he first had contact with Martí through *La Revista,* to which the Cuban patriot would contribute. The relationship between them seemed to flourish later during meetings at literary and political events. Martí's first letters to Figueroa date back to 1890; in 1891, Figueroa was a member of the Cuban club "Los Independientes," to which Martí also belonged. Once the CRP and *Patria* were established in 1892, Figueroa actively participated in both institutions, always beside Martí. He was editor and director of *Patria* for a long time, and the newspaper was printed at Figueroa's printing press for many years. He was the president of the Club Borinquen (attached to the CRP) as well as secretary for the party's Cuerpo de Consejo (council board) in New York (the structure that coordinated the work for the CRP clubs).

Figueroa was Martí's close collaborator in the production of *Patria.* During his repeated trips out of New York City to fulfill his duties as delegate of the party, Martí entrusted Figueroa with the management and publication of the newspaper, as proven by the many letters he wrote to Figueroa. In one of the letters, Martí tells Figueroa: "*Patria* is safe in your hands, in your pure heart, and in your good judgment" (1975 vol: 2, 352).[9] Figueroa's work for the newspaper was recognized years later by Rafael Serra, another contributor to *Patria* and an intimate friend of both Figueroa and Martí. Years later Serra and Figueroa also published the newspaper *La Doctrina de Martí*:

We have to put on record, since it is time that we say so, that the most decisive assistant that Martí found while publishing *Patria* was our Figueroa. Since the first moment, he contributed with financial resources and despite working during the day for *La Revista Ilustrada*.... he contributed to *Patria* to the point that during the first years of admirable propaganda, when Martí had to make those astonishing trips throughout this republic and other countries in free America, his articles, along with those by Gonzalo de Quesada, were the best ones published. (Serra 1897)[10]

Figueroa came to develop a close friendship with Martí, as the letters from the Cuban leader show. This friendship was not only based on their collaboration in the newspaper and political struggles, but also on mutual admiration and respect. On several occasions, Martí recognized Figueroa's dedication and political devotion. In the noteworthy article "Vengo a darte patria," Martí qualifies Figueroa "as the natural leader of Borinquen's ideals in New York," and "the spiritual son" of Betances, the "generous and brave Sotero Figueroa" (1893a—document no. 51). Martí's words in the short article "La imprenta Figueroa," which is actually a thank-you note to the Puerto Rican, are perhaps the most intimate public comments on his behalf on his friend and collaborator:

We should not speak well of those of our own stock, or those whom we love and consider dear to us—regarding the merit that their assiduous work affords such honored talent, because righteousness is taken for flattery according to the world's shameless perspective. The award-winning biographer and energetic Puerto Rican poet Sotero Figueroa, our brother in hope and in toil, is so highly esteemed for the order and innate quality of his reasoning, for his elegant and concise speech, and for his active and edifying patriotism. (1894g—document no. 71)

As Martí states in this quote, he never wrote long articles about his close friends for fear that they would take his words as empty flattery. However, Martí does have a long report on Figueroa's work and deeds that was published in a Havana newspaper in 1892:

Sotero Figueroa is one of the most deserving children, one of the most proven characters, and one of the most energetic and known writers from Puerto Rico. He had a teacher whom we cannot remember without affection: the Maestro Rafael.

...In the political controversy of his country, Figueroa has only had equals; he does not set aside nor does he forgive offense. He tries to right wrongdoings at their roots, and wants human rights respected and claimed for all. His is an energy that never gives up until the moment of negotiation, nor does he reach arrogance. His writing is extensive, without unwanted words, nor recycled thoughts, and music full of accents and sense.

From his work, besides his continuous and industrious work with the press and his noteworthy comedies, the most famous is his collection of "Estudios biográficos" (Biographical studies) from Puerto Rico, which has won an award from the leading organization in Ponce. It is a literary work that already reflects Figueroa's strongest qualities (although not to say they will not continue to develop): coherence of ideas, laborious investigation, elegant style, and indomitable and ardent patriotism. Today he acts as one of the main editors of *La Revista Ilustrada* in New York; over in New York he has published *Reparos Literarios*, a collection of letters dealing with Latin American literature in which, in addition to new and excellent biographic accounts, he highlights the uniqueness and ignored richness of Latin American arts; it also shows the profoundness and sharpness with which he has understood the problems of America, that many should already understand, and the close connection between the Antilles and the American problem. (1975 vol: 4, 370–4)[11]

We can see once again Martí's talent for making fair judgment of those who are close to him; in this article, Martí shows an exact knowledge of Figueroa's work and personality, even in a time where their friendship and close collaboration had not yet flourished.

If Martí's influence on Figueroa and other Puerto Ricans is well known, it is also certain that Puerto Ricans in general and specific figures such as Betances, Hostos and Figueroa himself equally influenced the Cuban hero.[12] A veiled influence by Figueroa exists in Martí's writings on Puerto Rico. Martí was a voracious reader and without a doubt, he was familiar with the historical writings on Puerto Rico (1895b—document no. 56), and as we have seen, before his friendship with him, he already knew about Figueroa's written work. As countless letters and accounts by Martí and

Puerto Ricans close to him, the Cuban leader enjoyed close meetings as well as political and literary gatherings in which he spent time with Puerto Ricans. Martí mentions several times this type of gathering in *Patria*.

Martí must have heard many stories, accounts, and anecdotes about Puerto Rico in these gatherings, especially from his closest Puerto Rican friend and collaborator, Sotero Figueroa. Martí has an account related to the interpretation of events in Puerto Rican history in which one can acknowledge his connection with Figueroa: "El 22 de marzo del 1873: La abolición de la esclavitud en Puerto Rico," published in *Patria* on April 1, 1893 (1893b—document no. 52). In this article, Martí recounts in extreme detail the events and characters that led to the celebration of such an historic event in Antillean and Puerto Rican lives: the abolition of slavery in Puerto Rico. It is as if Martí was present, which he never was, since he never stepped foot on Puerto Rican soil. Martí gives at the end his source of information:

A young man with a fearless demeanor and indomitable gaze came forward—arm in arm with two beautiful women, and followed by the entire multitude—to offer Primo de Rivera the tortoiseshell staff which the Círculo presented him with as a token of that great day: Sotero Figueroa was that young man, the Círculo's secretary. The Spaniard listened, his hand on his heart, and his eyes full of compassion; the Puerto Rican—that virtuous son of both bloodlines—spoke to him with modest assurance about Captain Correa, the Arecibeño who—with might and machete—fell, swimming against the British invaders; and of the brave Amézquita who—when the Dutchman, Boudewijn Hendricksz, challenged him to a singular duel at El Morro—struck down all of Holland. The Puerto Rican spoke to the Spaniard of his country's vigor and independent spirit from his own natural sense of freedom. (1893b)[13]

Martí not only informs us that the story comes from Figueroa, but he also makes him a protagonist in such an important event in Puerto Rican history, which seems to be an obvious act of kindness and recognition towards his beloved Puerto Rican friend and comrade.

Another moment when Figueroa's influence on Martí is evident is in his concept of Puerto Rican autonomism, specifically his thoughts on Baldorioty de Castro. Martí analyzes the leading figure of Puerto Rican autonomism in an article with the same epigraph previously mentioned. Martí, who was carrying out a very intense campaign against Cuban autonomists (and annexationists) through the pages of *Patria,* surprised many with this writing by having words of praise and admiration for the Puerto Rican autonomist. However, what is more surprising is the resemblance in ideas of Sotero Figueroa's concept of Puerto Rican autonomism (previously presented in relation to José Celis de Aguilera):

Autonomy was not, for him, a toast with amenable generals, who tomorrow send to the gallows those they played chess with yesterday. Rather, the genuine defense of freedom was always foremost in his mind—whether in prison, adversity, or exile—because freedom for Puerto Rico was never so far off that Baldorioty did not aspire beyond it. For Baldorioty— that righteous and pragmatic Criollo—autonomy was a way of uniting, through geography and history, each country's irrepressible forces. This unity, necessary under any system of government, was required so that when the deficiencies and duplicities of autonomy were confirmed—as they would have been soon after either its institution or unattainability—they could seek a more auspicious system without risk or chaos. (Martí 1892j—document no. 50)

Martí shared Figueroa's belief that autonomy was a path towards independence for autonomists like Baldorioty de Castro and Figueroa himself. María M. Solá comments on this writing: "Martí, who was almost never willing to praise autonomists, pays tribute here to Baldorioty's unwavering virtue as well as the respect that his friends' admiration for his teacher inspires" (1974, 95). We can also add that Martí paid tribute to his friend, whose political path changes from devotion to autonomism to unswerving separatism.

The defense of Martí's legacy

Martí was the greatest historical figure in Cuban nationalism in the late nineteenth century and represented more than any other individual in the Cuban revolutionary movement the connection between Cubans and Puerto Ricans in the struggle for independence. It was Martí who included independence for Puerto Rico as an aspiration of the CRP (Article 1 of the CRP platform); it was Martí who constantly promoted, on the political grandstand or in the newspaper *Patria*, the ties between the Cuban and Puerto Rican exiles; and it was Martí who, throughout his thought, work, and specially charisma, continuously attracted hundreds of Puerto Ricans to join the Antillean liberation movement. Martí's death represented for thousands of Cubans the loss of a beacon that shed light for both Antillean countries in their struggle for independence. It also meant the loss of an ideological and spiritual guide that raised the separatist movement to heights never seen before. The same way that the pages of *Patria* served as an instrument in spreading the Cuban's thought and work, they also served in praising the heroic and transcendental figure of Martí.

One of the personalities who most prominently highlighted the historical figure of Martí, but most importantly, the weight of his work and thought, was Sotero Figueroa. From the moment *Patria* announced Martí's death in Dos Ríos, Figueroa was one of the writers who earnestly dedicated himself to praising the work and thought of who was once his guide and mentor. Figueroa knew how to assess Martí's significance in Cuban history, and his early commentaries on the latter's death proclaimed the importance that the Cuban's life and work would have in the future.

Patria made public Martí's death (which had already been a rumor for weeks) in the June 25th, 1895 issue. The leading front page article in honor of Martí's life and thinking—entitled "¡INMORTAL!" (1895a—document no. 57)—was written by none other than Sotero Figueroa. From the very first paragraph, Figueroa begins to delineate the importance of his *maestro*'s death; Martí "rose to the heights of immortality to live on in time and history. His lessons on patriotism became all the more irresistible, for they were sanctified by his exemplary evolution—not his death." Figueroa then expresses himself on a personal level demonstrating what Martí's death meant to him (and to thousands of Cubans and Puerto Ricans who followed Martí):

To those of us, the forever faithful, who shared his hopes and concerns and suffered with him along his bitter path, Martí has not died; he lives on with ineffable life, and we feel him more than ever in our modest hearth. He is an exceptional friend who is but absent from us; yet wherever we go, our thoughts overflow with the immensity of his name, with the remnants of his benevolence, and with the splendors of his pen. From him they came and to him they shall go, these vehement affections that subordinate the head to the heart; these intimate letters that were not penned for indifferent readers, but for those select friends who admired the agitator, followed the activist, and supported the teacher... (1895a)

In this elegy for Martí, Figueroa gives us a characterization of the Cuban national hero that would be in unison with future biographies. He defined Martí's personality in the following way: "Restless, passionate, vehement in nature, he could never remain passive or indifferent when faced with any iniquity. A soul tempered for sacrifice and with a clear vision of human perfectibility..."

Figueroa, like many other Cubans and Puerto Ricans, knew the "irresistible" Martí closely, the overwhelming personality that attracted anyone nearby.

In his social affairs, José Martí was irresistible. He coupled a beautiful heart with extreme affability, and all those who met him instantly became his friends. The poor, the lowly, and the unfortunate were always given support, warmth, and affection. In his ranks, there were neither categories nor hierarchies...

Figueroa emphasized the integrity of Martí's character, but more than anything else his dedication to the cause for the country and for those he had close by:

He could have been rich, but he scorned wealth by continuing to be the voice of Cuban independence. He corrected without insult; he was firm without arrogance; quick to praise, slow to censure, and an effective and benevolent teacher to his working-class brothers...

Figueroa, who like Martí maintained high political and moral values, knew how to appreciate at an early time the true value of his friend and mentor. In an opinion that historians and biographers would support in the decades to come, Figueroa knew how to measure the worth of what was and would be Martí's main contribution to the Cuban and Antillean people:

His most accomplished work, though—which continues to resonate in posterity and places him among the world's great liberators—is having stoked the Cuban protest to a potency even greater than that of the Spanish aggression and having preached through his word, restraint, and martyrdom this heroic awakening of the Cuban people to a life of independence. That indelible and sickly body was transformed on the podium and inspired even the most incredulous and disheartened to answer the call of duty. He united disparate and displaced elements in exile; he erased the animosity and distrust that had endured as an inevitable consequence of earlier unsuccessful attempts. Sparked by his prophetic and fervent speech, prestigious leaders once more contemplated victory; the troops of the Ten Years' War again filed into the ranks and impatiently awaited the voice of command; the sons of enterprise—those contributing laborers—shored up their faith, and, with more vigor than ever, they hunched over their work tables and divided their day's wages between family needs and the no-less-sacred demands of the homeland. Revolutionary clubs sprung up wherever there were groups of Cubans or Puerto Ricans, throughout the whole of the American republic, and the war, systematized around harmonious and substantive bases, did not appear as the dream of some overheated imagination or persistent neurosis, but as an easily remedied problem if the perseverance and intelligence of Cubans abroad were united with those on the island through a sense of common cause and magnanimity.

This paragraph brilliantly summarizes what would endure most from Martí's revolutionary work: the unique ability to *aunar voluntades* (join wills) which made possible the creation of an organization that gathered the support of all Cuban factions above race, social class, or ideologies to fight an organized war against the colonial yoke and present a concept of the nation and the future republic based on high moral and ethical values.

An elegy for Martí cannot fail to mention one of his most beloved creations (likewise for Figueroa): *Patria*. Figueroa tells us that Martí considered *Patria* "his warrior *palenque*, his doctrinal pulpit, the prestigious flag that was unfurled..." Martí's "agitator soul has been poured out" in this publication, as one can notice in any study of Martí's work as a whole. In a note written with highly emotional content, where intimate memories are combined with political devotion, Figueroa recalls Martí's dedication to the newspaper: "Martí, who was of a sweet, serene nature, only turned severe when he believed that others did not pour into *PATRIA* all the effort that he himself demonstrated in decisive moments to ensure that the project did not falter..."

Figueroa was not the only Puerto Rican to feel and express pain by Martí's death. In the same commemorating issue, J. M. Terreforte (1895—document no. 58), a veteran from the Lares uprising, expressed his dismay and pain from the loss of the Cuban patriot in "Nuestro hermano" by saying: "Antilleans! Let us mourn the loss of José Martí!" The Club Borinquen, which received so much attention and affection by Martí, highlighted the Latin American character of Martí's personality and work:

Puerto Rico is in mourning. The Puerto Rican Martí has died. Venezuela laments the loss of her favorite son; they have just lowered the Venezuelan Martí into his tomb. Argentina is inconsolable over the premature death of one of her kin; the Argentine Martí. In a word, all of the Americas are grieving, because Martí did not just dedicate his entire life to the redemption of his patria; rather he employed it in the service of all the nations of the Americas. (Los Clubs 1895—document no. 59)

These displays of affection for Martí reflect the deep connection between the most revolutionary faction of Puerto Rican exiles with his work and thought. They also indicate that Puerto Ricans were present at the moment of paying tribute to the fallen patriot and friend.[14]

The changes that took place following Martí's death in the party as well as in the Cuban war encouraged several Cubans and Puerto Ricans to promote Martí's legacy as a standard for values and struggle. One of these individuals was Sotero Figueroa. In a report of the assembly that proclaimed Tomás Estrada Palma as the new Delegate of the Cuban Revolutionary Party, whom Figueroa said was "surrounded by Martí's halo" (rightfully so, since the post was created for and by Martí), the journalist dedicated more paragraphs to the martyr in Dos Ríos than he did to the new delegate. Figueroa believed Martí "must have enjoyed a most lofty triumph, since the revolution he predicted, organized, and nourished with his blood on the field of battle is still alive today, stronger than ever" (1895b—document no. 60). Figueroa then compared the figure of Martí with other illustrious Americans such as Washington, Bolívar, Hidalgo, San Martín, Juárez, and Louverture, and finished by comparing him with the figure of Christ, an image he had previously used while Martí was alive:

Like Jesus, the great model of Christianity, Martí can present himself to posterity with unbloodied hands and a heart brimming over with good deeds. How then not to envy and exalt this Cuban Nazarene, who fell valiantly clutching his messianic cross and commanded admiration even from his implacable executioners. (1895b)

The newspaper *Patria* as well as the party suffered notable changes in their structure following Martí's death. The election of Tomás Estrada Palma as delegate of the CRP and director of the newspaper transformed the ideology and program of both institutions. The conservative faction of Cuban separatism took over both institutions, created by Martí to lead the struggle of the Cuban people and guide the revolutionary process. Even factions that opposed Martí moved in to hold leading positions in the party and newspaper. This situation inspired a revolutionary faction that sought to maintain the ideology and program established by Martí to take action against the conservative faction's influence. Rafael Serra, a black activist and founder of the Antillean League (an educational organization for Cuban and Puerto Rican laborers where Martí and Figueroa converged before 1892), established a newspaper appropriately titled *La Doctrina de Martí*. This newspaper rescued and preserved Martí's thought against what they considered was harassment on behalf of the conservative faction and anti-revolutionary Cuban exiles.[15] Sotero Figueroa and Pachín Marín (who acted as a war correspondent once he joined the army in the Cuban manigua) were among the newspaper's contributors. Figueroa continued raising awareness through *La Doctrina* by writing articles on Cuban patriots and important events of the liberation war. Furthermore, Figueroa wrote a series of seven articles (from September 1896 to March 1897) entitled "Calle la pasión y hable la sinceridad" (Hush passion and let sincerity speak) where he defends Martí's legacy against attacks by Enrique Trujillo. Trujillo, who had been a personal enemy of Martí and was driven out of the party by him, returned once the Cuban patriot died. Starting in August 1897, Figueroa contributed as a correspondent and later editor of the influential magazine *Revista de Cayo Hueso*, which represented the most revolutionary faction of the Cuban exile at the time.

The War

Martí created *Patria* not only as an organizational and propaganda instrument, but also to incite unrest. Hence, the prevailing elements throughout the newspaper were articles analyzing the political situation and news that the traditional and leading press did not cover. Before the war began in 1895, there was plenty of news on the state of unrest in the Antilles; once the armed conflict erupted, news on the preparations for the war were highlighted.

Puerto Rico became part of this organizational scheme and propaganda. Many Cubans—of which Martí himself stands out—and Puerto Ricans contributed in presenting the situation in Puerto Rico and praising the Puerto Rican separatist movement of the time. The news articles on Puerto Rico published in the newspaper had the purpose of not only informing Puerto Ricans and Cubans of the situation on the island, but also serving as an instrument in mobilizing the revolutionary movement. The article "For Puerto Rico," published on June 23, 1894 (Por Puerto Rico 1894a—document no. 46), emphasized the influence of independence on the island, therefore contradicting the official stance of the colonial government on the movement's nonexistence. The article "Por Puerto Rico," published on July 28, 1894 (Por Puerto Rico 1894b—document no. 47), warns about the dangers of repression under the colonial regime and the habitual position of reformism of autonomists. Subsequently, the article "Agitación en Puerto Rico," published on December 8, 1894 (document no. 48), informs about the existing concerns that the colonial regime and autonomist Creoles have about the tense situation in Cuba—already in a prerevolutionary state—and how they could affect Puerto Rico.

The content of *Patria* was affected by the war's outbreak and Martí's death. On one hand, the situation in Cuba deserved the attention it demanded since a liberation war against Spain was taking place, while in Puerto Rico, the separatist fervor never manifested itself. On the other hand, Estrada Palma's position in the party distanced Puerto Ricans and their cause from the party. Estrada Palma—as well as the conservative faction of Cuban rebels—was not engaged with the cause of independence for Puerto Rico, a cause that Martí supported and had been established in the party's platform. Estrada Palma confirmed his viewpoint on several occasions, including organizational meetings in which he acted as delegate of the party. He had reasons to justify this: the escalating situation in the Cuban manigua and the lack of revolutionary fervor in Puerto Rico. Another reason was the conflict the delegate had with the conservative leaders of the Puerto Rico Section beginning in 1897. The presence of Puerto Rico in *Patria* was affected both quantitatively and qualitatively by this situation. Attention towards Puerto Rico in the newspaper was also affected by the departure of Puerto Ricans like Sotero Figueroa, who was already having ideological differences with the conservative faction of the party (and with the PRS). One of the few times Puerto Rico is mentioned in the newspaper is in April 1897, on two dispatches detailing the Yauco uprising. The article "El movimiento de Yauco," published on April 14, 1897 (document no. 81), reflects the hope that Puerto Rico will imitate Cuba and that the Cuban freedom fighters finally raise a second warfront that will weaken Spain and facilitate a victory.

The year 1898 brought substantial changes in the Cuban War for Independence. The conservative faction in Cuban separatism—entrenched as the party's leadership headed by Estrada Palma—yearned to end the war by intervention of the United States, a position that was greatly opposed by the most revolutionary factions that were fighting in the manigua. During 1898, Estrada Palma dedicated himself to his political work as a diplomat in Washington, seeking the intervention that he longed for in the conflict. Consequently, the pledge to support the cause of independence for Puerto Rico became a possible obstacle for US intervention in the Cuban war. Therefore, Martí's commitment to Puerto Rico was not only abandoned, but the Cuban conservative leadership also adopted a stance on accepting the annexation of Puerto Rico to the United States.

The Cuban Revolutionary Party and *Patria*'s new position on independence for Puerto Rico had already been evident since 1897. The article "La única solución, published on October 13, 1897 ("The Only Solution"—document no. 83), and which clearly responded to the official ranks of the party, rejected Spain's offer of autonomy to its Antillean colonies. Even though the abovementioned autonomy did not apply to Cuba, the article, however, did accept it for Puerto Rico; Spain was urged to hurry and "implement an autonomous regime in Puerto Rico before it is too late; a regime that the sister island has been seeking for a great number of years..." (La única solución 1897). During 1898, very few articles mention Puerto Rico; the majority of them appear in the "Las noticias" section, where *Patria* republishes articles from other newspapers. The initial purpose of this section was to inform readers about the war, but *Patria* expressed their position by only publishing certain news items without editorial comments. The same happened with the news of the US invasion of Puerto Rico. For example, a dispatch was published in the July 23, 1898 issue (document no. 86)—two days before the invasion in Puerto Rico—, in which the following is stated: "The United States' policy toward Puerto Rico will be to annex the island" (Las noticias 1898a). Later, on July 30, 1898—the island already having been occupied by the United States—, another report (document no. 87) published in *Patria* says: "Cuban independence and the cession of Puerto Rico remain completely beyond debate" (Las noticias 1898b). Although these statements were taken from other newspapers, they reflect the party's and newspaper's position on Puerto Rico at the time

It is no one else than Betances—a clever observer—who best expresses the concern of Puerto Rican revolutionaries about this change of program in the CRP and *Patria*. Betances, a diplomat for the CRP in Paris, understood diplomacy in war, and knew about the United States' aspiration of expansionism. His letters from months before and after the invasion reflect his dislike of the CRP abandoning its commitment to independence for Puerto Rico. His letter dated June 23, 1898 and addressed to Estrada Palma, delegate of the CRP, expresses the opinion on the annexing of Puerto Rico:

I am not satisfied; and it is with great sorrow that I see we are treated indifferently by the Delegation, when the issue of Puerto Rico, the way Martí understood it, is closely tied to Cuba's. To abandon it is to give up at no cost a Cuban province; and I believe that, without any expenses, it would suffice for the Delegation to give the American government the right indications so that they will be satisfied in giving us our independence without wanting to absorb us. (PRC 1941–1946 vol: 3, 143)[16]

Betances understood very well the importance of Puerto Rico's independence for that of the Antilles, Cuba, and America, since he deeply shared the same sentiment in Martí's maxim: "the Antilles are at the center of the Americas." Independence for Cuba without independence for Puerto Rico—in Martí's thought—would never be guaranteed, simply because it would feed the voracity of US expansionism.[17] Those who knew him said that the pain of seeing his beloved island under the US yoke shortened his race against death.

The invasion and occupation of Puerto Rico by the United States could not go unnoticed by *Patria*. In the editorial "Lección de Puerto Rico" on August 6, 1898 (document no.89), the newspaper says that the invasion "undertaken by the North Americans to complete Hidalgo, San Martín, and Bolívar's work" would free Puerto Rico from Spain, but it does not comment on the plans the Unites States had for the island. The invasion is described as follows:

It was not a significant act of war, as not a single shot was fired, nor was it the result of adept strategic planning, as the invaders, up until the present, have seen only the backs of their fleeing enemies. It seems that the Americans carry the magical trumpets of Jericho, whose blasts alone brought down its fabled walls. (La Lección de Puerto Rico 1898)

Patria attacks the Spanish colonial regime in Cuba and Puerto Rico and concludes, rightly so, that the cause for the immediate fall of the Spanish regime in the Island was the contempt that the population had for it:

Spain occupied Puerto Rico for nearly four centuries; during this considerable amount of time, her domination has never been seriously challenged. The sunny island has not experienced the tremendous convulsions that have twice unhinged Cuban society. However, the Americans have hardly planted their feet on Borinquen soil and the colonial infrastructure has begun to tremble—shaken to its very core—and will collapse on its own. (Lección de Puerto Rico 1898)

The US occupation of Puerto Rico becomes accepted as fact and no comments are made about its independence. By presenting "war reports" from other sources as news, *Patria* emphasizes the differences between Cuba and Puerto Rico regarding the US invasion of both islands. One example is how the "news" of the arrival of US troops to the city of Ponce is reported (Las noticias 1898c—document 88):

- On Wednesday afternoon, the city of Ponce surrendered to Commander Davis of the Dixie.
- Not a single shot was fired.
- General Miles and a number of his troops arrived at the city on Thursday morning.
- It was a day of great celebration. The American flag was hoisted above many of the city's main buildings, and the invading army was greeted with music and enthusiastic cheers.
- Twelve hundred Spanish soldiers from the garrison joined in the festivities.
- In his proclamation, General Miles declared that the war is not against the people living on the island, but against Spanish domination.
- The Americans have become enchanted with the island.

Martí's commitment to the cause for Puerto Rican independence had been completely abandoned.

The last news on Puerto Rico that was published in *Patria* reflects the Puerto Ricans' reaction to the US invasion. In a small section of the newspaper ironically entitled "A bit of everything" on August 6, 1898 (Algo de todo 1898—document no. 90), the dissolution of the Puerto Rico Section is reported. This action not only indicates the end of the ties that joined Cuban and Puerto Rican separatism in the nineteenth century, but also represents the final outcome of a long history of the Puerto Rican independence movement of that period. Distraught by the US invasion of the island, the only Puerto Rican rebel organization was dissolved. The newspaper section also informs about the creation of the Liga de Patriotas ("Puerto Rican Patriots League"). On September 10, 1898, *Patria* published the manifesto of the League (Hostos 1898—document no. 91), signed by its president Eugenio María de Hostos. The League set out to educate the Puerto Rican people on life in democracy so that they could choose their own destiny. It also set out a campaign in the Island and in the United States for Puerto Ricans' right to vote in a plebiscite that would determine their political future and allow them to decide whether they wanted or not to become a state of the US federation.[18] In this document, Hostos expresses his belief that US action towards Puerto Rico will be based on the moral and political principles that characterize the American nation, respecting the "natural rights" that Puerto Ricans have to decide their own future:

[T]he Constitution of the United States and the traditions, customs, and solid foundation of justice, impartiality, and liberty that form the foundation of this potent American federation grant us the opportunity to exercise our natural right to advocate for justice and the good of our land; we are endowed with all manner of substantial rights that will be essential and useful resources during the life of this society. (Hostos 1898)

The Manifesto states in one of its sections the hope of many Puerto Ricans that the United States would allow them to democratically decide their future:

We will go to the plebiscite and exercise our natural right as human beings, who cannot be treated like objects; our rights as accidental citizens in the American Union who cannot be compelled against their will to be or not to be what they do not want or aspire to be. In the United States, there is no authority, force, power, or will that is capable of imposing on any people the shame of an annexation achieved through armed violence or of conspiring against that most developed civilization currently in existence among men, resorting to the ignominy of conquest in order to subdue spirits. (Hostos 1898)

It did not take long for many Puerto Ricans, like Hostos, to open their eyes to the true intentions of the United States. The annexation of Puerto Rico was an irreversible event that would transform the structure of Puerto Rican society, up to today. Hostos never returned to live in Puerto Rico; like Sotero Figueroa, Lola Rodríguez de Tió, Juan Rius Rivera, and many other Puerto Rican separatists, he preferred to live in exile before living in an American colony.

CHAPTER 3

EN NUEVA YORK: CUBAN AND PUERTO RICAN ECONOMIC AND POLITICAL LINKS TO NEW YORK CITY DURING THE NINETEENTH CENTURY

It is no coincidence that Cuban and Puerto Rican revolutionary exiles met and joined forces in New York City. Martí, like many other Cuban patriots, never traveled to San Juan. Betances, Hostos, Figueroa, and many other Puerto Rican leaders had never visited Havana. They met and joined forces in *Nueva York*, like scores of other Latin American and Caribbean revolutionaries before them. Economic forces linked New York City to Latin America and the Caribbean, particularly to Cuba and Puerto Rico. Political events brought Latin American revolutionaries to New York City during the nineteenth century. The city became a safe haven to Latin American rebels, including Cubans and Puerto Ricans. The history of Puerto Ricans in New York City, which even today remains as the largest and most important Puerto Rican community in the United States, began much earlier than 1898, long before the United States invaded and colonized Puerto Rico.

The story of how New York City became a safe haven for Cuban and Puerto Rican exiles fighting for the independence of their *patrias* from Spanish colonialism at the end of the nineteenth century must go back some decades, perhaps even a century. The city was a growing trade and financial center of the rising American nation, with economic links with Latin America since American independence. But New York also provided a place of refuge for Latin American revolutionaries trying to gain independence from the Spanish empire. It was in New York City that Francisco de Miranda, one of the founders of the independence movement in Latin America, declared: "I formed a project for the liberty and independence of the entire Spanish American continent" (quoted in Wallace 2010, 26). It was from New York where Miranda organized one of the first expeditions for Latin America independence with men and weapons. A year later, the *Libertador* Simón Bolívar visited the city. Once the war of independence began in Latin America, New York merchants, always eager to make a profit, began to trade with the rebels, and very often also with Spain. After independence, many Latin American countries found in New York a preferred place to do business.

The economic links between New York City and Latin America, Cuba, and Puerto Rico expanded greatly after the end of the Civil War. Freed from its internal conflict, the United States began its economic, political, military, and territorial expansion that culminated in the so-called Spanish-American War of 1898 (a most representative symbol of the end of the nineteenth century and the beginning of what has been called "the American Century"). New York City companies linked to Moses Taylor, J. P. Morgan, James Scrymser, William R. Grace, and Meyer Guggenheim, among others, provided the capital to finance mining, telegraph, shipping, and oil companies throughout Latin America. By the 1890s, US investments in the Caribbean and Central American reached $350 million; in Cuba alone they topped $50 million (Burrows and Wallace 1999, 1211; Wallace 2010, 39–42). Many manufacturers, financiers, and traders with headquarters in New York were among the strongest supporters of the "splendid little war" that began with the invasion of Cuba, the Philippines, and Puerto Rico in 1898. It was from the streets of New York City that the two newspapers moguls of the time—Joseph Pulitzer and William Randolph Hearst—competed in vociferous support for war in Cuba as they tried to outdo the other in sales for their newspaper, the *World* and the *Journal*, respectively. The sinking of the Brooklyn Navy Yard-made *USS Maine* gave the US government—with more than a little help from Pulitzer and Hearst—the perfect excuse to declare war on Spain (Burrows and Wallace 1999, 1212–7). As New York City historian Mike Wallace states: "New Yorkers went wild over America's emergence as an imperial power, with Gotham its de facto capital" (Wallace 2010, 51).[1]

It was in sugar and tobacco investments and production that New York City became significant for Cuba and Puerto Rico (since the nineteenth century for the former, mostly in the twentieth century for the latter). During the nineteenth century, New York was a significant trade center for sugar from Cuba and Puerto Rico, mostly for the former. By 1865, Moses Taylor controlled nearly one-fifth of the entire US-Cuba sugar trade; by 1860 the Havemeyer brothers made Brooklyn the world's greatest sugar-refining center in the world, producing almost half of the American sugar supply during that year. In 1860, New York City ports received 211,000 tons of sugar from the islands: 171,000 from Cuba, 22,000 from Puerto Rico, representing two-thirds of all US sugar imports that year. By the 1870s New York was already a very important center for American financial, manufacturing, and trade interests. Following the example of Standard Oil Trust, New York corporate lawyer Elihu Root—later to become the architect of the American overseas empire as Secretary of War under presidents McKinley and Roosevelt—structured the Sugar Trust for the Havemeyers, joining 17 sugar refining companies that represented 78 percent of the nation's capacity. When the Trust was declared illegal, Root converted it into a corporation: the American Sugar Refining Co., which in a few years controlled 98 percent of national output. The Sugar Trust was at the center of what sociologist César Ayala (1999) called the "American Sugar Kingdom" in the Caribbean, the sugar empire built on the aftermath of US overseas expansion after the war of 1898. No wonder that the Sugar Trust was the most important economic interest behind the American imperial venture at the turn of the twentieth century. Following the example of the Sugar Trust, the American Tobacco Co. settled in New York in 1890. By then, the city was not only the largest US urban market for tobacco but a leading center of tobacco manufacturing for over a century. The Tobacco Trust was a major winner in Cuba and Puerto Rico after the US took control of both islands. After a few years, it became the leading tobacco producer and manufacturer on both islands, controlling over 90 percent of the Cuban Havana cigars trade to the US, and 98 percent of cigarette manufacturing and 42.7 percent of cigar production in Puerto Rico (Burrows and Wallace 1999, 1044–6, 1218; Wallace 2010, 29–31).[2]

After the successful conclusion of the war for independence in Latin America, Cuba and Puerto Rico remained as Spain's last two colonial territories in the Americas. With the 1814 Cédula de Gracias (Royal Decree of Graces), Spain signaled its intent on making these two colonial outposts into profitable ventures, allowing for foreign investments and trade with the islands, more immigration to stimulate social and economic growth, and land distribution to encourage agriculture. This policy was effective in promoting in Puerto Rico an agricultural economy for export based on three main cash crops (sugar, coffee, and tobacco.) It also led to the growth of a Creole landowning class, the *hacendados*, which would be in constant economic and political tension with the Spanish colonial regime on the island, particularly with Spanish merchants. The expansion of this economic structure led to an increase in trade with the United States, which by 1830 was the island's major source of imports (with 27.2%) and market for exports (with 49%). Spain tried to curtail this relationship with the imposition of tariffs, particularly on sugar. But the United States remained an important trade partner, accounting for over a fourth of the island's imports by the end of the century, particularly in sugar, but also—given the island's lack of production of food staples and Spain's lack of a manufacturing basis—in imports like wheat and beef, machinery, and other manufactured goods. New York and other areas of the East Coast were Puerto Rico's main trade links with the United States. But trade was always linked with social and political ideas. For the Creole elite, demanding reforms to the Spanish colonial regime on the island, trade, and economic liberalism was linked to their demands for political liberalism, for a more democratic and representative political system. Many Creoles admired the United States not only for its vigorous capitalism, but also for its democratic and liberal political regime (Meléndez 1988, ch. 2; Quintero-Rivera 1976, pt. 1).

Sugar, coffee, and tobacco were Puerto Rico's three main agricultural products during the second half of the nineteenth century and dominated the island's exports. Production of sugar increased from 112 million pounds in 1850 to 206 million pounds in 1871, reaching a period-high of 340 million pounds in 1879, followed by a constant decline that reached 94 million pounds in 1893 (with an increase to 126 million pounds in 1897, certainly related to the war in Cuba). Coffee production also experienced a dramatic increase during this period, from almost 12 million pounds in 1850 to a period-high of 67.1 million pounds in 1879, followed by a relative decline afterwards, reaching 51.7 million pounds in 1897 (Colón 1930, 290–1).

The increase in the production on these two crops was reflected in the increase of the island's exports throughout this period. Puerto Rico's yearly average external trade increased from $11.5 million in 1861–1870 to $22.4 million in 1897-1900 (Perloff

1975, 17). Sugar and coffee dominated Puerto Rico's exports during this period. In 1864, of exports totaling $4.94 million, sugar provided $3.76 million and coffee $1.01 million. In 1870, total exports reached $7 million, out of which $5.75 were in sugar and $1.04 million in coffee. The relative position of sugar and coffee with regards to total exports changed by 1885; on this year, of $12.99 million in total exports, sugar amounted to $5.78, while coffee increased to $6 million. This relative positioning remained the same until the end of the century: in 1892, of the $14.2 million in total exports, sugar amounted to $4 million while coffee represented $9.4 million; by 1897, total exports were $17.4 million, out of which $4 million corresponded to sugar and $12.23 to coffee (Colón 1930, 289).

The export market for Puerto Rico's top three agricultural crops was very different. The United States was the main market for Puerto Rican sugar (2.4 million pesos in 1897), followed by Spain (2.27 million pesos). Coffee's main market was Spain (3.56 million pesos) followed by France (3 million pesos), Cuba and Germany (2 million pesos), and Italy (one million pesos), among others. Cuba was by far the main export market for Puerto Rican tobacco with almost a million pesos, followed by Spain in a distant second (114,729 pesos) and the United States an even more distant third (33,906 pesos) (Carroll 1975, 154). As in Cuba, Creole sugar interests in Puerto Rico were the main social force behind the pro-US annexationist impulse on the island, though never as strong as in Cuba, given the disparity in the size of the sugar industry between the two islands. During the last third of the nineteenth century, Spain gave preferential treatment to the island's coffee industry, while placing limits on investments and trade on the sugar industry. Puerto Rican sugar planters kept demanding bigger trade with the United States during this time (see: Meléndez 1988, ch. 2; Ramos Mattei 1981).

Cubans were already the largest group of Latin Americans living in New York City during the first decades of the nineteenth century. This settlement was fueled mostly by Cuba's trade links with the United States: by 1835, the island was the third American trading partner behind England and Canada. Although their initial numbers were small compared to Europeans, and mostly involved in trade, it was sufficient to merit publishing a Spanish language newspaper: the *Mercurio de Nueva York*. In 1830, the Sociedad Benéfica Cubana y Puertorriqueña was created to promote trade between the two countries. By 1850, there were some 207 Cubans living in New York City, mostly in Manhattan (particularly in the area of lower Manhattan, Greenwich Village, and in the area between Union and Madison Square) and some in Brooklyn. By 1860, there were more than six hundred Cubans in the city, with a more diversified social composition, including clerks, artists, teachers, cigar workers, and small businessmen (Wallace 2010, 34–5). After the end of the American Civil War and the abolition of slavery, New York displaced New Orleans as the "center of Antillean emigration" (Vega 1977, 85). Using census numbers, Gabriel Haslip-Viera reports that the Latin American and Caribbean population of New York City increased from 3,605 in 1870 to 5,994 in 1890. In 1880, people from Cuba and the West Indies (which included people coming from

Puerto Rico) amounted to 3,480, or 65.7 percent of the 5,296 persons coming from Latin America and the Caribbean; Cubans represented 39.1 percent of this group (2,073 persons). In 1890, 3448 persons came from Cuba and the West Indies, representing 57.5 percent of the total; 1,421, or 23.7 percent, came from Spain (Haslip-Viera 2010, 34). Puerto Ricans living in the United States were not disaggregated as a group during the nineteenth century. The US Census indicates that there were only 678 Puerto Ricans living in the United States in 1900, the first time they were counted as a group.[3]

New York City as Safe Haven for Cuban and Puerto Rican Revolutionary Exiles

As discussed earlier, New York City became a safe haven for revolutionaries from Latin America in the struggle for independence from Spain in the early decades of the nineteenth century. For Cuban and Puerto Rican revolutionaries, the city played an important role in the efforts by exiles to organize the movement for the independence of their homelands. The United States, and New York City in particular, represented the ideals of democracy and freedom sought for the colonized homelands. For example, in their significant manifesto "To the Puerto Rican People" (Club Borinquen 1892–document no. 30), the Club Borinquen argues that they lived "in the great metropolis of New York, whose admirable institutions guarantee freedom in its highest expression..."

Such ideas also come to the fore in "La grandeza de un pueblo" (1894) published in *Patria* on July 8, 1894. Here *Patria* reproduces an article celebrating the American Fourth of July from a Cuban newspaper in Tampa. In its preface to the article, *Patria* argues that "those who still do not have a patria and wander in foreign lands joining our efforts to establish ourselves in sovereign nationality" also celebrated "the great day [when Americans] finally broke their chains of slavery and became sovereign of their own destiny." But in that Fourth of July, in "reverently saluting the solemnity of this great day," they also associated the name of Washington to that of Bolívar, San Martín, Hidalgo, and the other "libertadores de América..." In "4 de julio," the article reproduced from the Tampa newspaper *Cuba*, Cuban revolutionaries contend that "North American independence was the beam of radiant light that illuminated for other oppressed peoples the path to freedom." The article added that "the light of July 4th brightens like a blaze on the dark horizon of the subjugated peoples and consolidated the principle of modern democracy... America is free! This is the Fourth of July. Washington first; Bolívar followed." To these revolutionaries, the independence of the United States had meaning in regards to the independence of other colonized peoples and for those still struggling for freedom. But the article makes an even greater jump when it argues that the work of Washington was left incomplete and it was up to Lincoln to complete it with the abolition of slavery: "One achieved independence, beating the English leopard; the other consolidated the Republic by freeing four million slaves... Glory to the freest nation in the world: the United States of the North."

This view of the United States as a symbol of colonial freedom and liberty, of democracy and rights, does not mean that Martí and other revolutionaries had a simplistic view of the American nation and society. It was common for Martí and others to point to the negative elements in the United States concerning racism, class exploitation, territorial expansion, and the subjugation of native peoples, and the growing impulse for imperialism. In the above-quoted manifesto by Club Borinquen, Puerto Rican revolutionaries opposed annexation of Puerto Rico to the United States on the basis that "we must not aspire to surrender ourselves to the absolute absorption of our race by another, one that does not seduce us to the point of wanting to forsake our language, customs, traditions, sentiments... everything that constitutes our physiognomy as a Latin American people..."

In "La verdad sobre los Estados Unidos" ("The Truth About the United States"), published in *Patria* on March 23, 1894, Martí presents one of his most succinct reviews of society and politics in the United States. He begins by stating that "In Our America it is vital to know the truth about the United States" (Martí 1894b). He points to all those people that came to the United States to work under servitude, all those that came from Africa as slaves, and to the conquered Mexican territories, as well as Native Americans exterminated and pushed away from their lands:

What the honest man should observe is precisely that it was not only impossible to fuse the elements of diverse tendency and origin out of which the United States was created, within a period of three centuries of life in common or of one century of political awareness, but that compulsory social intercourse exacerbates and accentuates their principal differences and turns the unnatural federation into a harsh state of violent conquest. (1894b)

The American political system, so admired by peoples all over the world, is in a state of decomposition: "... the reasons for unity are weakening, not solidifying; [...] the various localities are dividing and irritating national politics, not uniting with it; [...] democracy is being corrupted and diminished, not strengthened and saved from the hatred and wretchedness of monarchies." He questioned the goals and reasons of those seeking annexation to the United States, be it from "an excessive love for the North" based on "an expression of such a lively and vehement desire for progress" that they are blinded to certain obvious truths, or by those whose "Yankee mania is the innocent result of an occasional leap of pleasure..." (Martí 1894b) As he said many times, you had to live in the United States to really know this society. Martí promises to keep talking about the United States in the pages of *Patria* to "demonstrate two useful truths to Our America: the crude, uneven and decadent character of the United States, and the continuous existence there of all violence, discord, immorality and disorder blamed upon the peoples of Spanish America."[4]

But the United States nevertheless provided a sanctuary for Cuban and Puerto Rican exiles conspiring to end the colonial regimes in their homelands. One of the first Cubans forced into exile for political activism against Spain was Father Félix Varela, an outspoken critic of Spanish colonialism who came to New York City in 1823. Father Varela remained in New York for decades, reaching important positions within the city's Catholic hierarchy. That same year, the poet José María Heredia came to New York fleeing Spanish punishment for his rebel activities. New York City also became refuge for Cubans fighting against Spain, but seeking annexation to the United States. The well-known Cuban planter Cristóbal Madán made the city his home during the 1840s and from there planned rebel activities. After escaping from a Spanish prison, the writer Cirilo Villaverde made it to New York, later publishing the pro-annexation newspaper *La Verdad*. It was from New York that former Spanish General Narciso López launched in 1848 his first failed attempt at a revolutionary expedition to Cuba; he later moved his base of operations to New Orleans (Pérez 2010, 97–103; Poyo 1989, ch. 1; Wallace 2010, 34–8). Lisandro Pérez describes the allure of New York for Cubans at this time: "The choice to live in New York City was to be repeated in subsequent decades by Cuban exiles who wished to stay close to their native island and remain active in its affairs. In terms of economic, political, and socio-psychological distance, the closest place to Cuba was New York, and it was New York's commerce with the island that made that distance appear so short. The commercial ties and the intense ship traffic served to attract and sustain a growing expatriate community" (2010, 99).

Many of the early pages of Bernardo Vega's landmark history of the formation of the Puerto Rican community in New York, which remains one of the best accounts of this period, center on how islanders came to the city during the nineteenth century. Cuban revolutionaries as early as the 1820s had made New York their "center of operations." They received the support of Puerto Rican general Antonio Valero, who was immersed in the independence wars in Latin America (Vega 1977, 78–9). Vega finds that contact between the two islands and New York City increased after the end of the Civil War, when New York replaced New Orleans as the center of trade with Cuba and Puerto Rico. He notes that with the end of the conflict and the abolition of slavery in the United States, New York became the center of stateside Antillean emigration (Vega 1977, 85). With the arrival of Ramón Emeterio Betances and Segundo Ruiz Belvis to New York in July 1867, the conspiratorial activities of the Sociedad Republicana de Cuba y Puerto Rico—created in 1865 by the Cuban Juan Manuel Macías and the Puerto Rican José Francisco Basora—began to flourish again. The group transformed the organization into the Comité Revolucionario de Cuba y Puerto Rico. In 1869, after the Grito de Lares, several other Puerto Rican exiles came to New York, including José Julio Henna, Eugenio María de Hostos, and Juan Rius Rivera (on his way to joining the war in Cuba, where he became army general). According to Vega, the revolutionary activities of Puerto Rican exiles in New York came almost to a halt after Betances and Hostos left the city in 1867 and 1870, respectively. Hostos came back to New York in 1874 and, along with Antonio Molina León and Flor Baerga, founded *La Voz de Puerto Rico*, the first Puerto Rican newspaper published in the city (Vega 1977, chs. 6–7).

The end of the war in Cuba in 1878 opened a new period in the history of the Cuban and Puerto Rican exile community in New York. Hundreds of Cuban exiles

who left after the war ended came to New York and engaged in pro-independence activism. As several Cuban scholars have noted, this wave of Cuban exiles changed the
political and ideological dynamics of the Cuban community in New York. Until this
time, the Cuban community in the city was dominated economically, politically and
ideologically by those linked to sugar, giving it a markedly conservative and annexationist inclination. Those exiles coming after the end of the Ten Years' War—hardened in the battlefields of the Cuban manigua—provided a more revolutionary and
republican orientation to the community's activities (Pérez 2010, 103–4; Poyo 1989,
ch. 4). Perhaps the most important event for the Antillean exile community in the
city at this time was the arrival of José Martí on January 3, 1880. As Vega and many
others have stated, Martí's charisma and thinking excited the Antillean community
in the organized effort to free Cuba and Puerto Rico from Spanish colonialism. Vega
recounts how it was during a meeting at Clarendon Hall on June 25, 1885, in a hall full
of Cubans and Puerto Ricans, mostly artisans and tobacco workers, that the city's Antillean exile community came to acknowledge Martí as its spokesperson for independence and revolution on the islands, as its "indispensable organizer, its ideologue and
maximum leader" (1977, 102). Vega details how after this event the number of Cuban
and Puerto Rican organizations multiplied exponentially, leading to the creation of
the Cuban Revolutionary Party and the newspaper *Patria* in 1892 (1977, ch. 9).

Perhaps nothing better reflects the link between New York City and the Cuban
and Puerto Rican revolutionary movements in the nineteenth century than the fact
that the Cuban and Puerto Rican flags first flew in the streets of Manhattan on May
11, 1850, and December 22, 1895, respectively. They became the official symbols for
their countries in the twentieth century, under different circumstances, of course.
Lisandro Pérez describes the birth of the Cuban flag as follows:

There is no better symbol of New York's role in the Cuban separatist movement than the
extraordinary event that occurred exactly at mid-century, on May 11, 1850, at the corner of
Nassau and Fulton Streets, the location of the *New York Sun*. Then and there, a flag identified
in that day's edition of the *Sun* as the "Flag of Free Cuba" was flying over Lower Manhattan.
No one had ever seen this or any other piece of cloth identified as a flag of Cuba. And it was
not just any Cuban flag, but the Cuban flag, the one that would be adopted by the separatist
movement and remains to this day, despite a turbulent history, the flag of Cuba. It was on that
day, in New York, that it flew for the first time anywhere, reportedly designed and sewn in a
Manhattan boardinghouse. (2010, 102–3)

What came to be the Puerto Rican flag was presented at the founding meeting of
the Puerto Rico Section of the Cuban Revolutionary Party held in Manhattan on December 22, 1895. It also had a turbulent history in the twentieth century. It was prohibited
immediately after the US established its colonial regime on the island in 1900, and it
was not until the 1930s when the Nationalist Party, under the leadership of Pedro Albizu

Campos, resurrected it as a symbol of the Puerto Rican nation. In 1952, it became (with a distinct shade of blue) an official symbol of the Commonwealth of Puerto Rico, to be displayed alongside the US flag. Nevertheless, for decades afterwards people were persecuted for showing the flag alone, taken to be a representation of nationalism and support for independence. But by the 1990s, even annexationists in Puerto Rico were using the flag as a signifier of Puerto Ricanness (Rosario Natal 1970). Today, it is widely used by Puerto Ricans in the United States as a marker of their heritage and ethnic identity.

Puerto Rican Exiles in New York City before 1898

Perhaps the two best-known nineteenth-century Puerto Ricans are Ramón Emeterio Betances and Eugenio María de Hostos.[5] Both spent most of their adult lives as exiles outside Puerto Rico due to their revolutionary activities against the Spanish colonial regime. Both came to New York City at some point of their lives to use the freedom of movement and ideas the city provided in their struggle for independence.

Betances, the intellectual and organizational mind of the Lares uprising, was universally acknowledged as the symbol of the Puerto Rican independence movement during his lifetime. He arrived in New York in 1867 after being banished from Puerto Rico for separatist activities, defying an order to return to Madrid for trial. He arrived with co-conspirator Segundo Ruiz Belvis and was helped by José Francisco Basora, a fellow compatriot who was the diplomatic representative of the Dominican Republic in New York. In New York, the three created the Revolutionary Committee of Puerto Rico, whose July 1867 manifesto calling for a revolution in colonial Puerto Rico is generally seen as the programmatic basis for the Lares uprising of 1868. The manifesto also called for Antillean unity, particularly among Cubans and Puerto Ricans in their common struggle for freedom against Spain. Several scholars agree that it was in his stay in New York that Betances developed his ideal of an Antillean confederation, an idea that alongside that of Hostos would greatly influence Martí (Ojeda Reyes 1992, 16–8). During this stay in New York, a controversial event in Betances's life occurred: on August 21, 1867, in New York's Supreme Court, he signed a sworn statement declaring his intention to become a US citizen. Betances historian Ojeda Reyes has argued that this act was linked to the Puerto Rican's independence struggle, since such document could provide him some protection from Spain's persecution, possible arrests, or claims for political asylum (1992, 18–20). Days later, Betances left for St. Thomas to begin organizing the Lares uprising.

Betances returned to New York on April 1869 and contacted the small group of Puerto Rican exiles in the city, among them Basora (later a member of the Puerto Rico Section's board) and José Julio Henna (Delgado Pasapera 1984). Months later, Hostos arrived in New York, although his relationship with Betances at this time was not very close. Finding the Puerto Rican exile group in the city too weak for any major endeavor and the Junta Revolucionaria fractured by annexationists, Betances left New York for Haiti on February 1870. He never returned to New York (Delgado Pasapera 1984, ch. 6).

Disenchanted with the lack of Spanish reforms in the aftermath of the Lares uprising in Puerto Rico and excited about the war in Cuba, Hostos left Puerto Rico for New York City on October 1869. There he contacted Cuban and Puerto Rican independence fighters through the Junta Central Republicana de Cuba y Puerto Rico. It was in that organization's newspaper *La Revolución* that Hostos began to publish his first essays on the need for an Antillean confederation. He had disagreements with the organization's leadership who were avowed annexationists. He left New York for a pilgrimage throughout Latin America in 1870, proselytizing for the independence of Cuba and Puerto Rico and seeking support and aid for the war in Cuba. Hostos would go back to New York in 1874 and again in 1876, only to depart quickly to Venezuela, where he got married, and then to the Dominican Republic for a longer stay there. After conflicts with the Dominican government, Hostos left for Chile, where he was living when the Cuban Second War of Independence began (Ojeda Reyes 1992, 66–75). Hostos returned to New York City on July 16, 1898, too late for any active intervention in the Cuban war and days before the US invaded Puerto Rico. He tried to participate in the discussions that the CRP's Puerto Rico Section representatives Henna and Roberto H. Todd were having with US officials in Washington leading to the US invasion of Puerto Rico, to no avail (Delgado Pasapera 1984, ch. 8). In the August 2 meeting, in which members of the Puerto Rico Section voted to dissolve the organization, Hostos (1898) made a call to create the Liga de Patriotas, whose manifesto was the last text by any Puerto Rican person or organization in the pages of *Patria*. As Bernardo Vega acutely observed, with the dissolution of the PRS, a whole period in the history of Puerto Ricans in New York City came to a close (Vega 1977, 120).

There are two distinct periods in the flow of Puerto Rican exiles to New York in the last four decades of the nineteenth century: after the Grito de Lares in September 1868 and after the *año terrible del '87* (the "terrible year of 87"). On September 23, 1868, a group of Puerto Rican rebels, led by Betances from exile, took the mountainous town of Lares and declared the Republic of Puerto Rico. The uprising lasted for over a week and was finally defeated by an upsurge of Spanish troops. Weeks later, on October 10, Cubans declared war on Spain on the Grito de Yara, leading to the Ten Years' War (Cuba's first war for independence.) The Lares uprising failed for many reasons, including the fact that, contrary to the initial plans, it began prematurely because the Spanish government was informed of a coming uprising; lack of general support (it was rapidly contained by the colonial regime and many of the revolutionary clubs spread throughout the island never got the order to begin fighting); and the weapons and war material sent by Betances from abroad never made it to the island (the cargo was confiscated in St. Thomas, arguably with intelligence provided by the United States.) Spanish authorities detained thousands of Puerto Ricans; many were tortured (Jiménez de Wagenheim1985; Delgado Pasapera 1984). Those revolutionaries already in exile, like Betances and Hostos, never returned to the island, but kept fighting all their lives for independence. Others that were persecuted after Lares opted for exile; some of them went to New York.

Among the most notable of these was José Julio Henna, who became president of the Puerto Rico Section of the CRP in 1895. The son of a wealthy family in Ponce, the center of Creole power and culture, Henna was imprisoned on sedition charges after Lares, although he was not directly involved in the uprising, but simply for his separatist ideas. He was freed under the general amnesty given by Spain to those imprisoned for the Lares uprising and soon thereafter left for New York, where he became a doctor of medicine and a US citizen. In 1872, he went to study in Paris, where he met Betances and developed a long-lasting friendship cemented in common interests (politics, separatism, and medicine) until Betances's death in 1898. Henna was Betances's main link to Puerto Rican separatists in New York during the 1890s. Although he favored annexation of Puerto Rico to the United States, Henna was disillusioned with the way the American government took over the island and never allowed Puerto Ricans to decide their own future. He remained in New York for the rest of his life and became a well-known figure in the city.[6]

A second wave of political exiles from Puerto Rico arrived in New York after the año terrible del '87. On March 10, 1887, the most radical faction of the Liberal Reformist Party (LRP) in Puerto Rico founded the Puerto Rican Autonomist Party (PAP) in Ponce. The LRP was founded in 1870 by several sectors of the Creole elite, a consequence of liberal reforms to the colonial regime in Puerto Rico by Spain in light of the war in Cuba and the Lares uprising in Puerto Rico. The PAP represented the most liberal and discontented sector of the Creole elite at the time, seeking broader reforms—not independence—to the Spanish colonial regime on the island. Spanish colonial officials and island "unconditionals" saw the PAP as radical and separatist and a threat to their social, economic, and political power in Puerto Rico. Using as an excuse the actions of clandestine groups—collectively known as La Torre del Viejo—against Spanish merchants, the Spanish regime launched a virulent and repressive attack on Puerto Ricans, particularly against the leadership of the recently formed PAP. The party leadership, not directly linked to the clandestine activities, suffered particularly from imprisonment and torture. Román Baldorioty de Castro, the PAP's founder and a symbol of Puerto Rican autonomism, was tortured in the infamous *compontes*.[7] Many autonomists, either because of the regime's persecution or because of disillusionment with a colonial regime incapable of giving even the most modest autonomist reforms, left the island and came to New York City. Many became prominent members of the revolutionary movement of Puerto Ricans and Cubans in the city. Among this group were prominent figures in the Puerto Rican exile community by the end of the nineteenth century, like Sotero Figueroa, Pachín Marín, Lola Rodríguez de Tió, Arturo Schomburg, and Antonio Vélez Alvarado (Ojeda Reyes 1992).

Foremost among this group was Sotero Figueroa, a close collaborator of José Martí in New York and a constant presence in the pages of *Patria* during Martí's lifetime. Born in Ponce, he was a typographer and well-known writer. Figueroa was very close to the PAP's Baldorioty de Castro, whom he considered his mentor. He married Inocencia Martínez in 1889 and right after left Puerto Rico for New York City, where both immediately became involved in the Antillean independence movement. Neither of them ever returned to Puerto Rico; they both settled in Cuba after its independence, although they had divorced by this time (Sánchez Korrol 2010).

Like Figueroa, the well-known poet and writer Pachín Marín had to leave the island after 1887 and, after a pilgrimage through the Caribbean, he arrived in New York City in September 1891. There he immediately established close links with the Cuban and Puerto Rican exile community, particularly with Figueroa and Martí.[8] In New York, he found his brother Wenceslao, who died in the Cuban manigua like Pachín would some time later, both fighting for the independence of their two patrias. As mentioned in chapter 2, Marín's (1896) elegy for Wenceslao published in *Patria* remains one of the most heartfelt and elegant pieces of writing published in the newspaper.

Another great and well-known Puerto Rican poet who came to New York after 1887 was Lola Rodríguez de Tió. She is best remembered in Puerto Rico for writing during the Lares uprising the revolutionary version of "La Borinqueña," which has been the national anthem for independentistas ever since (and with bland revised lyrics, the national anthem under the Commonwealth).[9] Several years after 1887, Rodríguez de Tió was banished from Puerto Rico due to her anti-Spanish activities and ideals, moving to Cuba in 1892 and right after to New York, where she was well-known in the Cuban and Puerto Rican exile community not only for her poetry, but also for her unrelenting proselytizing and support for the independence of the two sister islands. Several verses of her poem "A Cuba" are well-known by Cubans and Puerto Ricans of all ages: *"Cuba y Puerto Rico son / de un pájaro las dos alas, / reciben flores y balas / sobre un mismo corazón..."* ("Cuba and Puerto Rico are / the two wings of a bird, / flowers and bullets aimed / at one single heart..."). Like many others of this exile group, she moved to Cuba after 1898, where she died, refusing to live in a colonial Puerto Rico.

Cuban and Puerto Rican Tabaqueros in New York City

Cuban tobacco workers in Key West and Tampa, Florida, and Cuban and Puerto Rican *tabaqueros* in New York City were the backbone to the growth and significance of the Cuban Revolutionary Party and to the war effort in Cuba. Bernardo Vega reports the strong support these Antillean tabaqueros in New York City gave to the PRC, to *Patria*, and particularly to Martí. He recounts how, on Christmas Day 1893, New York's Cuban and Puerto Rican tabaqueros handed Martí $12,000 collected on what they called El Día de la Patria (Homeland Day): they each donated a full day's salary to the cause of Antillean independence. The Cuban revolution is full of tobacco-related symbols. According to Vega, it was in a cigar that the order signed by Martí to begin the war was sent from Florida to Havana; also wrapped in a cigar was the uprising's confirmation sent back to Martí (Vega 1977, 116).[10]

Throughout Martí's tenure at the newspaper, *Patria* covered the struggles and events of tobacco workers in the United States. One particular incident occurred in

August 1893 when, in reaction to the economic crisis affecting the United States and hitting its tobacco industry particularly hard, a group of Cuban and Puerto Rican tabaqueros (including Pachín Marín, Rosendo Rodríguez and Arturo Schomburg among the latter) decided to create an organization to fight poverty among the exile community (Martí 1893d—document no. 53). Spain's government and media argued that this was a sign of weakness among the exile community. The New York City tabaqueros replied: "Our poor will not be neglected. Nor shall the enemies of our freedom be able to benefit from a civic act—a simple act of compassion and foresight—by presenting it to the patria during these days of uncertainty as proof of our inability to its independence." In a declaration of patriotism and class solidarity, their manifesto concluded: "The Antilles shall be free and our poor brothers in New York shall be sustained by their brothers of all classes and colors" (Martí 1893d). Before making the manifesto public, Martí described the economic crisis affecting the tobacco industry in the United States, where large numbers of Cubans and Puerto Ricans worked: "Key West, the largest center of production, anticipates—at great expense—the imminent and inevitable hour when the consumption of current inventory will force buyers to make new orders. Tampa, which exists solely from tobacco, barely gets by on the little it produces. Whomever lives from tobacco suffers. New York is closing its factories or reducing production by half" (Martí 1893d). Like the *tabaqueros* themselves, Martí concluded his declaration by underlying the relationship between patriotism and class solidarity:

No conflict exists between patriotism and poverty, although Spain—with its concentrated influence—incites and encourages one. No one insults the poor man. And, if some scoundrel were to tell a cigar maker that, by being poor, he has stopped loving freedom—that by losing his position at the cigar factory, he has lost his brotherly love of man, his desire to find a happy home in his own land, the pain of his oppressed compatriots' humiliation, and all that comprises the purity and dignity of human beings—that unemployed cigar maker would violently backhand him and anybody who believed that, by losing his job, he has lost his honor. Tabaqueros, outlaws: the Indio Benito Juárez cast an empire into the sea and fought poverty with honor, reclaiming and securing his land's independence. (1893d)

In the same vein, Martí (1893c) acknowledged the economic support given to the party and to *Patria* by Key West tabaqueros in "El domingo, para la patria; los tabaqueros de la casa de O'Halloran" (April 10, 1893). Tobacco workers from this manufacturing house had devoted their Sunday pay to the cause of their motherland's freedom: *Patria* must "celebrate those Cubans who after working all week to sustain their families, worked, like many other times, their day off, their Sunday, to provide the funds with which they will achieve their honor as men and that of their brothers."

Another view of the relationship of tabaqueros to the exile community is presented by Pachín Marín in his lovely elegy to his brother Wenceslao, killed while fighting in Cuba (1896—document no. 75):

One day while I was managing a newspaper in New York with the fleeting halo of celebrity and fame encircling my brow, I had to visit many of the city's tobacco manufactures in search for support and subscriptions. In one of these establishments I found my brother priming tobacco, a job that has been taken here on sunless days by countless prominent men from all over Latin America!

Bernardo Vega (making reference to a report by Samuel Gompers) contends that there were 3,000 cigar manufacturing shops in New York City by 1894, out of which 500 belonged to Hispanic owners (Vega 1977, 114).[11] Vega also asserts that during this period some 3,750 people worked in *fabriquitas de cigarros* (small tobacco manufacturing shops), usually held in private apartments and worked by family members and relatives. These workers earned $2 less per thousand cigars made than those in the regular shops and had to strip the tobacco leaf for free. Many of these *chinchales* (buckeyes) sold their products directly to small stores, bars, or larger cigar manufacturing companies. They mostly used domestic tobacco leaves, but in some cases Cuban and (not very often) Puerto Rican tobacco. According to Vega, by this time most Puerto Rican tabaqueros lived around 100th Street and Third Avenue and many families coming from Puerto Rico by 1894 began to settle in Brooklyn around Jefferson, Johnson, and Adams streets (Vega 1977, 113).

Besides Vega's account, very little is known regarding Puerto Rican tabaqueros in New York City in late-nineteenth century or on how they got here. But developments in the tobacco and cigar-making industry in Puerto Rico during this time would have prepared them to get jobs in the city. After the middle of the century, tobacco growers and cigar makers on the island adopted the cultivation of Cuban Vuelta Abajo tobacco leaf and the making of Havana cigars, the standard of the industry by then. As the production of local tobacco expanded, cigar making also increased. The manufacturing technique of *habanos* branched out of Cuba as Cuban cigar manufacturers established in the United States, particularly in Key West, Florida, and New York City: in Florida because of its closeness to Cuba, in New York due to its trade links with Havana. These manufacturing techniques were adopted in Puerto Rico as well, so island tabaqueros would have no problem finding jobs in New York City among *habanero* cigar factories. During the last two decades of the century, the factory system and thus wage labor in cigar manufacturing also expanded dramatically in Puerto Rico, consequently making Puerto Rican tabaqueros familiar with this form of labor relations. Puerto Rican cigar makers, like those in Cuba, Florida, and New York City, were deeply involved in labor organizing and politics; they were very important in developing labor organizations in the nineteenth century and central to the creation of the Federación Libre de Trabajadores right after the US invasion and, later on, the Socialist Party in 1915.[12]

New York was a place where Cuban and Puerto Rican cigar makers could find jobs in the second half of the nineteenth century. According to the National Cigar History Museum's website, by 1885 the state of New York had 4,495 cigar factories, out of which 41 percent (1,875) were located in lower and mid-Manhattan. No other city in the world, not even Havana, had as many cigar factories as New York City then. There were 350 cigar factories in Central Manhattan, 12 of large size and 123 of medium size. Lower Manhattan had 1,525 cigar factories: 264 were midsize and 65 were large, 20 of which were capable of employing more than 500 rollers. New York City was the only place in the United States with such production capacity, rolling as many as a quarter million cigars a day. Cigar making in New York on the last decades of the nineteenth century was divided among those factories producing habanero cigars and those that did not. Cuban habanos were of higher quality and thus more expensive than other cigars. Most of the shops producing habanos were owned by Cubans and Spaniards, and employed mostly "Spaniards," i.e., Cubans, Spaniards, and eventually Puerto Ricans. These tabaqueros were deemed to be more skilled in making habaneros than non-Hispanic cigar makers and were paid accordingly: wages were higher than in other shops. These habanero shops used imported Cuban tobacco leaves, while American and European-owned shops used mostly domestic ones. The latter were owned mostly by Americans and Germans and employed mostly American and European immigrant labor (although as the ads in *Patria* attest, some Cubans and Puerto Ricans as well). Most New York tobacco workers were unionized and very few women worked in large or midsize tobacco factories. Most *tabaqueras* worked is the small chinchales that usually employed from three to ten people (Fair Cigar Fabricators 1887; The Makers of Cigars 1887).

Tobacco workers were among the most organized and combative sectors of the American working class by the end of the nineteenth century. In 1864, representatives from cigar makers' unions on the East Coast met in New York to form the Cigar Makers' National Union of the United States. In 1867, after joining Canadian locals, it became the Cigar Makers' International Union of America (CMIUA). In 1869, dissidents organized a new union, the United Cigar Makers of New York (UCMNY). In 1875, the UCMNY affiliated with the CMIUA and became Local 144; its president was Samuel Gompers, who, in 1875, was appointed an international organizer for the union, and in 1886, became vice-president. The CMIUA was very combative and led many strikes for better wages and working conditions during this period. The CMIUA played a very important role in the creation of the American Federation of Labor; Gompers later became its president.[13]

Both Hispanic and non-Hispanic cigar shops employed Cubans and Puerto Ricans, as indicated in *Patria* classified ads throughout its existence. The newspaper listed in its classified ads page (the last of the four-page newspaper) the names and addresses of tobacco factories employing Cubans and Puerto Ricans. The first issue of *Patria* published the list only for "tobacco manufacturing" with 27 names and addresses. By the third issue, it divided these into two categories: those owned by Cubans and Puerto Ricans, and those owned by Americans and Spaniards. Through time the former included the following names and addresses:

Aday, R. V. (34 Old Slip)
Agüero, J. M. (50 Fulton St.)
Aguilar, T. (236 Bleecker St.)
Balmaceda, Luis (932 Columbus Ave.)
Barranco and Co. (281 Pearl St.)
Betancourt, F. (29 Fulton St.)
Cosio & Co. (130 Maiden St.)
Cordero Bros. & Co. (213 Pearl St.)
Cordero y Miranda (185 Prince St.)
Fonseca & Co. (169 Front St.)
Juan Fraga (839 Fulton St., Brooklyn)
Galindo, R. C. (203 Fulton St.)
López Havana Cigar Co. (86 Maiden Lane)
Manresa, J. (32 Platt St.)
Martínez Ibor & Co. (89 Water St.)
Medina, Eligio (6 University Place)
Olivella, L. (149 Bleecker St.)
O'Fallon, S. (627 Columbus Ave.)
Perea Bros. (25 Fulton St., later 91 Barclay St.)
Quesada, F. (320 Fourth Ave.)
Rodríguez, L. (7 Cortland)
Rodríguez R. (62 E 14th St.)
Rodríguez, A. (5 Beckman St.)
Roig, J. (105 Maiden Lane)
Saume, J. (195 Allen St.)
Trujillo and Benemelis (18 Burling Slip)
Trujillo & Sons (90 Wall St.)
Xiques, J. F. (489 Broadway)

American and Spaniard tobacco manufactures that employed Cubans and Puerto Ricans also listed in *Patria* included:

Amo Pérez & Co. (Fulton & Front streets)
Arguelles, Isidro (172 Pearl St.)
Argüelles López & Co. (222 Pearl St.)
Díaz A & Co. (118 Maiden Lane)
García Pando & Co. (228 Pearl St.)
García y Vega (171 Pearl St.)
García y Guerra (23 Gold St.)
Ghio y Rovira (251 E 33rd St.)
Guedalia y Co. (409 E 70th St., later 54th St. & 3rd Ave.)
Jacoby, S., & Co. (E 52nd St.)

López, R. (16 Cedar St.)

Lozano Pendas & Co. (209 Pearl St.)

Monne & Bros. (39 Barclay St.)

M. Pérez (150 E 14th St.)

Ottenberg & Bros (2nd Ave. & 23 St.)

Torres, J. (93 Maiden Lane)

According to the National Cigar History Museum, S. Jacoby & Co. and Ottenberg and Bros. were among those large cigar factories that employed more than 500 workers. As discussed earlier, Manhattan's Lower East Side was the city's most important area for tobacco manufacturing in the later nineteenth century, and many of the tobacco factories that were advertised in *Patria*—both non-Cuban- and non-Puerto Rican-owned, as well as those with owners from the islands—were in that area, particularly on Fulton Street, Pearl Street, and Maiden Lane.

Ads for tobacco products were common in the classified section of *Patria* from its very first issues. An ad for El Progreso cigars appeared in the first issue of the newspaper. The ad read: "*Tabacos puros* (cigars); Made with Havana Vuelta Abajo leaf by first-class Cuban workers in Key West; on sale in all shops in the United States and particularly by Alfredo Ribas (Fulton & Broadway) and J. A. Agramonte (7 Astor House)." Also in its early issues appeared an ad for La Guayana Fábrica de Cigarillos (cigarette factory), owned by Juan Guerra Cisneros.

CHAPTER 4

THE CUBAN AND PUERTO RICAN LATE-NINETEENTH-CENTURY EXILE COMMUNITY IN NEW YORK CITY AS REPRESENTED IN *PATRIA*

Patria offers a window to study and understand the Cuban and Puerto Rican community in New York City at the end of the nineteenth century. *Patria* was not only a tool for proselytizing and propaganda for the independence movement, but was also a means for education and culture, an instrument for keeping the Antillean community informed about world affairs (the war, for example) and local issues as well. In its effort to keep Cubans and Puerto Ricans informed of current events on the city the newspaper provides us with a view of the political, social, and cultural developments in the exile community at this time. Furthermore, *Patria* also offered a very important view into the community by publishing classified ads advertising multiple services for the community. This allows us to gain a broader perspective of different social sectors of the exile community, showing in effect a diversified and integrated community.

The Role of Patria in the Exile Community

As discussed in this book's introduction, Martí saw the newspaper as, foremost, an instrument of proselytism and organizing for the independence of Cuba and Puerto Rico. This is nowhere clearer than in the fact that during his tenure at the newspaper, the CRP's *Bases* (platform) appeared on the newspaper's front page. In the very first issue of *Patria*, Martí described the political function of the newspaper in "A nuestra prensa" (Martí 1892c). Contrary to the press in democratic societies, even the most progressive media, the role of a revolutionary newspaper was very different:

But the press is something different when you have to face the enemy. Then, quietly, the signal is passed. What the enemy has to hear is nothing more than the voice of attack. That's *Patria* in regards to the press. It is a soldier. For our opponent it will be prudent with statements... The weapon is to hurt, the word to heal the wounds. But in our endeavor we do not recognize adversaries. Our virtue shields us and we wrap ourselves in it. This, then, is our hand for the common task. Whatever brings us together and teaches us together, that's ours... With brotherly love... we will stand next to the newspapers that support with indomitable tenacity and sacrifice and disinterest, the independence of the fatherland. (Martí 1892c)

Patria was, first of all, an instrument of *el exilio organizado*, the sum of all Cuban and Puerto Rican exile organizations devoted to the cause of their patria's freedom. In this sense, the relationship between the exile community and its organizations and the independence forces in Cuba was always an element of tension in the revolutionary movement. Spain was always promoting and encouraging internal fights to divide the forces of revolution in Cuba and Puerto Rico.

In the unsigned article "La espontaneidad del patriotismo," published on April 10, 1893, a year after the creation of the CRP, the author responded to those questioning the revolutionary fervor and organizational capacity of the party and the exile community. This text –which clearly follows the programmatic ideas of Martí-- the provides a concise, deeply thought and felt writing on the relationship between the CRP clubs and the independence revolution.

The powerful vitality of the Cuban Revolutionary Party lies in its clubs, and who does not acknowledges this will sin of recklessness or improvisation, or expects the triumph of the cause of independence idly or uttering bravados as a madman without creating anything practical and steady that will lead to cordially and cleverly preparing the democratic republic of tomorrow. The authority of the Cuban Revolutionary Party rises from its clubs, that is, the meeting of wills of all patriots who are sympathetic to the idea of independence, who delegate authority temporarily to a prestigious leader who has the duty to account for his actions, while at the same time limiting his functions to what the Party's Bases and Estatutos prescribe. ("La espontaneidad del patriotismo" 1893)

Later, the article elaborates on the organization of the revolutionary movement and the nature of the future republic after independence. It was the task of the exile community to prepare for the future republic beforehand:

We need to make habits, we must refine ideas, we must adopt fair procedures, we must distribute, with ample spirit of justice, that elective representation of the true republican system, and thus, the comparison between the despotic colonial system whereby Spain rules its colonies, and the democratic principles that the revolutionary emigrations practice in their preparatory work to establish an independent homeland, is and will be favorable to us. So it must be that we must continue adding what the Spanish administrative immorality is subtracting, so much so that our war guided by method and foresight will be final and fast, because the preparations carried by those outside answer to the yearning from those inside. ("La espontaneidad del patriotism" 1893)

The author questions those who promote an immediate war, one without the necessary organization and preparedness: "The lion does not sleep when preparing to give furious onslaught. Nature is never so calm as when the storm is ready to explode ... " The article then concludes:

We do everything we do in strict accordance with Cuba. The time, the people will tell us. Then we'll see how worthy is the spontaneity of patriotism, the virtue of savings, the organization of our clubs, of those overwhelmed groups of our brothers that in exile have joined together to redeem from slavery the Antillean islands, and with their behavior have written the most beautiful page, the one with more order and constancy in the history of peoples struggling for their freedom.

The party was essential in preparing and organizing the exile community for the coming revolution, something that was best done in silence to their enemies. *Patria* was not only vital for this task but also, and most important, in preparing Cubans for the future republic.

Revolutionary Clubs in New York and the United States

In fulfilling its tasks, as viewed by Martí and others, *Patria* also provides us a view of the political and organizational activities of Cuban and Puerto Rican exiles in New York City and other areas of the United States at the end of the nineteenth century. Starting with its very first issue, *Patria* published on its front page not only the CRP *Bases* (platform) but also the names of the CRP directory with addresses and the names and location of the CRP clubs. This gives us an idea of not only where the party was organized, but the name and location of its clubs. By mid-1892, there were 20 clubs organized in Key West, four in Tampa, five in Jamaica, and one each in New Orleans; Ocala, FL; Atlanta; Philadelphia; Chicago; and Boston. There were eight clubs in New York:

- Los Independientes (Juan Fraga, president, 839 Fulton St., Brooklyn)
- José Martí (Emilio Leal, pres., 213 Pearl St.)
- Borinquen (Sotero Figueroa, pres., 124 Chambers St.)
- Pinos Nuevos (Federico Sánchez, pres., 403 E 83rd St.)
- Independientes de Cubanacán (Gonzalo de Quesada, pres., 307 W 28th St.)
- Rifleros de La Habana No. 2
- Mercedes Varona (Inocencia Martínez, pres., 1342 2nd Ave.)
- Las Dos Antillas.

Two of them—Borinquen and Dos Antillas—were Puerto Rican clubs, although others like Los Independientes also had Puerto Rican members. Mercedes Varona, presided over by the Puerto Rican Martínez, was an all-female club with members from both islands. José Martí (120 Front St.) was the party delegate and Benjamín Guerra (281 Pearl St.) its treasurer. There were three Cuerpos de Consejo (council boards): in Key West, Tampa, and New York. The latter's president was the Cuban Juan Fraga (839 Fulton St., Brooklyn) and its secretary was the Puerto Rican Sotero Figueroa. The newspaper's administrator was J. A. Agramonte (214 Pearl St.). Already at this time, the party and newspaper's main leadership was located in lower Manhattan, in the tobacco manufacturing area, its main source of material and financial support. Fraga's party address (he was also president of the club Los Independientes), for example, was the same as his tobacco factory. *Patria* cost five cents and was initially published every Saturday.

By January 1893—a year after the party was created—the number of revolutionary clubs had grown dramatically: there were then 55 clubs in Key West and 15 in Tampa, and, in addition to the ones already mentioned, one in Jacksonville, two in Philadelphia, six in Jamaica, and two in Mexico. By this time, Jamaica had its own Cuerpo de Consejo. The number of clubs also increased in New York, with two new clubs in Manhattan (Cuerpo de Ingenieros and Guerrilla de Antonio Maceo) and one in Brooklyn (Henry Reeves No. 2). New clubs kept forming month after month: by April 1894, almost a year before the beginning of the Second War of Independence, there were 62 in Key West; 14 in Tampa; seven in Mexico; six in Philadelphia; five in Ocala; three in New Orleans; and one each in Gainesville, Jacksonville, San Agustín (probably St. Augustine), Thomasville (state not identified, but most likely Georgia), Chicago, and Boston. By April 1895, there were 120 CRP clubs in the United States and Latin America. Key West remained the center of the party with 62 clubs, followed by Tampa (15), New York (12 with the addition of the club Martín del Castillo), Mexico (7), Philadelphia and Jamaica (6), New Orleans (3), Costa Rica (2), and one each in Atlanta, Boston, Santo Domingo, Brooklyn, Jacksonville, Thomasville, Chicago, San Agustín, Gainesville, and Panama.

Patria is thus an important source in the study and examination of the organizational and political activities of the CRP clubs, particularly in New York City and especially the Puerto Rican ones. In *Patria*'s first issue on March 14, 1892, Martí (1892e) described in "La acción unánime" the meeting of the four existing CRP clubs in New York City joining hands and making a pledge to free their homelands: Pinos Nuevos, Los Independientes, José Martí and Borinquen. Sotero Figueroa and Pachín Marín spoke to the gathered crowd. On April 23, 1892, *Patria* reviewed the meeting of New York CRP's clubs on April 17 in Hardman Hall. Figueroa's speech that day was published in that issue (1892c—document no. 8). On August 6, 1892, the newspaper announced a coming meeting of New York's CRP clubs, at 59 E 25th Street, with José Martí expected to discuss plans and "the progress of the revolutionary ideals... [and] of the positions gained in this preparatory period the indispensable war, which is the war itself..." The review of the meeting by Martí appeared in the August 13, 1892 issue ("Las reunión de los clubs").

A meeting of New York's CRP clubs was reviewed in "La reunión de los clubs" in November 1, 1892. There the Party Delegate described his journey to Haiti, the Dominican Republic, and Jamaica seeking support for the coming revolution in Cuba and Puerto Rico. As usual, along with the speeches made by the Cubans Fraga, Gonzalo de Quesada, and Guerra, the Puerto Rican Figueroa also spoke to the crowd . Among those honoring the work of Martí was Pachín Marín. In the same issue of *Patria*, "El banquete" (1892) describes the meeting of Cuban and Puerto Rican friends to say farewell to the Delegate before his next trip. Among the many speeches was that "most tender toast to 'that good man José Martí' by the Puerto Rican [Modesto] Tirado."

In its February 4, 1893, issue *Patria* published "La reunión pública" reviewing the meeting of Cuban and Puerto Rican exiles to discuss the most recent events in their islands, including proposals of electoral and political reforms being discussed by the Spanish government. In a crowd that gathered "Cubans and Puerto Ricans of the most diverse occupations and fortune," Martí, Gonzalo de Quesada, and Figueroa gave well-received speeches (see Figueroa 1893a—document no. 13 for Figueroa's speech). On April 21, 1894, Sotero Figueroa made public the Actas or proceedings of the last meeting of New York's Cuerpo de Consejo on April 10, where the city's CRP clubs elected their own officials and those of the CRP. Once again, Martí was elected party delegate. Accompanying Martí on his entrance to the podium that night was General Máximo Gómez, on visit to New York at the time. In "Nuestro adiós al General" and "El adiós del general," on April 21, 1894, Martí described the general's tour of the East Coast and the latter's farewell words before leaving for the Dominican Republic, respectively.

The insurrection that launched the Second War of Independence in Cuba began on February 24, 1895. In its February 23 issue, *Patria* published a front page note, "El meeting," announcing a meeting by the CRP calling "all those that feel for the land of their birth, for their unfortunate *patria*." The circular to "All Cubans and Puerto Ricans" stated: "Duty commands us to meet to discuss patriotic issues. Never could our union and our aid be more useful than at the present time. We need to offer our moral and material support to those who work for the cause of independence." The meeting was to be in Hardman Hall. Interestingly enough, the note stated that "it is possible and very probable" that Martí would be at the gathering. But Martí left New York on January 31; by early April he co-wrote the Montecristi Manifesto with General Gómez and landed with him in Cuba on April 11. From this moment on *Patria's* main focus and concern would be the war in Cuba. On May 13, 1895, the newspaper published in its front page two letters from the manigua: one from Máximo Gómez and the other from José Martí. On its June 25 issue, *Patria* acknowledged for the first time the death of Martí in Cuba. The front-page essay, "¡INMORTAL!," was written by Sotero Figueroa (1895a—document no. 57).

Puerto Rican Clubs

The organization and activities of the CRP's Puerto Rican clubs were widely advertised in the pages of *Patria*. Always present in the pages of *Patria* was Club Borinquen. Martí was fond of talking about this club; in the very first issue of the newspaper (March 14, 1892), he wrote "La sesión del Club Borinquen" (1892f—document no. 2) reviewing their March 11 meeting, where in a "fervent assembly... the sons of Puerto Rico exiled in New York proclaimed their revolutionary faith." In the newspaper's second issue (March 19, 1892), Sotero Figueroa signs "En la ratificación" (1892b—document no. 3) in which the Puerto Rican club ratifies its adherence to the CRP, its platform and its delegate, José Martí.

In "Club Patriótico Borinquen" (1892—document no. 5), in *Patria's* fifth issue (April 10, 1892), Club Borinquen's secretary, Pachín Marín, presented the organization's proclamation of Ramón Emeterio Betances as honorary president during the club's foundational meeting on February 27, 1892. In "La proclamación" (1892g—document no. 7), Martí appraised the meeting of CRP's New York clubs. Representing Club Borinquen was Antonio Vélez Alvarado (vice-president) and for Dos Antillas, Rosendo Rodríguez. These two spoke for their respective clubs, as did Sotero Figueroa for Mercedes Varona and Pachín Marín for Borinquen.

On May 28, 1892, *Patria* announced the next meeting of Club Borinquen at 57 W 25th Street. It reported that a letter from Betances was to be read to the members, and that the general public was invited. That letter was read in a May 29, 1892, meeting reviewed by Martí in "El Club Borinquen y Betances," published on June 4 (1892k—document no. 9). On October 1, 1892, the newspaper published the note "Borinquen: Club Político Antillano" (document no. 11), a communiqué by the club's secretary, Pachín Marín, on the meeting to be held on October 5 on 203 E 54th Street, at Third Avenue. On the agenda were issues related to the organization of the upcoming October 10th event and the presentation of one more letter from Betances.

On April 17, 1894, *Patria* published "Club Borinquen," by José Martí (1894d—document no. 18), reviewing the club's meeting on April 5. Cuban exiles joined Puerto Ricans in renewing their commitment to the independence of the two islands. In that issue, *Patria* also welcomed General Máximo Gómez to New York City. On December 15, 1894, *Patria* published "Club Borinquen" (document no. 20) to discuss the latest meeting of the Puerto Rican organization. It announced a new club leadership, headed by the Lares veteran Juan de la Mata Terreforte as president, and well-known exiles Francisco J. Amy, Rosendo Rodríguez, and Domingo Collazo.

On March 4, 1895, weeks after the war began in Cuba, a brief communiqué in *Patria* by Terreforte and Collazo from Club Borinquen (document no. 21) called Cubans and Puerto Ricans for a meeting on March 4 at Military Hall (193 Bowery): "Cuba is standing and Puerto Ricans should not, cannot lie still. Do not forget that the seed planted today in the fields of freedom of Cuba is tomorrow's fertilizer for the redemption of our poor Puerto Rico."

On March 18, 1895, *Patria* published a small note, "Puerto Rico" (document no. 22), announcing the publication a new newspaper of the aforementioned title published and financed by five Puerto Rican "enthusiasts of Antillean independence." The newspaper was created "within the platform (*Bases*) of the CRP" and all the proceeds from the sale would be given to the party. On June 17, 1895, on one of the last mentions of these two clubs in the pages of *Patria*, the newspaper published two brief announcements by the two New York Puerto Rican clubs. Club Borinquen announced its next meeting on 101st Street and Third Avenue to discuss "important issues regarding the smallest of the Antilles." The note from Dos Antillas, signed by its secretary, Arturo Schomburg, announced that, given the number of meetings attended by its members, the club would start meeting every two weeks.

Along with Club Borinquen, Dos Antillas was the other Puerto Rican club that appeared frequently in the pages of *Patria*. On June 16, 1892, *Patria* announced an upcoming meeting of Dos Antillas on Sunday, June 24 at 2 pm at 203 E 54th Street, called to "discuss important matters." Another meeting was announced on August 20, 1892, for the next Sunday at the same address. In "Banquete patrio del Club Las Dos Antillas" (1893f—document no. 17), Martí acknowledged the patriotic commitment of this Puerto Rican club. In "La fraternidad antillana" (December 19, 1893), *Patria* reviews the latest meeting of the club. The flags of Cuba and Puerto Rico and the portraits of the Cuban Céspedes and the Puerto Rican Baldorioty de Castro hung prominently in the hall; Baldorioty de Castro, the father of Puerto Rican autonomism, is described as "the sagacious and evangelical politician who prepared those worthy Puerto Ricans for the life of freedom in the land that after all will throw off the yoke of foreign and embarrassing domination." Betances was honored and the name of José Martí "was deservedly acclaimed by the crowd and it was agreed to send him a congratulatory testimonial" in appreciation for his work, given that he was out of the country in a political mission.

Another club that appears in the newspaper's dispatches regarding the CRP clubs is Mercedes Varona, the first women's club in the party. An unsigned article (probably by Martí) on the August 27, 1892, issue titled "Nuestras mujeres" (Our Women) announced the formation of this club; the clubs' main purpose was to collect funds for the revolution. (In honor of this New York club the Mercedes Varona No. 2 club was founded in Key West later.) The article underlined the role played by women in the struggle for independence. Martí himself announced the creation of this significant club on November 1, 1892 (document no. 12). It was presided by the Puerto Rican Inocencia Martínez. The club was reorganized in early 1896 to support the war effort. In that news dispatch (Club Mercedes Varona 1896—document no. 27), *Patria* included a letter from Martí to Martínez where the Cuban martyr acknowledged the importance of this club: "I will come to the Mercedes Varona Club, before any other, to give an account of my work and my plans." On October 23, 1895, *Patria* announced the creation of the CRP club Hermanas de Betances in Philadelphia (Hermanas de Betances 1895—document no. 24) in honor of the Puerto Rican patriot and revolutionary "so that this eminent leader may see that he is not relegated to oblivion..." On February 1897 (document no. 28), *Patria* announced the formation of another women's club, Hermanas de Rius Rivera (1895), in honor of the Puerto Rican general; it was led by two Puerto Rican women: Inocencia Martínez (president) and Lola Rodríguez de Tió (vice-president); CRP president Estrada Palma and PRS president Henna were honorary presidents.

October 10th Celebrations and Other Political Gatherings

One yearly event that was very important for Cuban and Puerto Rican exiles, and particularly for Martí, was the celebration of "10 de octubre", the anniversary of the Grito de Yara, which launched the first Cuban War of Independence (1868–1878). On the first anniversary of the creation of the CRP and *Patria*, the newspaper made public the declaration by New York's Cuerpo de Consejo inviting the exile community to the event, signed by Juan Fraga (president) and Sotero Figueroa (secretary), on October 1, 1892. Given that Hardman Hall, where the event had been held in previous years, could not accommodate the number of people that usually gathered for the celebration, it was to be held that year at the Lyceum Opera House, 160-162-164 E 34th Street, between Third and Lexington avenues. The event was to be organized by Fraga, Figueroa, Emilio Leal, and Domingo Ubieta. The event was reviewed (the article was unsigned, but written by Martí) in the October 15, 1892, issue in an article titled "El 10 de octubre." It stated that the room was decorated with the portraits of Cuban heroes from the First War, and also that of Román Baldorioty de Castro, the leader of Puerto Rican autonomism (and Figueroa's political mentor.) Among the speakers was Pachín Marín, described as a "sympathetic face, sparkling eyes, easy and graceful movements, a tribune voice, this is the aspect of this fiery young orator. A soft and murmuring stream when sliding on sand or among the flower beds, surging, thunderous, impetuous when running between stones or tramples in his rough course the dikes that want to harness him and spins and jumps and turns around and overflows, here we have his oratory." The reviewer added: "Three times the speaker retreated, ending his speech and as many times he had to go back to the podium, called back by the applause, cheers, and shouts of the crowd."

That was not the only praise for Marín in the pages of *Patria*. In the very next issue, on October 22, 1892, the newspaper included a piece saluting and welcoming a new Antillean newspaper: *El Postillón*, published by Marín ("El Postillón,' por Francisco Gonzalo Marín") . The author declares that "in Francisco Gonzalo Marín we must celebrate the opulent soul, broad and generous, the prudent sacrifice of his indignant and combative soul to the convenience, complex and delicate, of the motherland that he worships, and the high and orderly spirit that is reflected in the precision and robust force of his language."

More praise for Marín came on May 8, 1893, when *Patria* published "El meeting de Hardman Hall" (1893), a front-page review of a meeting called by the CRP to discuss the situation in Cuba, particularly news reported in the Spanish press regarding a rebel uprising on the island and its defeat by Spanish forces. The top brass of the Cuban exile community in New York was there and, as usual, Puerto Rican exiles also attended. Two of them spoke in the meeting: Marín and Figueroa. The reviewer said of the Puerto Rican poet:

To the vehement request of the audience rose to the podium F. Gonzalo Marín, already seasoned in the battles of the word. He had resolved, as stated in concise and easy sentences, never to speak in public again, but to demonstrate with concrete acts the fervor of his revolutionary ideas. But he obeyed the call that was made; he was upholding all of his previous statements and would go to fight for independence until he succeeded or died in the quest. This time the orator wanted to hide behind the patriot fighter; but the public remembered the former at the same time that took note of the offer of the latter, and to one and the other bestowed congratulations and applause.

The event's longest speech published in the newspaper was that of Figueroa. He restated Martí's and the party's commitment to an organized and methodic war in Cuba and the commitment of the exile community (*las emigraciones*) to support any patriotic uprising on the island:

Thus we can explain this beautiful concert of wills, this patriotic attraction that unites in a single front all Cubans scattered throughout the free continent of the two Americas, and that will impact, like a mysterious electric shock, that noble land that could have been overcome by praise or by the promise of justice, but never tamed in their natural aspirations, in their lust for independence and freedom. ("El meeting de Hardman Hall" 1893)

Thus even when the event was to discuss the future of the Cuban nation, Puerto Ricans were present to support the freedom of their sister patria. Both Marín (fighting and later dying in the Cuban manigua) and Figueroa (devoting his efforts to the fight in Cuba after the war began) were true to the words spoken at this meeting. A few weeks later, *Patria* reviewed the meeting called by the CRP to hear its delegate speak on the situation in Cuba and the party's and the exile community's role in the coming revolutionary war ("Otra vez en Hardman Hall," May 27, 1893). In this issue, the newspaper also published Martí's historic speech, "El Partido Revolucionario a Cuba."

The 1893 "10 de octubre" meeting was announced in *Patria* in a communiqué by Juan Fraga and Sotero Figueroa, president and secretary, respectively, of New York's Cuerpo de Consejo, on October 6, 1893 ("Comunicaciones oficiales: El diez de octubre en Hardman Hall"). Alongside was an article by Martí on the meaning of the Cuban celebration ("El diez de octubre"). That year's meeting in Hardman Hall was reviewed in "En Hardman Hall" in *Patria* on October 14, 1893. Hundreds of Cubans and Puerto Ricans attended the meeting, in a full auditorium with the "revolutionary flags of Yara and Lares" adorning the podium. As on other occasions, Sotero Figueroa was the Puerto Rican speaker addressing the exile community (see Figueroa 1893b—document no. 16).

On October 2 and 10, 1894, Fraga and Figueroa once again announced the New York Council's proclamation for the October 10th event that year, to be held in Hardman Hall. This event of "respectful admiration" for the Cuban uprising was opened to "those in exile that await the time of complete vindication," to "all men of good will and love of justice." That year's celebration was reviewed by *Patria* ("En Hardman Hall") in its October 13th issue. Along with the Cubans Fraga, Estrada Palma, Guerra, and De Quesada, Sotero Figueroa was again one the speakers at this event. He emphasized the goal and duty of exiles in the coming independence struggle: "Today, with the Antillean exile community already organized, with clear awareness of the past, with deep faith in the future, we are moving with the Cuban Revolutionary Party to the final conquest of independence. The jealousy and rivalries, the factional struggles, the irrelevant questions, everything that could make us falter in the fulfillment of our magnanimous goal has disappeared." Following Martí's ideas, he calls for a brief and successful war for independence.

Patria reviewed the 1895 October 10th celebration in "Diez de octubre en Chickering Hall" (October 12, 1995). It was the first of these celebrations after the war erupted in Cuba and after the death of Martí in Dos Ríos. *Patria*'s review reflected the changes in the party and in the newspaper in the post-Martí period. None of Martí's close collaborators spoke in the gathering. None of the speeches was reproduced in *Patria*, as was the norm until then. Estrada Palma, the party's new leader, gave the main speech. But other orators included Enrique Trujillo, an avowed enemy of Martí who was excluded from the party during his leadership. And although *Patria*'s review characterized the event as a "numerous, extraordinary gathering composed of Cubans, Puerto Ricans, and North Americans," none of the Puerto Rican leaders that previously participated in this event did so this time. The only one mentioned by the review was Gumersindo Rivas, not known to be close to the CRP and a close associate of Henna and Todd in the pro-annexationist faction of the PRS.

In what came to be the last writing by a Puerto Rican in the pages of *Patria*, poet Lola Rodríguez de Tió (1898) expressed once more the devotion of Puerto Rican patriots to the Cuban cause and to the October 10th celebration. In "¡Octubre 10!", published in September 28, 1898 (document no. 78), when US forces had already occupied Puerto Rico, Rodríguez de Tió expressed her heartfelt sentiments about her life's devotion to the cause of Puerto Rican and Cuban independence. For her, the October 10 Grito de Yara marked an important day: "From that glorious day, my life has been but an offering to the exquisite ideals of our homeland!... My only thought was to see our nation rescued from her ominous yoke and united with Cuba by unbreakable bonds of love—for our pains are one and the same, as is the cause of our sorrows!" After a life devoted to the cause of independence for her two homelands, characterized by "exiles, disappointments, and misfortunes due to expatriation," she contemplated the fate of Cuba and Puerto Rico, which she once described as the two wings of a bird: one moving towards independence, the other under US rule: "Overwhelmed by my infinite sadness, I see the splendor of glory glisten on the brow of the victorious, those who have known how to fight for the most sacred of causes—Independence! I yearn for the broken wing of that lost ideal, and, among the shadows of an eternal nostalgia, I hear that still-fervent echo: Forever! Forever!" Rodríguez de Tió lived the rest of her life in Cuba; like other Puerto Rican patriots—e.g., Hostos, Figueroa—she could not endure to live under colonial rule in her native patria.

Exile Organizations in New York
Patria also offers a glimpse of the Cuban and Puerto Rican community in New York City at the end of the nineteenth century. Since its very first issue, the newspaper

published in its classified ads page a list of professionals—mostly Cubans, Puerto Ricans, and Latin Americans—offering their services to the Antillean community. Particularly significant is the number of doctors listed in May 1892 (29, including the Puerto Rican Henna at 8 W 40th St.) and dentists (6). The overwhelming majority of them listed their addresses in the Upper East and West sides of Manhattan, reflecting their class background and position in New York society. There were 27 merchants listed, most of them with addresses in Lower Manhattan, within the tobacco manufacturing area; this might reflect their links to this industry or simply closeness to a neighborhood particularly important for Cubans and Puerto Ricans at the time. There were eight lawyers and four notaries with addresses throughout Manhattan. There were nine music teachers listed, all but one with Manhattan addresses. Seven engineers were listed, all except one with Manhattan addresses. Listed also with Manhattan addresses were three *boticas*; without any references, these are difficult to assess, since these might represent drugstores, a meaning common in Spain and Latin America, or a shop for spiritist products and practices, as is known in Cuba and Puerto Rico and remains so common today in New York City. Two *logias* (masonic lodges) were listed: Estrella de Cuba (Benjamín Goberga, Venerable Master, 118 Wall St.) and La Fraternidad (M. Andrade, Venerable Master, 230 East 15th St.).

Also listed since the early issues of the newspaper were a series of Sociedades Cubanas y Puertorriqueñas (Cuban and Puerto Rican organizations): Ignacio Agramonte (J. F. Silva, pres., 214 Pearl St.), La América (Francisco Lahena, pres., 214 Pearl St.), La Equidad (Gregorio Graupera, pres., 1777 Third Ave.), La Igualdad (Manuel Coronado, pres., 944 Third Ave.), Los Treinta (P. Caldera, pres., 233 Sullivan St.), La Liga (Rafael Serra, pres., 74 W 3rd St.), and San Carlos (Eusebio Díaz, pres., 1372 Third Ave.). Most of these were probably *sociedades de ayuda mutua* (mutual aid societies).

La Liga, the organization founded by the Afro-Cuban Rafael Serra to promote the advancement of black Cubans and workers, particularly *tabaqueros*, was a constant presence in the pages of *Patria* during Martí's tenure in the newspaper and the party. Martí, as well as Sotero Figueroa, worked with and supported the work of the organization. On May 14, 1892, a news brief tells of "Lunes en la Liga" (Mondays at La Liga), where an excited crowd gathers to enjoy literary discussion and learn French. La Liga is described as "a true coalition of selfless hearts that support education and spread love among men of good will." On May 21, 1892, Juan Bonilla, on a request from his "cariñoso Maestro" (Martí), reviews the latest "fiesta" in La Liga, an evening full of music and poetry and good food. In the November 1, 1892, issue there is a review of a meeting where Martí discussed his trip to Haiti, the Dominican Republic, and Jamaica. The reviewer (Martí) states: "La Liga is a home of study and love, where men do not go to see how under the pretext of color, or the transitional pains that come from it, make the curare that will poison the motherland where they will have to live..." (Martí 1892o).

On January 28, 1893, *Patria* reported on an event sponsored by La Liga in honor on Cuban and Puerto Rican women and their role in the struggle for the independence of their beloved islands. Many were the speeches by honored women and also by some men, including Serra, Martí, and Figueroa. In "Noche hermosa de La Liga," published on November 4, 1893, the meeting of this working-class organization is described in great detail by Martí. La Liga is characterized as "the home of affection and teaching where a tenacious group of real men meet in the heat of the stove paid by the poor." It is "the home of ideas that for many years, with the sacrifice of their meager wages, is paid by a few Cuban workers, workers of color..." where the tables and bookcases are full of books of world literature, politics, history, and science; where a sickly merchant goes to teach grammar and a doctor full of goodness teaches English; where someone is always playing the piano and women go to relax from the hard chores of the day and can enjoy the evening along with the men.

Other exile organizations appeared in the pages of *Patria* as well. On September 17, 1892, *Patria* announced the creation of La Liga Antillana, a mutual aid society formed by *señoras y señoritas cubanas y puertorriqueñas*. It stated that "Puerto Ricans and Cubans in New York have now, apart from their work or political associations, a charitable organization in which the worker, every month or every week, deposits the contribution that is to be used if illness or death paralyzes his energies." On November 7, 1892, *Patria* reviewed the meeting of the Sociedad de Beneficiencia Hispano-Americana de Nueva York with a transcription of the report by its secretary, CRP leader Gonzalo de Quesada. The Cuban stated: "In this metropolis—where there is no emigrant group that does not have an organization to relieve their poor—we felt the need of gathering under an effective leadership, the means to help our brothers when afflicted by disease and misfortune." He contended that there were 150 members in the organization.

Literary and Cultural Events

Also common in the pages of *Patria* were announcements for literary and artistic events of interest to Cubans, Puerto Ricans, and Latin Americans in general living in New York City. As mentioned in the introduction to this book, perhaps the most prominently featured non-political Puerto Rican figure to appear the pages of *Patria* was the pianist Ana Otero. On November 1, 1892, *Patria* reviews the *velada lírico-literaria* held by the Sociedad Literaria Hispano-Americana de Nueva York in commemoration of the fourth centenary of the discovery of the Americas. As described by the reviewer, it was a politically and socially diverse crowd with representatives of all Latin American and Antillean nations and peoples. The highlight of the event was a piano concerto by Otero:

And then came the time awaited by all with real impatience: the first-time appearance among us of the distinguished pianist of Puerto Rico, the gentle *Borinqueña* Miss Ana Otero. Much we expected from this artist given the fame that preceded her; but reality exceeded our hopes. *Señorita* Otero has all the qualities of a first-class pianist: clear and distinct notes, clear execution, and a tender courage and expression are what we

found most remarkable. She played with true perfection a 'Polonaise in B' by Chopin and 'Invitation to the Waltz' by Lazare, along with several encores, and retired laden with flowers and applause. We hope that this charming artist, who carries in her eyes all the fire of her beautiful land, promptly gives us another occasion to hear and admire her again. (La Sociedad Literaria 1892)

On December 17, 1892, *Patria* published a brief note announcing Otero's upcoming concert in Chickering Hall. Those who heard her play before, it stated, would no doubt go back to "admire the real merits of the remarkable artist," and all Cubans and Puerto Ricans would be there to "applaud her in the night of her concert. The glory of this meritorious *Borinqueña* is our glory." A few weeks later—on January 21, 1893—*Patria* announced that her upcoming presentation would be held on February 3, 1893, her first public concert in New York. The dispatch concluded: "There she will receive from the hands of peoples from other countries the applause that every artist who honors their art deserves; but moreover, will the beloved sister know, by its fire and pride, that of her fellow Cubans and Puerto Ricans?" On January 28, 1893, *Patria* reported the excitement leading Otero's concert and published its program. On February 14, 1893, an ad for "Ana Otero, music teacher" appeared in the classified ads for the first time; the address was 313 W 14th Street, her residence (this is the address for a *casa de familia* that announced rooms for rent for Cubans and Puerto Ricans). On June 17, 1893, *Patria* published the news bit "Ana Otero," announcing the pianist's trip to Humacao, Puerto Rico, to take care of her ill father. It expressed the hopes that she would return to New York, "where so many fraternal hands are eager to applaud her again... fortified by love and faith, to continue on the path traced by her vocation and in whose summit shine the great masters of harmonic inspiration."

Other artistic and literary events were announced in the pages of *Patria*. On September 9, 1893, a brief note appeared in the newspaper asking for amateur tenor and baritone singers for a "recreational Hispanic-American society" interested in *lírico-dramática* representations for the "educational entertainment of our large colony." Those interested were asked to contact Imprenta América (owned by Sotero Figueroa) on 298 Broadway, third floor. On November 4, 1893, *Patria* published the speech given by Martí in honor of Simón Bolívar on October 28 to the Sociedad Literaria Hispano-Americana in New York.

Another Puerto Rican whose name and writings appeared frequently in the pages of *Patria* was Pachín Marín. On November 1, 1892, *Patria* published a small ad for *Romances*, "a beautiful volume of verse" by F. Gonzalo Marín, sold in the newspaper's office for 50 cents. In "El periódico," *Patria* announced the publication of the most recent newspaper published by Marín, from which he—until the war erupted in the sister islands—would fight his enemy with the written word. A news item on June 17, 1893, reproduced the beautiful prose that opened the new newspaper:

And you, patria of my love and my elders; distant asylum of the outlaw that observes you every day under the unclear veils of the dying afternoon; you, rebellious Cuba, sick Puerto Rico; my two slaves and sad pueblos, lying haphazardly, as two bands on the high-sea blue Caribbean waters; you, my beautiful Republic of tomorrow, greeted by emerging brilliance of the next century, forgive me, Oh patria, if for today's offering I will have sometimes to tear your pale flesh; forgive me if, to love you best, I have to drop my contemptuous slap on the cheek of one of your children. (El Periódico 1893)

A year earlier, on December 17, 1892, a brief note by F. Gonzalo Marín had appeared in *Patria* announcing that for health reasons his newspaper *El Postillón* was to be shut down. It asked all those with paid subscriptions to retrieve their refunds in the newspaper's office at 113 E 114th Street.

A well-known Puerto Rican newspaper in New York was *La Gaceta del Pueblo,* published by the renowned Puerto Rican revolutionary exile Antonio Vélez Alvarado. On April 16, 1892, *Patria* published Martí's "Palabra generosa" (1892h—document no. 6), in which he thanks the newspaper for its gracious welcoming of *Patria*. Martí acknowledged the contributions made in this newspaper by Pachín Marín, "a man of generosity and fire." On June 11, 1892 Martí presents a brief review of several exile newspapers in the United States, including *La Gaceta del Pueblo*. On June 29, 1893, an ad for *La Gaceta del Pueblo* appeared in the ads section in *Patria*; it was printed by Tipografía Gaceta del Pueblo, 134 World Building, NY.

One well-known institution in the Cuban and Puerto Rican exile community in New York at this time was Imprenta América, the print shop owned by Sotero Figueroa where *Patria* was printed for a long time. On June 24, 1893, an ad appeared for the first time in *Patria* for Imprenta América (on 298 Broadway, between Duane and Reade streets in lower Manhattan). The ad stated: "This printing establishment is open to favor those who speak our language and have our same ideals and artistic feelings, guarantees the goodness and correction of all work entrusted to us no matter how lengthy, difficult, or complicated it is. We can take care of all kinds of translations from Spanish to English, French, German, and Italian, or vice versa."

One institution listed and advertised in the pages of *Patria* since its early days was Instituto Estrada Palma for primary and secondary education, founded by its namesake in 1885 and located in Central Valley, Orange County, New York. One it its ads read: "Several students of Hispanic America have been prepared in a short time in this school and have successfully entered the University of Medicine and at Cornell, Ithaca." Also listed as a *colegio* was that of "Flora y Leopoldina Quesada" at 60 Lexington Avenue.

As a voice of the Cuban and Puerto Rican exile community in New York, *Patria* very often published small notes on the affairs and events of the exile community. Notes of condolences appeared from time to time. One of particular interest to this book was published on September 9, 1893, on a tragic event to the family of Sotero

Figueroa and Inocencia Martínez: the tragic death of their young child (although unsigned, the author might have been Martí).

Delight of the home, exemplary and noble, of the Puerto Rican Sotero Figueroa was that butterfly fluttering full of life and joy: Julia. A painful disease, which struck the little girl only two years old, and as an angel going to heaven, she soon flew, with the smile of suffering on her lips compressed with pain. In the white coffin she resembled a dove of the purest white quietly sleeping in the nest of her innocence. With grieving heart distressed by great pain, the mother pressed against her chest the siblings also crying, and standing between the snowy draperies, the father, with the lowered head and dull eyes.

And to have to bury the children of your soul, for lack of a patria, in a foreign grave!

Deep-felt words to console a dear friend and comrade in the struggle for independence.

Lodgings and Food

Ads for hotels and lodgings catering to the Antillean community were also common in the pages of *Patria*. One of the institutions that advertised in the classified pages in almost every issue was Hotel América, on Irving Place and 15th Street. It advertised single rooms for $1, or $2.50 with meals, per day; its owners were Arturo T. Berntich and E. Spinetti. A few months later, it began announcing a branch in Paris (60 Rue Lafayette), and in 1893, it opened a branch in Chicago on 1469 Michigan Ave. ("The only Spanish and Hispanic-American hotel, located in the most elegant and aristocratic part of the city"); the price of rooms were a bit higher in Chicago than in New York, $3-4 per day. Also advertising by 1893 was Hotel Central on 154-156 W 15th Street, calling itself a "classy hotel, especially for Latin-American families." The ad also read: "Spanish, French, and English is spoken; the agent of the house will be in the docks on the arrival of the steamers." *Patria* also featured an ad for the Plavano Hotel and Restaurant at 28 East 23rd Street ("In front of Madison Square Garden; Good food, affordable rooms, our customs").

Also advertising in the pages of *Patria* were rooms for rent, usually boarders in family apartments. For example, there were two such ads in the July 9, 1892, issue. One read: "Family house (*casa de familia*) for Cubans, Puerto Ricans, and Hispanic Americans in a central and comfortable place—313 W 14th Street; Cuban customs, Cuban food; room and board from $7 weekly." The other read: "Furnished room $1.50 weekly, a block from the Park—71 E 109th Street—Cuban Family." In a later issue, another *casa de familia* ad read: "In Brooklyn, 32 Poplar St., two blocks from the Bridge and 3 from Fulton—Cuban food, Cuban customs, furnished rooms—affordable prices; Misses Estenoz."

Several *bodegas* were also listed and advertised in the newspaper since its first issues, with addresses mostly in lower Manhattan. One ad for Bodega Española in

Maiden Lane read: "Everything imported for the consumption of our colony in the New World." It advertised the selling of foodstuffs and products from Spain and Cuba. This raises an interesting question: might this be the origin for those Puerto Rican and Dominican bodegas so famous in New York City for most of the twentieth century? In Spain the term is usually related to wine cellars or to warehouses, usually for wine, but also for other products, although in some places, like it is common also in Latin America, it might refer to an *almacén* or general warehouse. Restaurants also placed ads in the classified section. One such ad read: "Julián Moreno Cuban Restaurant: The food is Cuban, it is good and cheap; Home delivery of food canteens–173 Spring St."[1]

Patria was more than the organizational and propaganda tool for the Cuban Revolutionary Party in its struggle to gain the independence of Cuba and Puerto Rico from Spain. As this chapter has shown, the pages of *Patria* can be used to depict the social and political activities and daily lives of the Puerto Rican and Cuban community in New York City in the late ninetieth century. It serves as evidence of the fraternity developed between Cuban and Puerto Rican exiles in literary, cultural, and mercantilist milieus, showcasing the camaraderie that existed between the two, aside from or rather, in addition to, political organizing. The applause for Pachín Marín's verses or Ana Otero's piano concerts, for example, epitomizes this mutual support. *Patria*'s inclusion of Puerto Rican exile organizations in addition the Cuban counterparts, evokes what Martí made clear through both his word and action: just as Cuba seeks her own liberation, so too does her sister wing. Martí insisted that Cuban liberation efforts that failed to take into account Puerto Rico's independence would simply be in vain. In this way the newspaper can be used to document the historical record of the nascent Puerto Rican community in this city and remind current generations that the origins of the Puerto Rican presence in New York goes back to years before the US invasion of their *patria* in 1898.

PART 2

Section 1
EL PARTIDO REVOLUCIONARIO CUBANO

Doc. 1
"Platform of the Partido Revolucionario Cubano"
March 14, 1892 (#1)

Proposals made on behalf of the Key West exile community, approved by the Tampa exile community and by the Cuban and Puerto Rican Clubs of New York, with which this newspaper complies and upholds.

Article 1: The Partido Revolucionario Cubano is hereby established to achieve, through the united efforts of all men of good faith, the absolute independence of the island of Cuba, and also to promote and aid in the independence of Puerto Rico.

Article 2: The Partido Revolucwionario Cubano does not intend to hastily precipitate war in Cuba, nor to launch at any cost to the country a poorly prepared and divided movement of forces, but to organize a noble and expeditious war, depending on the number of active and honorable factions who join it, aimed at securing the prosperity of the inhabitants of the Island through peace and hard work.

Article 3: The Partido Revolucionario Cubano will assemble the revolutionary elements currently in existence and will gather as many new elements as it can without unprincipled obligations to any country or man, to establish in Cuba by means of war, republican in spirit and practice, a Nation capable of ensuring the lasting good fortune of its progeny and fulfilling, in the historic life of the hemisphere, the difficult mission that marks its geographic situation.

Article 4: The Partido Revolucionario Cubano does not intend to perpetuate in the Republic of Cuba the authoritarian spirit and bureaucratic composition of the colony through new structures or changes that are more superficial than fundamental, but to establish, through the open and righteous exercise of the legitimate rights of man, a new country based on true democracy which is able to overcome, through the organizing of genuine efforts and the balancing of social forces, the dangers of sudden liberation in a society created for slavery.

Article 5: The Partido Revolucionario Cubano does not intend to take to Cuba a victorious group that considers the Island its prize and dominion, rather to organize the war that must be undertaken for the honor and good of all Cubans with as many efficient means as permitted by the freedom of exile, and to deliver a free homeland to the entire country.

Article 6: The Partido Revolucionario Cubano is established to found a wise and prudent Cuban *patria*, one in which each of its preparatory efforts is arranged to protect it from the internal and external dangers that threaten it, and to replace the economic chaos under which the public Treasury system suffers with the immediate opening of the country to the diverse enterprises of its inhabitants.

Article 7: The Partido Revolucionario Cubano will guard against attracting, through any injudicious act or declaration in its propaganda, the ill will or mistrust of countries with which interest or friendship encourages or obliges the maintaining of cordial relations.

Article 8: The Partido Revolucionario Cubano includes the following as its purposes:

I. Unify, in a sustained and common effort, the actions of Cubans residing abroad.

II. Encourage open relations between the historical and political groups, both inside and outside the Island, that which can contribute to the rapid triumph of the war and the greatest empowerment and efficiency of the institutions that, after it, are established and seek to embody its principles.

III. Propagate knowledge of the spirit and methods of the revolution in Cuba and bring together the inhabitants of the Island in a favorable disposition toward victory by means that do not put Cuban lives unnecessarily at risk.

IV. Collect funds for the realization of its agenda and access a wide range of sustained resources for the war effort.

V. Advisedly establish relations with friendly countries that may serve to accelerate the success of the war and the founding of the new Republic, which is essential to achieving hemispheric balance, with the least bloodshed and sacrifice possible.

Article 9: The Partido Revolucionario Cubano will be governed by the secret Statutes agreed to by the organizations that form its base.

Doc. 2

José Martí, "Club Borinquen Session"

March 14, 1892 (#1)

On March 11, a passionate meeting confirmed the decisions reached at this memorable session where the progeny of Puerto Rico, exiled in New York, proclaimed their revolutionary commitment. The actual location of the meeting, which was formal in nature, only added to the impressive nobility of these proceedings. The men spoke briefly, and their words were like fire.

Those assembled approved a resolution that was declared exemplary as proof of the heartfelt courage—which is censured by small-minded and distrustful individuals who lack foresight—by which the peoples' republican spirit must be measured. They proclaimed as honorary chairmen of the Club three Antilleans who have long been joined in the closest sympathy born of a common desire to see the progeny of their country fully realized in the fruition of their prosperity and dignity: Ramón Emeterio Betances, who, like the ancient Persians, kept the fire of the nation burning in the desert and sheltered in the castle of his heart; Eugenio María de Hostos, who presented the Americas as living proof of the superior strength and order that can be achieved through virtuous deeds; and that Cuban who is devoted to Puerto Rico, José Martí.

Then, with a strength and conviction that would have served as lesson enough to the natural enemies of altruism and nobility, Club Borinquen agreed to proclaim its full solidarity—the solidarity of a closely knit and dynamic family—to the platform and statutes of the Partido Revolucionario Cubano.

Doc. 3
Sotero Figueroa, "At the Ratification"
March 19, 1892 (#2)

From the momentous meeting at which the Cuban and Puerto Rican Clubs of New York ratified their allegiance to the Platform and Statutes of the Partido Revolucionario Cubano, *PATRIA* has recorded three significant notes: the prudent discourse of Sotero Figueroa, the germane phrases of Rafael Sierra, and the noble and ardent remarks by Miguel González Ortiz's son.

Sotero Figueroa said:

Gentlemen,

We have no need for declarations that are better made in the heart than on the lips; but reaffirming our faith in the patriotic ideal we hold dear and invigorating the enthusiasm that agitates us is indeed crucial to uniting us in a common effort—in a single binding force—that no one person or thing can destroy, regardless of how great the obstacles thrown in our path.

We gather here to ratify our sincere allegiance to the revolutionary Antillean project. The platform was already accepted by each and every one of the Clubs of New York as a banner that will make us an organization fertile for certain victory. We come here to collectively and publicly confirm our vote in favor of that platform, which has been submitted for approval to all the Clubs already organized, and which has been recognized by all as a judicious endeavor born from enlightenment and experience.

Whereas, it can no longer be considered the isolated expression of a specific group of patriots, but the unanimous voice—the spontaneous and formidable manifestation of all the exile communities in the United States that strive to make a free country of their enslaved homeland.

To those impoverished of spirit; to those who think it insane to break with old colonial models; to those who still have not wanted to fully comprehend the irrefutable power of our ideas; to those who, believing we are weak and aiming to discourage us, dare say that in the struggle for existence the stronger side always triumphs, we tell them that there is a rational and humanitarian principle which contradicts that distressing theory: it is that of *alliance in struggle*.

The weak can do nothing by themselves; but all who, like them, refuse to be humiliated or annihilated can join their side. Then, the strong falter; persecution escalates because they fear defeat; and they seek mercenary collaborators to help them. But these are actually foreign elements who are not bound to the soil and lack the spirit fortified by that bond. The struggle becomes inauspicious for those who thought themselves absolute overseers; and in the end, defeat lets them know that the weak triumph if they know how to ally themselves, in spirit and truth, with the emancipatory struggle. And there is, gentlemen, no power that can withstand a people who long and demand to be free!

Nothing is as invincible as unity. One strand of hair is easy to pull out; but a fistful is extremely difficult. The skin will sooner be ripped off before any strands in a section of hair.

Let us imitate, then, the conduct of the assiduous and diligent ant. If an ant sees a dead elephant blocking its path, he does not think it impossible to take the elephant to his anthill: he studies the surroundings, examines the colossal prey, and, once he has assessed the elephant's nutritious value, quickly reports back to his companions. Within minutes, the massive body is surrounded by hundreds of thousands of ants struggling together to carry it. Since there is intelligent leadership and commendable discipline, none tend to rebel when it comes to the common good; all join forces toward a given purpose; and—oh, the wonders of alliance!—the elephant is removed and, in no time, it is triumphantly hauled to the anthill.

Club Borinquen is pleased to reiterate its fullest allegiance to the revolutionary agenda that has brought such an extraordinarily honorable and commanding messenger as Mr. Martí, who contributes a life of patriotic sacrifice and benevolent engaging instruction. Nonetheless, if there should come a time when the principles set forth turn out to be deficient in practice, he would respectfully propose to the rest of the patriotic Clubs the reforms he deems necessary.

Doc. 4
José Martí, "Borinquen to *PATRIA*"
April 3, 1892 (#4)

PATRIA would be silent if its only purpose were to personally acknowledge the flattering praise extended by Club Borinquen; but it cannot be silent because its pages express the pure spirit and the magnificent honesty with which those not intimidated by time, obscurity or any of the other obstacles enter into this decisive campaign and direct the furies of the soul—the single soul of the battle they fight together—with the power of intellect, the intensity of great enterprises, and the genuine dedication of strong men, both Cuban and Puerto Rican. And, more gratifying still is the acclamation from Club Borinquen, in both mind and heart for its worth and weight, to *PATRIA*, which reads as follows:

"To the Editorial Staff of the Newspaper *PATRIA*,"
At the Board Meeting held last night by Club Borinquen, it was agreed to congratulate the newspaper *PATRIA* for launching such a brilliant campaign for Antillean emancipation, with which this Club, as a whole, allies itself.
New York, March 31, 1892.
CHAIRMAN, S. Figueroa. —SECRETARY, Gonzalo Marín.

Doc. 5
"Patriotic Club Borinquen"
April 10, 1892 (#5)

OFFICE OF THE SECRETARY

As a matter of public business, Club Borinquen today publishes in *PATRIA* the communication that announces to the noble Puerto Rican, Ramón E. Emeterio Betances, his appointment as honorary chairman of the Club and the note that informs the Secretary of the Steering Committee of the Club's endorsement of the Partido Revolucionario Cubano.
The communications reads as follows:

MR. RAMÓN E. BETANCES
Highly distinguished compatriot,
On the 27th day of the current month, in this city, Club Borinquen was formed by Puerto Rican patriots in exile who have joined together with other Antillean patriots. One of its most noble resolutions—one which raised storms of applause—was that of your appointment, as well as that of the Puerto Rican compatriot, Eugenio María de Hostos, and the Cuban compatriot, José Martí, as honorary Chairman of our organization, which thus recognizes your indisputable eminence and the sacrifices you have made fully and completely to, first, educate our people in the pursuit of a free and independent life and, then, to struggle vigorously to establish it as a sovereign na-

tion, and which, if unable to triumph in this most noble undertaking, has nonetheless kept alive the regionalist idea that today flourishes mightily again. We are pleased to raise this glorious banner around which all those who seek to achieve a free *patria* gather—without hatred or condemnation—on the path toward justice and dignity.

It was agreed to send two copies of the platform to you, along with the statutes by which we govern ourselves, and several copies of the manifesto, which we felt compelled to draft to direct the Puerto Rican people.

By fulfilling this most gratifying duty, Club Borinquen has written the most noble document of camaraderie—the one on "gratitude"—which exalts all who proclaim it and glorifies all who are worthy of it.

Patria y Libertad

New York, February 28, 1892

Secretary

F. Gonzalo Marín

Approved by the *Chairman*

Sotero Figueroa

Patriotic Club Borinquen
OFFICE OF THE SECRETARY

Distinguished party member,

At the General Meeting for the definitive constitution of this Club held on the 27th day of the current month, it was agreed to bring to your attention these Puerto Rican patriots who, upon joining their efforts to those of Cuban patriots working toward independence, accept in their entirety the platform and statutes for the constitution of the great revolutionary party that will lead us to the attainment of our rightful aspirations and support the *righteous and singular* movement, without which we could not lay the foundation for a free country.

As the current Secretary of the Steering Committee, please engage all the Clubs from that historic Key in our cause, express to them our feelings of solidarity, and greet them effusively as the brothers that we are in this redemptive project.

Patria y Libertad

New York, March 1892

Secretary

F. Gonzalo Marín.

Approved by the *Chairman*

Sotero Figueroa

Secretary of the Steering Committee

Key West

Doc. 6
José Martí, "Benevolent Words"
April 16, 1892 (#6)

What springs from the soul resonates and, with the soul, is redeemed. Thus, *PA-TRIA* appreciates the eloquent greeting from the Puerto Rican newspaper *La Gaceta*, which comes from the land of Antonio Vélez Alvarado. The newspaper has recently published invaluable articles about Cuba and also counts on the talents of a generous and ardent man, Francisco Gonzalo Marín. He who loves us will have no cause to stop. All which we defend, we will defend each day with even greater vigor and sincerity. We will strive to deserve the following noble acclaim:

"There is a new newspaper in this city. It was born the other day and it is called *PATRIA*.

"It is the voice of encouragement in the anguished silence of the colony. It is the battering ram that tomorrow will break through and bury old, corrupt ideas; the doctrine of political faith for men of conviction and perseverance; the resurrection of a country destroyed by the murderous hand of the abuses perpetrated by the Overseas Ministry. It is a newspaper that holds more than ideas. A home where ideals thrive; a Decalogue of revolutionary commandments; and a tome with sources that include the defiant Cuban as well as the derided Puerto Rican: this is *PATRIA*.

"Those who stand with liberty stand with *PATRIA*. Divorce is impossible.

"We commend *PATRIA*; we recognize that its vocation corresponds to that intense longing in our souls. With its clear course, well-defined principles, and manifest aspirations, we wish it as long a life as necessary for the attainment of Antillean independence."

Doc. 7
José Martí, "The Proclamation"
April 16, 1892 (#6)

The hall abounded with people, and both flags together presided over it. Juan Fraga, the chairman-elect of the New York Board of Advisors, stood before the crowd and declared the Partido Revolucionario Cubano officially established: Fraga's words were like a bouquet of swords. Seated around him at the table were Sotero Figueroa, who chairs Borinquen and functions as secretary of the Board of Advisors; Emilio Leal, the chairman of Club José Martí and respected activist; Gonzalo de Quesada, the beloved young chairman of Cubanación; Antonio Vélez Alvarado, the vice chairman of Borinquen; Federico Sánchez, the enthusiastic leader of Los Pinos Nuevos; Rosendo Rodríguez, founder of Las Dos Antillas; and Justo Lantigua, the sincere and exuberant orator.

And, must it be said that in those passionate and spontaneous remarks, which were genuinely beautiful and flashed with ardor, there occurred, without warning, a concert of sugar cane stalks waving in unison, seeking the sun and obeying the wind? Must it be said that what was remarkable at the meeting was not the effusive enthusiasm, but the urgency and firmness of each word? It was not giddy, naïve confidence, but the judicious conviction of consummate patriots. It was not revolutionary recklessness, but the vigilant passion of the republic. It was not the haughty and guarded display of one social class, but the magnificent and sincere communion of all.

The patria is a home for all; and all must have a voice in it. The patria is not meant to profit from the land, nor should one live off of it, like the worm off the tree. Rather, we are meant to give everything over to it, as parents give themselves to their children. The patria is not vengeance, forever excluding those who have sinned, nor a village where there is no room for those who live outside its borders. Rather, it is a heart with room for all. The Party is not a ship that will run aground on the beach. Neither is it a network of the Clubs of Cuba, which may be infiltrated by spies from podiums. It is the entire exile community that, in a spirit of equality, stands up along with those purified by experience to establish an American pueblo.

Lantigua, a criollo of visionary speech and clear mind, spoke for José Martí; Sotero Figueroa spoke elegantly for Mercedes Varona; Las Dos Antillas brought the voice of Rosendo Rodríguez, who spoke with singular composure in his exuberant speech; the speakers from Borinquen were Antonio Vélez Alvarado, whose discourse was fiery and inventive—vibrant and novel in spirit—and Francisco Gonzalo Marín, a man who belongs on a lofty pedestal. Gonzalo de Quesada spoke for Cubanacán with austere and rousing refrains; Benjamín Guerra spoke to the aims of the meeting with emphatic and incisive economy. But the greatest moment of the night, when the proclamation appeared complete and true to all, occurred when Leopoldo Acosta recounted past mistakes with the spirit of a natural-born orator, the momentum and good sense of one who does not fear nor obscure, and with an edict proclaimed in the open air that breathed life into those honest souls. He deferred to the spirit of the republic on this new day, publicly declaring his heart's sincere and solemn conviction and that of the entire hall. Lawyers, businessmen, journalists, engineers, and doctors stood up to embrace that worker who is also an orator, a *guajiro* orator. Such are the times in which we live!

Doc. 8
Sotero Figueroa, "Speeches at the Confirmation of the Proclamation of the Partido Revolucionario Cubano (Hardman Hall, April 17, 1892)"
April 23, 1892 (#7)

Sotero Figueroa, Secretary of the Board of Advisors and Chairman of Club Borinquen, stated:

Antilleans,

Eight days ago—a momentous date for the Cuban people—all the wills here in the exile community who are inclined toward establishing a populist sovereignty in the liberated homeland joined together and confirmed the great Partido Revolucionario, which was definitively established for the independence of those two oppressed islands bathed by the Caribbean Sea. The Guaimaro Constitution—the Code of a sovereign Cuba—was the banner around which gathered all those who believe that the hour of vindication had arrived on April 10, 1892. The commemoration of this great date—when the founding document that restores to a people their innate dignity was written, a dignity expropriated by the despotic and inconceivable right of conquest—could not have been better celebrated.

And today, on this august day for humanity that commemorates the glory of Christ, who laid down the principle of justice on solid foundations wherefrom modern law originates, we come to solemnly ratify the sworn proclamation and bind our redemptive effort to that of the humble Nazarene, who raged against the iniquities of the ancient world, transformed slaves into citizens, and planted the seeds of hope in what was an inferno of sorrows.

And, how many similarities exist between that enduring saga, which began in that miserable stable in Bethlehem, and the patriotic endeavor we pursue today, which originated in the little town of Yara and is on the path to glory, having already walked the streets of bitterness and soaked the cliffs of its Calvary with blood!

Likewise, this redemptive movement, which acts upon the conscience and soul, does not emerge from the privileged classes. Those on the bottom rise to the top, which is why it will surely result in its justified triumph. It is the humble—the gentle of heart—who spread its message with a lofty spirit of justice without violence or hatred. For that reason, they carry within themselves the seed that will fortify it and make it triumphant. In the great uprisings for justice, leaders do not emerge from the affluent class, which finds itself perfectly sated by the established order, but from the suffering masses and the dispossessed, who carry inspiration in their minds, torment in their hearts, and truth on their lips. Neither the arrogant nor the haughty have the authority to lead the popular masses. Nor can presumptuous intellectuals set themselves up as mentors of the clarity and simplicity that, if it were to surrender to rigorous and thoughtful reason, would never become Olympian pretension or humiliating notoriety. It is strength; it is transparency; it is modest knowledge; and it is the righteousness of intentions that the people ardently welcome. And he who embodies these charitable qualities will be the leader and mentor whom the multitude will follow in moments of radical transformation.

Such was Jesus, that eminent martyr of the democratic doctrine that was written in unsparing blood and recorded in the annals of honorable peoples. According to the sacred Christian legend, he was born to parents so miserable that they did not even have a home in which to shelter him. He grew up to be a poor, insignificant, and vulnerable carpenter. He reached manhood and—having already been educated in the school of misfortune and fortified by redemptive truth with both a faith that moves mountains and sufficient abnegation in his soul to forgive trespasses, dismiss attacks from fools, and give his life for the redemption of his people—he embarked—poor and uncertain, alone and defenseless—on a journey through Judea to establish a kingdom of justice in the hearts of the people and to abolish the caste system by preaching a doctrine that enlightened minds and elevated humanity, all of which is embodied in these three sublime words: Liberty, Equality, and Fraternity.

Soon thereafter, the cedars of Lebanon and the palms of Jericho whispered the teacher's consoling words; and the banks of the River Jordan and the Sea of Galilee lovingly spread the echoes of that inspired voice. Cana and Bethsaida, Capernaum and Nain, Bethphage and Bethany—all the borders of ancient Galilee trembled with ecstasy upon hearing that doctrine of grace, which raised the moral standing of man, gave it character, and recognized its rights.

Little by little, the multitudes gathered around. First, they came to cheer him and later to follow him. The scribes and Pharisees—those who prospered from Caesar's favor—laughed disdainfully at that wandering man, that strange madman preaching such absurdities. There would be time enough to silence him when he upset them just a bit. But the converts quickly numbered in the hundreds of thousands. Jesus had to instruct the twelve apostles so they could preach the new doctrine; and they were modest fishermen, simple and unlearned men. Yet, they possessed a great love for humanity in their souls, these men he chose to bring his work to fruition. The wave of sacrifice had to crash against the hard rock of egotism, and the Teacher did not enter imperious Jerusalem gently; it was amidst cheers and waving palm fronds. He thundered against corruption and scorned the powerful; he expelled the merchants from the temple with lashings when the full force of imperial domination—which did not realize that the redemptive seed had taken root in the people's hearts—came crashing down on him in the foolish decision to silence the messenger. The death of the Righteous One would do nothing but encircle his triumphant redemption in everlasting glory. Only through the martyrdom of its most dedicated champions do great ideas gather strength. Thus, Jesus could not have reached his victorious transfiguration at Mount Tabor without first having suffered the horrible tortures of Calvary.

His example is moving and comforting to supporters of redemption for the Antilles. Up with the meek in this beautiful awakening of souls! Show the path of political dignity—the path that leads to the definitive constitution of *la patria libre*—to the colony's vain and proud men.

The revolutionary idea has triumphantly traveled through the patriotic exile communities in Tampa and Key West. It is the inspired agent that has commanded enough strength to not retreat a single step, when all others succumbed to vacillation or belief in the false promises of liberalism. The righteous man educates the working classes to consciously march toward the fulfillment of their rights, and the modest man carries himself without pretensions to bring wills together—as did the best of the models I have presented for your consideration tonight. This idea does not hate or condemn; it inclines toward the rule of justice in a place where the palms are more magnificent, the sun's rays more brilliant, and the flowers and fruit more varied, more succulent and sweet. It has had its Peters of denial. But, as in the

biblical tale, they recognized justice and reason, and they have returned—respectful and prudent. There might also appear a Judas to betray it. But, were that to be the case, the benevolent messenger's words whisper of a disarming alliance.

When, on that Passover night, Jesus said to his apostles, "Among you is one who will betray me," and the indignant disciples asked his name so that he could be punished, Jesus replied firmly, "Why do you need to know it? Punished is he in his conscience."

Let us, then, forge ahead and not let the obstacles that might cross our path intimidate us, nor be discouraged by the pessimism of those who **do not believe** in resurrection, because it is very easy to be a patriot without solidarity.

Onward! And, may it be very soon, at another celebration of Christ's redemption, that we also celebrate the political redemption of Cuba and Puerto Rico.

Doc. 9
José Martí, "Club Borinquen and Betances"
June 4, 1892 (#13)

The meeting held on May 29 by Club Borinquen—today the house of the purest and most judicious patriotism, of fellowship and reason, where the liberty that guarantees the future welfare of the worthy island is practiced in the present by broadening the contentious discussion of issues, ideas, and all the trials and tribulations that life presents—was not, as in other public cases, the result of a fleeting alliance between political novices who elevate the fire of adolescent rebellion or the benevolent enthusiasm of their aspirations to the status of patriotic solutions. Rather, it was one of those events that unites the hearts of the people, polishes and refines temperaments, revives the faith of the weary, reconciles differences in method and approach into a greater harmony and leaves, in both the devout and skeptical soul, the same feeling of greatness—the greatness of the loyal man and that of sympathetic men.

There was not an empty seat in that noble hall—none of the steadfast of yesterday or their counterparts of tomorrow was absent from the meeting—when the chairman of the Club, Sotero Figueroa, stood before the flag of Lares and, in a tone at once gentle and firm of one who has sworn himself selflessly to freedom, gave an account of the great organizing effort the club has carried out in its already distinguished career and of its strong relationship with loyal Puerto Ricans for whom the abhorrence of tyranny and the fear of ever-growing poverty has set out on the quest for liberty and support from around the world. He spoke of the evident and rising influence of the ideal of independence in the country of Puerto Rico—which had placed absurd hope in a prostrate ideology—unquestionably provoked by the disdain from a metropolis by nature imperious and oppressive; that is, a politics opposed to the character and conditions of the incompetent and bewildered nation that would grant it. And, the silence was reverential when, at the chairman's request, the secretary, Francisco Gonzalo Marín—as one who lifts his soul as well as his body from his seat—read the communication in which that eminence of charity and purpose, of benevolence and sincerity, of solidarity and judgment, Dr. Ramón Emeterio Betances accepted with youthful ardor his appointment as honorary chairman of Club Borinquen, as he was named with fraternal reverence. And, in that instant, as if lifted to an extraordinary height, a determination of spirit—that clandestine ardor which men once bound by glory neither forget, nor scorn, nor ever abandon—burst forth from the eloquent lips, eager arms, and spirited gaze of those present. It seemed that a nation was being born!

Beautiful it was indeed, to see the moment when the commanding and compassionate words of Betances' letter—words of conviction and combat—fell like brimstone on those expectant souls, as if suddenly awoken from a slumber, joining hands, clinging to their enthusiasm, and letting tears fall from their eyes. Those souls belonged to *Lareños* who had borne arms on the September 23, 1868. They belonged to those young men from Cabo Rojo and Ponce, from Arecibo and San Juan, who sat respectfully and in solidarity alongside Cubans who would angrily turn against whosoever dared suggest that in Puerto Rico they were not at home, or that they would not be together at the hour of redemption, joined as equals as much in their suffering spirit and indomitable hope as by the whim of the sea; the two islands joined in their passion for liberty, their brave spirit, and their intense devotion to the heroes they share; islands whose lips swear the same hypocritical oath, bear the same shame on their backs, and whose bare hands carry the same chains.

Beautiful it was to see, as the address intensified, that impressive speech about the birth of the republican ideal; the kind of speech that judiciously shapes future law in its liberal enthusiasm; the righteous and unwavering speech of those who do not seek the victory of one faction or class in the triumph of their ideal, but seek harmony for all through justice and the reconciliation of their people to the geography and history in which they live. Beautiful it was to see how that gathering of youth—where those who already comb their grey hair are considered young men, and men seasoned by secrecy and ignominy display their precocious maturity—rose in a spirit of full recognition to praise, without the envy that corrupts ambitious novices, the man whose virtue has reached such heights that reason itself guarantees his thundering prophecy. The only given for those who arrive after is the difficult task of emulating it.

But more beautiful still, in the serenity of his self-sacrifice, is the magnificent sage himself—the son of wealth and culture—whose natural talents lifted him to the elegance and comforts of life. Those things he put aside when he saw that they must be acquired through sheer cunning and at the cost of his honor. Rather than toil in the public service, allowing an ideology that debases humanity and obstructs the path to happiness to persist in his patria—America—he preferred always to work toward a political ideology that would lift the human condition and firmly establish its enduring happiness. With his feet rooted in history and his eyes fixed toward the future, he saw the independence of his homeland in the opportune combination of concession and resolve, and in the honest treatment of all the country's principled and constructive elements, rather than—foolishly and small-heartedly—in the cruel and indifferent treatment of its various elements. Noble is the man who is obstinate in rational virtue, devout in his heart, and tightly bound to good judgment. Noble is the man who has devoted his life—a somber shadow voluntarily cast over it—to rescuing the patria through the united efforts of both the great and the humble.

And now—having paid a tribute of well-deserved admiration to the dignity, fervor, and determination evidenced by Club Borinquen at its May 29th session, to the qualities of a lofty patriotism and unifying politics of solidarity which reveal the Puerto Rican spirit—it is *PATRIA*'s duty to give a detailed account of that memorable meeting.

After having read and approved the minutes from the previous General Meeting, the chairman gave a brief summary of the tasks carried out by the Board; the most significant of which follow:

Club Borinquen has established cordial and patriotic correspondence with all the revolutionary clubs established by our brothers and sisters in this republic.

It has roused public opinion in Puerto Rico with its manifesto directed at the Puerto Rican people, which has been the subject of spirited debate in the press of the small Antillean island.

It has communicated with other Puerto Rican exile communities outside the United States.

It has been able to attract to its ranks—through good judgment and concord—other invaluable elements here in New York who have expressed their apprehension and resistance, and who believe that the work of the club might be unformed and inconsistent or unruly and impetuous.

It has gained new members who have joined voluntarily and attest to how the Puerto Rican exile community thinks and how it feels.

Lastly—and this is the most admirable and uplifting triumph of Club Borinquen, the one that must make it prouder than any other, and strengthens its noble undertaking—from Paris, the illustrious Betances, that most prominent figure in the annals of Puerto Rico's history of emancipation, that highly distinguished scientist who is beloved and respected in the mind of the entire world, allies himself with the club, bringing all his influence, knowledge, and integrity to bear on its mission.

"The secretary," concluded the chairman, "will now read the inspired communication from that assiduous patriot, which must undoubtedly be for all of us—as it already is for the Board—the most glorious mark of honor on our place in the Partido Revolucionario Cubano."

Here is that response, which was read by the secretary, Francisco Gonzalo Marín, in a voice that lifted eager hearts:

Paris, May 9, 1892
Messieurs.
S. Sotero Figueroa................Chairman
Antonio V. Alvarado...............Vice Chairman
F. Gonzalo Marín..................Secretary
of Club Borinquen

New York
My esteemed gentlemen and worthy compatriots,

On the first of this month, I had the pleasure of receiving your communication dated February 28, whereby you informed me that the patriotic Antillean group, Club Borinquen, had dignified me with the title of honorary Chairman. I have also received two copies of the Party's platform, several copies of the Club's statutes, and the manifesto you directed to the Puerto Rican people.

I am so deeply moved by such a spontaneous display of consideration from those who—due to their freedom in exile and their work in the fullest exercise of their rights as patriots—are the true representatives of the people of Borinquen, that I do not know whether to express my gratitude or congratulate you for having given our country the recognition it deserves. The sacred name of that club serves as a constant reminder of what each and every one of us owes to our homeland. I join in the task that you so valiantly assume with the most heartfelt solidarity. And I, who have been, am, and will die a separatist, will always joyfully hear the cry of protest issued by my comrades—a cry which must guide you on the path to victory, and which I repeat today with everyone, after twenty-five years of exile:

Long live the revolution!
Long live Borinquen, free and independent!

Betances

A thundering applause—long, sustained, and affectionate—reverberated in the meeting hall and, immediately afterward, the visibly moved Chairman said:

"Thank you, compatriots, thank you for that resounding applause that bursts forth from the soul and will reach Betances as the sure promise of future victory."

Let us learn from his enduring influence—the distance, the haze of years, and the treachery of men—to remain firm in our position and not retreat in face of any of the obstacles that cross our path or the insinuation of pride that, at times, breaks with the most noble and sacred sentiments that can blossom in our hearts.

No one more than he could have reason to be discouraged; yet he burns with all the fire of youth upon affirming the allegiance sworn to his country's independence twenty-five years ago in Lares and thirty, at least, since he pioneered his emancipatory instruction. Indeed, half of his life has been spent spreading his tenets of freedom for all men and the other half, waiting for the joyous triumph of his cherished ideal!

And, do not think, gentlemen, that what you just heard are merely the conventional slogans of a grateful patriot. No! In his intimate disclosures, in the memorable letter which I am honored to receive from the noble sage who spent 125,000 pesos on the Lares Revolution—all of his fortune—he is even more vehement, more devoted, more fervent.

He believes that today we are in a better position than at the time of the Lares Revolution, and he applauds as we come together in the Partido Revolucionario Cubano, adding these deeply heartfelt lines:

"Today you find yourselves united and, consequently, in a better position to achieve victory, as seen from, oh! so far away by Bassora, Ruiz, Rojas, Brugman, Braoín, Parrilla, Hostos, Lacroix, and by me."

After, he spoke of his Memoirs, which he considers writing if he were able to enjoy any respite and, if not, he added—blaming himself instead of the degenerate colonists— "and if not, there is oblivion for those who have not had the good fortune of achieving for their fellow citizens the golden dreams of prosperity, independence, and dignity."

His final paragraph must necessarily move us all with its passionate fervor and noble patriotic impulse.

"My heart fills with bitterness and my eyes with tears upon remembering my enslaved patria. Therefore, whatever I am capable of doing—now and always—is for her, and I am a friend to all who, like you, work for her wellbeing, which is entirely impossible without her independence.

"Salute all the members of Club Borinquen in my name."

Now you know, gentlemen: Betances fervently salutes you. May that salute form a bond of permanent unity between Club Borinquen and that unwavering exile, and may no one be exempt or grow weary of contributing to the redemptive task by thinking that, if Betances has sacrificed everything for his beloved Borinquen—his mind and eyes fixed on us—the least we can do for the patria is organize elements to aid in its imminent emancipation.

May other inspired words and other indomitable figures—defenders of the patriotic ideal—come to encourage us in our efforts.

At the Chairman's encouragement, Secretary Marín asked for the floor, and—as always—in a heartfelt, impassioned, and enthusiastic address, he spoke instinctively and ardently, beyond political thought or the vestiges of his ideological and argumentative discourses. He spoke of the wrenching of a heart whose pride bleeds from guilt-stained offenses. So said, with an honorable and compelling admiration for virtue, the elegant tribune:

GENTLEMEN:

Yesterday, when our modest Club was born, when those of us who know the revolutionary spirit of our people, launched an fiery Manifesto to Puerto Ricans residing in this metropolis calling them to the breast of the Partido Revolucionario Cubano; when, after being condemned to four centuries of oppression as servants of the colony, we did not place our faith in the rebels from the exile community, and we swore in a covenant with our consciences to sacrifice everything for the sake of the country's independence; then, gentlemen, we were thought to be deluded, the sin of impatience was thrown in our faces, and we had the honor—yes, gentlemen, the honor—of being the target of invectives from those who, like us, resented the degrading whip on their backs, but who, unlike us, have not had enough courage to confront the Spanish nation and declare before it in humble tones of integrity and dignity: "the hour of emancipation has arrived. We were slaves in the nineteenth century, but we must be free in the twentieth."

Pueblos mature; and they are emancipated on the day when the flame of Liberty ignites in all minds and a sense of contempt takes root in all hearts. The outlaw that rises with vigorous protest and rebels against the disgraceful and injurious whip is no outlaw, nor is he worthy of being called such. Leave the ignominy and the vile profits he exposes to those who, either from an attachment to the colony or from a cowardly tolerance for usurpation, keep their lips pursed and ready to kiss the hand that beats them.

"Deluded!" And, why did they call us deluded? Oh! Now I understand them, gentlemen. Sane is the nimble acrobat who understands the failings of balance on the topic of tightrope walking. Sane is he who accepts the comfortable construct that the geographic position of a country must necessarily debase the character of the individuals who inhabit it, and resigns himself to it. Sane is he who prefers the voluptuous enticements of the official dance to the sorrows which result from an exile that is endured with firm tenacity and singular honor; and, finally, sane are they in Boricua [sic] who upon joining their fortune to a most faithful and affectionate woman—as is the Puerto Rican wife—do not stop to think that their firstborn will be born a slave, the vassal of a monarchic Constitution, and the subject of an alien government.

If by affiliating itself with the Partido Revolucionario Antillano, Club Borinquen were only to have served as a disgraceful stain for the incensed men who attack it, today the name of Betances—which bears the hallmark of our aspirations and our benevolent ideals—would have been sufficient to fulfill its glory.

And, is not Dr. Betances the contemporary figure who emerged in our political lives and before whom, either zealously or unwittingly, uncivil people prostrated? Dr. Betances is the illustrious *Caborrojeño* whose fervor they have been unable to undermine after twenty-five years of exile; Dr. Betances is that same man who, by not colluding with treason when treason offered the prestige of wealth, earned the title of martyr in the incipient consciousness of his people; Dr. Betances is that sage, that apostle, who at every opportunity bowed the head of apostasy and contemptible corruption, triumphant; and it is Dr. Betances, gentlemen, who is the most capable and accomplished to lead our partisan movement within the Antillean Revolutionary Party; he, who as a young man—very young—began contemplating the emancipation of his Homeland, and as an old man—very old—must be amazed by the first cry of the glorious Republic...!"

With his innate warmth, gentle in form and profound in purpose, the magnanimous chairman—perceiving that eloquence of open hearts that rarely alights on men—saluted Cuban patriotism in the honorable representative visiting from indefatigable Florida that he had there before him. He saluted one of the firm and impartial leaders of independence in Key West—that city allied by Cuban industry in the Yankee desert. Teodoro Pérez, in turn, with the friendly and fluent words that come to men who are sincere in their emotions and nourish faith in human dignity, saluted in the chairman the passion that sustains and the benevolence that attracts. In the Club, he saluted, for both himself and the Key where he lives, the ordered and exemplary patriotism that removes the greatest obstacles. And he saluted the flag of Lares, as if his own.

The Club speaker and secretary of the delegation for the Partido Revolucionario, the equally fervent and pensive orator, Mr. Gonzalo de Quesada, then addressed those invited to the event. His emphatic words of just aim and ardent form sprung visibly from a very deep place in which the young orator put to one side Antilleans on crutches, the irrevocably timid, and encouraged the boldness of Antilleans determined to walk on their own; in which, with intimate tenderness, he praised the merits of the ideal Antillean, the *Borinqueño* whose soft heart finds no obstacle to great resolve, Betances; in which he painted patriotism as a crystalline river leaving on its banks the dead leaves and silt that hinder its course.

The latest to answer the call; to signal the scope of that manifest spirit; to distill from it the patriotic lesson of genuine democracy, which must be learned in these decisive times by all patriotic congregations; to praise—with honor and candor—the strict party discipline at the core of the revolutionary club of Puerto Rico; to define a future politics of inclusion and equity with which the Partido Revolucionario Cubano hopes to save the sister islands from the hidden dangers of the colonial republic; to illuminate the figure of Betances with the intense colors of his soul—stamping impatiently before injustice, activist in the colony, stoic in exile, compassionate in his bitterness—was José Martí, the current delegate of the Partido Revolucionario Cubano. What he said did not matter; rather what mattered was the ardent spirit of those who listened to his loving description of that man who, from the solace of his work, neither small-heartedly recalls the wealth he invested in the seeds of liberty for his patria's future prosperity, nor cowardly vacillates, but courageously stands up at the appointed time alongside the brave men who are forging the future, his fine compatriots in whom dignity takes refuge. Thus, concluded the Club Borinquen session on May 29 in a spirited celebration with repercussions of singular importance.

Doc. 10
José Martí, "Our Newspapers"
June 11, 1892 (#14)

Cuban books and Cuban newspapers cover our desk. Our desk is undeniably beloved by Cubans, and none could love it more, nor with more tenderness or greater humility.

But, we cannot merely acknowledge in passing the noble first issue of *La Revista de Florida*, where an uplifted spirit and pure patriotism shine; we cannot simply acknowledge in passing the courageous article in which it vigorously and resolutely champions the Partido Revolucionario Cubano.

It is not here, in these hasty scribblings, that due recognition should be accorded to the commendable ambition and positive influence of *La Nueva Era*, which a Cuban has begun publishing in Havana, and—having known him since his beginnings—in whose ultimate purpose we place great hopes: the meticulous and freethinking writer, Martín Morúa Delgado.

Certainly, hurried words cannot not suitably express our gratitude to *La Gaceta del Pueblo*, the spirited journal by the Puerto Rican, Antonio Vélez Alvarado, for the article in which—using his best style and the warmth of his pure heart—he informs readers, with the singular greatness that belongs only to decisive times of America, about our hemispheric ideals and the growing influence of the Party in which Cubans and Puerto Ricans have joined together to complete our mission in America.

Nor should we, in this eleventh hour, applaud *El Yara* for two splendid editorials on statesmanship: the interview in which a Cuban revolutionary declares that war will be futile as long as an integrated ideological war is not also waged; and the article that, in describing the scenes of Camero's failed lynching, cries out in anguish for the defense of our native soil—the only soil where we will be safe from the hostile and covetous foreigner.

Doc. 11
"Borinquen: Antillean Political Club"
October 1, 1892 (#30)

To discuss matters pertaining to October 10, report on the impact of our ideological message and, once again, heed the authoritative ideals with which our illustrious honorary Chairman empowers us with from Paris, this Club will hold a special general meeting at eight o'clock in the evening, next Wednesday, October 5, at 203 E. 54th St., at the corner of 3rd Avenue.

We request punctual attendance, since the meeting will be officially called to order with those members in attendance.

Individual invitations will not be distributed.

Secretary

F. Gonzalo Marín

New York, Sept. 30, 1892

Doc. 12

José Martí, "Club Mercedes Varona"

November 4, 1892 (#34)

Who moves hearts? Who brings both the rich and the needy together? Who suggested to the Cuban women of Mercedes Varona—those modest wives and mothers—the celebration with which, from their diligent hands and under the protection of glorious crests and the double flag, they received those who see no way out other than sacrifice—a sacrifice that purifies and unites, that uproots and engenders—from the elusive and incomplete existence that the houses of Cuba and Puerto Rico carry throughout the world?

There, around the table, some of them with children in their arms, Puerto Rican and Cuban women of modest means presided over the hall—that hall where the affluent lady sat side by side with the *Cubana* of lesser means—to hear, trembling with compassion for the suffering and sacrifices of Cuban women, the sermon—poetic as only the truth can be—from that veteran of Lares, the loyal Terreforte; the abounding impetus of Ernesto Rossel; the warm, spontaneous remarks of Marín; the magnetic verbal assault of Leopoldo Acosta's candid oratory; the welcoming conversation of Delgado; and at which even the very humility of María Acosta, the chairwoman of the event and symbol of the Cuban woman's modest spirit, drew an audience for her speech, where she expounded in paragraphs which she arranged like bouquets— "bunches of flowers gathered in the tropical forest which the brave *mambí* would hang after victory above the thatched palm door of his beloved"—the politics of compassion and dignity in which we Cubans are embroiled; the unalienable right and capacity of these intrinsically pious women to help emancipate the only land where their children can progress from the degradation toward which it is headed. She presented eloquent examples of the glorious history of the women of Cuba, which floated over the deeply moved audience like the aroma from a chalice. She spoke of the need for sacrifice from those with the most wealth at the hour of the inevitable conflict between two great duties: the obligation of restraining the spirit as a sacrificial offering to the homeland, and safeguarding here an army of reinforcement—sustained by men and enlivened by women—that with daily, tangible labor replenishes the forces which the army over there will certainly lose constantly. What beautiful oratorical sketches came from Carolina Rodríguez; from Juana Sandrino, Gómez's daughter and a compatriot herself; from both Maceo's mother and wife; from a lady of revolutionary lineage who said—standing upright among her three sons—that it must be so, even though the war that took her father were also to wrest her sons from her bosom! Class solidarity, the purging of the pusillanimous, and a deep abiding affection for the Antillean women of Mercedes Varona, who—during the privation of the long, hard winter—found the faith and precious means for these celebrations, so exemplary of the homeland. Everything—accented with vigor—dissolved against the Delegate's passionate farewell speech, in which he described an emancipated island and our women, "their hands worn to the bone from work and widowhood," saluting the march toward victory with the raised hands of their martyrdom. And, as the meeting rose up in a united spirit, on the finger of one woman shone a diamond and in the eyes of more than one shone tears. Once again, the Delegate bade us farewell: He will be accompanied on his journey by both the rich and the poor, and by the sympathies of both the newlywed and the modest mother—the voices of America!

Doc. 13
"Sotero Figueroa" (Speech)
February 4, 1893 (#48)

Fellow Countrymen,
An inevitable duty which I cannot shirk brings me here under these solemn circumstances, even though I understand that I lack the oratorical skill to stand at this podium where only the eagles of philosophy, who soar through the infinite spaces of sublime ideas and lend eloquence to patriotic exaltation, should be heard.

I would have come here tonight with my head obediently bowed, as a disciple convinced that he has arrived to receive lessons of political integrity and consequence from conscientious apostles and indomitable champions of Antillean independence who have all the authority to give them. But this, gentlemen, is about shedding light on the decisive course that public opinion on our suffering islands has begun to turn against those who worship the power that demeans and ruins us. And all those who have convincing evidence, all those who can present reliable facts to strengthen that claim, must come forth to testify as principal witnesses under the penalty of being taken for accomplices of those who swindle our patria and opportunistically collude with them. These are who supply the noble impulse that moves me and the sincerity of my statements, despite my inadequacy in this medium of expression, which I lament today more than ever, since I will be unable to seduce you with that enticement of spoken discourse—optimism.

Why does the Partido Autonomista Cubano now emerge from the justified reticence in which it had locked itself up, and for what purpose? Perchance, have the causes that forced it to distance itself from active struggle ceased, leaving its impenitent adversaries with the responsibility for the certain and immediate failure of its corrupt and oppressive policies? Has the metropolitan government done justice to the honorable aspirations of our oppressed and exploited people? Not in any way, shape, or form: the Central Directorate of the Party of unwavering hope continues to part from the expectant attitude in which it has remained. Since the tax rate has been slightly reduced, it opts for electoral struggle without ever warning us that the decade of milk and honey—if there can be milk and honey in that paltry concession— is merely an indicator to support for the farce known as representation in the *Cortes*, and that the electoral process tends to legally sanction the administrative corruption that has invaded all spheres of our public life by the constituents of the enslaved region.

And, that Directorate has chosen quite a striking moment to convene the Autonomist electoral body to lend itself to this game—in which the producer country always loses—and to the conservatives who resist supporting anything not aligned with their own self-interest and debilitating leadership! They have chosen to do so at a time when an economic class has had to confess its impotence to save regional production from imminent ruin; when exorbitant taxes agreed to by Spain's Overseas Minister, Romero Robledo, intensified poverty, displaced hard-working laborers, paralyzed employment, incited the people to rise up, and caused the blood of resolute compatriots to run in Puerto Rico. They have chosen to do so when transferring customs tariffs has been considered not only to continue paying exorbitant salaries to employees whose ineptitude is revealed by the vacuity of their results, but also to guarantee the metropolis one hundred million pesos—the equivalent of throwing a grain of salt into the bottomless pit of national debt—and to pay those profiting from the business an obscene incentive. They have chosen to do so at a time when a loss is predicted that will orphan the monarchic institution of that irresponsible entity obliged to reign over the Spanish people; when the republican factions commanded by Ruiz Zorrilla, Salmerón, and Pi y Margall have gathered intelligence, allowing them—by degree or by force—the reins of power that today are held by the collapsing restoration; when the Partido Revolucionario Antillano stands up as a single united front, and, from the icebergs of the Behring Sea to the scorching climate of the Strait of Magellan, vows to press on with the redemptive task which resulted in the pathetic truce that is the Zanjón Pact. Something akin to a volcanic eruption is being felt in Cuba; loyal patriots shake hands; skeptics brace themselves; and distinguished heroes ready the weapons of combat, their eyes gleaming with the light of victory because the days of great struggle are nigh—days of noble sacrifice and Homeric feats, of the blessed victory that will deliver us a free homeland. When every anachronism is at the point of collapse because the contemptuous metropolis has insulted Cuba's Partido Autonomista by throwing it a trifle of representation; and this party has decided to share the responsibility for the catastrophe, instead of stepping aside and allowing the country the freedom to act and determine with dignity, as it must, its future destiny. The proponents of autonomist policies do not understand—nor do they want to understand—that the Spanish government uses them to contain the vigorous and radical demands of the Cuban people. In the same way that, after the allegedly charitable policies of the Zanjón Pact, they obligated the unconvinced to barricade themselves in an expectant attitude—letting time take care of enforcing its evolving policies of transfer—today, they blindly and unpatriotically insinuate themselves between just and necessary revolution and galling, vitiating domination.

But, let us say this, in honor of our working classes and as proof of their capacity to participate in civil society: the producer country—made up of *criollos* who are loyal to their beliefs and the banner of redemption—looks disdainfully on the new electoral law in Cuba. They show no signs of enthusiasm, nor do they rush to register in electoral rolls. And, it is not surprising that the Cuban people shut themselves up in such a telling posture, when the incomprehensible reality is that the very same ones who advocate for electoral engagement have no faith in the potential of the process and say, along with the sincere orator, Fernández de Castro, that they will continue joining the ranks of pawns in this governmental farce; that they will serve as touchstones for reactionary conservatives who, by contrasting their efforts with autonomist ones, will organize themselves and unite to pave a smooth and peaceful path for the government by instituting the law through its complacency, so as to maintain peace in Warsaw. And, with those phrases—possessing, as they do, such conviction and exposing such bitterness and irony—they now agree to go to the ballot box with the resignation of Islamic fatalism...!

Where is the vitality of unconquerable wills? Given the homeland's oppressive despair, there is no room for the humiliating phrase *it has been written in stone*, only for the revolutionary *non serviam* (I shall not yield).

Regarding Puerto Rico, the letters and newspapers we receive from the unfortunate island tell us that the Partido Autonomista there will not be participating in the next elections as merely an ornamental figure because the liberals refuse to be *third-class* Spaniards. Today, more than ever, that attitude is justified in long-suffering Borinquen.

There, as in no other place, the government travesty has been bloodier and the disillusionment, deeper. I, gentlemen, joined the ranks of the Puerto Rican Partido Autonomista because I considered it an important force, an educational instrument aimed at preparing our people for greater fortunes. In good faith, I put my meager abilities toward achieving the triumph of the liberal principles deeply instilled in its credo. But, upon seeing how ignoble defamation has assailed patriotic conviction—how a conspiracy was hatched to take degrading practices to their extreme, to fill the prisons with prominent politicians, and to impose horrible tortures on innocent workers—and upon seeing that those abuses went unpunished, that the eloquent voice of our representatives in the Cortes remained mute, and that a sense of impunity incited contemptible persecution, I understood that there was no redemption for our people while bound to colonial servitude. And I abandoned the land where so many iniquities were perpetrated, and, from the land of liberty, I took refuge under the tricolor flag that ennobles the battle cry for Antillean independence. Afterward, the patria's tyrants were rewarded;

those who at first suffered tortures were vanquished—if not, they died from the assault of grief. The Autonomist Directorate continued, docile and complacent, begging for freedoms and leaving their fellow countrymen with no personal protection, since they did not demand reparation for the atrocity of the assault, nor did they retreat into decorous reticence when the Delegate suggested that public opinion was, in fact, the maleficent source of the *Componte*. In the end, voter abstention came more from the directed than the directors, and it is indeed difficult to break free from that situation while humiliation still burns their cheeks.

So, let us exhort our compatriots to practice the exemplary virtue of not yielding to any type of pressure, and to keep faith in the great ideal of a democratic republic within *la patria libre*. Soon, very soon—judging by the signs of the times—our flag with its solitary star shall comfort us all amidst its beneficent folds.

I have finished.

Doc. 14
"Communication from Sotero Figueroa to José Martí"
April 16, 1893 (#57)

Partido Revolucionario Cubano
CUERPO DE CONSEJO
Office of the Secretary
Honorable José Martí, re-elected Delegate to the Partido Revolucionario Cubano,

I am extremely pleased to inform you that you have been re-elected unanimously by the Clubs of New York as the delegate to the Partido Revolucionario Cubano in the elections that were just held, and that the distinguished compatriot, Benjamín J. Guerra, has been re-elected General Treasurer.

With both illustrious incumbents having verified the proclamation at our formal meeting on April 10, I respectfully fulfill the duty of communicating the electoral results to you. I express my hope that, under your honorable leadership, we will soon have the great fortune of succeeding to establish a democratic republic in our enslaved Antilles.

Patria y Libertad.
New York, April 11, 1893.

S. FIGUEROA
Secretary

Doc. 15
"Sotero Figueroa" (Speech)
April 29, 1893 (#60)

Fellow Countrymen,

The Partido Revolucionario Cubano has come together on this solemn occasion to ratify all its previous declarations; to insist today, more than ever, in its redemptive ideology, which cannot lead to failure, but to certain victory because it does not organize partial, inadequate, or poorly prepared movements.

The party has fortified its sphere of action, extended its methods, and disciplined its army. It has cultivated, first, the army's sympathies and, then, their respect for the young republics that arose from Bolívar's spirit. The homeland's wealth has already increased to such a degree that were our brothers in Cuba to rush united onto the battlefields—securing with their blood the right to be free—they shall not, from the first strike, want for continuing and enduring assistance from the Antillean exile communities.

Clearly, discretion and a sense of responsibility have had to precede all their actions. Only after extraordinary and repeated proof of the purity of intentions, the integrity of principles, and just and capable leadership can the trust of the wise and the visionary—the discouraged and the skeptical—be won.

This cannot explain that communion of wills [*concierto de voluntades*], that patriotic affinity which unites all Cubans dispersed across the free hemisphere of the two Americas into a single united force—a mysterious and galvanizing revolution—that will reverberate throughout our noble land, and which risks defeat by treachery and the hollow promise of justice. But its natural aspirations—its intense longing for independence and liberty—can never be tamed. Thus, we believe that the revolution will expand to reach Cuba. A fistful of valiant men—impatient to break the chains that shackle the island to a painful past which fails to recognize its citizens' full character and inalienable rights—have temporarily retreated to the *palenque* in preparation for armed struggle and, from the remote mountains of Holguín and Las Tunas, have issued forth the exalted cry: "¡Cuba libre!"

What should the position of the Partido Revolucionario be under the present circumstances? The same one it has staunchly proclaimed and supported without deception or restraint: It does not intend "to hastily precipitate war in Cuba, nor to launch at any cost to the country a poorly prepared and divided movement of forces, but to organize a noble and expeditious war, depending on the number of active and honorable factions who join it, aimed at securing the prosperity of the inhabitants of the Island through peace and hard work," as stated in Article 2 of its platform. But, should the war break out in any particular place, this will in no way prevent us from lending our resolute support and pushing to extend it so the heroic sacrifice will not be in vain and the precious blood of brave and sacrificed men will not be squandered fruitlessly.

Now is not the time to question the belligerent posture assumed by the indomitable men in the eastern region, who have once again unfurled the flag—with its the solitary star—at precisely the moment when the Partido Revolucionario Cubano was lighting the fuse that will accelerate widespread insurrection. Now is the time for swift and vigorous action. If our brothers-in-arms can keep the ground they have taken, then our invincible leaders, our veteran soldiers of the Ten Years' War, and our youth who long to inherit from their elders a position of power in their homeland—which is currently subjected to the avarice of a despotic oppressor—will very soon run to fill the ranks of the liberating army. Meanwhile, fervent exiles—those who have sworn never to return to their native land until they can sing the blessed hymn of independence at the top of their lungs—will not cease to invest their resources in the arsenal of abnegation. Many souls of Spartan and noble character will take the bread from their own mouths and those of their children so that a patriotic soldier will not go without any of the basic elements for combat—those elements which must necessarily clear away all corruption and lift the opprobrious shadow of slavery from their eyes so that they may gaze at the heavens with gratitude; there, they will make out the smiling faces of the heroes who saw their earthly shell exchanged for the glories of immortality in reward for their valiant deeds.

And, this is not, compatriots, the vain display of a hollow promise. Immediately after it was announced that war had broken out in the eastern region, the clubs affiliated with the Partido Revolucionario Cubano stood up to swear their allegiance to the cause of independence. Resources are multiplying; consensus has been reestablished throughout the entire exile community; and any differences in the methods employed to reach our aspirations no longer exist. A triumphant *sursum corda* springs from all lips. We close our ranks until there is no opportunity for discontent or apathy to enter, and we all join together in one strong embrace. There are no factions when facing a common enemy; there are no club members or non-members. We are all believers, and we all share the same belief: the independence of Cuba!

But mysterious telegrams from suspicious sources claim that everything has already ended in the region of Santiago de Cuba: the revolutionaries have meekly surrendered, and peace once again reigns in Warsaw. To *corroborate* these reports, some claim that the press has not been gagged; the state of siege has not been lifted in the communities where the skirmishes occurred; and formidable reinforcements continue to be sent to places supposedly already *pacified*. Each day, gunboats patrol the coasts with greater zeal; the wires are monopolized by the colonial government; and only news confirming *complete pacification* is allowed. In short, there is no longer absolutely anything to fear.

But experience has made the Partido Revolucionario Cubano prescient. It continues steadfast—more faithful today than yesterday—amassing resources, consolidating different faction, and, with weapons raised high, fixing its eyes and heart on the land of Cuba. Much more is happening there than what is fabricated in these Spanish telegrams. We shall not let ourselves be caught off guard by barbarous tactics, nor shall we stop aiding those who fight so valiantly for the homeland's independence to the best of our ability and with the greatest effectiveness.

As for us, we believe that when a volcano is about to erupt, it would be inconceivably foolish to think that the mouth of the crater might be blocked; the fire already burning within will explode in a hundred different directions. And, woe to those who insisted on stifling the first eruption!

Compatriots: We are witnessing the beginning of the end.

Keep the faith and march onward!

Doc. 16
"The Honorable Sotero Figueroa" (Speech)
October 14, 1893 (#82)

CUBAN AND PUERTO RICAN COMPATRIOTS,

If passion for the patria's independence were not so firmly entrenched in our hearts, I would not, on this magnificently grand and solemn evening, rise to this noble podium, which was erected in exile to praise our illustrious heroes—our legendary combatants of that unforgettable decade who fell facing the enemy, and cried out as they embraced that flag with its radiant star set in a red triangle: "¡Viva Cuba libre!"

And, I would not rise to this podium if you, as I, think that the greatest glory we can give our revolutionary forefathers is an impressive tomb in our still enslaved land. Like you, I believe that the time is nigh for us to free her through our efforts: that blessed land which has been consecrated with the tears of our women, the valiant protests of those who refuse to yield under the yoke of reckless and incompetent Spanish domination, the noble outbursts of our proud youth who refuse to sell themselves to capricious overseers, and that most noble torrent of blood spilled by those who showed us the path which, if it could lead us to Zanjón, was but a moment's pause on our unified ascent—healed of factionalism and distrust—to the summit where the Capitol beckons with its attendant rights.

But, if I dare to stand in this place—shielded by the benevolence of your untarnished patriotism—it is because a mysterious voice from my innermost soul calls out and tells me that this 10th of October is more than a commemoration of the great date on which the flag of our national sovereignty was unfurled into the wind. It is the confirmation of revolutionary protest from all Antillean émigrés who stand up and make their veneration known—from exile to the immortals of La Demajagua—by saluting and telling their Cuban and Puerto Rican brethren: "Keep the faith and march onward: The great days of epic feats did not disappear, never to return. Intense jubilation rouses the soul; something akin to a vision of glory flashes in the eyes of the brave men who wait impatiently to begin the magnificent new journey toward liberation. Today, more than ever, conviction in the immediate success of our cause incites all hearts. Keep the faith, and march onward!"

Gentlemen, in both the spiritual and physical world there are certain internal cataclysms which are nothing more than early warning signs of the deep clashes that shall somehow transform the usual course life and nature. Prescient men do not ignore these warnings. On the contrary, they seek to act as they occur. Impetuous men—like the grasshopper in the fable—live carefree, and disaster eventually makes them victims of their own impudence. To those who do not see this just and restorative revolution—which permeates the air, impels all consciences, and joins the exile communities in a brotherly bond—vehemently and forebodingly manifested in the discontent from the working and producing classes of our enslaved islands; to those who do not see the revolution in the increasingly respectful treatment accorded the Partido Revolucionario Cubano by Cuba and elsewhere, including the United States and all of South America, and who are ignorant of the immense work it has realized—the wills it has united, the resources it has amassed, and the invaluable groups that endorse it—in short, of the integrity and certainty it has used to advance the arduous mission under its charge; to those who do not see the revolution in the auspicious consent of so many eyes afire in this grand hall—so many strong arms and proud minds harmonized with the patriotic community of ideas; to those who do not see the revolution made palpable in such uncontestable signs, as well as others that discretion best keeps unnamed: we must pity those men blinded by obstinacy because—like the grasshopper in the fable—the winter will catch them by surprise since they have failed, during the summer, to stock the provisions of unity and consensus among revolutionary supporters. The freezing, icy blizzard will blow them off course without a care for their tirades and tantrums.

As for us, we feel possessed by an ineffable vision. The fathers of our independence—those who shall never perish in our hearts' devout reverence—appear around us, not with the frowning countenance of years past, but beaming with joy. The murmur of palm trees caresses our ears; the blazing sun quickens our pulse; the breeze, infused with the aroma of our intoxicating flowers, refreshes our brow; the Caribbean Sea, with its undulating and crystalline waves—all of these things recall the peaceful days of childhood. A resplendent sky displays its deep, translucent blue as never before. The light, fragrance, and harmony—along with liberty, integrity, and justice—evoke the image of a joyous and independent homeland.

Could it be that we are near the end and a hopeful premonition anticipates our desires?

We do not know. But as the great revolutionary Muhammad left written in his sacred book and *PATRIA* repeats: "Paradise lies in the shadow of swords." I have finished.

Doc. 17
José Martí, "Patriotic Banquet of Club Las Dos Antillas"
November 21, 1893 (#87)

As its name suggests, both Cubans and Puerto Ricans make up Club Las Dos Antillas. Since they understand the logic and prudence behind this revolutionary movement and—through the strength of their sincerity and camaraderie—stand more resolutely before every trap that might be set. These compatriots seek to express their conviction in a public forum. They will cover Borinquen's table with the cloth of hard work, and good men will sit around it as if Betances presided over them; as if Hostos were to speak; as if Gautier were to recite verses; as if Baldorioty, who bore his people within his heart, and Ruiz Belvis, who was assassinated in the pursuit of his country's freedom had returned from their tombs. We shall sit proudly at that immaculate table.

Doc. 18
José Martí, "Club Borinquen"
April 17, 1894 (#108)

PATRIA extends a warm greeting to this patriotic Club, which never allows its history to fall into oblivion, and which actively and enthusiastically ratifies its sworn conviction to the ideal of Antillean independence.

The divine souls of Ruiz Belvis and Parrilla have no reason to recoil in shame because those who have had the freedom to do so have returned from exile; they retrace those hallowed footsteps and arrive for the ultimate triumph of their nation along with their Cuban brethren. The respected and beloved names of Betances and Hostos—those indomitable revolutionaries—remain symbols of valiant resolve worthy of noble emulation. There is not a single Puerto Rican who does not feel reverence before them, nor can anything divide what is indivisible: the intimate joining of two sister pueblos in both hope and sorrow.

Such was the reason for the consensus meeting convened by Club Borinquen on the fifth evening of the current month and year.

Some twelve new members joined the existing ones, and one of the decisions reached that evening was the appointment of Dr. Fermín Valdés Domínguez as an honorary member— just tribute to his honorable merits and a show of gratitude to the brave vindicator of students who has written and presented Club Borinquen with a fiery and original pamphlet to raise funds for this organization of fervent patriots.

The board of the aforementioned club was constituted as follows:

Chairman, Sotero Figueroa. Vice Chairman, Félix S. Yznaga. Treasurer, Juan Fraga. Secretary, Domingo Collazo. Representatives, Isaac Delgado; Vicente Fernández; Leopoldo Nuñez; J. Vega.

And, now, march onward with our revolutionary struggle, which the faithful shall not abandon until the consummation of Antillean independence.

Doc. 19
Sotero Figueroa, "Declarations"
June 30, 1894 (#118)

New York, June 28, 1894

Friends of *PATRIA*,

In order to assuage the rumors, which should not be dismissed merely because they are inclined to debase one's character or distort the rectitude of one's intentions, I feel a personal obligation to make the following declarations:

1. I am not currently the editor in chief of *PATRIA* as has been printed, although I will not stop lending my humble support to the newspaper, which is a shining star of our aspirations.

2. I have not, nor will I ever, subordinate my conscience as, undoubtedly, neither would any of you, my good friends, to anything that is not worthy, noble, and beneficial to the cause of independence. Political involvement does not nullify one's own dignity; it only strengthens it.

3. I believe that there are no rancorous dictatorships imposed upon the editorial offices of *PATRIA* because were they to exist, I would not be able to make these frank declarations in the columns of this very publication, nor would I meekly and obligingly accept it, since I, by nature, rebel against any despotic imposition. The editors of *PATRIA* work **in a particular manner**, as they see fit. But, as journalists, they maintain an objective approach when it comes to any people or things that might threaten the work of the revolutionary exile communities.

4. I do not attempt with these lines to satisfy the whims of my wounded pride, rather to preserve the honor of my political convictions and personal dignity.

And, that is all.

I remain forever your loving friend and fellow countryman,

S. FIGUEROA

** (Author's Note: Due to a series of personal and financial problems, Figueroa resigned from his official positions in the Partido Revolucionario Cubano and *PATRIA* during this time, although he continued collaborating with both organizations. Figueroa issued these "Declarations" to refute the "rumors" spread by malicious people who sought to undermine his personal honor and political integrity.)

Doc. 20
"Club Borinquen"
December 15, 1894 (#141)

This patriotic organization held a memorable session on the evening of the 10th of the current month during which important decisions were made that, in due time, will yield worthwhile results for the cause—today more certain than ever—of Antillean independence. Its new governing board was constituted as follows:

Chairman,
Juan de Mata Terreforte
Vice Chairman,
Francisco J. Amy
Treasurer,
Rosendo Rodríguez
Secretary,
Domingo Collazo
Representatives,
Manuel Budet, Candelario Calor,
Marcelino Piedra, José Budet

These distinguished and eminent new individuals, who are to be commended for their service and who come to decisively impel Club Borinquen's effective action, include the upstanding and unquestionable patriot from Lares, Mr. Terreforte, and the distinguished intellectual and rebel against all Spanish domination, Mr. Amy.

We are pleased to welcome the new board of *Borinquen*, and we have no need to provide them with any form of incentive because, as good men, they hold the most uncompromising incentive present in their consciences, even in the darkest hours.

Doc. 21
"Meeting Announcement from Club Borinquen"
March 4, 1895 (#151)

Last Saturday, the following leaflet was circulated throughout this city:
CLUB BORINQUEN

———

CALL TO MEETING
———To all worthy Puerto Ricans.
May no Cuban or supporter of Antillean independence fail to attend Military Hall, 193 Bowery, Monday, March 4, at eight o'clock in the evening.
Cuba is at war, and we must prove our patriotism through action.
Cuba is on its feet, and Puerto Ricans cannot and must not remain seated.
Let us not forget the seed that was planted today in the fields of Cuba's freedom; tomorrow it will enrich the redemption of our ill-fated Puerto Rico.

J. DE M. TERREFORTE,
Chairman

D. COLLAZO,
Secretary

The meeting was held last night, and we are pleased to report that the large hall was entirely filled with club members and supporters of the revolutionary ideal.

Among the opportune decisions that were made during this crucial time, we should mention the following, albeit hastily, because time is pressing and space is limited: Membership fees have been raised to one dollar a week, without limiting those individuals who can or want to contribute greater sums.

A manifesto shall be drafted to rouse public opinion in Puerto Rico and prepare the people for future events. Lastly, extraordinary fundraising efforts were initiated that yielded quite satisfactory results; the funds will be immediately deposited into the Party's Treasury.

Many new members joined, and the discussions heard there revealed a full awareness of their right and desire to go to war, setting out on the wide open paths cleared for us by the Partido Revolucionario Cubano.

March onward, Club Borinquen!

Doc. 22
"Puerto Rico"
March 18, 1895 (#153)

A new collaborating newspaper bearing this title has surfaced in the city and within the base of the Partido Revolucionario Cubano; it is written and financed by five Puerto Ricans, all devoted believers in Antillean independence.

Revenues from the sale of the newspaper are to be donated to the reserves *Partido Revolucionario* and, judging from the first issue, we have no doubt of its ability to fulfill its mission.

This new colleague joins us at a most auspicious time because the independence of Cuba is also that of Puerto Rico.

Doc. 23
Notes from the Clubs of Puerto Rico
June 17, 1895 (#166)

"Interesting Meeting" (Club Borinquen)

Club Borinquen will convene a meeting at eight o'clock sharp this Wednesday on Third Avenue and the corner of 101st Street.

We request the punctual attendance of all active members, since the meeting will address an important issue for our small Antillean island.

Cubans and Puerto Ricans who are not club members, but who wish to participate in this session, are also invited. –Chairman, J.M. Terreforte. –Secretary, Domingo Collazo.

****

Club Las Dos Antillas

The Office the Secretary of this revolutionary club sent us the following letter for publication:

New York
June 5, 1895
Honorable Editor of *PATRIA*,
At the last regular meeting held by Club Las Dos Antillas, it was agreed and approved "that some members of this club were also associated with other clubs and that since they had to attend meetings so frequently, in the future it would be advisable to hold club meetings biweekly, instead of weekly." For this reason, the change was published in the meeting notice that appears in the official newspaper of the Partido Revolucionario Cubano. These meetings will take place on the second and last Tuesdays of every month.

I bring this to your attention in accordance with what was agreed.

Patria y Libertad
Secretary,
Arturo Schomburg

Doc. 24
"Hermanas de Betances"
October 23, 1895 (#189)
Philadelphia
October 11, 1895
Honorable Editor of *PATRIA*
New York

Dear Sir and Fellow Member,
I hasten to bring to your attention the following report for publication in our official newspaper. This event is of great urgency since it arrives at a critical moment in our sacred battle to victory or to death for the freedom and independence of our

beloved islands, Cuba and Puerto Rico. I hereby request that the name "Hijas de Betances" be registered in the list of clubs in this city which *PATRIA* publishes in honor of that champion for the rights of our enslaved sister island, and so that this eminent leader may see that he is not relegated to oblivion, but that he lives on in the hearts of Puerto Ricans, Cubans, and Americans.

On behalf of myself, this new club, and Silverio del Prado No. 1, please receive our most cordial thanks.

Yours truly and faithfully, fellow member,

J.A. Lucena

Doc. 25
Gumersindo Rivas, "Speech by Mr. Rivas"
October 30, 1895 (#191)

Citizens of a free people, I salute you in the name of freedom, and with this greeting, I am pleased to affectionately bear testimony to the deep solidarity of the liberal Venezuelan youth who look proudly upon you, admiring your conviction and your struggle for the sacred ideals of *patria* and *libertad*.

We salute those who, like us, were born in those virginal lands of the Antilles, inhaled its natural fragrances, and contemplated the radiance of its starlight. We salute those who, like us, have laid their heads on their mothers' laps when it came time to rest, and who are prohibited from planting the kiss of sacred love on their mother's austere brow; those who cannot keep a fire burning in their homes because of the harshness of their peculiar and unsettled situation and who, upon leaving their native land, make a pact of honor to not tread on the virtue of the region. It suffices that we receive the pure and gentle breeze of its redemption. We are so pleased to participate in this eternal struggle—the glorious commemoration of a valiant protest already recorded in the portentous pages of History.

Those of us who seek the independence and redemption of our native lands do so not out of hatred for the imperious nation that rocked our parents' cradles. We seek it because, within the legitimate authority of our sovereign rights, we can no longer continue being colonial subjects when we could be citizens without the shameful abdication of our name, history or future.

Do you know why the glorious Revolution of 1868 did not triumph, despite all the sacrifices made, all the energy it had at its disposal, and the distinguished lineage of its brave lieutenants? It was because that movement was the surge of a wave before it crashed. It was, we might say, the liberal upper classes of the Cuban people wanting to break free from the burdensome yoke of Spain's dominant elite.

And do you know why the current Revolution has now taken such an uncompromising turn, one that astounds the heroes of Numancia, sows terror among its ranks, and triumphs—as it inexorably must—even if Spain were to station all its military forces across the island and surround it with warships? It is because this Revolution is the popular movement of the Antillean people; it is the cry of sovereignty from humble workshops where tongues turn to fire, and the Antillean worker's sweat—transformed into a brilliant pearl—will fill the coffers of the Revolution and become war munitions to be transported to Cuba's countryside, fortified by struggle, the spirit of redemption, and the sovereign rule of law.

Oh! immortal ghosts of Céspedes and Martí, of Agramonte and the Agüeros brothers, and so many other noble fighters in our great struggle, sleep peacefully in your graves. The Homeland and History will do you justice.

And, you may rest in peace and tranquility, triumphant leaders, because the homeland does not sleep the debasing sleep of the colony. She is agitated and rebels, and—from one end to the other of those immortal fields where your names are whispered by the pure breeze of the forest and encircled by the perpetual light of immortality—the clarion of war rings out again, combative, with beautiful notes of resounding courage.

The current warriors—the unconquerable soldiers of this new phase—are guided by the magnificent flash of light that shines radiantly from the Sinai of our independence called Yara, the anniversary that we commemorate today. And, they flee, as one who flees the site of his degradation—that bleak place so shrouded in darkness called the Zanjón Pact.

In the present historic battle we celebrate today—in that honorable conflict entered into between the Colony and the Metropolis—there can be no vacillation or middle ground. It must be the Capitol or the Tarpeian Rock; graves abandoned on the battlefields or a ray of light shining down on the promised land of History.

Thus, we understand that those valiant champions who lead the new generation like prophets—the expert Gómez, the indomitable Maceo, and the persevering Massó—have entered into this decisive struggle with the self-reliance of those who find inspiration in the great and sublime responsibilities of duty.

That is why we see the Revolution walking in the footsteps of victors. If you wish for examples, you need only to consider Bayamo and sublime Boyacá in the current battles for a free Cuba.

And, that is how, gentlemen, we will see the peoples of Latin America answer the cry of outrage proclaimed by Amparán on the 19th of September in Caracas over seventy years ago, in fulfillment Miranda's initial plan—the culmination of the Venezuelan Convention which occurred on July 5, 1811.

And, it shall not ring true—neither liberty in the Americas, nor the unified political and historical life of the Latin American family joined together on this side of the Atlantic—until that supreme moment when Antillean independence has been achieved.

Gentlemen, it is before the great drama that unfolds in Cuba today, through its extraordinary enterprise and the battles fought by its heroic warriors, that the most sublime epic wars of antiquity—their glorious hymns sung to us by History at every moment—fade and lose their shape.

We have nothing to envy any nation in the world. Character, we have; courage, we have more than enough; virtue, there you have (pointing to the stage) the honor and virtue of our wives and mothers. And, it is good that the crumbling nations of Europe know this. If they present the heroic lives of their soldiers as the standard of their greatness—counting among them the Cid, Pelayo, Napoleon, Nelson, and all of their epic heroes—we need to take only one name from our shared tropical heritage to illuminate the world with its moral greatness: that name is Toussaint L'Ouverture.

March onward, then, beloved compatriots! Destiny guarantees the magnitude of our cause. Let slanderers rebuke us; let blasphemers curse us; do not heed those who already dream of our internal conflicts and divisions.

We do not approach this state of independence from the audacity of luck or the providence of extemporaneous maneuvers. We approach it from sound induction, from our own reasoning, and from our shared enlightenment.

If we were not a people prepared for a just future, would the date December 6, 1892 ever have come into being—that glorious date which Martí called Día de la Patria (Day of the Homeland) and which will be celebrated throughout our history as the date when the Cuban worker gave a portion of his noble wages to the cause of nationhood and independence? Perchance, could the nation that develops a passion for liberty despite its proscription and neglect ever cease to be anything but great?

Who could—snatching bread from his child and garments from his wife to clothe our *patria* in liberty and dignity—be anything but an honorable citizen, a hopeful portent of the model magistrate?

In whom could future generations and history see a citizen worthy of immortality and glory, if not in those who have extinguished the fire of their own hearths to give its smoldering embers to the greatness of their homeland?

In that case, gentlemen, you will find that you represent the most magnificent union of all heroisms.

In the name, then, of the ideals of Patria and Libertad, with our thoughts dedicated to the memory of José Martí—that Christ of the new redemption—and his greatness, as well as to his disciples fighting in the countryside or in the city to bring us communal prosperity and a shared home, I salute from the core of my patriot soul.

Doc. 26
"In Paris"
January 22, 1896 (#215)

In a Paris newspaper, *La Renaissance*, we read the following, which gives us cause to rejoice:
"The latest Cuban victories have produced such great enthusiasm among the

Island's great heirs living peacefully in Paris that some have finally decided to openly defend the cause of a free Cuba. They have approached Mr. Betances, the representative in Paris, to establish a committee and collect resources for the task of liberating their brethren to fruition."

Doc. 27
"Club Mercedes Varona"
January 25, 1896 (#216)

With the enthusiasm of those heady days of patriotic inspiration during which the passion for the cause of independence was evidenced at every moment by purposeful action and with blessed charity—often to the neglect of their own domestic necessities—the Club Mercedes Varona, that preeminent women's Club established in New York when the unforgettable Martí laid the foundations for the Partido Revolucionario Cubano, has been reestablished and returned to the fore.

In these glorious moments, it returns to its place of honor among our arsenal for liberation, and it is called upon by all good patriots wishing to provide genuine support—for which no effort should be spared—to hasten our imminent victory.

New and valuable elements have joined existing ones and, in the honorable meeting held for its reconstitution on the evening of January 17, the following Board of Directors was announced:

Madame Chairman, Inocencia M. de Figueroa; Treasurer, Luisa de Arteaga; Secretary, Miss Gloria de Céspedes; Representatives: Estella Rodríguez, Mercedes Martínez, and Teresa Bernard. Delegation and Advisory Board representatives: Dr. Buenaventura H. Portuondo, who, in a noble and spontaneous outburst, has made a donation to create a lavish silk flag, which will be raffled to augment the resources already being collected.

The distinguished Mrs. de Barranco, who was present at the session, humbly declined the position of acting Madam Chairman. But we understand that she will be elected honorary Madam Chairman in recognition of her merits and as venerable tribute to the dear name of Manuel Barranco, her unforgettable husband.

The meeting ended by reading the beautiful letter from that illustrious martyr of Dos Ríos, which he wrote during the time when he embarked on the first of his commendable trips to Santo Domingo and Haiti. And, after the New York Board of Advisors, Club Mercedes Varona was the first place he visited, as promised, and where he recounted the invaluable results he hoped it would achieve.

Here is the uplifting letter:

Partido Revolucionario Cubano Delegation
New York, April 24, 1893
Madam Chairman of Club Mercedes Varona **

My Distinguished Compatriot,

News of the Club's meeting tonight reaches me at precisely the moment when I am embarking on a trip that I hope will not be futile for our homeland. And, I do not know, my sisters of this Club, if my health will be sufficiently robust to meet the demands of my trip. If Club Mercedes Varona were to perish, if its example and spirit were to fail, then certainly my own health would also fail. And, I will be sure to conserve it, if, during the course of my arduous tasks, I receive news that the Club exists. There is much malice in the world and many obstacles to genuine freedom: there is no greater solace and strength than the knowledge that moral beauty shines from those who generous nature has given us as companions and the prize of life. I will come to Club Mercedes Varona before anywhere else to recount my work and efforts.

A proud greeting to my sisters of the Club on your election day,

Delegate José Martí

[**Author's Note: Letter to Puerto Rican Inocencia Martínez de Figueroa, Chair of Club Mercedes Varona at the time.]

Doc. 28
"Hermanas de Rius Rivera"
February 13, 1897 (#326)

The new women's club, which was just founded in this city under the fine name Hermanas de Rius Rivera, deserves special mention.

Under the singular name of that resolute and indomitable champion who, upon arriving at Pinar del Río, managed to gain the absolute trust of the great Maceo and who, when betrayal or heroic faith caused this great man's fall, opposed the full force of the Spanish mercenary troops; and under the remarkable name of the man who—along with Maceo—did not acquiesce to Zanjón, Puerto Rican and Cuban women have hastened to form a new, robustly born club. From exile, it will provide invaluable support to the war for independence and hope to Antillean women who sympathize with us and who, alongside us, proceed toward glorious victory, since proceeding into catastrophic defeat—which would close our path to freedom for what might be several generations—is unthinkable.

The following Board of Directors was constituted at a cordial meeting of Cuban and Puerto Rican women:

Honorary Chairman, Mrs. de Rius Rivera. —Acting Madam Chairman, I.M. de Figueroa. —Vice Chairman, Lola R. de Tió. —Treasurer, C. Bosch. —Secretary, M. de Acosta. —Assistant Secretary, José Crespo. —Representatives, M. Martínez, Mmes. de Macías, de Méndez, de León, and de Valdés. Honorary Chairmen: Messrs. Tomás Estrada de Palma and Dr. Julio J. Henna. —Representative to the Board of Advisors, Luis

Castro López. —Club Sponsors: Sub-Delegate Dr. Joaquín Castillo Duany, Professor Emilio Agramonte, Dr. Luis A. Baralt, Dr. H. Lincoln de Zayas, and Eduardo Yero.

With such valuable members, there is no doubt that *Club* Hermanas de Rius Rivera will serve as an example and an impulse for the enthusiastic and ever-sacrificing exile community.

We applaud you, and march onward toward the independence of Cuba and Puerto Rico.

Doc. 29
"New Newspaper"
February 5, 1898 (#428)

The Sección Puerto Rico of the Partido Revolucionario Cubano has begun publishing the newspaper *Borinquen* as its official organ. This newspaper will direct its energies toward working vigorously and tenaciously for the independence of our Antillean sister island. These paragraphs are from its article "Programa:"

"At these very moments, due to the imminent triumph of the glorious Cuban Revolution, a deceitful autonomist constitution has been drafted and promulgated in Puerto Rico in the hopes of reconciling fleeting crises. Those characteristic signs of a centralizing and tyrannical system are completely laid bare by the reporting of the activity of political organizations to the overseers in Madrid and keep public offices in the hands of enemies and exploiters.

"There has not been, either for the Puerto Rican or for the Cuban people, any other solution than the definitive severing of the ties that bind it to the metropolis.

"Nor is there any other way to proceed than by force. Latent rebelliousness must become concrete and strident action very soon; and, on that happy occasion, which will be glorious and fruitful, on that day, we will begin to act more as harbingers than journalists.

"In the fight for emancipation, the sons and daughters of Puerto Rico have supported us wholeheartedly, while we have directed our efforts to first give aid to the struggle in Cuba, so close to its glorious triumph. They have also rallied around all our patriotic ventures and will continue to do so, along with those who—unable to abandon their miserable homes—uphold the indomitable hope for their redemption while surrounded by peril in the enslaved homeland. By our side also stand all the Cubans—ardent and resolute in their support—who have included us in the platform of their Homeland, which is an inseparable part of the plan for our own island, as we are both sisters in suffering and ideals.

"Cubans and Puerto Ricans—joined as an indivisible force and unified in organization, direction, and with perfect discipline—must triumph over the opposition of our shared tyrant; and, if they have proceeded us in history and may, perhaps, precede us in victory, their help and example will clear the path to achieve the same triumphs that destiny has reserved for their victories and heroism."

The mission that this new colleague has set for itself is admirable. It is a mission in which we cannot help but take interest because it is the cause of both Cubans and Puerto Ricans against Spain, their common oppressor. In it, we see a champion that stands with us to publicize the hardships of battle. And, in our eagerness to see *Borinquen* become a reality, we welcome it enthusiastically.

Section 2
THE INDEPENDENCE OF PUERTO RICO

Doc. 30
Club Borinquen, "To the People of Puerto Rico"
March 14, 1892 (#1)

Chairman: Sotero Figueroa
Vice Chairman: Antonio Vélez Alvarado
Treasurer: Modesto A. Tirado
Representatives: Gonzalo de Quesada
Leopoldo Núñez
Agustín González
Rafael I. Delgado
Secretary: F. Gonzalo Marín

We, the undersigned, in our own name and on behalf of Club Borinquen, which we represent, have come together on this day to carry out an act, compelled by conscience and patriotism.

Having seen the tortuous course the Autonomist Directorate of San Juan has been imposing on the party that has welcomed into its ranks all those born on the island of Borinquen, and believing that such a Directorate had always known how to preserve unscathed the principles that ensure all rights inherent to the human character and all ideals that feed regionalist sentiment and which have always shaped the acts of our political life, we appeal to the liberals of this nation to protest, as necessity dictates, against the illogical conduct and against the brazen behavior of said Directorate, which has fittingly unveiled the crowning glory of its repulsive dictatorial project, namely, the deplorable Manifesto dated December 19 of last year.

When in November 1886 the so-called "Ponce Plan," which was designed to reorganize the old Partido Liberal Reformista, was publicly proclaimed, the men who today head the Autonomist group, forgetting the righteous instructions stamped on the notice circulated for such purposes by the author of said Plan, the prescient Baldorioty de Castro, which, in sum, stated that "when considering and amending each part of the document, which is presented as material for further study (and was the result of extensive considerations and uncommon political acumen), do not lose *sight of the dominant relations between those parts and the whole.*" These men heading the Partido Autonomista Puertorriqueño, we repeat, were most resolute and determined in openly breaking with the Ponce Plan. Title I was supplanted with remnants from the colorless Autonomist foundations set forth by Mr. Labra and fragments of various articles from the Constitution of the Partido Liberal Cubano, while other articles in this Plan were amended or altered, thus leveling a well-reasoned work of good judgment and foresight.

In other words, that self-contained, harmonious, and essentially democratic Plan that was so methodically constructed—in which all parts fit so seamlessly together and aligned with the previous liberal political ideology (for it did not yield, but raised on high the glorious Reformist flag, that flag which Puerto Ricans have revered since 1867, when the illustrious members of the Junta Informativa de Reformas para Ultramar cloaked themselves with it)—proved to be a half-bred monstrosity, contradictory on more than a few points, and lacking a political doctrine that is uniform, ample in breadth, and truly democratic. The name Partido Liberal Reformista was replaced by Partido Autonomista, thus depleting invaluable strengths from the old banner, which was never meant to be retired. An alliance was made with Cuban Autonomists, an alliance that, proving insincere, was later dismissed or ignored, and thought of no more.

Reactionary animosity was furiously unleashed upon seeing that, in accordance with Autonomist sermonizing, it was advised to not conduct business transactions with *peninsulares*—who had been dominating as if they were lords of the manor—but with fellow islanders instead. Therefore, a vast conspiracy for rebellion, born from the severing of these economic ties, was believed to have been hatching, and the people paid, with horrible martyrdom, with the tortures and ignominious brutality of 1887, the sad reality of today being called *insolent*; and the same people who added the yeast of boycott to the bread of their Autonomist aspirations now try to disassociate themselves from their involvement.

We are unaware of the existence of secret societies in Puerto Rico, but the facts allow us to state that, if they do exist, their organizers have not been miserable and ignorant campesinos. No doubt, those who today damn and defame are not free from guilt—grave guilt—by forgetting that only he who is deemed without sin *may cast the first stone*.

Would government persecutions have been unleashed, would the deep division—which today weighs heavy on the Partido Autonomista Puertorriqueño—have befallen them, had the steadfast voice of the incorruptible Baldorioty de Castro been heard? Undoubtedly, no, for, despite the fact that the Ponce Plan was in essence more radical, more autonomist than what had been approved—for it granted *the greatest measure of POLITICAL and administrative power* to the provincial and municipal leadership and recognized individual rights as *beyond legislation*—it did not stir up spirits with hollow words, nor did it baptize the reorganized party with an ostentatious name, evoking suspicion and animosity among the legions of the opposition—a name that is as explicit as it is untrue, since, actually, there is no such autonomy, rather only assimilation to the metropolis with regards to everything political and a shameful decentralization of the economic life within the province.

Baldorioty de Castro was soon compelled to resign as chairman of the Autonomist party. Ailing; overwhelmed by obstacles set forth by of adversity; not entirely free from the gloomy dungeon where he was imprisoned; his life in danger as a result of General Palacio's fabricated conspiracy; his greatest merits, unknown; and accused, with blatant injustice, of being passive in his duties when the liberals of the nation refused to move in terror of the dragonnades of '87 still overpowered their consciences; disappointed in mankind, but never in the ideas he had preached, he went off to die in the solitude of his home, without the slightest complaint rising from his lips.

With him fled circumspection and common sense, and individual authority took root in the heart of the newly formed Directorate. As a sign of protest, more than a few distinguished Liberals retreated into their private lives, and those who placed themselves at the head of the now waning liberal forces unscrupulously permitted a system of excommunication, which the Integrist party has so used and abused, to reign. And, as embarrassing as it is to say, those who previously had sustained with Spartan determination that there were no conspirators at the Autonomist camp, in effect, upheld General Palacio's politics of repression by implicitly admitting to their existence when they identified and condemned secret societies with illicit purposes as deserving severe condemnation.

A Directorate that so clearly accuses its members is a suicidal Directorate, one that is incapable of realizing patriotic ideals. This is the reason behind the fading enthusiasm and why in cities such as Ponce and towns such as Cabo Rojo, where intransigent Conservatives who had never been able to win in a fair fight, nowadays triumph and dictate the law of the victors over their adversaries. This is the reason why, no matter how many threats the Autonomist Directorate directs at its fellow members to reorganize and contribute to lifting the charges against the Party, no one—or very few—answer the call. This is the reason, in sum, why the party will dissolve like a lump of sugar in a glass of water, because it has not resolved, as in Cuba, either to retire or become extinct.

The Autonomist Assembly that recently convened in the city of Mayagüez deigned to inform us, the exile community, that the consequences of these mistakes are now being felt and that it was the lack of foresight with which the Ponce Plan was examined that planted the seed of divisiveness. It was undoubtedly those unconscionable henchmen of the people's cruel persecution in 1887 that brought such a confusion of ideas to the proceedings and such blatant contradictions in the exposition of doctrine that the Party could no longer move forward without making certain changes to the Constitution, which had been solemnly proclaimed in Ponce. Therefore, those who today lead the Partido Autonomista—who are, as we have already stated, the same people who initiated and sustained the campaign against the Ponce Plan and who, at the aforementioned Assembly, opted for the name Autonomista, which the party now bears—most uselessly proposed to alter the name of the party in order to attract the invaluable figures who so prominent in the old Partido Liberal Reformista. They exhausted their persuasiveness with remarks that the party should make truly nationalist statements; that it be made explicitly clear that Puerto Rican Autonomists sought no future outside the arms of the motherland; and that it be implicitly acknowledged that it was not these Autonomists who, by any means, formed the ranks of reputedly illicit societies. In this Assembly, Mr. Labra was given full authority to affiliate the party to the political group in Madrid, which he considered most appropriate. Furthermore, funds would be raised so that Mr. Labra might establish a newspaper in Madrid that would promote the ideals of the Party, all the while, hard-working newspapers on the island, such as *La Razón* in Mayagüez, are allowed to disappear, perhaps because devotion to a leader is carried to the point of idolatry, believing he might somehow procure...what the government refuses to give.

Without a doubt, the Directorate's numerous affirmations of *españolismo*—which Integrists reject in light of how frequently they are bandied about, whether relevant or not—are a show of appreciation from the Autonomist group toward the metropolitan government for having chosen as *Diputado* to the Spanish Cortes for San Juan the odious name of don José Gallart—one of the ruthless triumvirs which public opinion considers as the henchmen of the 1887 compontes and, moreover, as responsible for perpetuating that very same administration and upholding the theory of castes, all of which assured overrepresentation in the polls, an advantage they then used to secure political domination of reactionary peninsulares. This offensive injustice is what brought about the complete withdrawal of the Partido Liberal Cubano.

This inconceivable and unlimited delegation of authority granted to Mr. Labra has been received with expressions of great disapproval, shedding light on the dictatorial manner upon which it was agreed and how improper it is, under sound democratic doctrine, to cede the will of an entire party and rest it on the shoulders of one man. Such distinguished and well-intentioned Puerto Ricans like Messrs. Cortón and Abril have already honorably and whole-heartedly battled against it, and the Directorate gets the worst end of the deal with such severe, yet just, charges.

And to add insult to injury and further thicken the haze of precaution measures the Directorate has created with its hostilities, it pronounced its manifesto, dated last December 19, which is so harsh and brash that it does not come across as the pondered and conciliatory product of an illustrious body, rather a blind and hostile attack by an intransigent adversary.

It is precisely this document that has compelled us to submit our unequivocal protest. From it, we extract the following two paragraphs to provide a proper response, since we believe that these lines were meant for us:

Perhaps this new account of principles and objectives—which are unique to the Autonomist party—may seem useless or redundant, recorded as they are in all clarity in our Constitution, but the Directorate does not believe it superfluous to recall them, considering that with each step our critics fail to remember them; that day after day malice and bad faith insist on attributing to us purposes and doctrines openly opposed to those which we seek and profess; and that, at times, impatience and pretension from rash party members —or the treachery and hypocrisy of those who act as such—have passed through our organization with WICKED

INTENTIONS, all of which have served as the pretext to create an artificial atmosphere of despicable suspicion and stolid skepticism surrounding our party, which we wish to dispel.

Political parties are not a closed camp where permission is needed to enter and leave.

Everyone is free to call himself an Autonomist without having to be one, and it is not up to the Party to put an end to it. The Party does, however, have the right and the duty to reject—as it strongly does—all solidarity and communion with the INSOLENT ones who abuse the name to embarrass the party and proclaim to the four winds that those who embrace other principles and cultivate aims aside from those set forth in letter and spirit in our credo are, in fact, not Autonomists and have nothing in common with them; neither do those who, in order to carry out these principles and aspirations, follow or intend to follow procedures that are not of the strictest legality, to which our party sternly adheres, recognizing as it does, BEFORE AND ABOVE ALL, national sovereignty and the rule of law.

We shall not breach the sanctity of intentions to inquire as to what degree those statements are sincere; but it is in line with our forthrightness and with the integrity of our sentiments to make it known to the Partido Autonomista in Puerto Rico—and we have the right to be believed, for we act under no coercion or suggestion whatsoever—that our current political conduct may not be agreeable to the men of the Directorate. Our beliefs, however, deserve all due respect for they are inspired by the objective of broadening the horizons for the land of our birth.

Those here, who belong to the expatriate community in New York and hail from the Puerto Rican Autonomist camp, have no reason to be apologetic. They had affiliated themselves with the most progressive party—considering the existing colonial situation—and their attitude was proper and disciplined while they were members. After the tempestuous period of 1887, the unforgettable year when they resigned themselves to suffer the same fate as those of similar beliefs, they refused to engage any longer in dealings with evil and, while by no means meek, agreed to live under an artificially imposed moral peace that undermines public prosperity, diminishes character, and demands continuous declarations of loyalty in order to tolerate the political actions of a tame liberalism, all without ending repression—increasingly carried to extremes against the criollo—and without erasing the *stain*—considered vile by those who do not comprehend the full nobility of the idea embodied in the people's redemption.

It is true that certain valiant Puerto Ricans wished to remain in the thick of things, upholding in newspaper columns the innate pride of the worthy patriot, and in this admirable campaign they indeed gained the people's gratitude; however, government persecution crashed upon them. They were struck down by the anathema of the Autonomist Olympus, and some either had to appeal to the liberals of the nation for the justice denied them by the Directorate—having to accommodate to those they fear and with whom they continue to sustain a campaign as titanic as fruitless—or abandon their beloved post, convinced that it is impossible to contend with the formidable obstacles of tradition and where there seems to be no room, except for the malleable and complacent or the passive and tolerant.

Those who, being able to live peacefully in foreign lands where the entire breath of their rights are fully guaranteed, struggle in noble emulation to free a nation from colonial enslavement are not treacherous and hypocritical people.

Those who took their freedom to act abroad and, thus, do not intervene in any way with the Autonomist party's disastrous course, did not pass through that organization with wicked intentions. If an atmosphere of despicable suspicion and stolid skepticism has enveloped the Party, it is you—the leaders—who are to blame. You encouraged rash enthusiasm; in your political catechism, you tolerated and even recommended those economic ties that the people carried to extremes, diving off the embankment of caution. Yesterday you stressed doctrine, and today you defame and speak abominations of the disciples you appointed to preach. First, you denied the issue of secret societies; now you acknowledge their existence, although you say they have nothing to do with your political beliefs. You were optimistic in Ponce, hesitant in Mayagüez, and in San Juan, slanderous against your fellow countrymen. About what and whom are you complaining?

Reject the *insolent ones* who abuse the name of the party to embarrass it!... But who are these insolents ones? Those who unleashed the compontes or those who suffered them? Those who showed themselves to be ardent worshipers of regionalism or those who today go to the Governor General's mansion and genuflect before him? Those who today recognize, *before and above all*, national sovereignty or those who yesterday put principles before this sovereignty? Oh, men of the Directorate, wield your double-edged sword! Passion is bad counsel, and never should communications be addressed to the public when under her influence. It is not right; it is not proper that illustrious and sophisticated democrats with enviable political careers should aid in the work of intransigent reactionaries.

When, in 1867, General Marchessi—along with other most honorable Liberals—judged as suspect the man who today is the chairman of the Partido Autonomista in Puerto Rico and banished him, the sympathy and respect of his fellow countrymen followed. And when soon after, in 1868, he was accused of being one of the fomenters of the Lares insurrection, he found no Puerto Ricans who could substantiate the accusation or who would publicly call him *rash and impudent*. Before, on the contrary, the stain of hostility toward the Spanish government did nothing but add new titles to the honors with which he had been bestowed, and his countrymen were able to triumphantly name him Diputado to the Spanish Cortes as soon as colonial life was reestablished itself, despite the fact that those were times of real danger for those who promoted expansive, decentralizing ideas.

Compare this behavior to what can be observed today from supporters of absolute autonomy, particularly now when the Supreme Court in Madrid has recognized that emancipation propaganda is not punishable as long as it does not incite armed rebellion. One must agree that, as struggling patriots and selfless Puerto Ricans, Autonomist leaders have much to learn from the old Liberal Reformists, whose flag—emblazoned with the motto REFORM—they have not successfully flown; a reform that signifies "acknowledging the past, but always taking a step forward," until reaching the solution we hold to be the most rational and logical in the sovereign lives of nations.

We will now offer a few explanations, which we owe our brothers in Puerto Rico to justify our political conduct abroad.

In the great city of New York, where admirable institutions guarantee freedom in its highest form, there is no room for transitional, transactional or middle-ground parties because our concept of *nation* has already been founded on unshakable ground. In colonies where there is an artificially imposed political atmosphere, there must still be a sense of balance, so that democratic pronouncements may be tolerated, albeit, with more than a few restrictions.

The parties that alternate in power here are fundamentally radical on the subject of administrative procedures, for they understand that these cannot be permanent; and this radicalism—which is born from the protection and respect for ideas—is passed on to the political clubs founded by Antillean émigrés longing to break the old molds of colonialism to lay the broad, generous foundations for a free country.

Following this expansive trend, there exists in the American Union two parties on diametrically opposed paths that try to advance new horizons for the only two nations that still remain enslaved in the Americas. One desires absolute emancipation; the other, the annexation of the Spanish Antilles to the Colossus of the North. We cannot participate in the latter for we must not aspire to surrender ourselves to the absolute absorption of our race by another, one that does not seduce us to the point of wanting to forsake our language, customs, traditions, sentiments... everything that constitutes our physiognomy as a Latin American people, nor do we wish to do so.

One must have lived in this country a few years to understand that this race does not have a propensity to perfect or improve, simply through contact, those it believes inferior and has no other reason to abandon this proud belief—save for material advancement—as if man, in fact, does live *by bread alone*. For this reason, it exterminates, in its victorious march, elements that pose resistance by refusing to be absorbed.

One can discern from the foregoing that we do not renounce our race nor do we defame our origins. If we favor emancipation, it is because it is the natural law from which neither pueblos nor individuals can escape. And, just as the son wants to establish a separate home for himself upon reaching the fullness of reason—regardless of how good he is to his parents, for he cannot pursue his heart's desires or invest his own energies in sowing healthy young crops— so colonies—nations under guardianship while they cannot yet rule themselves—react against all pressure, against any yoke—as mild as it may be—for they are but nationalities in an embryonic state and behave as the stream, which is stagnant when contained, but furiously breaks its embankment, spreading out at will through the lowlands when sufficient volume has accumulated, proving itself an irresistible force. Then, balance is restored, and the beneficial waters fertilize the land and wipe away any sickly vegetation. Happy are the parents—happy are the nations—who teach prudence and prepare their children—prepare the colonies—to fulfill their eminent duties in concert with society.

Annexation is an embarrassment for Spain because, in hoping to erase from the colonies the signs of their conquering domination, it breaks all the ties that the metropolis had created and sets out, like a slave of a bad master, to sell herself to a different master, who is believed to be wealthier, more just, and more humanitarian.

Therefore, when choosing between the two inevitable extremes—annexation and emancipation—every good Spaniard who jealously guards his citizenship and admires the glories of the motherland must resolutely support the latter, which does not extinguish, but improves upon the work that the metropolis initiated, yet has been unable to bring to its noble fruition.

If it is to be, if it is the law of history—as has been acknowledged by more than a few shrewd Spanish politicians—that emancipation is to come inevitably (a triumphant day, which is not far away), it is patriotic and prudent to channel this redemptive movement in the high spirit of justice, without defamation and without hate. Let us find that magnificent formula that leads to a free country for all, where the process of ensuring the common good is not at the mercy of those who have set out to dominate the Spanish Antilles, but is rather tied to those who have been born there. Let us not strive for a false autonomy that will forever be subordinated to the conquerors—becoming slavery in disguise—but move toward the absolute emancipation of those pueblos that reach maturity and demand their rights—rights which have been accorded to them by nature, reason, and history.

To our Puerto Rican brothers who do not wish to trample on political decorum and patriotic honor: Move aside and let the dignitaries struggle in the void you leave. To those who today condemn yesterday's apostolic work and are now invited to the Palacio de Santa Catalina, not to perform *acts* that bring to mind the works of Acosta, Corchado, Alonso, and Ferrer—who were all able to *steer clear* when they became convinced that they had only succeeded in playing along with distinguished, yet intransigent reactionaries—but to entertain flattery and smiles in exchange for unthinkable favors, even when the government carries humiliation to extremes: Imitate Autonomists worthy of the actions of your fellow party members in Cuba, who solemnly promised to dissolve the party—precipitated by the latest humiliating provisions of Spain's Overseas Minister, Mr. Romero Robledo—and await the hour of great vindication.

Regarding our political opponents, understand that in us you have honest and loyal adversaries, not hypocrites or slandering, underhanded deviants who give rise to suspicion and fuel hostile distrust.

We do not work in the shadows, we stand in plain sight, and may impartial History pass judgment on each and every one of us when the time comes.

Sotero Figueroa

Antonio Vélez Alvarado

F. Gonzalo Marín

Doc. 31

Sotero Figueroa, "The Truth about History, I"

March 19, 1892 (#2)

Subjugated peoples [*los pueblos subyugados*] always tend to recover their independence, just as the caged bird struggles to own the air. Hence, it is no wonder why a sense of dignity is so deeply entrenched in *los pueblos*, and this is why wise and prudent Nature gave wings to birds, so that they might live in a space without boundaries.

Freedom is such a precious gift that we cannot accept it secondhand. It is an imprescriptible and inalienable right that is born with us, and, just as we cannot be deprived of our life or our land without committing a crime or a monstrous usurpation, there ought to be no attempts on our freedom, for we shall unflinchingly rise up until we succeed, either peacefully or by force.

Therefore, judge for yourself how odious tyranny can be when exercised not against an individual, but against an entire pueblo. Hence, just and sacred are the revolutions that tend to bring independence to the homeland. And these, according to irrefutable law, always triumph. It is of no consequence that oppressive regimes might win partial victories, leading them blindly and haughtily to intensify their severity. This only serves to prolong the battle until definitive victory comes to bring to triumphant conclusion the redemptive efforts borne by patriots who refuse to be slaves.

Hence, *pueblos conquistados* never passively accept the yoke of their conquerors, but always fight to break the chains of slavery until they ultimately succeed.

Puerto Rico, like Cuba, has not been able to escape this influence of dignity. Perhaps they are childish tactics or attempts to divert suspicion so as not to be accused of being accomplices or sympathizers, but they have sung and repeated the chorus of the Puerto Rican liberal faction: that in the smallest of the Spanish Antilles there are no separatists, nor have there every been any. As the popular saying goes, this is to block out the sun with two fingers, for this absolute negation tends to deny historic truth and make of Puerto Ricans—who are conscientious about their future destiny and who have consistently fought for their freedom—faithless and debased helots without regional aspirations who tolerate insult, seek no redress with pride, and accept their punishment by submissively kissing the hand of their abuser.

How could the idea of emancipation have not found resonance on the island of Puerto Rico when its landscape is bordered by *pueblos soberanos*, saturating it with freedom, like oxygen does the lungs? If adaptation to the environment is a sociological truth from which neither individuals nor societies can escape, then Puerto Rico must surrender to the influx of political expansion conveyed by pueblos that were able to bring to triumphant conclusion their own redemptive efforts during the first quarter century. These pueblos have not ceased to look upon us with sympathy, nor have they ceased to lend support to any insurrection carried out in the two Antillean islands that are still subject to Spanish dominion, for they are convinced that, as long as these islands have not been liberated, Bolívar's magnum opus will remain incomplete, and, in the concert of American republics, the two beautiful islands that serve as watchtowers to the new continent will be absent.

While it may be true that Puerto Rico does not have a vast territory to hold its population of nearly one million inhabitants—and this makes those in favor of emancipation wary of attempting a surprise attack, since there is barely a handspan of unpopulated land on the island—there are very important and strategic locations for revolutionary preparation nearby, namely, Santo Domingo and Saint Thomas, which are only a few brief hours away, as well as Curaçao and Venezuela, which lie only a short distance from our shores. Santo Domingo, above all, has always been an invaluable supporter of the cause of Antillean emancipation. That vibrant nation has always seen in their Puerto Rican brothers-in-bondage a need for redemption at all cost, and has offered on so many occasions to contribute to the independence efforts and has been unstinting in moral and material support.

In 1821, when the old Hispaniola was not yet entirely free from the yoke of the metropolitan power, the president of the new republic, José Núñez, addressed Gonzalo de Aróstegui, who then was Captain General of Puerto Rico, inviting him to complete a plan for the emancipation of the Antilles and appealing to his sense of justice and freedom (which naturally spring forth in the human heart) and to his heritage as a citizen of the Americas (which should compel him to stand for the hemisphere on which he was born and not for the subjugating nation). This request did not have the desired effect, and all of Mr. Núñez's subsequent efforts had to yield to the need of building his own country—for energies and resources could not be distracted in such a risky and uncertain enterprise—and given that the Spanish government had been forewarned and had reinforced its military presence in Puerto Rico.

This attempt was enough to establish a precedent of political solidarity in the Antilles, and we, Puerto Ricans, ought to place José Núñez first on the commemorative wall honoring the cultivators of our independence. The seed had fallen on fertile ground, and by 1824, it had sprouted forth lush and robust. At that time, Saint Thomas was the center of agitation for Puerto Rican independence. Revolutionaries Carlos Rigoti and Andrés Level de Goda actively and productively corresponded with prominent Puerto Ricans, and a rebel agent from Tierra Firme, whose last name was Moloni, had recruited a solid contingency of patriots... José Escuté was in Bogotá campaigning for an armed expedition in support of Puerto Rico, and Castro, the Do-minican—we regret not knowing his given name—enthusiastically contributed to the efforts and firmly believed that not a year would pass before Puerto Rico, like Santo Domingo, would see the shining star of independence.

Unrest on the subjugated island itself was by no means less intense. Bolívar's ge-nius triumphed in the American hemisphere. Heeding his call, inspired independent nations emerged from slave colonies, and the desire for emulation clearly flourished in the hearts of all Puerto Ricans. Now it was not only the people who desired free-dom everywhere and at every moment, but also a sizeable number of government employees, as well as the clergy, more than a few officials, and even the most influ-ential families sympathized with the fomenters and heroes of hemispheric indepen-dence and were willing to endorse it.

Puerto Rican patriot, José Ignacio Grau, one of the movement's most prominent leaders, wrote to José de Luque, an agent for Colombian revolutionaries based in Saint Thomas, who, after taking inventory of a great many number of the most in-valuable people committed to the imminent uprising, stated the following: "If I were to give you a list all of those devoted to this cause, I am afraid that there might not be enough paper. But I end my letter by telling you that three and half of Puerto Rico's four corners are firmly in our favor." The source of these remarkable and redemptive pronouncements was Manuel Coronado, Francisco Dueño, Manuel Otero, and the aforementioned José Ignacio Grau.

Why did Antillean independence not triumph this time, when public opinion in Puerto Rico declared itself so resolutely in its favor? Oh! Because they were waiting for the armed expedition that victorious Colombia had offered. But the United States of America was opposed to this very last emancipation. Spain, having been defeated on the continent, fortified the Antilles with troops that were no longer needed in South America by then, and—as it redoubled persecution after the fall of its consti-tutional system—exiled or threw those Puerto Ricans regarded as traitors in dun-geons. Patriots lost heart when they realized that they would not be counting on the assistance offered, and more than a few of those who most fervently supported the overthrow of the Spanish government—when they deemed it an easy enterprise—became its most enthusiastic defenders, either for fear of punishment or for having found a shameful reward for their contemptible actions. When has the god of Success refused the incense of adoration from mercenaries and purchasable men who traffic in honor and conscience?

This heart-wrenching failure lulled the separatist cause into dormancy until 1838, when it prevailed as an irresistible force in the hearts of Puerto Ricans who love in-dependence more than life in the wretched bowels of slavery. This time, the Granada regiment had agreed to support the revolutionary movement. The plan was to launch a surprise attack and capture Governor General Miguel López de Baños, as well as officials who opposed the movement; take control of the forts and other strategic points around the capital city; and proclaim the independence of Puerto Rico. The strategy was quick and easy to execute—counting, as they did, on an army—but no less daring. Nevertheless, there was a Judas in their midst who reported the conspiracy to the authorities. After identifying our compatriots, Andrés and Juan Vizcarrondo and Buenaventura Valentín Quiñones, as leaders and Sergeants Francisco Salinas and Ezequiel Santillana as dissenters in the army, they were all sentenced to death.

The Vizcarrondo brothers managed to escape to the coasts of Venezuela as soon as they realized that the plan had been uncovered. The unfortunate Buenaventura Valentín Quiñones was imprisoned in a horrid dungeon, where he was found the next day hanging by the neck, having crafted a noose from a silk scarf and attaching it to the end of the hammock where he was to sleep. Sergeants Salinas and Santillana— sons of Andalusia, whose generous hearts were devoted to the noble cause—were executed by firing squad on October 6, 1840.

Over in Venezuela, Puerto Ricans who reached the gracious city of Caracas would have found, as of a few years ago, a venerable old man with a white beard and expressive eyes who would cry at the thought of his lost homeland and, with a father's love, would welcome any of his fellow countrymen who crossed the threshold of his home. The snows of years past never cooled the fire in his patriotic heart, and by 1869, he had planned to disembark on the shores of Puerto Rico with a great expedition of brave Americans to fight for the independence of the island, hoping to be fortunate enough to one day see, before dying, his homeland free and independent. Such sweet aspirations did not materialize due to insurmountable obstacles, but the attempt is a testament to the nature of this patriot, who was none other than the indomitable Andrés Vizcarrondo. When Puerto Rico finally takes her place amidst the *pueblos redimidos* and becomes the arbiter of her own fate, the remains of this illustrious patriot should rest in the land he so venerated. As so, we honor his memory, and we shall emulate his valiant consequence.

And now we arrive at Lares, which deserves a separate chapter.

Doc. 32
Sotero Figueroa, "The Truth about History, II"
April 3, 1892 (#4)

The Lares revolution was not a pitiable and miserable pronouncement by a few disgruntled men, nor was it a disorganized skirmish led by a wretched and ignorant mob seeking not the procurement of the noblest ideal, but the satisfaction of their instinct for greed and extermination.

The liars who attempt to disseminate such statements apparently know little about the people of Puerto Rico. No, the Lares revolution—aborted because of the imprudence of two emissaries devoted to the cause who decided to converse aloud in the middle of the road about the imminent uprising, clearly believing that the night's shadows would keep their secret in the folds of her cloak—was an eloquent demonstration of a *pueblo altivo* wanting to break the yoke of enslavement: It was the culmination of the people's regionalist sentiment which materialized and laid the foundations for a *patria libre*; it was the reassuring result of the emancipatory ideology that started to be felt in 1821 and that today can and will restrict overpowering force, which will not succeed in annihilating this passion—even if the persecution persists and spreads—for there are eternal laws of the physical and moral order from which neither nature nor societies can escape.

Bodies always fall on the side toward which they lean, and so do *pueblos subyugados*, always leaning toward freedom. Medicines will do nothing but prolong the sickness. Heroic remedies are what kill or save, and—given that the Spanish Antilles cannot perish, for they enjoy robust conditions to live autonomously—they will be saved through the heroic remedy of revolution, even if the metropolis refuses to understand that it is as impossible to contain the separatist ideal in the Americas as it is ridiculous to use doors to enclose the air. Therefore, for the glory of the patriotic efforts that were demonstrated at Lares, we come to vindicate the respect for Puerto Ricans who do not traffic in the shame of the homeland, who do not abdicate their rights, and who do not scorn or forget the saviors of yesteryear or curse their revolutionary work. Abandon at once the urge to strip all consequence and grandeur from one of the most significant political events ever recorded in the annals of Puerto Rican history and in which those who distinguished themselves in this enterprise will exult as a badge of honor, if they are still alive—or their descendants, if they themselves have passed away—when Puerto Rican nationhood has been proclaimed; and when, by its freest will, the nation of Betances and Ruiz Belvis, of Baldorioty and Corchado, of Padial and Vizcarrondo, becomes part of that Antillean Confederation we can now see outlined on the horizon of our hopes, making this trinity of islands—which bathe in the Caribbean and offer the promise of a friendly welcome which the free Americas will always bestow on the brave ships that promote trade relations and spread the triumphs of human ingenuity across the earth—prosperous and happy, respected and loved.

Do not be alarmed with the current state of affairs, you conformists, for we will not disturb your palatial meals with our inconsiderate story-telling, nor will we rouse animosities with virulent statements that confer neither clarity of judgment nor rectitude of intentions, but muddle the spirit with a blind intemperance that does not persuade or unite the good people of the colony toward the betterment of the nation. What follows is taken entirely from *Historia de la Insurrección de Lares* written by a Spanish Integrist, Mr. Pérez Moris, who certainly had access to all the official documents that were gathered for such purposes. He corrupted his sources to wield them as illicit weapons for the party, thus casting in a bad light the rectitude and impartiality that History must inspire, the result of which could never undo—in any period—ideological fanaticism or the caste system hierarchy. It is logical reparation that speaks for the undeniable law of compensation. What was written to slander and persecute will serve to ennoble and sanctify. The painting that was all shadows will seem full of light in its easternmost corner. Those with greater authority and knowledge of historical fact than we have will soon come to examine it in full detail and present the truth in a memorial celebrated in honor of worthy Puerto Ricans.

Lares, like Yara, has a glorious ancestry. The Junta Informativa de Reformas para Ultramar, meeting in the Spanish metropolis between 1860 and 1867, embraced the illustrious commissioners from Cuba and Puerto Rico who firmly and unwaveringly requested reforms consistent with human dignity. José Morales Lemus, for Cuba, and Segundo Ruiz Belvis, for Puerto Rico, were the most prominent figures at the Overseas Commission and, therefore, directed the debates that had been proposed. The Junta de Información was dissolved on orders of the government, and the result was none other than the maximizing of persecutions throughout the Spanish colonies and unleashing the wrath of the omnipotent supporters of slavery against Antillean informants, since they had dared to vigorously advocate in favor of the immediate abolition of slavery. The valiant protests were succeeding, so repression was instituted to ferociously extinguish them. Hence, in 1867, several Puerto Rican patriots were exiled from the land of their birth, among them the two most noble and prestigious figures of the Regeneration movement: Segundo Ruiz Belvis and Ramón Emeterio Betances. The same relentless persecution was unleashed in Cuba, and among those who marched proudly toward forced expatriation figured Ruiz Belvis' illustrious colleague: the wise activist, Morales Lemus. These two patriarchs were not cast from the same mold as are meek, patient helots, who resign themselves to live without personhood and without rights. They fought tenaciously and resolutely to deliver their enslaved homeland. They were not given the ineffable good fortune of seeing their ideals triumph, but their work has been more than enough to win them admiration, their names becoming a glorious banner around which today all parties championing emancipation have gathered. Ruiz Belvis died in Valparaíso as ambassador of Antillean patriots, and Morales Lemus, here, in the American Union, working resolutely for the independence of his homeland. These two men will shine eternally in the pantheon of martyrs for independence, and their fellow countrymen will, in time, show them the everlasting adoration of grateful nations.

Still standing, firm and lively, without succumbing to blandishments or threats, was the incorruptible Betances. His name would command the respect of his bloodiest enemies. The people would see in him the spokesman for their freedom. The needy would see him as their providence. The sick, as destitute as they were, would never seek his medical assistance in vain, so much so that he was known as "the poor man's doctor." A well-deserved chorus of praise followed him wherever he went, and he took pleasure in the lavishing of good deeds. Educated in France, he fed on the words of great thinkers and selfless republican activists in its capital city, where he studied Medicine. When he settled in Mayagüez, that elegant city on the west coast of Puerto Rico, he dedicated his time to establishing his practice with such zeal and philanthropy that the author of *Historia de la Insurrección de Lares*, Mr. Pérez Moris, felt obliged to state that Betances "observed a strict rigorousness regarding his duties as a good doctor and readily gave the sick and impoverished not only medical assistance, but also financial support, when they were in need. His philanthropy extended so far as to establish a hospital in his own house, where any poor man or woman who arrived at that charitable refuge was admitted free of charge." To deflate the significance of these acclamations, it did not occur to the author to suggest that this was all a "calculated" charity.

But that incomparable Puerto Rican went even further in his catechism. The wretched slave—struggling in the bleak inferno of the sugar mills; watering the furrows that he plowed with his tears and leaving streaks of blood over the sweet grasses—saw in Betances the merciless flogger of his executioner and the savior of his hapless children. He and Ruiz Belvis founded a charitable society to buy the freedom of the disgraced fruit borne of the slave womb at the baptismal font for the price of twenty-five pesos. And when the time came to appoint the commissioners to the illustrious Junta de Información, he exerted all of his influence to ensure the election of Ruiz Belvis, the vehement abolitionist who wrote the memorable report demanding the immediate abolition of slavery, with or without compensation, "for while it exists, humanity and justice will not be served."

It is easy to understand the widespread prestige that this distinguished patriot would acquire in his homeland and how his voice would unite all followers of all inclinations. Dormant spirits would awaken, and those who once felt and who now feel the doctrine of free nations stirring in their very being consider him a guide for their regionalist aspirations. Having said this, a preparatory movement led by a man as pure and selfless as Betances; an insurrectional movement that thundered out of the vast field of patriotic societies, communicating through "codes" known only by their most prominent affiliates; a movement that received all or most of the bright minds that shone in these oppressed lands—despite government pressures—with funds aplenty and armaments readied to uphold the right to independence; a movement in close communications with support centers in Saint Thomas, Santo Domingo and New York, acting in joint accord with Cuban patriots, whose insurrection would coincide with the Puerto Rican uprising; a movement so organized, so skillfully planned cannot be considered a mere uprising attempted by "inexperienced," "crazy," "crude," or "dissolute" men. It was the transcendent work of Bolívar, which lent itself to completion. It was the irresistible expansion of freedom, which is innate to all pueblos, that eloquently expressed itself and powerfully awoke the inspired voice of the man who—like Jesus to Lazarus—was able to tell his people: "Come forth!" And he would have walked with a sure and steady pace—that Puerto Rican Lazarus—for he had already stretched his limbs, which had previously lain motionless from the weariness of the years, if only fate had not forced the abandonment of such patriotic efforts and such noble and well-directed endeavors.

But if the structure collapsed, it was not due to the incompetence of the one who directed the project, but to an unforeseeable and fortuitous event. However, the wreckage has resisted the sands of time, and from it the lasting structure of Antillean independence will be erected, one that is even more solid than before—if that is at all possible—for time does not touch men or matter without consequence, but purges what needs to be purged. Betances remains in Paris—steady as a defiant rock in the midst of a stormy sea—awaiting the hour of magnanimous struggle to take his place, called forth by his past deeds and his steadfast commitment. Club Borinquen is overflowing with pride for having proclaimed him honorary chairman, and because of him, Puerto Rican exiles have joined the patriotic efforts.

But we are still at the threshold of Lares, and it is now time to move forward.

Doc. 33
Sotero Figueroa, "The Truth about History, III"
April 16, 1892 (#6)

In our previous article, we declared that the abandoned insurrection at Lares was not an isolated or fortuitous event without preparation or plan, but a spontaneous and unanimous response of an entire people who, aware of their own worth, decided to march resolutely toward armed rebellion, fed up with dishonor and oppression, and tired of waiting to no avail—with the eternal expectation of tolerance in which they had been interned—for their infringed rights to be recognized.

Lares completed Yara, and surely these two sister islands, united by common pains and aspirations, would have figured today in concert with the free nations of the Americas, if the revolutionary movement of the former—which should have coincided with the latter—had not failed. To substantiate these statements, the following true facts are put forth: On November 30, 1866, by virtue of news passed on by the Minister Plenipotentiary for Spain in Washington, the Captain General of the island of Cuba informed his counterpart in Puerto Rico that there existed "a vast conspiracy, which was very close to eruption, to proclaim the independence of the two Antillean islands."

To this communiqué, officials in power in Puerto Rico replied that, up to a certain point, the news corroborated their suspicion that on the island conspirators were preparing and organizing themselves, which meant that they were working together with the rebels in the largest of the Antillean islands under the direction of the main Junta based in New York, which was probably headed by Joaquín Goicuría, who was believed to have gathered in Cuba and Puerto Rico a mixed commission of peninsulares, Cubans, and Puerto Ricans. Afterward, the Governor General of Puerto Rico added the following, which is best to copy verbatim, for the lessons of the past should inform us on the things to come:

For some time I have been exercising extraordinary vigilance over certain suspects because of their background, some of whom hail from that island (Cuba), such as Dr. Luis Leiras. I most humbly submit to Your Excellency information on this person's background, as well as information on the subject of his reputation here, for his continuous and frequent trips from one town to another cast much doubt in my mind on the real objective that has brought him here, even though he is said to be following a lawsuit pending in this Audiencia. I harbor some fears that it is mainly on this island where the revolutionaries now intend to carry out their plans, no doubt to draw the attention away from Cuba with a surprise attack, even if it is ultimately frustrated. So I find good reason in need to assemble forces in this port. Their resources and preparations at this time must be considerable, for some aversion and withdrawal is obvious in the case of certain people, which is a sure symptom of the desire to conceal their plans.

By royal order dated the previous 27th of June, I was then informed of a certain movement within the Junta in New York, which Your Excellency's government was made aware through the Spanish Consul there, to divert the revolutionaries' attention away from these islands with illusory projects to increase Juárez's forces in Mexico, but in truth the enlistments, which then amassed a number of at least three thousand men, were intended to support an uprising on this island. However, they withdrew the attack that time for they found themselves lacking funds to see the enterprise through and were hoping to receive them from the forgoing.

Before continuing, we have wanted to faithfully copy a good portion of the communiqué dated December 13, 1866, which the Governor General of Puerto Rico addressed to his Cuban counterpart in order to gather three eloquent lessons we should not forget, considering the current state of affairs:

1. We should be cautious and stealthy in the revolutionary cause for, while the Spanish government may not develop a despotic system of control in this republic, it makes use of espionage to frustrate and destroy the patriotic cause.

2. Our message should be cordial and attract rather than repel, for great ideas prevail due to their own potential; and, hence, the mixed commissions of the Antilles of 1866 featured hard-working peninsulares who are loyal supporters of our emancipation.

3. The collection of funds to deliver the patriotic cause now underway at all clubs founded by Antillean exiles should be our main objective, for we have already seen that in June 1866 Puerto Rican patriots, even under favorable circumstances, had to discontinue the revolutionary enterprise due to lack of funds.

Communications exchanged among the authorities appointed to the islands of Cuba and Puerto Rico resulted in increased persecution on both islands, and in reaction to a seditious act that occurred mid-1867 at the artillery garrison in San Juan—which ended with the execution by firing squad of Corporal Benito Montero and the imprisonment of private Rafael Miguel for withholding information, both of them peninsulares—a great number of Puerto Ricans were violently banished from the island, among them the following distinguished patriots: Segundo Ruiz

Belvis, Ramón Emeterio Betances, Pedro Gerónimo Goico, Julián E. Blanco, Rufino Goenaga, and Carlos Elio Lacroix.

This unlawful measure gave wings to the cause of emancipation, and Lares responded with the conviction of ineluctable strength. Saint Thomas was the point of convergence for Puerto Rican patriots in exile, and from December 7, 1867 (when Betances arrived in Santo Domingo by way of New York) to September 23, 1868 (when the insurrection broke out) he was actively and ceaselessly seen toiling for the satisfaction of seeing his beloved land free from all humiliating foreign domination.

Usually, he resided in Saint Thomas, from where he kept active correspondence with patriotic societies in Puerto Rico, "particularly with those in the capital and in the Buena Vista sector in Mayagüez, to keep them abreast of the advancements made abroad regarding the cause of emancipation." He maintained the fire for independence forever burning in the people's hearts by sending encouraging and eloquent proclamations to Puerto Rico, which inspired emulation, and with the money received from revolutionary organizations on the island, he bought military equipment, which shrewd emissaries passed on to the interior. He also made frequent trips to Santo Domingo to further mobilize preparations for the redemptive launching of freedom.

On January 2, 1868, Betances returned to the capital of the Dominican Republic to meet with Juan Manuel Macías, representative of the Junta Revolucionaria de Cuba y Puerto Rico in New York; with Pujol, the agent of a band of patriots from all reaches of the Americas; and with Cabral, Baez's opponent in the Dominican Republic presidential race.

It was agreed that the general uprising on the island should take place on the night of September 29, 1868 for they had been informed that around this date, an insurrection would break out on the sister island of Cuba and, in Spain, a powerful republican revolt would topple the monarchic government. It was further agreed that the hacienda of the patriot Rojas, leader of the forces that would enter into operations, would serve as headquarters because of its strategic location—merely a league from Lares, in Pezuela, and surrounded by settlements as determined and resolute to take action, such as Bartolo, Mirasol, and Latorre—which allowed for ease of communication with the patriotic centers at Mayagüez, San Germán, Arecibo, Aguadilla, Yauco, Adjuntas, and Ponce. In the words of Mr. Pérez Moris, "it was a place that had been well studied, chosen, at first, as a meeting place, and later, as the meeting ground for the army, so they might descend, when the time was right, on the peaceful and defenseless town of Lares, which was undeniably better suited to serve as the insurgents' base of operations than Yara." Therefore, everything was perfectly positioned for the spirit of independence to triumph once more in the Americas and for the islands within the American hemisphere to be free and sovereign as is this one. They had invaluable support from abroad, intelligent leadership, resolute patriots, and—as never before—the moment was right. Puerto Rico was to precede Cuba on the path to emancipation, and once both Antillean islands had risen up in arms, it would be impossible for victory to fall short and not bring to these redemptive efforts triumphant conclusion. But behold an unforeseen event: Ten days before the date that had been set for the general uprising, the revolutionary plan was uncovered, and the day of the revolt had to be moved forward. All plans were thwarted, and the efforts, which had been so skillfully combined, failed. Behold how this unexpected disaster came to be.

On the night of September 19, two men on horseback met in the outskirts of the town of Quebradillas. One was leaving this town; the other traveled toward him from the town of Camuy. They introduced themselves to each other as revolutionary patriots, which was enough to initiate a conversation about the impending movement. Without keeping the necessary precautions, they specified the date, mentioned the resources they had, and the tactics to be employed. They finished by saying goodbye, completely unaware that behind some shrubs, very close to where they were standing, a captain of the militia—by the surname Castañón—had heard the essence of their conversation, for he had hidden there just moments before, compelled by a call of nature.

The following morning, on the twentieth day of said month, when Castañón was preparing to head out to Arecibo—the main city of the department, which was about two leagues from Quebradillas—to inform Military Commander Iturriaga of what he had heard the night before, Castañón found out from a militiaman, Antonio López, that he had been offered veiled propositions to take part in a revolutionary movement and that the leader of that revolutionary cell was patriot Manuel María González. That night Iturriaga knew enough to immediately proceed with González's arrest and the seizing of his documents. He headed for his house, located in the Palomar sector of Camuy, about three leagues from Arecibo. By the twenty-second, González was in prison, cut off from all communication, after having been apprehended with important papers detailing the particulars of the revolution.

After being discovered, the Puerto Rican patriots at Camuy rushed everything, deciding to attack and free González from jail and proclaim independence. We shall see in another article how Lares fell to the few patriots who had pushed the date of the revolution forward despite their haste and poorly led plans, but the movement did not take hold in this key settlement, which is practically at the heart of the island, because they did not have sufficient forces and because the rest of the island did not respond to the patriotic efforts—no doubt ignorant of what was taking place.

But first, let us quickly state that in this brief historical overview of the Puerto Rican struggle for emancipation, we have not mentioned any names other than those who are free from all persecution, either because they are no longer with us or because they live away from the island—proud of their meritorious work, which is worthy of their fellow countrymen's eternal gratitude—steadfast, noble, and eager to resume their efforts whenever necessary. Similarly, we shall keep to ourselves all that prudence counsels, for we are not so candid that we may inform our shrewd enemies, who never sleep, or direct victims to exile in this new awakening of patriotic souls. All those who have forged the path upon which we walk and keep themselves circumspect, yet unconquerable, shall forever hold a place in our hearts.

Doc. 34
Sotero Figueroa, "The Truth about History, IV"
May 21, 1892 (#11)

On the evening of that memorable day of September 23 in the year 1868, a substantial contingency of revolutionaries from Mayagüez, armed mostly with knives and machetes, joined the main body of liberating patriots from Lares in the vicinity of the hacienda owned by Rojas, as we have said before, the General in Chief of all forces that were to enter into operations.

The opportunity to descend upon Lares could not have been more favorable. Despite the fact that some peninsulares sensed the surprise attack that was brewing, the population maintained its usual repose. Local authorities suspected nothing, so they did not even take the slightest precautionary measures. The townspeople who provided intelligence to the revolutionaries seemed so calm and indifferent that they did not raise any manner of suspicion whatsoever. Some of the Spaniards residing in the surrounding areas of the besieged town attempted to warn the authorities, but regardless of how cunning they tried to be, and for all the diligence and shrewdness they displayed—choosing winding trails and impenetrable or less traveled paths—they could not the evade the extensive surveillance of the sentinels which Rojas had posted all along the outskirts of Lares, and any Spaniards who ventured on such an excursion were temporarily detained.

The shadows of night had not yet begun to stretch out across the hills and valleys hills when the revolutionaries headed toward Lares, almost two leagues from their point of departure. The entire region of Lares was fast asleep, when at midnight the spirited group of patriots advanced into the town, determined to take the town and proclaim a republican government and a free nation, or selling their lives at a high price. Their number barely reached one thousand, but they trusted that the people would take their side and join in the uprising, and that victory for the redemptive cause would soon transform hope into glorious reality.

The town awoke to vehement cries, to thunderous cheers for freedom and an independent patria, and to the sound of horses galloping over the cobbled streets, gunshots (discharged more to frighten than to internationally do harm because, so far, they had no enemies against whom to battle), hurried steps, the voices of commanding officers, and the unusual unrest which always precedes great popular upheavals. However, no one, either individually or collectively, opposed the movement that came to transform the established way of the colony. Therefore, there was no struggle, and the patriots peacefully took control of the town.

Is it not admirable, having no precedent in the annals of revolutionary history? One might say that a village that implicitly gives itself over without protestations of any kind is in agreement with the doctrine of emancipation, and that those who made this doctrine viable did nothing more than rightly interpret the wishes of the majority. But there is more, which speaks very strongly in favor of the cause of independence. This was not a movement fueled by hatred or destruction, but by equitable reparation. And, once achieved, complaints and grievances were traded for generous pardon. This is why there were no bloodstained reprisals. During the prolonged and oppressive domination, those who suffered all manner of humiliation, endured all kinds of unlawful detentions, whose interests were affected, who were treated like serfs, and more than a few were persecuted or exiled and had to lament the misfortunes of their homeland in a foreign country—they did not impose on their oppressors the retribution of an eye for an eye during the brief moments in which they completely controlled a portion of the subjugated land. Only three or four stores owned by *peninsualres* were sacked during the first moments of chaos and confusion, and one or two harsh words were uttered by the most impetuous men to a few Spaniards, thus staving off vengeance and use of force to conquer their domination—these are all the charges that could be brought against the revolutionaries in Lares. But these accusations turn out to be a model of decency compared to the riotous gang of soldiers unleashed by the world powers against a tyrannized people—and they had no other offense to avenge than the natural inclination to secure what they have been denied.

And what were the authorities doing in the meantime? Nothing. They thought themselves impotent to repel force with force, and they decided to take no measures at all. Finally, the *alcalde* and the town clerk decided to rush to the streets to find out for certain what was happening, but after only taking a few steps, they ran into a band of revolutionaries who invited them to join the triumphant movement. They resisted and were led without humiliation or insult to a prison cell where they were isolated. Half an hour later, they were called to stand before the Junta Revolucionaria and were read the declaration of independence, which had been drafted and signed by all those present. They were forced to adhere to it, relinquish the authority vested in them, and surrender keys, files, and all the official pertinences.

Having founded the provisional government of the Republic of Puerto Rico at the town hall, we must recognize the rectitude and integrity of those who formed it, for their honor and for the cause that they defended. Not one important piece of paper or document was removed from the archives, and not a single object was missing from where it was placed the day before—except for the portrait of Queen Isabel II, which was set aside as a useless and farcical item to have hanging in republican chambers. They could have demanded that the depositary surrender the public funds under his charge, but they did not. They could have surrendered to flames all that reminded them of the ominous past that they wanted to forget, but they did not. They were not miscreants or arsonists, and when the structure they had begun to erect collapsed, they could come forth with clean hands and a clear conscience.

Not even during the first moments of instinctive hostility against the oppressors was the sense of justice forgotten, which is so characteristic of the frenzied masses. A group of revolutionaries tried to break into the shop of one Spaniard, Mr. Márquez.

But this man told them that he had made his money working in this land, and he had no love for the children of his own country. "This house must be respected," said a commanding voice. And the hostile group retreated without the slightest objection.

Regarding the first actions of the provisional government, they could not have been more restrained, despite the evident vacillations that are typical of great moments of transition. Minutes were taken to record all the agreements reached that memorable night, but, together with the declaration of independence and other important documents, they were probably destroyed by reactionaries when they fiercely and despotically regained control of the colonial administration. The following solemn notice was affixed in public spaces so that the noble purpose the Puerto Rican patriots pursued might be understood:

Having agreed that the time had come to take up arms to honor the cause of their rights, those leading this revolutionary movement declare that they are determined to die before living another day under Spanish rule. And to dispel any thoughts suggesting the nature of a coup or a lawless protest, so that it be considered a patriotic movement intended to throw off this ominous yoke and create a free patria, they put forth this declaration, so that it may be known to the whole world. –Lares, September 23, 1868.

(Signatures follow)

Not one injurious word against the dominating forces that had so humiliated them as men and offended their dignity as citizens! A decree was issued declaring that every son of the nation was obliged to take up arms in support of the quest for freedom and independence for Puerto Rico; that every individual, regardless of nationality, who should voluntarily take up arms would be welcomed and deemed a patriot; and finally, that every slave who should take up arms would be free by this act alone, and so would all who are not able to do so for reason of physical impediment. Lares came before Guáimaro in the sacred efforts to deliver man from brute exploitation by another man! A circular was distributed among landowners, announcing that no obstacles of any kind would be permitted to employment and that freedom taken from laborers is slavery in disguise and, thus should immediately cease so that work may be a reflection of one's own will. And, finally, *estancieros* or *hacendados* were advised to cooperate with the revolutionary movement by dispatching good-willed and able-bodied men for the purposes of securing the republic, and by contributing a few horses to the mounted force and a few head of cattle to feed the army.

On the next day, the 24th, the neighborhood of Lares awoke without fear or fright. The interim government ensured respect for the lives and property of all. It threatened revolutionaries with severe punishment if they were to commit the slightest excess; and, as proof of the honest rectitude of their intentions, the various negligible items that were needed were acquired with vouchers so as to reimburse their nominal value as soon as funds were made available. At eight o'clock that morning, the parish priest sang a *Te Deum* in thanksgiving at the request of the newly-founded republican government, which was attended by the supporters of the cause for independence.

Such were the most salient acts carried out by the free government of Puerto Rico during its short life, and history will always do justice to its decency and good intentions.

How and why did this benevolent work of patriotism collapse?

Doc. 35
Sotero Figueroa, "The Truth about History, V"
June 11, 1892 (#14)

The tranquility of the town of Lares did not lead Puerto Rican patriots to linger in blind confidence. They assumed that the other departments on the island had reinforced the emancipation movement, but the complete lack of communication began to trouble them. Nevertheless, on the morning of September 24, the reduced forces of the liberating army left spirited and determined for the town of San Sebastián del Pepino, where they were counting on a sure victory by the many invaluable people committed to supporting the movement. But the town authorities had already been forewarned. On account of confidential messages he received from persons friendly to Spanish rule, the "alcalde" had sent an express rider to the military commander of Aguadilla the previous day to alert him of the coup that was organizing and to request that he send the forces under his command to repel the revolutionaries. Seeing that the plan had been uncovered, the San Sebastián militia, which had promised to help the patriots, had surreptitiously turned to support the regime that oppressed their fellow countrymen, and when the patriots arrived at San Sebastián between eight or nine on the morning of September 23, they found enemies among those they had counted on as friends, and dejection that spread among the ranks was a sure sign of defeat. However, this did not convince them to abandon their efforts, and judging from the official report issued by the Corregidor of Aguadilla to the Captain General of the island, who was there leading the defense, "the rebels, located on the S.E. corner of the church, sustained constant fire against the militiamen, who were supported on the S.W." Seeing how the resistance was becoming more pronounced—despite the fact that the patriots in general only carried machetes as weapon—the militiamen were given the order to charge, and they all stormed patriots. They retreated to the road leading to Lares, but the militiamen, who had chased them back to the town, did not dare enter. The patriots charged again, but since the San Sebastián defenders had provisioned themselves with an abundance of cartridges, the enemy ran out of the few they carried. This situation—together with the voices clamoring, "Fall back, the veteran troops are coming. We don't stand a chance," and one observation that the troops were laying an ambush that would to fall upon them if they dared to enter the town again—

forced the patriots to disband and fall back to the protection of the *maniguas*. There was one death among the ranks of the liberators and several injured on both sides.

Rojas—followed by a good number of the patriots—headed toward his hacienda in Lares to deliberate with the interim government about future actions, for they suspected that the rest of the island had not responded to the precipitous movement. At his farmstead, he met with other leaders, as well as members of the provisional government, who, having heard of the regrettable failure, had justifiably agreed to abandon Lares, which would be impossible to hold if the uprising had not spread.

"Lares stood alone," says Pérez Moris in his account of *La Historia*. "The peninsulares who had not been imprisoned fled during the night. With no weapons and no encouragement, those who loyally remained there—both islanders and peninsulares—did not even risk organizing a defense against the second assault?" Ah! But if the other revolutionary centers on the island had responded to the patriotic efforts at Lares, surely victory would have crowned their hopes. A few days later, our sister island launched a revolution for dignity and justice. Meanwhile, in the Spanish metropolis, the Bourbon monarchy was collapsing. A few more drops of revolution, and the two sister islands would have been singing today the anthem of free nations.

At the Rojas hacienda, the patriots began deliberations to agree on a logical and appropriate plan. No one, of course, thought of surrendering to Spanish authorities. They doubted that the entire of the island would have had time to revolt, but they took it as an unquestionable fact that, at the very least, the crucial revolutionary cells in Ponce, Mayagüez, and San Germán would have launched into battle with better luck. So they agreed to wait—weapons in hand—in the rugged hills and dense wilderness for the cry of independence to be heard before they continued to lend their services to the cause of a free Puerto Rico, so that their blood would not be shed in vain. Why did the Lares movement not catch on, when it was a redemptive movement with such vast ramifications and possessed such invaluable representatives of all social classes—these forces which began with only a few civil servants and eventually consolidated hard-working and passionate people of Puerto Rico?

Let us heed the author of the concocted *Historia de Lares*, which is a prime example of the viciousness and hatred with which he has always characterized the Puerto Rican people. Much to his regret, he makes these precious statements, which attest to the gravity and significance of the aborted revolution.

With only a hint of reflection, it can be easily understood why the premature spark on Lares did not produce the conflagration that unquestionably would have occurred on September 29, the day of Saint Michael.

First of all, (patriotic) societies should have received—one after the other and with an interval of no more than two days' time—two very different bits of news: the first, notifying them that the 29th was the day for separatism, when men had agreed to raise the battle

cry against Spain; the second, informing them that the government had captured their leader and the documents belonging to the Lanzador del Norte society. The conspirators who did not or could not know that the imprisonment so carefully effected by Colonel Iturriaga had been carried out without an order from his superiors. And, by virtue of a number of random and isolated reports, the conspirators naturally believed that General Pavía had awoken from his genuine or feigned slumber of blind indifference and managed to uncover all the threads of the revolutionary plot. That they had been discovered; that they were under surveillance by the authorities; that the sword of the government had been raised high over their heads, ready to fall as soon as they took the first step on the path to insurrection—these should have necessarily been the first ideas to occur to the conspirators when they received the order to move forward the movement, along with what, for them, was the ill-fated news that the government was aware of their plans and that they had already captured González and seized his documents.

While it is true that they would later receive news of the capture and taking of Lares, they would also know that several military columns were sent in pursuit of the patriots and that the well-organized militias of the towns were on alert. Therefore, they decided that it would not be wise to launch the battle.

The spirited men of Lares solely sacrificed themselves, but an example had been set, and the "failure" of that moment was to serve as experience for future redemption.

Subjugated pueblos do not resign themselves to being slaves in perpetuity, and the more the tyrannical nation unleashes its fury, the more it feeds the inextinguishable bonfire of patriotic independence.

The capture of the Lares revolutionaries and the judicial rulings regarding the armed rebellion are to be discussed in the next article—the last of the series dedicated to proving that in Puerto Rico the ideals of liberation have not ceased to forge a path or produce self-sacrificing patriots.

Doc. 36

Sotero Figueroa, "The Truth about History, VI"

July 2, 1892 (#17)

To be ferocious in battle and magnanimous in victory—this is the rule of conduct which must be observed by those caudillos who have been forced, by the law of circumstance, to resort to war and subject the predominance of collective aspirations to its caprices, which are thought to be just and reasonable. Did the military forces that went out in pursuit of the dispersed army at Lares—who did not defend themselves for they had neither weapons nor supplies to do so—abide by this generous rule? Was there a reason to pursue them as if they were heartless bandits, offering no truce to those who decided to fight for the noble ideal of freedom, which spontaneously sprouts in all subjugated peoples, just as the planted seed struggles to break its outer shell and rise robustly toward the unlimited dominion of light and air? We leave these questions to the impartial reader. We shall only add that we find it foolish to punish a captive bird for fighting to break the bars of its cage and reclaim its independence.

Let us examine the facts. News of the Lares separatist rebellion spread with the swiftness of lightning to all corners of the island, and all the military commanders of the different departments—following the Captain General's order on September 25, 1868—hurried to dispatch forces in pursuit of the patriots, who had already been defeated by their own countrymen who did not endorse the movement. The entire island was invaded by a multitude of flying columns and, although they found no enemies against whom to fight, they took prisoner numerous campesinos who they capriciously thought suspect, struck terror in the faint of heart, interfered with farm work, and, with victorious alacrity, left behind tears and torment in devastated homes. A general search was organized covering all the rural towns, forests, and fields of Puerto Rico after establishing numerous prisons in the town centers, which resulted in the capture of some six hundred campesinos—all peaceable and unarmed—for having been deemed suspects or accomplices.

Regarding the prominent patriots and leaders of the aborted revolution, they were all seized by the military forces, save for Matías Brugman and Baldomero Bauren—who was apprehended fast asleep in the impenetrable undergrowth in wee hours of the morning on account of a breach of trust by those who had hidden them away—were finished off by a torrent of bullets propelled by their assailants, without any humanitarian mercy. The same sad ending found the spirited Joaquín Parrilla, whose lips pronounced these heroic words when a flying column tried to capture him in the mountains of Yauco, calling for his surrender: "Joaquín Parrilla does not surrender." Then, he fell, riddled with bullets.

The implacable hunt lasted some twenty-seven days, ending when the rainy season was at hand and the veteran troops grew tired of the futile and painstaking search. The six hundred or so prisoners were transferred to jails in Arecibo and Aguadilla, where—stacked up like a pile of refuse, malnourished, poorly dressed, without ventilation to refresh the pestilent atmosphere in which the miserable writhed—seventy-nine of them died from a fever that erupted in these nauseating prisons. The devastation would have been greater if the survivors had not been distributed among other jails—which were as abysmal as the two mentioned, but where the victims of colonial ferocity were somewhat more comfortable—and if hospitals had not been improvised to treat the sick. The courts of justice quickly began to take action, so quickly, in fact, that in just over four months proceedings reached such colossal proportions that they produced fifty-two thick case files.

This is in addition to the fact that the courts of first instance issued a writ of prohibition to the military jurisdiction regarding those it determined to be the chief promoters of the skirmish in the town of San Sebastián del Pepino and, as a result, placed the following prisoners under the charge of the war council, which had been formed in Ponce: Manuel Rojas, Andrés Pol, Ignacio B. Ortalaza, Pedro Segundo García, Rodolfo Echevarría, Leoncio Rivera, and Clodomiro E. Abril, all of whom were sentenced to suffer the ultimate penalty in the fateful gallows.

A general clamor of anguish was heard in all reaches of the island, and the word *"indulto"* (amnesty) was pronounced fervently by Puerto Rican mothers. Thousands of signatures—some of them under heartbreaking circumstances—were collected and addressed to the superior authority on the island to seek a pardon for all those who had been sentenced. This time, sweet, benevolent Mercy did not have to hide her wounded countenance away from the ferocity of men. By the island's great fortune, a gallant soldier had expressed his desire from the beginning to have his conscience spared from the blood of political adversaries, who fortune did not celebrate as heroes. And General Pavía never felt so ennobled or slept so soundly as when he made use of the prerogatives bestowed on him by Law 27 of Book and Title 3 of the Laws of the Indies and by Royal Order of March 27, 1857 to pardon the accused Pol, Ortolaza, García, Rivera, and Abril and commute their judgment for an immediate sentence to be meted out in one of their penal institutions in Spain. At the same time, he suspended the sentence that had been imposed on Rojas and Echevarría due to conflict of jurisdiction between the Alcalde Mayor of Ponce and the investigations in Arecibo.

General Sanz, who succeeded Pavía in the government of the island, pardoned Rojas and Echevarría—influenced by the winds of freedom blowing across the sea from Spain, where traditional monarchy had given way to a representative government—and wanted to inaugurate its advent with magnanimous acts for which the people are always grateful. And the result was, without a doubt, a far-reaching amnesty accorded to all those prosecuted in reaction to the separatist movement at Lares, which was dictated by the provisional government on January 20, 1869, ordering Overseas Minister to promote a greater use of pardons and consultations for dismissals by judges of the courts of first instance for cases that, because of the importance of the matter, should have been elevated to the Superior Court.

This is how the cause of Lares came to an end, but the legitimate aspirations of emancipation did not; they continue to forge their path and will ultimately triumph, for while all great ideas rooted in the consciousness of pueblos may suffer momentary eclipses, they shall not perish since the longing for independence—which is inherent to the human heart—cannot perish.

To govern is to foresee, and governments that do not understand the signs of the times are lacking foresight, thus constricting the redemptive movement rather than channeling it. It is an undeniable law that all nations and islands of the Americas shall be free, and any despotism that seeks to oppose this law shall be in vain.

Doc. 37
Francisco Gonzalo Marín, "A Slap in the Face"
March 26, 1892 (#3)

The time for futile sacrifice had come to an end. General Palacio was now somberly moving away from the oppressed island, whose fate and honor were, for a period of a few months, at the mercy of that bloodthirsty and asinine head of state.

The sinister sound of the gendarmes making their rounds through the streets—which at times mimicked the avenues of a cemetery—was suddenly followed by silence, a dead silence, the kind in which colonies live after having felt the heel of the despots on their brow and the shame of defeat weighing on their very hearts.

The reactionary mob—the one that broke into festive cries at the pain extracted from its victims, the one that tried to sink the country into a boiling cauldron of blood, the one that lives sycophantically off of prosperity and, like a raven, does not miss any occasion to pluck the throbbing livers from the fallen—the reactionary mob in Puerto Rico, finally, after a cowardly win, retreated to its camp to taste the delight of victory in the drunkenness of silence ...

But was there really a battle? Were there victors and vanquished? Would it have been fitting to welcome a Caesar under an arch of triumph and with martial hymns on his return from a conquered Gaul?

In horror, I turn my eyes away from this bleak page in the history of my country!

Perhaps I have spoken wrongly. No matter how much I try, time and time again, I shall never be able to wrench the memory of those terrifying days from my soul. It is not that vengeful resentment springs from the tranquil recesses of my conscience, nor is it that my misfortunes—pitiably contemptible because they are mine—which attempt to lend dark relief to that dismal painting in which the contorted and greenish countenances of the innocents stand out. Likewise, it is not my disposition to descend into the pond, where so many miseries hide, to collect sufficient deposits of lime to mask the faces of the executioners of a pueblo. No, but, I can only say that the further away I go from my patria, the closer I find myself to its disasters. It is just that [apostasy] reigns, uneasiness takes root, shameful capitulations stand tall, and dejection takes hold with each passing day. Therefore, as the son of a country which is still shrouded in the darkness of slavery, I feel more obliged to live concertedly with the torment of my patria and not lose sight of it for one instant, and, meanwhile, to remind my own people that patriotism, like an alert sentinel, should await at the ready.

On the other hand, is Spain responsible for its governments? Are these governments responsible for the faults committed by their leaders? Could these same men at times be able to answer for their own mistakes? Clear and somber proof: General Palacio.

This contemptible panjandrum was surrounded by cronies culpable for Puerto Rico's unforgettable anguish—not for having been born in Spain, but for being bad

Spaniards. Champagne flowed on the governor's table; palatial music flit about in his ear; the caresses of lovely courtesans distracted him... Below, the people dug their nails into their chests.

These were the cronies who kept the country at the mercy of an irresponsible despot; at their mercy were Puerto Rico and the governor.

Three men comprised this inquisitive Aeropagus; and it is fitting that these names should join the Roman Circus that has become public anathema: Ubarri, Infiesta, Gallart.

May your images be carved in stone!

...

I recommend this unpleasant task, and, I say again, peace seemed to be returning, while in the winter quarters where the army had retired, *crowned by the laurels of victory*, the reactionaries devised a new plan, which was to be the last assault in the people's dignity and the glorious, honorable, and magnificent culmination of the bloody journey.

The asinine ruler fled, but the offensive trinity remained on the war path.

If 1887 was for Puerto Rico the year of mourning, 1891 is the year of shame. The idea is not new to my lips. Something resembling the vague shape of a democratic process confirms it.

In 1891, I repeat, Puerto Ricans celebrated elections, and the booths practically vomited a ballot designating one man as the delegate to the Cortes of the accursed country: Gallart.

The entire inbred administration elected him Diputado. That ballot should have been black—black as bile; black as the hearts of those who unconstructively voted so to make us seem not as men who are steadfast against insult or as citizens of an educated people, but as miserable Central African hordes in the eyes of the occupying metropolis and of the civilized world.

And Gallart, that monster, holds a high post in the Spanish chambers. There he still remains, caustic and cynical. There he stands, scornful and proud, flouting the anger of the wounded colony. There (he says) he was placed by the will of the people. There (we repeat) he was placed by deception, treachery, and the weakness of a party that meanders through the drawing rooms of the palace. Those who cannot or do not want to withdraw in time—defeated, if you wish, but not humiliated—and who prefer to abandon their own, forgetting the honors they received, to fall with honor on the wide path of a noble protest, swaddled in the cloak of the Homeland.

You who call insolent those who, in exile, have come to encourage the first newborn cries of the Puerto Rican revolution; you who, from the pontifical pulpit of ridiculous pride, issue certificates attesting to their quality as *shrewd and discerning liberals*, and lead the herd of sheep, avoiding dangerous paths and high cliffs; you—overly pious or dissolute, Autonomist or courtesan—who are flattered by the Interior Minister's smile and are mortified by the complaints of a selfless and impatient people, heed the sincere and honest voice of an exile who aspires to nothing, except to spill his blood for the dignity of the nation, for blood and dignity course through these very veins.

The election of Gallart as Diputado to the Spanish *Cortes* is a slap in the face, and still, numb is the hand that dealt it and red the cheek that received it!

Have you pitted yourselves against popular sentiment? Then, rise to the occasion!

Francisco Gonzalo Marín

Doc. 38
José Martí, "Facts and Ideas"
April 3, 1892 (#4)

As in the pages of books, major newspaper articles tend to communicate essential ideas that should be taken from their wrapping and placed plainly before your very eyes. Such are these, which have been excerpted from *PATRIA*, for they must not be forgotten.

So says the Puerto Rican patriot, Sotero Figueroa, in his colorful article "The Truth about History," on the struggle for independence for our beautiful Borinquen:

"Why did Antillean independence not triumph this time—with Grau and Coronado, with Otero and Dueño—when public opinion in Puerto Rico declared itself so resolutely in its favor?

"Oh! Because they were waiting for the armed expedition that triumphant Colombia had offered. But the United States of America was opposed to this very last emancipation."

And below he says:

"Sergeants Salinas and Santillana—sons of Andalusia, whose generous hearts were devoted to the noble cause—were executed by firing squad on October 6, 1840."

And in another article from *PATRIA*, he states:

"If revolution is the creation of a free and just *pueblo* out of a broken people, even from within the known evils of a noble colony, then the revolutionary project consists of establishing and guiding the people so not a single soul acquires a disproportionate predominance over another which, through distrust, loosens the bond with others or, as a result of unfairness by either the ignorant or the educated, places the revolutionary project in jeopardy."

Doc. 39
Sotero Figueroa, Antonio Vélez Alvarado, Francisco Gonzalo Marín, "Let Us Have a Discussion (To the Puerto Rican Press)"

May 7, 1892 (#9)

The manifesto which Club Borinquen addressed to the people of Puerto Rico has had the honor of the circulating through all the newspapers on this, the smallest of the Greater Antilles, and, as we expected, those who became the most irate—not toward it, but toward those who signed it in their name and in representation of said Club—are the organs of the Autonomist party. We comprehend the reason behind the aggressive and personal attacks, although we cannot defend them. It must be proven that in the Palacio de Santa Catalina, residence of the Governor General, the toler-ance accorded by today's friends of the crown—yesterday's insurgents—is not a lie; that expressions of national allegiance are exploited and professions of españolismo are cultivated. Those who show themselves to be sincere men without disguise or subterfuge are scorned, no matter how far beyond in the jurisdiction of their con-science these prestigious men of extensive political background acknowledge that those who do not equal them in significance or notoriety within the limited scope of the homeland are on the side of the unyielding law of history; they follow the inevi-table force of reason and act on this benevolent impulse from which nations, upset and dejected in the expression of progress and freedom, never escape.

Yet it is indeed curious what occurs in certain liberal publications in Puerto Rico: they constantly anathematize the brutal colonial system; they become enraged with the shameful inequality to which criollos are subjected; they list the humiliations inflicted upon Autonomist colonial subjects; they express grief over the constant exo-dus of spirited youth who bid farewell to their beloved land because in it they find neither the dignified means of earning a living nor the inherent guarantees of a free citizen; they envy the progress made by those who were once slave colonies and are today sovereign nations; they sing of the heroism of those who fought tenaciously and arduously to seize their independence; they admire Cuba when she rebels and praise her when she stands tall, threatening the dissolution of her Autonomist par-ty—which will be the signal to launch the great redemptive cause; they cry *alea iacta est* with the terrible force of despair. In other words, they awaken the revolutionary spirit that lies dormant in the heart of the people, and when their compatriots—who feel the pains of the homeland more strongly in exile—want to take the correct and practical solution that lends itself to establishing a perfect order in line with the mes-sage that is taking root and the pressing dictates of reason, they angrily turn against those who think differently, calling them mad or impetuous for wanting to help the people escape from the cesspool in which they struggle, and they swear they want to continue being subjects of Spain and slaves of Ubarri.

Fortunately, these are not the same Puerto Ricans who suffered the dreadful compontes of 1887, nor are they the same people who would ever reach a compro-mise with their executioners. If there is someone who prefers to waste away point-lessly in the colony, putting up with scorn and humiliation, jail and ruinous fine—de-spite their valiant protests—and welcome Caesar as a proper gladiator even when the vigorous quill is plucked from his hand, then we regret his downfall, but we believe it to be fair punishment for his blindness to the nature of the colonial subject, no matter how well he knew the iniquities of the colony.

We will not begin to dissect, point by point, everything that the Autonomist press and one or two newspapers loyal to the Unconditional party have spitefully said of the Manifesto signatories. These comments are as trite as they are pretentious, and we are not here to ascribe merit. Good deeds are what give men reputability, not vice versa. Therefore, we do not admit a comparison between those who grapple onto the pulpit of arrogance to speak out publicly against those who are more constant than they and fight to deliver their country from slavery, and those who—modestly and gently, yet firmly and resolutely—warn their unruly adversaries: "You may strike, but listen first."

If we were to discuss merit, the Autonomist subjects of the colony who oppose us know quite well that in our ranks there are those who are thoroughly familiar with the facts and people of the homeland, not by reference, but by intimate and systematic study for the better part of sixteen years of public life—a modest, yet honorable and substantial span—and there would much to say regarding the prestige and reliability of those who believe that great ideas cannot be born in noble and refined men, but in ostentatious and conceited ones, inconstant and pusillanimous men, when strength of conviction and civic valor are most needed.

To weigh the significance and transcendence of the position put forward by Club Borinquen, it is important that those who try to reference it out of context know that the Lilliputian press of New York has made clear, through its most authoritative newspapers, that it has given it serious and deferent attention due to the noble purposes it pursues; that the most active reporters have been moving to take notes and disseminate patriotic thought; that the free Americas view this awakening of Puerto Ricans who want to accompany Cuba—that 10-year warrior—in the attainment of its complete freedom with love and respect; that we are a part of the Partido Revolucionario Cubano, without which it would be madness to seek the emancipation of our island. We will not embark on disorganized and poorly prepared actions that leave our brothers in the colony exposed to persecutions and humiliations. Rather, we will propagate patriotic ideas, join wills, awaken sympathies, collect funds, and seek to centralize valuable groups abroad by all the noble and generous means that will propel decisive action when internal elements believe they must work without exposing themselves to a lamentable failure. Finally, we are not those we lead; rather, we collect materials for the great patriotic undertaking. We have our illustrious leader, Betances. And, before this name, before this glorious flag that adversity did not lower or enfold the amnesia of the ungrateful, the slaves of the colony must be revealed. If we do not have the great good fortune of seeing it wave over our free country, we will be satisfied in having brandished it so that no one may forget its colors or the redress it symbolizes.

Regarding the *Unconditional* newspapers which—like *Boletin*—have combatted us without disregarding journalistic etiquette, we say to them that they are entirely within their right. We like to do battle in the field of ideas, but combat with legitimate weapons—the ones which lift the heart and mind so they are not dragged through the underworld of insolence and insult, the ones which injure those who squander them more than those they target. For that reason, we will not hurl rude invectives against Spain and the Spanish people for this would neither credit the virtue of our cause nor lead us to any practical solution. We will triumph not so much by conviction, but by discretion. And, if we have great love for our fellow countrymen—even those who oppose us blindly or thoughtlessly— it is our pleasure to deliver justice to the Spaniards who prove themselves worthy of it. We believe our forthright attitude will please our Unconditional adversaries more than the delusion that shrouds those in the colony who want to act as the Pharisees of our redemptive idea—cursing in secret that which they praise in public.

To the Autonomist newspapers which, like *El Criterio* from Humacao, discretely discuss the extent to which they are allowed to express their arguments, given government pressures, and recognize the right of all peoples to revolution, yet disagree with us on account of their expectations that the Spanish Republic will do justice to the proven loyalty of Puerto Ricans—we assure you that you are sadly mistaken. Yes, the Republic will accord certain liberties to Puerto Ricans, but they shall be for the **usufruct** of Spaniards on the peninsula, who will always enjoy **a better condition** than Spaniards on the island. It is that *mancha de plátano,* that indelible mark that brands us as *Puerto Rican,* which has been articulated so well by Mr. Frelles—Spaniard by birth, Puerto Rican at heart, and editor in his own right of *El Cañón,* a newspaper that dispatches its commentary from the town of Cayey. The truth should have made *El Criterio* more astute, but, at the end of the day, this Autonomist mouthpiece disagrees with us only in opportunity, and, hence, this is a sign of integrity.

El Clamor, which is the main organ of the Autonomist Directorate, calls upon the people to **define themselves** along separatist or autonomist ranks. This has a particular flavor of mockery and irony in which the noble people of Puerto Rico will most certainly not indulge. *El Clamor* knows too well that there are no guarantees whatsoever that a separatist party can be formed in Puerto Rico, and he who so **defines** himself will pay a high price for his naïveté. If said newspaper (because its writers are in good standing with General Lasso and Secretary Cano) manages to pass a law shielding all supporters of the emancipation of the Antilles from persecution and ensures that this law is permanent in nature and duly upheld, without exceptions or reservations, we promise our colleague that every Puerto Rican, even the writers of *El Clamor,* will immediately declare themselves to be separatists. This is a nascent feeling in the Puerto Rican heart, and any attempt to extract it by force or terror will be futile, and it shall grow robust when needed.

La Democracia from Ponce callously insults us. We forgive their unwarranted resentment in light of the strong campaigns that they have launched against the despots and the fence-sitters of this colony. We trust that they will come to know us and come to understand that our ideas cannot be defeated by fighting words, but only by solid arguments offered with the respect that is characteristic of its editor and his noble outbursts of unselfish patriotism.

After all we have said, the readers of *PATRIA* might have noticed that the Manifesto penned by Club Borinquen has not been successfully refuted in the field of doctrine or principle. This is the truth. It is still standing after the devastating downpour that has befallen its signers, with the notoriety attributed to them by the same ones who disapproved of it.

We invite the Puerto Rican press to discuss it both as a whole and in detail, with the promise to defend its integrity.

Let us then have a discussion.

S. FIGUEROA

A. VÉLEZ ALVARADO

F. GONZALO MARÍN

Doc. 40
Sotero Figueroa, Antonio Vélez Alvarado, Francisco Gonzalo Marín
"Domination and Independence, I"
July 16, 1892 (#19)

El Criterio, the Autonomist republican newspaper that was established in the town of Humacao on the island of Puerto Rico, has finally decided to respond to our article "Let Us Have a Discussion," which was addressed to the Puerto Rican press and, specifically, to this publication.

We really should not impugn that zealous champion and defender of a domination that is collapsing due to its own mistakes, for we realize that it must take great efforts to suppress certain eloquent expressions—those of a patriot who will never acquiesce to being an obedient colonial subject before the insatiable voracity of the metropolis, no matter how much the former heroically guarantees it—from bursting forth in the arguments penned by his honorable quill. However, we do not want to be judged as ill-mannered, especially when the aim is to convince us with words worthy of educated polemicists. And so we proceed to topple the house of cards *El Criterio* has laboriously erected because we comprehend the fragility of the structure and how easy it is to demolish.

El Criterio begins by recognizing the right all peoples have, *in certain circumstances*, to revolution, but regarding the Spanish Antilles, it believes that it is opportune for them to remain tied to the metropolis.

We do not understand how this is opportune when it systematically—and for almost four centuries—has borne bad fruit. We do not understand how this is opportune when it keeps the colonial subject under perpetual servitude, constricts his freedom, and overwhelms him with countless tax burdens that only serve to support an extravagant administration imported from the dominating metropolis. And, since he has no emotional attachments or deeply rooted assets in the land where he has arrived as a privileged gentleman, little does it matter to him that the country is drowning in bankruptcy, if from the administrative disorder he can withdraw intact his lavish allowances, which he will later enjoy far away from the wretched and ruined colony. We do not understand how this is opportune when it denies Puerto Rico institutions of higher learning; does not guarantee the waning rights which were granted by the generous acts of better times, rather than the good will of the metropolis; and imprisons and inflicts unspeakable torture upon campesinos for their conspiratorial daydreams, and later bestows generous rewards on the instruments of violence, leaving the victims without their due redress, so that all those who suffered torture may realize that they are mere serfs with no personhood, although they may naively believe that they are citizens of the Spanish nation. We do not understand how this is opportune when it heavily taxes colonial products in the metropolis, while it permits all manner of favorable terms for the introduction of peninsular goods into the colony, thus proving that there are two weights and two measures and that the legal one is not applied to the docile Puerto Rican. And finally, we do not understand how this is opportune when it enslaves an entire people and forces them to live averse or contrary to the expansive expressions of the circumstances in which they stir, and, no matter how much *El Criterio* insists on proffering this opportuneness, the facts—with their overwhelming eloquence—will tell the people that those who live in humiliation, shying away from their natural and legitimate aspirations, cannot be content with their fate. To maintain this system of submission and servitude is to be contrary to the wise laws of democracy, just as it is a similar monstrosity to maintain that the exploitation of one man by another is opportune because for it protects the slave from the crack of the whip which he would otherwise have received from omnipotent slave traders or supporters of such commerce. It is pitiful—for lack of another word—to uphold the theory of domination of the strong over the weak.

To our statement that "the Spanish Republic will accord certain liberties to Puerto Ricans, but they shall be for the usufruct of the Spaniards on the *peninsula* who will always enjoy a better condition than Spaniards on the *island*," *El Criterio* replies that it has witnessed the magnanimous events of 1873, and can, therefore, reach very different conclusions.

We are sorry to spoil our colleague's exuberance, but we owe it to the rectitude of our principles to maintain our assertion, which we have not made without previously performing an examination of conscience.

It is true that the Republic extended Title I of the Spanish Constitution, but only in theory and not in practice. In fact, Spaniards on the peninsula continued to subjugate the land, and the criollo remained as exploited and humiliated as during any other regrettable period in our memory.

Indeed, we were allowed to sing Riego's anthem, but only harmonized with the unheeded cries of the unfortunate who felt the crack of the whip and who, for whatever slightest offense, were hauled away to the San Juan prison. We had representation in the *Diputación* and in the people's *ayuntamientos*, but these were mired by reactionary peninsulares, who began a spirited campaign against the newly established order and, aided by a conservative metropolitan press, managed to impose their views on the local authorities, thereby neutralizing the effects of free representation. We were accorded the democratic Constitution of 1869, but it was interpreted by the usual military heads of state, which was tantamount to placing it at the mercy of the intransigent ones, for these men resolutely supported it with the all-embracing power of the saber and derived from it the better part of their despotic power. And whereas, *in theory*, we were given citizenship for no other reason than to curtail any motive for rebellion—since Cuba was warring for her freedom, and the metropolis would not have been able to support two campaigns overseas, as well as the Cantonalists in Spain—the peninsulares held in *usufruct* the profits of the small island; meanwhile the criollo worked for his dominators, lived under the most contemptuous burden, all the while exulting himself in his Spanish citizenship.

It was then that the infamous words were spoken on the "despicable elements, unworthy of frequenting the *ayuntamientos*." It was then that the persecution of the colored race was carried to extremes, setting the army and volunteers against them, for the peninsulares had fabricated and spread a rumor that the blacks would hurl stones at the armed forces. Then, the Republican journalist, Pablo E. Rodríguez, was assaulted by a staff officer. The editors of *La Araña* and *El Estado Federal*—both peninsulares, yet Republicans—were beaten (the former) and threatened (the latter). As a result, the former had to leave the country and the latter, the spirited quill with which he fought his adversaries. Then rebellion could be seen rising from proud loyalty, jeering at Captain General Baldrich, threatening to send General Latorre away—as it did with General Dulce in Havana—and disrespectfully whistling at General Primo de Rivera from the heights of the Spanish Casino when, positioned at the main balcony of the Palacio de la Intendencia, he gave thanks to the people—who had come together in a jubilant response to the proclamation of the abolition of slavery in Puerto Rico—for their impressive displays of gratitude.

Never had Spaniards been more emboldened as they were then—or more omnipotent or in such a better situation than Puerto Ricans—when Puerto Rico enjoyed the most freedom. But it was freedom with no consequence, for there were no solid foundations and the line between *here* and *there* had not been erased simply because it is impossible, for it will always continue to exist to our detriment because the dominators will not easily resign themselves to treating us as equals.

But *El Criterio* will tell us that it is the Republic to which we owe the abolition of slavery. This is true, and we will not be sparing with our appreciation to the Republican chambers for this act of justice, which has enshrined them in glory. Nevertheless, slavery was already mortally wounded by universal disapproval, and abolition was a political act that found favor in public opinion and lent itself to strengthening any government that would carry it out. Since Spain received several million pesos from England to put an end to the slave trade and free the slaves in all her possessions, she was morally obliged to follow through, according to the codes of humanity and justice. In addition, the constant threat to public peace implied by maintaining 30,000 human beings in ignominious servitude, together with the most meritorious and unforgettable abolitionist campaign directed by Julio Vizcarrondo from Puerto Rico, led to the breaking of the accursed chains without protestations when it came time to cast the solemn vote. However, as a shameful sequel, the *patronato* and the *libreta* still remained as slavery in disguise, enchaining the laborer to his exploiter.

Therefore, do not be deluded, *El Criterio*, by thinking that if the Republican regime is established once again in Spain the children of other provinces would have no *special treatment* over Puerto Rico. We have seen how, within the Spanish republican form of government, the peninsulares have always ensured their usufruct over public freedoms and taken advantage of whatever was profitable, while discrediting whatever was not beneficial to their liberticidal ends through a reign of terror. They fought the *Diputación*, and today it is the very lifeblood of caciquismo. They fought the *ayuntamientos*, and today they serve to reward apostasies and support the meek henchmen who have been able to secure a *greater majority* (in the words of the intransigent Pontifice) when there is an urgency to triumph at all costs. They fought the provincial institute of higher education, and today it houses the staff officers of their invincible army. They fought the Governor Generals who did not yield to their law of castes, and today the Fortaleza, from the first floor to the last—that is to say, from the Minister of the Interior to the Captain General—is at their beck and call. They fought assimilation, and today they reap the benefits of this equivocal system of colonial administration. Have the metropolitan conquerors and dominators—all of them from Ponce de León to the present—not profited from this *usufruct* or have they simply not enjoyed it to the fullest? They have changed the system in response to the logical evolution of the times, but not their intentions or their all-engulfing domination. Failure may break them, but it will not bend them toward a justice that is absolutely equal to all.

That tame and harmless autonomy—which preaches allegiance with the metropolis in all things pertaining to politics, and is satisfied with administrative *decentralization*—might be implemented in Puerto Rico, but from the time and place it is proclaimed, the entire *decentralizing* organism will be in the hands of those who hold in *usufruct* the lands of the Americas. And does *El Criterio* know why this is so? Because we are not thought to be *essentially* Spaniard, no matter how many flowery protestations of españolismo we make. Because, within our fits of loyal adherence, beat the hearts of the children of America who long for freedom; because the desire to break the bonds that limit or pervert our sphere of action grows; and because it is considered dangerous to hand over provincial administration to the children of a subjugated land.

Hence, the parties of the Republic keep a telling reserve when it comes to the autonomy of the Antilles—despite *El Criterio*'s optimism—and if they do release a few statements, they are careful to make the appropriate disclaimers so as not to be labeled bad Spaniards who wish for the dismantling of the motherland by encouraging a regime that is believed to be the bridge to independence.

Therefore, enough of blind credulity and futile efforts. See what is currently happening in the Spanish Antilles, where exploitation is taken to the absurd with ordinances and customs duties, and tell us if there is no other dignified route to our aspirations as an educated people surrounded by sovereign nations.

And here we find some of the not so gracious charges presented by *El Criterio* against a free hemisphere, which still suffers the pains of regeneration and fights to cast far away the terrible vices instilled by the conquerors. But this is a matter that deserves to be studied in greater detail, and this article is already long enough for the columns of *PATRIA*.

To be continued.

Doc. 41
Sotero Figueroa, Antonio Vélez Alvarado, Francisco Gonzalo Marín,
"Domination and Independence, II"
August 6, 1892 (#22)

El Criterio practically walks us through the independence of the South American continent after examining, in light of undisputable facts, what Spanish domination has meant to the two Antillean islands that Spain still holds from Columbus' magnificent legacy.

Let us first examine the statements made by *El Criterio*, copying their words verbatim to attest to our integrity in this discussion:

As of today, [they certainly say,] we have many a just claim to voice against the metropolitan government to vindicate our rights and rectify the injustices that we are dealt in certain instances. Having said that, Colombian free thinkers can still envy Puerto Ricans, who are free—when they want to be—from right-wing despotism, and because journalists from Venezuela and Santo Domingo can only wish to enjoy the liberty with which our newspapers can—and certainly do—discuss their issues. In sum (save a few unforgettable exceptions, such as those of 1887), a citizen of Puerto Rico has more freedoms than in the Latin American republics.

El Criterio further adds, with an optimism most unsuited to the ostentations of front-page bold typeface:

We are too small and weak to build a nation with our effort because, with each step, we

risk being ridiculed by another, more important nation; nonetheless, the Spanish flag will
always have prestige aplenty, so that we may have nothing to fear now on that account

Venezuela, Santo Domingo, Colombia, and other republics should serve as examples and
warn us not to long for what cannot be sustained without order or prestige.

A reactionary and intransigent newspaper—the kind that appears on that small
Antillean island and denies any influence of españolismo—could not have expressed
itself with greater flattery toward the omnipotent dominators. Where did *El Criterio*
learn such an immoral doctrine of submission, thus breaking completely with republican practices of free nations? So you say that there are *many* a *just* claim to make to
the Spanish government to *vindicate* the rights of Puerto Ricans; and yet, despite this
fact, the oppressive noose and despicable slavery is subserviently accepted because
we are too small and weak to build an independent nation which other more important ones would not *ridicule* and because Spain will always have *prestige aplenty* so
that we may have nothing to fear *on that account?*... It is certainly true that a resolute
character will falter within an unnatural and corrupt environment, and the sense of
what is right and just will clearly be lost! In other words, that shameful guardianship must be accepted to avoid the offenses that a covetous neighbor might perhaps
inflict on us. The little bird must remain in its cage for fear that the hawk might *perhaps* snatch it with its talons. The longing for freedom, which is innate to the human
heart, must not be satisfied for it might *perhaps* be ridden roughshod by the brutal
omnipotence of despotism. But this does not take into account that there are laws
regulating international relations, and that it is not easy to openly violate them without incurring the wrath of other nations, which might equally feel *ridiculed*, since respect shown toward smaller nations is a guarantee of security, recognition, and fond
respect for the powerful ones. In any case—and according to the theory expressed by
El Criterio—it is better to accept the current and continued ignominy that robs us of
our personhood and bars us from actually enjoying real rights (no matter how they
are accorded in theory) than to have our own far-reaching independence for fear that
it might come to be and never be recognized.

But now let us address the charges raised in passing by *El Criterio* against certain republics of the Americas in order to conclude that Puerto Rico has more liberal
rights [*sic*] than the free countries of South America. It is clear that the Puerto Rican newspaper has failed to realize that the poisoned dart it aims at the republics of
Colombia, Venezuela, and Santo Domingo—which are specifically mentioned—will
ultimately harm the guardian metropolis.

Indeed, if these independent nations have not yet been able to erase the footprint of individual predominance and despotic servitude, whose fault is it if not the
conquerors, who carried to the virgin soil of the Americas their own power struggles,
their mortal hatred for territorial domination, and their unquenchable thirst for con-

trol? Did Spain teach the peoples of the Americas to live the life of free citizens or, perhaps, to be the eternal slaves of money-hungry heads-of-state who come to the subjugated land only to seek prosperity?

And since *El Criterio* has already reproached the nations of the Americas for the vices which Spanish domination has bequeathed them, could they tell us if the prestigious nation to which they wish to remain bound is more auspicious in this regard? Is not the saber still *triumphant* in the homeland of Daoiz and Velarde? Are bureaucratic ambitions not the cancer that corrodes the insides of the wretched Spanish people? Is freedom of conscience, in reality, well established in Spain, when reforms to separate Church and State still have not been implemented? Is the nation of Lepanto and San Quintín, of Bailén and Pavía faring so well that Spanish overseas subjects have nothing to envy their truly autonomous English counterparts in Canada? And do not forget this fact, *El Criterio*, so you may be all the more fair in your accusations: Since Covadonga to the present day, Spain has been a free nation for more than a thousand years, yet she still has not been able to establish herself as a Free State in the true sense of the word, despite her heroic battles for freedom. The nations of the Americas have barely experienced one hundred years of independent life from the time that they were Spanish colonies, yet they follow a republican system, which is *permanent*. What is *transient*, namely, their internal divisions—which are a sad legacy of Spanish domination—are disappearing by leaps and bounds. Nothing greater can be said of nations that in less than a century broke away from their opprobrious past of moral and material slavery, set the foundations for a democratic government, created laws, established rules for civil conduct, and increased their sources of wealth. We challenge *El Criterio* to list other nations that in the same span could have completed such an admirable enterprise—save for the United States, which was not formed by the *indigenous races of the Americas*, but is rather the refined product of the English civilization, that is to say, the European nation with the most elevated concept of *practical* freedom of all times.

We shall see in another article—for time is pressing—what is really behind the liberal *rights* enjoyed in the Spanish Antilles compared to those of the free republics of the Americas.

Incidentally, we say to *La Revista de Puerto Rico* that we have set aside their well-reasoned article—which is as gallant in form as it is plentiful in proper colonizing doctrine—to which we shall respond as soon as we are finished responding to *El Criterio*.

S. Figueroa

A. Vélez Alvarado

F. Gonzalo Marín

Doc. 42
Sotero Figueroa, Antonio Vélez Alvarado, Francisco Gonzalo Marín,
"Domination and Independence, III"

August 20, 1892 (#24)

Unless they have been blinded by a reprehensible sense of hostility toward South American nations, *El Criterio* must have realized from our previous article that these good, sister republics have accomplished a gargantuan task in less than *three-quarters of a century* of independence, and that it is highly unfair to ask for more exemplary acts or greater progress in developing autonomy, when the metropolis that educated them instilled its vices for domination and tried at all times to antagonize the unrestrained, revitalizing, and regenerating spirit of freedom.

Although it is true that *no one can give what he does not have,* and if Spain has continuously fought to expel administrative centralization and religious fanaticism as far away as possible but has not succeeded in doing so (nor will succeed for a long time), it would be naïve to believe that Spain would grant her *possessions* in the Americas what she herself does not enjoy. Hence, Cubans and Puerto Ricans have learned, through sorrowful experience, that to ask the metropolis for a form of government that broadly ensures their freedom and allows them to manage their own interests is to dream the impossible dream. And so they have set out on their own initiative to seize what nature and history have accorded, namely, democratic institutions within a Free State.

But *El Criterio* assures us, with the Machiavellian approach of Unconditional Spaniards, that the Colombian free thinker may envy Puerto Ricans who are free—when they want to be—from right-wing despotism, and that journalists in Venezuela and Santo Domingo can only wish to enjoy the *liberty* with which Puerto Rican newspapers can and certainly do discuss their issues, and concludes by stating—without a tremble of the quill—that for the most part, a citizen in Puerto Rico has more freedoms than in the Latin American republics.

Someone once said that comparisons *are odious,* and it was never as true as in the case at hand, for we are dealing with sister nations who cannot be held responsible without us sharing some of the blame. Every nation of the Americas, including the Antilles, is a branch of the same tree, and they cannot be snapped off without also spilling our own sap.

So you say that we are free from right-wing despotism? Very recent events indicate otherwise.

El Criterio should know that not long ago a gentleman from San Juan—the capital of Puerto Rico—was publically buffeted by an Evangelical priest for, in exercising his freedom of conscience, he had refused to remove his hat as a procession passed by. The injured party went to court and—to add insult to injury—he was ordered to pay a fine and most of the litigation costs. For appearances' sake, the priest was handed a milder fine, which has given him the impression that he may continue to slap any irreverent *passerby.* Does it not seem to *El Criterio* that this is a good example of citizens who are as meek as lambs and are free from this same despotism?

In Humacao, right under *El Criterio*'s nose, the young Mr. Nova renounced his affiliation with the Free Masons to have a canonical wedding in San Juan—that nest of the black ravens. He, another apostle who, like Him, preached the doctrine of meekness and brotherly love from the pulpit of the Holy Spirit, has impunibly humiliated Free Masonry to the point of having most indecently confessed that the women belonging to this philanthropic institution must *sacrifice their virtue.* These are clear, ennobling examples of how Colombian free thinkers can envy Puerto Rican colonial subjects. We have even ignored the many times an ecclesiastical burial has been denied to those who did not observe the practices of the Catholic Church, unless, of course, they paid for a lavish funeral, in which case *a camel can go through the eye of a needle.* Believe it or not, *El Criterio,* a country in which government imposes religion, pays for it, sustains it, and tolerates its excesses and animosities is a country that cannot boast of being free from despotism, nor can its newspapers become judges of nations who are masters of their own destinies and can thus be seen victoriously ascending, leaving behind the impurities of degrading servitude.

El Criterio, defender of Spanish domination in Puerto Rico, has assured us that the press can and certainly does discuss all issues pertaining to the colony. This preaching may be acceptable from the opposition, or from newspapers in China or Hindustan where people may be oblivious to Puerto Rico, but not here by our Antillean neighbor where countless Puerto Ricans have gone, preferring to live free in foreign lands than as slaves in their beloved *patria.* How can one believe that freedom of the press is guaranteed in any country where vile kidnappings are still practiced with unusual cruelty and ruinous fines and ignoble imprisonment can be imposed on a journalist who arduously battles against the abominations of colonial administration? What more could journalists from the independent nations of the Americas desire from our laws governing the press? What if every small-town mayor were to pounce on the journalist when his deeds are condemned and silence him with impassioned severity, either by destroying the publication with excessive and continuous fines or overwhelming this same journalist with proceedings that are as unfounded as they are theatrical? In the end, even if the journalist is found blameless, compensation for damages may not be exacted from the omnipotent panjandrum who firmly holds his post and who continues to ride roughshod over the writer who does not buckle under despotic pressures. Galo Rosado, a journalist from San Germán, has just been released from prison, yet the editors of *La Democracia* (Muñoz Rivera) and *La Nación Española* (Arnau Igaravides) have more than once visited those same prison cells during these times of merciful concessions to the colony. We do not wish to outline the proceedings or the cowardly traps that have befallen certain liberal writers, for this would be never-ending. And there are the *freedoms* that the press enjoys in Puerto Rico, *given* that there are no newspapers that oppose the government, as may perhaps occur in *certain* republics in South America. And if in this comparison someone seems to have the upper hand, it should be the free nations which *El Criterio* mentions, for silence is worth more than empty protests and, yet, even more transcendent is the refocusing of energies, which condenses the lightning bolt in the atmosphere of nations, than the childish opposition which colonial rulers listen to with disdain, knowing that their promises are but faint summer showers that will barely moisten the parched ground.

And now we have come to *El Criterio*'s great carillon of an argument, which undoubtedly must have sounded agreeable to intransigent Spanish ears. "A citizen of Puerto Rico has MORE FREEDOMS than in the Latin American republics." Whichever way you look at it, it is an audacious statement, and we cannot say to what degree *El Criterio* can fully justify it.

To live in the land of your birth dominated by the conquerors, who are the favorites of the regime and are flattered by lucrative administrative posts; to be forced to accept the steep taxes imposed by metropolitan legislators who pay no heed to the complaints raised by a people who have been bled dry; to see the children of our hopes grow up with no future for their aspirations, for one must either submit to the leaders in order to secure an insignificant seat at the official banquet or seek a dignified post abroad that is suited to one's aptitudes, or, otherwise, be humiliated in anguish—which only proves that an individual is not free from shameful invectives during the tragic days of government wrath, and a home can never be safeguarded from the profanations of flatfoots when conspiracies are fabricated to justify a show of force. In other words, to not have any initiative of one's own, to be bound under strict and pernicious guardianship, no matter how much we are accorded liberal laws which are never enforced—these are the better freedoms which Puerto Rican *citizens* enjoy, and, despite *El Criterio*, they are not the envy of the Latin American republics.

The Puerto Rican newspaper to which we respond imagines that it enjoys more freedoms than our hemispheric brothers because it is given the right to complain all it wants. But take notice of the reason: Like the fearsome dog, enchained even after a filing of its fangs, it would be excessive precaution to also apply a muzzle. In the free nations of the Americas, the fierce dog is on the loose and has very sharp fangs. Hence, the need to apply a muzzle, which is not sufficient to contain its ferociousness when it is goaded and violently pouncing irresistibly on its abuser.

Otherwise, it is better to live humbly in your own home than to live comfortably—yet ashamed and degraded—in someone else's.

Does is not seem to *El Criterio* that *PATRIA* was right when, in a sudden cry of dignity, it printed the following?

"What must be said is that, since we live in continuous anguish, in continuous insecurity, and under continuous threat, it would be better to live so in our own home—where the natural love of the land would begin to heal our illness, where the fruit of our possible depredations would remain within our country and among our children, and where the sudden dignity of our life would reveal its supreme obligations to our refined spirit—rather than live in agony knowing that only foreigners benefit from the fruits of our labor."

The esteemed newspaper from Humacao says that it will join our ranks when convinced that not even the Spanish Republicans can do justice to the righteousness of Puerto Ricans.

So, until then, colleague.

Doc. 43
Sotero Figueroa, Antonio Vélez Alvarado, Francisco G. Marín,
"Domination and Independence, IV"
September 17, 1892 (#28)

To *La Revista de Puerto Rico*:
We are pleased to contend with loyal adversaries who endeavor to add to the sound-ness of the argument that deferential courtesy which elevates all discussions to the sphere of principles. Personal attacks, boorish words, and idiosyncratic ill-suited expressions belong to the banal and arrogant troublemaker, who, with hollow and pompous words, only confirms a lack of sound reasoning, which was intended to con-vince instead of confound. Arguing with those who recognize that the true calling of the press—which is to illuminate public awareness with the light of truth—will always be fruitful, even if a satisfactory agreement on the issues cannot be reached.

Hence, the reason why today we will draw our sword against the *Revista de Puerto Rico*, a newspaper that hails from the cultured city of Ponce which, by re-sponding our piece "Let Us Have a Discussion," stands on dignified ground where common ruffians dare not tread. As polite gentlemen wielding sterling weapons, like Fontánez's paladins, they know to salute their adversary when they hit and wound.

The illustrious Autonomist newspaper begins by doing justice to our honorable intentions by asking to discuss the separatist credo proclaimed by Club Borinquen and, with it, other patriotic associations, which total more than one hundred and among which the following deserve a warm mention due to the important names they bear: Las Dos Antillas in New York, Cuba y Borinquen in Boston; Lares y Yara in Key West, and Guarionex y Hatuey in Port-au-Prince (Haiti).

La Revista then states that we have placed ourselves "on the only workable and hon-orable ground available in these times of open inquiry," and makes these categorical state-ments, which, because of their honesty, integrity, and truthfulness, we hold in high regard.

This publication never considered denying the possibility of independence to the colonies for it does not believe in the perpetuity of domination, however gently exercised.

It believes that the colonies are called to secede from the metropolis when they have reached a certain degree of moral and material culture and progress, and thus achieving equal standing and becoming allies and friends in life and death.

It believes that Spain's mission in the Americas is to turn her colonies into pros-perous and independent nations.

And, finally, it believes that the separatist ideal is noble and sacred for it lends itself to elevating the status of our country, transforming it from simple colony to independent nation.

Up to here, we are perfectly in agreement with *La Revista*, which shows that it is fully aware of the scientific and rational theories that make a metropolis respectable and a colony progressive. These are not *extensions of the homeland*, as one of the most eloquent Spanish orators once said, but nations in an embryonic state who are subject to guardianship while the conditions for viability have not been met. But once these conditions come to pass and the cultural development of its inhabitants demonstrates that it is not inferior to the dominating nation; once the metropolis has given the colony all that it could give, and the latter, by means of the environment, strives to become the master of its destiny in order to infuse life into its progressive endeavor, it is sensible to promptly release them, so as to avoid extreme resolutions, which Justice alone will ultimately settle through force—if, unfortunately, there is no other way.

And it is futile to state with pompous imprudence and without considering the lessons of history that Spain will play her last card and spend her last cent to maintain her domination over the Americas. No matter how great her power, no matter how strong her grasp, no matter how vast her resources, Spain will not win the final battle, for victory always belongs to the oppressed who desire and deserve to be free. What cannot be sustained through the ties of vain affection will be perpetuated through imposition. The struggle will intensify time and time again; it will be passed down from father to son; the offense will grow in proportion to the excesses; and Spain will play her last card and spend her last cent, and the Antilles shall be free, despite iron-fisted repression, and perhaps before anyone has expected. Could, perchance, bodies be kept from falling on the side toward which they lean or rivers from flowing downhill?

But, since we have already offered the logical arguments presented by *La Revista*, let us now examine its erroneous deductions.

The Ponce newspaper follows the beautiful *credo* we have transcribed above with an uncharacteristic lack of reasoning. Like *El Criterio* from Humacao, it denies the possibility for secession:

Because it believes that Puerto Rico has not reached maturity;

Because Puerto Rico lacks the strength to survive on its own;

Because Puerto Rico has no experience;

And because Puerto Rico lacks its own resources with which to subsist.

Fine. Every prudent father, who is ever humble and honorable, expresses himself as *La Revista* has when his first-born attempts to establish a separate home for himself.

He denies him the opportunity, as if nature itself were not imperiously contradicting it.

He assures him that he is too young, since in parents' eyes, their children shall always be children.

That he lacks strength of his own, when he is a strapping lad as strong as an oak.

That he has no experience, as if that could be acquired in anticipation of future events.

And that he lacks resources with which to subsist, when it is obvious that his own industry will shield him from hardship.

Yet the son insists vehemently on his desires. The father becomes furious, and then comes the painful fallout: the son is emancipated from his father's guardianship, and he prospers. Happiness smiles upon him, and he does not envy the prosperity of other homes that, perhaps, are not as peaceful as his own. Is he unhappy? Patience, this is how it should be. In any case, the human race continues its course, and there are no fewer marriages among the poor, regardless of whether happiness or misery reigns in his neighbor's home.

We hope that from this example our colleague will understand the full scope of our philosophy and be able to apply it to *small* nations.

Does our colleague even understand how dignified it is to be in one's own home, even if one is not very comfortable or well off in it? Does it not find the poor English peasant's pride admirable, when he exclaims before his ramshackle home: "Here, without my bidding, the wind and the rain may enter, but not the King of England." A Spanish colonial subject could never say this.

But *La Revista*—which is so logical in discussing the principles of modern democracy and recognizes that no nation can be enslaved eternally—becomes incomprehensible and lacks clarity of thought when it tries to justify Spanish domination *in Puerto Rico* without questioning the prospect of independence for Cuba. Let us see how it is stated:

"Hence, it is completely beyond doubt that Cuba—as much for its size, its riches, and its geographical situation, as for a thousand other reasons—can be independent within a *more or less* short period of time. But, is Puerto Rico on equal footing? Can it aspire, like that greater Antillean island, to a life of independence?

["]Are Club Borinquen's pretentions utopian, or is it a viable aspiration within the realm of possibility and utility, considering as possible and useful what a prosperous life—as opposed to an anarchic and demagogic state—means to Puerto Rico?

["]As far as we are concerned, *we deny the possibility of independence*, not because Spain would deny it come the opportune moment, but because Puerto Rico—not for ethnological reasons, but because of its very limited physical size—cannot be expected to form an independent State."

Behold how, in a few lines, the Ponce newspaper tramples upon its previous sound arguments that "colonies are expected to secede from their metropolises when they have reached maturity and hold the immoral principle that nations of limited size cannot be the arbiters of their own destinies.["] As if the right to national sovereignty had gradations according to territorial expanse, geographical area, or material prosperity! If we were to follow this complacent solution, Switzerland would not be independent because it is small next to the great European nations; Portugal would not exist as a kingdom nestled in the southwest corner of Europe; nor would Denmark or Holland or any of the independent European states that are relatively small compared to the great world powers.

And regarding our America, the Central American republics have no right to independent life as a result of their limited territorial size. And may very well *La Revista* say that we have overextended their arguments, yet such a conclusion can be reached when there is no awareness of the universal principle of justice, which demands sovereignty for nations everywhere and does not consider greater or lesser geographical extension.

Regarding Puerto Rico, we will soon see to what degree the *Revista* has lost focus in its final statement, which could not be more regrettable.

However, this matter deserves a separate chapter.

New York, Sept. 1892
S. Figueroa
Antonio V. Alvarado
F. Gonzalo Marín

Doc. 44
Sotero Figueroa, Antonio Vélez Alvarado, Francisco G. Marín,
"Domination and Independence, V"
September 24, 1892 (#29)

To *La Revista de Puerto Rico*:

Does the smallest island in the Greater Antilles have the appropriate and vital conditions to rule itself independently?

La Revista de Puerto Rico argues that it does not, even though this publication does not believe "in the perpetuity of domination, however gently exercised."

We believe that it does, according to the universal principle of justice, which concedes neither individual slavery nor collective subjugation.

And, on what does the Ponce newspaper base its arguments to have fallen in it lacks its own resources to subsist.

Let us see how *La Revista* paints a picture according to its own whims.

The island of Puerto Rico measures 931,700 hectares in surface area, and has a population of approximately one million inhabitants. Regarding actual sources of wealth, and going by the official data of 1887—which offers the most recent statistics available—in said year Puerto Rico exported goods valued at $10,994,993.17 and imported around the same amount. The culture of her inhabitants is demonstrated by the fact that there are countless criollos who have resided in Spain, France, England, Germany, and the United States, either traveling for pleasure or practicing an honorable profession in these centers of science and industry, and the numerous compatriots who wander freely throughout the continent honor their beautiful island, some with their industry, others with their erudition, and all with their prudence and good judgment which sets the name of Puerto Ricans in good standing.

There is no need to fear a future conflict between the two predominant races on the island: slavery has been abolished; all social classes stand together on ideals and noble aspirations; the Ethiopian race holds no perverse instincts; indeed, crimes committed by the slaves of yesteryear are scarce; revitalized is the race of "Caucasians by migration and the meeting of one with the other, resulting in their entwined harmony. And, a transformation toward progress is visible, which banishes all fear of internal discord." In the year 1887, there were 485,000 white residents and 329,000 of color, abounding in this latter class the most invaluable of people who have been able to secure a respectable post by their industry.

If we compare this progress with what other free nations in the hemisphere have attained, we shall see that Puerto Rico is better prepared for independent life and there is no reason to establish any cause for colonial domination by appealing to the futile pretexts of its immaturity and geographical smallness.

In 1885 (we do not have any statistics more recent than this), the Dominican Republic, which has an area of 53,343 square kilometers, supported a population of 500,000 inhabitants—almost half of Puerto Rico's—and exported $2,544,403 worth of goods.

In Paraguay, with an area of 238,290 [sic] square kilometers, there were 430,000 inhabitants in 1886, including uncivilized Indians. The country's exports totaled $1,621,000.

Bolivia, with 1,139,250 square kilometers, exports the equivalent of approximately 10,000,000 bolivianos.

Ecuador, which covers 643,295 [sic] square kilometers, exports the equivalent of 8,000,000 sucres.

And now, a glance at the Central American republics: Costa Rica, with 750,760 [sic] square kilometers and 230,000 inhabitants, exports $3,297,000; Nicaragua, with 133,800 square kilometers and 300,000 inhabitants, exports $2,236,000; Honduras, with 121,382 square kilometers and 360,000 inhabitants, exports $1,600,000; San Salvador, with 18,720 square kilometers and 650,000 inhabitants, saw its exports increase from 5 to 6 million pesos. With a surface area of 121,140 square kilometers and a population of 1,400,000 inhabitants, Guatemala's exports do not exceed $6,736,000.

With these figures that we have provided, *La Revista* can judge if Puerto Rico has sufficient *strengths of its own* for independent life and may become convinced that territorial extension is not always a sign of progress or vitality. Nationality does not define a *pueblo*, but, vice versa; and governments will be stronger and more respectable in accordance with the support and development of the sources of production. So what can be saved from *La Revista*'s argument, if it cannot withstand the logic of history, the principles of equity, or these enlightening and irrefutable figures?

But *La Revista*, feigning ignorance of our position within the Partido Revolucionario Cubano, says that we acknowledge and understand the reason it puts forward regarding Puerto Rico's limited size, since we are counting on Cuba's independence to achieve sovereignty for ourselves. Hence, it proposes the following violent conclusion:

Conceding that Cuba becomes independent and, at the same time, can procure independence for Puerto Rico, what is more suitable for this island: being a state of a nation during a period of organization or remaining a dependency of a European nation that is strong and well established?" And it concludes—as one would suppose given its political affiliation—by stating that "the salvation of Puerto Rico, as much for herself as for Spain, lies in the implementation of an autonomist regime, so that its own inhabitants may be the ones who govern it.

As the skilled propagandist that it is, this newspaper that we are contesting aims to tip the scale toward its own political ideology. But let us examine its arguments piece by piece.

We hold that Spain, despite her frequent struggles for freedom, is not well established, and this, *La Revista* cannot deny for it would be an offense against known facts. In the Spanish metropolis there are two political factions fighting for power, which frustrate the proper functioning of public administration, if not altogether nullify the projects implemented by their predecessors. Hence, there is no sound situation, nor does the metropolis enjoy the prestige it should have, given her history and influence in this hemisphere. Therefore, the possibility of belonging to a *strong and well established* European nation can be ruled out.

Premier world powers (and certainly not the weaker republics) make pacts and alliances to protect each other from a common enemy, yet this fact by no means undermines their authority, nor are they seen as being dependent on the other nations from which they seek support as allies.

The Puerto Ricans in Club Borinquen believe that joint action between Cubans and Puerto Ricans will facilitate the cause for independence, and they unite in this supreme effort, but not to become a state within the Cuban nation during a period of organization. Cuba, which denounces this inauspicious guardianship, would not impose herself on those who pursue the achievement of total freedom with her, nor would Puerto Ricans accept such a disgraceful situation.

Regarding autonomy, this is only a transitory formula which could not entirely deliver our aspirations because—and there should be no confusion, *La Revista*—as long as Spain exercises its national sovereignty, Spaniards will always be the ones to benefit from every new administrative system implemented in *her* colony. This is in addition to the fact that the autonomist ideology loses prestige every day, while the powerful ideal of independence continues its ascendency. Solid proof resides in the fact that *El Clamor del País* could not manage to make the Puerto Rican people demonstrate in protest against the position which Club Borinquen had taken and how the Autonomist Directorate in San Juan—which anathematized those who wanted to forge broad horizons for the homeland from abroad and abjured the ideas for which some of its members suffered persecution and humiliation—could not find support in popular opinion, despite their pressing campaigns. Hence, the Autonomist Directorate has finally understood what we told them in our manifesto: They had played a contemptible role at San Juan's Palacio de Santa Catalina—serving as accomplices to *Unconditional Spaniards*—when they announced their absolute withdrawal from the elections, convinced that Ubarri would triumph for a long time in patient Puerto Rico, unless vehement demonstrations for dignity break out, which—I might add—have already become more evident, thanks to the disastrous measures taken by Romero Robledo.

The peaceful evolution that *La Revista* presented is a tempting morsel of propaganda when hope is not yet lost. But we include ourselves among the disappointed and those who believe that freedom must be *seized* for it is an inalienable right, one that must not be *asked for* as a favor.

Consequently, revolutionary clubs are not excessive measures, nor are proclamations that elevate the Puerto Rican character.

Let us get to work; the outcome will reflect our noble efforts.

We have said our share.

New York, Sept. 1892.

S. Figueroa
Antonio V. Alvarado
F. Gonzalo Marín

Doc. 45
Antonio Vélez Alvarado, "The Puerto Rican Anthem"
September 3, 1892 (#26)

Nations roar, thirsty for freedom and gorged on bloody despotism; they forge ahead on the glorious path that will lead them to the pinnacle of civic greatness or the summit of their sublime desires. Over the galvanizing jubilation of crowds possessed by rapturous mania that chokes the roar of combat and the clamoring of the frenzied popular masses can be heard, that dreadful and divine cry that rouses the spirit, soaks the infernal battlefields with torrents of passion, and moves every fiber of every generous heart, stimulating in every being a panther-like sense of fearlessness that wanders from town to town—from world to world—and in the arms of each generation, the strings of resonant instruments, and the throats of the *Adelinas*, enduring together through the centuries.

Captive *pueblos* languish, poisoned by the noxious air that they breathe; they writhe in the agony produced by a disgraceful and absurd guardianship; they march sorrowfully with their heads clouded by a shameful shadow; and in their days of defiant rejoicing, during the revelry that brings out a hint of the patriotism that boils in their veins, in those early symptoms of popular fever, they tend to wail in pain—the gut-wrenching cries of a soul suffering from a longing for freedom, which overtakes present and future generations, like the glorious anthem that will incite them in that sublime moment when they contend with the gargantuan task of reconstruction, like the lament that confesses pain, the demeanor that denotes character, and the notes that harmonize the aspirations of a people succumbing to the horrific ergastulum of tyranny.

It was a night under a clear and beautiful moon, the French writer narrates. De Lisle took up his violin and instinctively began to play. He was inspired, and both the music and the words converged simultaneously in his volcanic mind. It seemed as though the same spirit of *la patria* had possessed his very soul, as if freedom herself were dictating those patriotic words to him. He wrote, played, improvised, and revised, inspired by the memory of beautiful France. When the first rays of dawn shone upon his face, De Lisle had already written six verses and composed the music for his immortal song. The tempest that once crushed the civic spirit would be swept away—along with thrones, arrogant despots, and their haughty followers—and radically transform indomitable France. And that immortal song still rings forth in the heart of nations, for "La Marseillais"—no matter how much it may be condemned by the usurpers of public rights—shall continue to topple despotism and undermine thrones. So has Riego's anthem continued to smolder within the Spanish heart since 1868, setting the stage for the coup that will vindicate the memory of Lanuza and Padilla.

To the world, the Puerto Rican Anthem still does not possess the political significance or the glory of those two sovereign hymns. One cannot yet know for certain what the people will do once enchanted by its magical cadences, but the day will come for the Antillean islands and all of the Americas when it will carry equal significance as Rouget de Lisle's sublime work does for France.

Whether "La Borinqueña" was written under a clear night sky or in physical darkness, or whether the first rays of dawn surprised the author while he was penning this singular composition is unknown. We do know that it is the work of a Spaniard, that it was not commissioned by a group of patriots as a war song during times of national crisis and suffering, and that when it was first made public, it produced precisely the intended effect among enthusiasts.

When it first appeared, "La Borinqueña" was exclusively a dance piece, one of those popular *danzas* that distract Puerto Ricans, drunk with pleasure, as they gently glide to the musical chords across the ballroom, perfumed with evergreens and lilies, hugging the svelte waists of their more graceful compatriots—all with penetrating eyes and angelic faces.

As a musical composition, "La Borinqueña" is not like the usual Puerto Rican danzas, or divine "musical nonsense." Those who can actually play it are only the gifted musicians from that privileged, yet disgraced land, whose children, it seems, also have the exclusive talent to dancing to it with the same grace and charm as their merengues.

And if the music of "La Borinqueña" is of the enduring kind, the lyrics are wanting. But this is how it was sung when it was given its subversive tinge; this is how it was sung by toiling *jíbaros* early in the morning when performing their agrarian duties, and this is how it must live on in the memory of every soul. "La Borinqueña," however, has other verses: the patriotic and incendiary lyrics that are sung privately, despite intransigent colonizers.

When it first appeared, "La Borinqueña" was the favored danza in all social circles. It was performed and danced at soirées hosted by the best families, as well as in the most humble of gatherings. Its cadences inundated the haughtiest of ballrooms and the most humble of shacks, in both the city and the countryside.

But the people, when they heard "La Borinqueña," felt something more than just the desire to be swept away by an enchanting danza. There was something inexplicably electrifying: the deep and languid wail of a nation writhing under the horrors of a cruel guardianship. And that ineffable something unveiled itself during one glorious day of popular rejoicing. The Spanish government had just announced the decree freeing the black man who had been beaten like an animal under the rule of the white slave, owing this to the constant and determined efforts of two illustrious Puerto Ricans. News spread throughout the island, leaving behind a frenzy of great elation in every noble heart, and the civic demonstrations with which the people eloquently, yet rarely, expressed their emotions overflowed uncontrollably in every single settlement. In the capital of the colony—despite it being the lair of high-ranking panjandrums, of those who maintained the immoral and offensive trade of human flesh, and other indifferent elements of society (if not to say outright enemies of all liberal reform)—the masses burst into tears of joy and filled the streets with resounding orchestras, singing praises to the god of destinies for the offense that had just been extinguished before the very eyes of the country.

An orator addressed the people from the balconies of a public building. Demonstrators silently reached the square before the ardent tribune and listened solemnly to the eloquent words of this patriot. With fiery expressions, he lashed out against those who had instituted the enslavement of the black man and had torn away those who lived happily and freely along the shores of the Calabar River only to turn them into slaves of slaves. He would extol, with the utmost elocutionary prowess, the giant step that had just been taken on the path to national freedom. The people listened with reverence when suddenly an explosion of cheers and hurrahs rippled through the city, and, as if by magic, as if compelled by an electric shock, all the orchestras that had gathered there flooded the air with the divine chords of "La Borinqueña."

And from that moment onward, that inexplicable something within the popular danza became clear; that something which infused "La Borinqueña" with such political significance that the authorities had it outlawed under severe penalties. Since then it had only been tolerated, until recently, when it again has been forbidden by the country's despots, clearly on account of the revolutionary movement that Antilleans have been organizing from abroad.

But "La Borinqueña" will never perish, despite the attempts made by those who believe it to hold the ember of hope that might fuel the hosts of independence. Its cadences—like the moans of the suffering—bring joy and enliven the most withdrawn spirit. And when in exile at intimate gatherings on harsh winter nights, or on clear days at meetings among souls of good faith, when ladies—perhaps beautiful angels who have escaped from the heavens—who feel the pangs of their distant homeland infuse life into it on the piano, it sounds like the plaintive voice of the adored homeland calling her children to die in the struggle for redemption—in the efforts to release her from bondage—as the patriotism swells in men of good faith to the tune of the sublime "Borinqueña"—an anthem which will resound throughout every free nation, for it incited the spirit of a people for whom fate had reserved the privilege of placing the last emerald on the glistening diadem of freedom in the New World.

LA BORINQUEÑA

By Félix Astol
Piano arrangement by Ana Otero

1
Most beautiful Borinquen
It is Cuba whom you must follow,
You have borne brave children
Who want to go to battle.

2
Your genteel air, which inspires our patriotism
Vibrates in our very core,
And what would suit you well,
Is the great sound of war.

3
Slaves we no longer
Wish to be,
Our shackling chains
We will break and be free.

4
War drums
Signal with their sound
That the rugged countryside
Will be our meeting ground.

....

[Author's Note: The lyrics to the original version of "La Borinqueña" come from a poem written by Puerto Rican poet Lola Rodríguez de Tió after the Grito de Lares in 1868. The music associated with this anthem comes from a danza composed by Félix Astol in 1867. A different version with lyrics written by Manuel Fernández Juncos in 1903 became the official anthem of Puerto Rico under the Commonwealth status in 1952.

The original Spanish version presented by Vélez Alvarado in this document is as follows:

Bellísima Borinquen
A Cuba has de seguir
Tú tienes bravos hijos
Que quieren combatir.

2
Tu aire gentil, patriótico
Vibra en el corazón
Y te sería simpático
El ruido del cañón

3
No más esclavos
Queremos ser,
Nuestras cadenas
Se han de romper.

4
El atambor guerrero
Nos dice con su son,
Que es la montaáa agreste
El stitio de reunión.

Although some verses in Vélez Alvarado's account are found in Rodríguez de Tió's version, the latter is a far longer text. Rodríguez de Tió's original poem (in Spanish) is as follows:

¡Despierta, borinqueño
que han dado la señal!
¡Despierta de ese sueño
que es hora de luchar!
A ese llamar patriótico
¿no arde tu corazón?
¡Ven! Nos será simpático
el ruido del cañón.
Mira, ya el cubano
libre será;
le dará el machete

su libertad...
le dará el machete
su libertad.
Ya el tambor guerrero
dice en su son,
que es la manigua el sitio,
el sitio de la reunión,
de la reunión...
de la reunión.
El Grito de Lares
se ha de repetir,
y entonces sabremos
vencer o morir.
Bellísima Borinquén,
a Cuba hay que seguir;
tú tienes bravos hijos
que quieren combatir.
ya por más tiempo impávido
no podemos estar,
ya no queremos, tímidos
dejarnos subyugar.
Nosotros queremos
ser libre ya,
y nuestro machete
afilado está.
y nuestro machete
afilado está.
¿Por qué, entonces, nosotros
hemos de estar,
tan dormidos y sordos
y sordos a esa señal?
a esa señal, a esa señal?
No hay que temer, riqueños
al ruido del cañón,
que salvar a la patria
es deber del corazón!
ya no queremos déspotas,
caiga el tirano ya,
las mujeres indómitas
también sabrán luchar.
Nosotros queremos

la libertad,
y nuestros machetes
nos la darán...
y nuestro machete
nos la dará...
Vámonos, borinqueños,
vámonos ya,
que nos espera ansiosa,
ansiosa la libertad.
¡La libertad, la libertad!

Doc. 46
"For Puerto Rico"
June 23, 1894 (#117)

The shallow critics of Antillean politics—upon seeing the apparent beatific attitude with which the people of Puerto Rico have endured the most unjust excises and scandalous violations of individual liberties—might declare that the character of the men and women who had once risen up against Spanish domination is now degraded. However, those who have carefully researched the situation of exploitable colonies know very well that they have never ceased to fight for expansive freedom and, on more than one occasion, have had their noblest aspirations for independence written in blood. They know that today more than ever the political climate of the Puerto Rican homeland is electrically charged, and as the asphyxiating calm constricting the people's conscience grows stronger, the greater and more inexorable the attack will be when they attempt—with the holy wrath of regional pride—to overthrow the imperious and overconfident usurper who oppresses and suppresses the same land which they have not been able to fertilize with their sweat or keep free from infuriating depredations.

It could be said that the only the thing left of the Autonomist party on that small Antillean island is just the name. Its hosts of enthusiastic and militant followers—who once believed that they would triumph immediately over the stubborn and eternally-pampered Integrists—no longer respond to the call of their leader. Romero Robledo, the man who carried out inconceivable acts as Overseas Minister, gave them the *coup de grâce* by producing an artificially inflated electoral body in order to dilute the Autonomist taxpayer vote. Withdrawal was imposed with all its eloquent consequence, and no matter how much the Autonomist directors rushed to say that it was only a partial withdrawal—only in terms of the elections for Diputado to the Spanish *Cortes*—experienced soldiers saw how they were being entertained by futile skirmishes with no positive outcome for the great ideals of *patria* and *libertad*, after the thick cloud that had kept them in plausible unity during combat had dispersed, so they made their partial withdrawal absolute. The ardent protests of the Central Committee were made in vain, for while they did in fact make tepid demonstrations against the treatment of liberal Puerto Ricans as third class citizens, they did not openly break with the Olympic Jupiter at the Palacio de Santa Catalina, but continued to genuflect before the government and receive mortifying disappointments in exchange for their unconditional adherence to Spanish dominance.

It is clear that the distinguished men of the Autonomist party—having no moral authority among their fellow party members—could no longer carry on with such unflattering attitudes and accomplish their objective of receiving the petitioned representation in the government in order to rise in their esteem. Thus, the Directorate felt obliged to surrender its authority in favor of the younger generation, which had said through one of its higher-ranking leaders that the Directorate deserved "a vote of gratitude for having stepped down." Although these passionate youths are struggling to return to the party its past splendor, their reiterated attempts are useless: Lazarus does not rise and leave his tomb.

One can gather from this disappointment that nothing and no one within the colonial system can be pulled out by their root. Faith in a colorless autonomy, which will always be the remedy to the current system of Spanish government, has been lost. Sights are set on a free hemisphere for the Americas. If domestic discord persists, it is understood to be the poor bequeathed us by the conquerors. Broader horizons are sought for the future. We look back on the past by venerating the heroes who fought for the independence of the homeland. LARES, cries out the heart, compelled by throbbing patriotism; BETANCES, pronounce the lips with fervent gratitude. The Partido Revolucionario Cubano, whose flag is inscribed with "ANTILLEAN INDEPENDENCE," keeps an altar in the recesses of every heart that longs to seize national sovereignty and longs to be a citizen in his own right.

"This must go," says the Puerto Rican character after painting a somber picture of the island's prostration. "We cannot wait for a remedy from Spain or from those meticulous politicians who call themselves Autonomists, yet acquiesce by serving as accomplices to the Conservatives who dominate here. Revolution is at hand and, when that day comes, a legion of Puerto Ricans—more numerous than expected—will be waiting in the flanks."

The same Autonomists who follow the radical inclinations of those who still call themselves a party are not afraid of writing paragraphs such as this one:

"If the prevalent idea is that there is no government here except for the kind that wrongs the nation's children with all manner of insults; if the preconceived notion that only exploitation is sought so that a few may seek profit from prosperous business, either by the appreciation and depreciation of the currency in circulation, budgetary mismanagement, or depressing public resources in any way so as to increase the riches of certain civil servants and private individuals; if, through the misuse of the inauspicious Sergeant's Bill, the ayuntamientos are made into puppets; if men are expressly appointed to the Ministries so they may shamelessly manipulate the electoral register by means of the most dishonorable measures and all manner of provocations, it is logical to deduce what the result will be, and it bears down on all our consciences."

And further on, when proposing the theory for the emancipation of pueblos, they add:

Los Pueblos have two paths toward redemption: either through resolute and unrelenting activism until they reach the progressive ends sought by the apostles of liberal ideas or through revolution, but never by tolerance of the same people who are the source of offense and savage treatment. Los pueblos are not dogs that lick the hand of their abuser.

When such eloquent protests are made by a pueblo as peaceable as Puerto Rico, it is because ominous clouds charge the horizon, and the tempest is upon us.

Never do colonies reveal such solemn calm as when they first withdraw before deciding their future destiny.

We await in hope.

Doc. 47
"For Puerto Rico"
July 28, 1894 (#122)

Through correspondence received from its Puerto Rican colleagues, *PATRIA* has been informed that there, as in Cuba, a reactionary situation prevails, along with all its consorts: corruption, misery, and caprice. But since the laws of morality and justice are not violated without consequence, threatening protests are beginning to spring up everywhere, which in due time will be translated into eloquent and transcendent fact, the kind that radically transforms valiant pueblos.

***

The political parties do not come to a mutual understanding. They seek new favors, and the hard-working country turns its back on them to face the horizon, as if demanding more light and a better path. Intransigent conservatives have held a general meeting, which has done little to alter the situation among their supporters: divided, as they are, into two factions that cordially detest each other. The more reactionary of the two is captained by Santurce's own count and livestock farmer, Mr. Ubarri. The other—which possesses more flexible and illustrious members and, thus, is not hostile to certain reforms—is obedient to the whims of Messrs. Valdés, Ledesma, and Mendizábal. Both factions struggle to obtain support from the government, and the working classes of the country already know that by one snap of this wolf's jaw they will wind up injured, as usual.

***

Autonomists show no signs of life. They withdrew from the electoral struggle, and it seems like they are no longer satisfied by the colorless autonomy that was preached by their party's orators. Nothing else can be gathered from the stance assumed by the writers of *La Revista de Puerto Rico*—a newspaper founded by Mr. Cepeda and which was the standard-bearer of the Autonomist credo—who have abandoned this newspaper in favor of a new one called *El Independiente*, which will have a more encompassing range of political views. It will consider a wider sphere of political dogmas and "strive for more progressive solutions than those sought by the current Autonomist party, more in harmony with the demands of the era and the colony."

It is easy to understand what these advances, as proposed by this prescient colleague, actually mean. He surely will launch a formidable campaign, and the government will carry its cruelty to extremes, but he will find the country ready for revolution, which will soon arrive at our camp, ... if time allows it.

***

And regarding the smaller Antillean island, which is facing a period of widespread resolutions, a monument must be erected to the incorruptible Baldorioty de Castro, that visionary politician who promoted broad and radical autonomy within the educational system for the ultimate realization of independence. If this inclination was overlooked at the time when the Ponce Plan was discussed, it is not Baldorioty who should be held to blame, but the fainthearted who agreed on the name but changed the essence of what was a truly autonomous credo.

A circular inviting the people of Puerto Rico to contribute to this monument was signed by Martín R. Corchado, Juan Iglesias Genebriera, Luis Muñoz Rivera, G. Villaronga, Pedro Fournier, Ramón Marín, and Herminio Díaz, all of whom were invaluable figures in the Autonomist movement and possessed the means and influence to carry the project to fruition.

The people of Puerto Rico have enthusiastically embraced this vision, and liberal newspapers have begun to print its long lists of subscribers.

Praise be to those who have managed to repair the memory of this great teacher, for there were those who, at the eleventh hour, tried to undermine his exceptional service to the cause for freedom in the Americas!

***

Persecution of the press that expresses independent judgment is fiercely carried to extremes.

By reprinting an article that first appeared in *La Bandera Federal* in Valencia (Spain) entitled "Los mismos perros" (The Same Old Dogs), Mr. Matos Bernier, editor of the Puerto Rican newspaper *La Libertad*, was prosecuted and sentenced to prison.

No wonder *La Democracia* in Ponce exclaims:

"Mr. Matos Bernier is in prison.

And where is justice?"

But, there is more. There is a weekly newspaper that appears in the town of Fajardo, entitled *La Voz de Oriente*. It is printed in the capital city of San Juan, and occasionally it is somewhat delayed in reaching the town where it is intended to circulate. So, after said newspaper was distributed two days late, the Alcalde placed its editor *under house arrest* and issued a pernicious report against him. Matos then released a separate article detailing what had happened, and he has now been indicted for nothing less than *disobedience and contempt of authority*.

Today, the editor of *La Voz de Oriente* is in all likelihood traveling at his own risk between Fajardo and Humacao to testify at the ridiculous proceedings against him, and the Alcalde is quite satisfied with having dealt a serious blow to a liberal and is eager to spread more abuses, convinced that anything small-town men conjure up can be carried out with impunity and without consequence.

And still, there are colonial subjects who do not want the redemption of revolution!

***

But, if there are those who yearn for war on that Antillean island—with its cordillera set against an expanse of blue—and who, when the fearful colleague asks, "Will there be war?" without inquiring what kind it might be, they exclaim: "May the Heavens prevent it!"

And they base their desire to avoid war on the following points, which are somewhat naive:

"Puerto Rico is particularly unprepared for war.

"The only submarine cable available belongs to a foreign company...

"Regarding weapons, about seven thousand rifles distributed between soldiers and volunteers are far from enough to effectively defend our eternal union with the imperious nation from which we are descended.

"Not even the government has 25 or 35,000 good rifles in its possession to arm that many volunteers in case of an invasion...

"So, in case of war, we might find ourselves:

"1. Without cable communication and, therefore, ignorant of what goes on in the metropolis or even other locations within the national territory

"2. Without weapons or the knowledge to handle modern weaponry

"3. Without men who are sufficiently accustomed to frequent military exercises of the discipline, which they absolutely must acquire. In truth, if war were to come to our doorstep, great will be our suffering, for if we wanted to resist without weapons or with [unintelligible] compromise our tranquility...we would prosper."

This *diatribe* speaks for itself.

And here we can say with a wink, "Spain, this is the kind of revolution you can expect."

And that is all for today.

Doc. 48
"Agitation in Puerto Rico"
December 8, 1894 (#140)

The letters and newspapers which we have received as of late from our unfortunate sister island of Cuba—unfortunate by her origin, her prolonged colonial enslavement, and her redemptive aspirations—tell us of the disconcerting economic situation that reigns over official spheres and becomes more and more embarrassing, and the abject poverty that has taken root in so many homes—not so much for the shocking depreciation of the Mexican currency as for the disastrous administration by Spanish authorities who lend an indifferent ear to the complaints of the working classes and, instead, triumphantly act as lords of a manor which no longer has the means to support so many and such ruinous taxes.

The monetary conflict, about which Spain knows nothing and cannot solve, has enabled the Puerto Rican character to rise up with pride. In San Juan—the walled city where the metropolitan padishahs reign supreme, the Mecca of intransigent Spaniards—right in front of the Governor General's very eyes, the people have mutinied, armed troops have left the barracks and, once again, like during the memorable occasion of that unspeakable tariff legislation, some eloquent *guajiros* made sure that the people's rage was felt, and the injured—our brothers—proved by the drops of their very blood that there is resolution and power under the fleece of those who have been foolishly deemed to be as meek as lambs.

This time, the Directorate of the Partido Autonomista Puertorriqueño, who proclaimed the withdrawal after the charade regarding the electoral body—which had been inflated according to Liberals and reduced according to Conservatives—and had been scorned in official spheres and discredited among the decorous army that refused to engage in shameful compromises, has not even issued forceful statements, and nothing is left, not even a hopeful memory, which at times can galvanize moribund ideals.

The Liberal nation raised the flag of redemption once again, free from all obligations and fed up with scandalous fraud, monopolies, iniquitous privileges, and nefarious domination. In eloquent letters, they cry out for their prestigious leaders in exile and for the unforgettable men who stood at Lares. They long for revolution and, "Here we are," exclaim the strained, yet brave-hearted, echoing the general indignation: "Here we are, ready to raise the spirited protest in proportion to the offense. It is better to die a thousand times waving the sword of freedom than to live like a pariah, without dignity or rights. May revolution come, for Spain will not deign to release us from our vile yoke."

And we rejoice at this explosion of wounded patriotism for memorable times and glorious days await the people of Borinquen. The sun of independence did not hide away forever amidst clouds of blood and mists of tears atop the splendid peaks of Lares.

Go forth, good friends, for you will not be alone at the hour of great vindication!

Doc. 49
"For Puerto Rico"
May 4, 1895 (#160)

The revolutionary faction in Puerto Rico begins to awaken, and the Spanish government is showing signs of unease, sensing that its dominion in the Americas will soon come to an end as the smallest of the Antillean islands hurries to stand behind Cuba to support the struggle for independence.

The following is the alert given by a Madrid newspaper:

Separatism in Puerto Rico

Puerto Rico, following the pernicious example set by Cuba, is preparing a separatist coup.

The effort has begun with the establishment of separatist clubs in New York and Mexico.

The government still has time. The grave news that has been received will be officially scrutinized, and that gravest of dangers which now loom before us will be eradicated in time.

A certain Puerto Rican Diputado has received an exemplary manifesto by a Puerto Rican revolutionary club established in New York, which has widely circulated on that island, and incited its inhabitants to take up arms against Spain and help its Cuban brothers.

Said club is a branch of the great Cuban revolutionary circle in New York, where separatists from the small Antillean island have gathered.

The manifesto announces that the rebels have used Cuba to acquire funds, stating that since the last war, tabaqueros, *azucareros,* and other people with certain social standing in Cuba who are affiliated to the separatist cause have been contributing one *duro* a month. These funds are deposited in the coffers of the Cuban revolutionary club in New York and then used to maintain the enthusiasm of supporters, buy weapons, and prepare expeditions.

In Puerto Rico, separatists barely have any strength, but those infected by the Cuban example have established another club in Mexico, aside from the revolutionary club we have previously mentioned.

* * *

And *La Bomba*, a spirited colleague who hails from Ponce—the city of great emulation—ignites this spark upon receiving news of the first revolutionary skirmishes in Puerto Rico, which the Spanish government tried to present as if they were being carried out only by bands of criminals:

OUTBREAK

For a while now the following question has been posed:

What the hell is going on in Cuba?

To expect to be told the truth regarding this prickly situation is unimaginable.

We are already familiar with the caliber of the *bombas* that are traded here, there, and everywhere in analogous situations.

At first, we were told about gangs of bandits.

And then bandits appeared in almost every single department on that great Antillean island.

As is natural, there was no one on that little island of cordillera who did not open their eyes wide and turn an ear to the west.

Because we were in doubt.

"Bandits?" we asked.

However, let it be known that efforts in Guantánamo were admirably executed.

And yet, they still said that it was all on account of bandits.

But after further examination, we concluded that these were no more than ten.

Another suspicion quickly came to our attention.

According to a telegram that had evidently slipped by Cuban authorities, the Matanzas expedition had multiplied to three hundred men.

As our readers will understand, three hundred men acting in concert can no longer be deemed bandits.

Hence, there is much more.

And it smells of gunpowder and the fearsome *manigua*; in other words, of independence.

However, our reservations do not end here.

A few battalions should soon be passing through this island's capital toward our own beaming island—to Yara and to the Ten Years' War.

And what is the purpose of all this?

What is the meaning of this formidable program?

Is the mobilization of seven battalions from the peninsula needed to destroy a group of miserable bandits?

The name Martínez Campos was also heard.

Pacification, with all that accompanies it.

Having said that, pacification is synonymous with smoke, and whoever cannot see that where there is smoke there is fire is thick-headed indeed.

What we have, then, is the decision from our brave brothers to reform themselves, which is the most efficient way doing things.

Good! Very well! This is how it should be done!

"The Americas for all Americans."

Do not falter, my dear brothers. Attack with might!

Four centuries of iniquitous repression is enough.

It is your turn for redemption.

Out with the *cachacos*!!

Section 3
MARTÍ AND PUERTO RICO

Doc. 50
José Martí, "The Antilles and Baldorioty de Castro"
May 14, 1892 (#10)

A spontaneous surge of spirit precedes great eras of action, as ripeness precedes the sweet, where one may observe the reality hidden from those who insist on seeing it crowned with flowers and who, upon seeing thorns, rush to deny its existence. On the one side, the tottering and dim children of the colony—who use only minimal effort to sustain imported colonial indoctrination and lack the strength to uphold the rights that they reasonably seek—are losing strength; on the other, the visionary forces who—protected by the sea and history—will use the colonial rubble, an instinctive sense of order, and propitious conditions to build the future nation grow stronger. It seems unlikely that the security of Antilles, eyed closely by rapacious forces, depends as much on ostentatious alliances, which are, in fact, insufficient and capable of inciting objections and justifying the use of force, as it does on a subtle unity—evident in everything and without the pretext of explicit provocations—between our islands, which must stand together or together disappear from the memory of free peoples. Agricultural rivalry, distinct customs and histories, or fear of provoking the enmity of a hostile neighbor could drive them apart and lead to the immediate collapse into factions of the natural alliance between the three islands, which—at the heart of independence and their aspirations for the future—extend their arms across the sea and face the world together, as three wounds of the same bleeding heart; three sisters guarding the true and righteous America that will ultimately triumph over the venal America. The lackey changes masters, and sells himself to the wealthiest and most powerful one. The truly free man refuses to give his heart over to a corrupt and subjugating freedom. He sees the triumph of the world as residing beyond decrepit Babylonian structures. He sees it in generous abundance; in that absolute commitment to justice that inspires respect for others as much as for one's self. In life, that visionary Puerto Rican, the invincible Baldorioty de Castro, was no lackey; and he was wisely paid tribute to yesterday during the celebrations in the heroic Dominican city of Azúa by the three Antilles, which must save themselves together or together must perish; those three sentinels of an open and enduring America; those three sisters who have been exchanging progeny and delivering emancipators for centuries; the three embracing islands of Cuba, Puerto Rico, and Santo Domingo.

Government promises, bound at times by a deferential cautiousness that injures the spirit, are perhaps less effective than the unfettered passion and the atmosphere created by a people steadfast in their support of a triumphant freedom triumphing for their region. What the administration cannot even attempt, gorged as it is on peace treaties and obsequiousness, can be achieved with the secret support of the country's spirit, which pushes forward with its unstoppable arms raised against the tyrants. The alliances forged between the souls of a people and signed by its purest sons before an altar where women and children offered flowers to a man whose only power was derived from his intellect and goodness are more lasting and desirable than pacts that favor political pursuits and wealth. The men who, on the anniversary of Puerta de Conde, fondly remember "the peoples of America who still weep and long for their freedom" will not soon let fall that weapon, which will secure independence in Cuba and Puerto Rico and which—without more confirmed allies than the twenty-nine from the Filantrópica and Trinitaria—was born under the cruciform flag to fulfill Duarte's ideals, Sánchez's leadership, and Mella's impetus at La Puerta, and written on that happiest of days, the twenty-sixth of February.

And, when, without the power of messengers, prior communication or bureaucratic negotiations, Puerto Ricans in New York decided to immortalize the memory of that unrelenting criollo who extolled the doctrines of hard work and justice in monumental form; that criollo who tore the newborn slave from the master and restored him, by amending the Moret Act, to his mother's arms; who seized the whip from the brutal master's hands, certain in the belief that "if institutions that are founded on injustice are not maintained by violence, they will inevitably perish;" who exchanged his superficial deference to the metropolis for the resolute and creative spirit that undermines them; who occupied himself during his frequent exiles by cultivating free souls and returned, as a father rushes to his daughter's defense, to attack and challenge the oppression of his bleeding island; who now lies in his tomb with his gaunt hands across his chest and an immortal light shining from his brow. The moment has arrived when Puerto Ricans, along with Cubans, have decided to cast in everlasting bronze that bust feared by evil and beloved by good—that sorrowful face of one who bore the weight of public grief which, like lightning in a storm, flashed radiant with fleeting hopes for redemption; those gentle and confident eyes which did not, like others, slip into duplicity, but shone with a sweet enveloping gaze, like a cloak of loyalty; that sharp and keen nose, typical of one who shields liberty with his instinctive courage, as the eagle shelters its nest; those delicate and anguished lips, guarded by a militant and judicious moustache; that diminutive and feminine beard, like those of men whose bravery is tempered by benevolence. The moment has arrived when Puerto Ricans and Cubans—convinced that showing gratitude to noble men is the republic's most fertile seed—announce their intent to consecrate, where all America can see, the *Borincano* who studied her, loved her, and served her with a son's loyalty. The Antilleans of Santo Domingo erected the *Altar de la patria* (Altar of the Homeland)—the singular and shared homeland—in their noble and courageous city of Azúa. The finest sons and daughters of this city, immortalized by the battle of March 19th, gathered around the altar to the applause of all Quisqueya, and three girls placed their floral crowns upon it in the name of the three sister Antilles—who must save themselves together or together must perish—and of the three embracing islands: Cuba, Puerto Rico, and Santo Domingo.

Was it the coerced temporizer, the ineffectual nationalist, the committed politician, the mere liberal reformist, or the Puerto Rican autonomist to whom, with liberated spirits and words, Cubanacán, Borinquen, and Quisqueya offered flowers? Was it to the Spanish government's commission to the 1877 Centennial Exhibition in which, like a dagger into a newborn, a clause of loyalty to the Spanish nation pierced that magnificent charter of freedom—that document which shall endure beyond the one it replaced—known as the Ponce Plan? No! It was not to the author of that clause, necessary at a time when there was no clear call or movement of public will to attain the fundamental rights denied man in his own homeland. Rather, it was to the author of the bill of rights that introduces that plan and which tomorrow could be transposed in its entirety to the constitution of the Puerto Rican republic! It was not to the obliging politician who, possessing mere vocal courage and, like the shrewd bullfighter, shows the bull his red cape from a distance and, once the bull is docile and willing, offers the bull his hand. Rather, it was to the man who—recognizing the inevitable reality and the high cost of sacrificing his pride—only used his weapons to tirelessly change and improve existing conditions, instead of perpetuating them, readying for the final and historic transformation of life in the Spanish colonies of America to independence! It was not to the cunning Indian, who feigns insincere loyalty to the metropolis in order to secure the means to defeat it. Rather, it was to the admirable prisoner who—disregarding any risk to himself and whatever unjust notoriety might say of him—asks the detestable warden for clemency for his prison mates and, perhaps, in return, might have gone so far as to consider showing clemency toward the warden himself. Nothing more! It was not to the Carrera de San Jerónimo—with its sloping roofs, its swords, and its bullfighter politicians. It was not to El Rastro, another name in Madrid for that market of excesses called "the Americas." It was not to Swiss chocolate or the almond soup of Fornos, or the *azucarillo* cakes from the Plazuela de Cervantes. Rather, it was to the man who—on a winter's day when his homeland ordered him—demanded from metropolitan authorities the restitution of all the rights unlawfully withheld by Spain, without compromising the honor or destiny of the island. He walked alone along the Plazuela de Cervantes, firm in his gait and his grip on his cane, chest open to the cold, and his face resolute and somber, while other delegates, all leather and lotions, disembarked from their fine carriages, dispensing greetings! Cane in hand, Baldorioty crossed the Plazuela de Cervantes, alone.

He was a pupil of the great educator, Rafael—of the black man, Rafael Cordero; the black man who "chopped down the tree, so that others could build with the wood." It was to this favorite student of Padre Rufo, who wanted his students to "die of hunger before committing a misdeed, and learn the gospel of Physics and Chemistry." It was to the man who, since his youth, urged his fellow countrymen to begin amassing the documents of his country's neglected soul in the Sociedad Recolectora de Documentos

Históricos de la Isla de San Juan Bautista de Puerto Rico. It was to that radical and kind educator, more partial to the substance of knowledge than its forms, who taught the new physics in the seminary itself; and who, in Santo Domingo—that country of coasts—headed the nautical school and later founded the prophetically named Colegio Antillano; who defended the Escuela Filotécnica as much as he could from the Jesuits and the mastiff that is the Puerto Rican press; who came already exhausted to the tasks of the Colegio Central Ponceño with assiduously nurtured dreams; who, in education as well as politics, wanted to create righteous, forthright, and honorable men forged from a shared cultivation of their innate humanity and capable of healing their own illnesses with their own remedies. It was this upstanding man that they celebrated; the one who felt his flesh depleted—as if his heart's blood were being drunk—when rights were scorned, or dignity was wounded, or body and soul were humiliated, or the innate freedom of any other man was demeaned or diminished in any way! It was to the man who saw the whip beat the defenseless slave—the slave who was the same color as his blessed teacher, Rafael—and who fought until his delicate hands seized the lash from the master and sat the slave by his master's side. It was to that man with hemispheric vision who, when the colony sent him to study the Exposition Universelle in submissive compliance to Spain's will, turned his gaze back to the land of his aspirations and devotion—the grand and righteous land of our united republics—and lifted the song of the Americas in the ardent heart of Europe. It was to the man who, with destiny as his invisible guide, spread his prophetic words throughout the islands, which must save themselves together or together must perish, and which—when its time comes and the wind clears away the colonial scourge that still buries his country's treasures—will unite the sister islands before the "altar of the homeland." It was to the poor defender of his dishonored and silenced homeland—his beaten, tortured, and bloodied homeland—who only recognized iniquitous courts to defend his homeland before them. It was to the loyal criollo who, with his sincere wisdom, recognized the particularly American nature of his homeland and the moral purpose he would necessarily be led to by its people. And he did not place himself as an obstacle before them, nor did he insist upon yoking them to a hopelessly reactionary metropolis or a fundamentally hostile and distant neighbor. Rather, instead of serving the country to deceive and betray it— instead of using existing conditions to impede its natural development and historic culmination—he deferred to those conditions, using them to establish a country determined by its people, reconcile its politics with justice, forge its destiny through the constant and concerted efforts of its men, and prepare for the country's natural ambitions. Autonomy was not, for him, a toast with amenable generals, who tomorrow send to the gallows those they played chess with yesterday. Rather, the genuine defense of freedom was always foremost in his mind—whether in prison, adversity or exile— because freedom for Puerto Rico was never so far off that Baldorioty did not aspire beyond it. For Baldorioty—that righteous and pragmatic criollo—autonomy was a way of uniting, through geography and history, each country's irrepressible forces. This unity, necessary under any system of government, was required so that when the deficiencies and duplicities of autonomy were confirmed—as they would have been soon after either its institution or unattainability—they could seek a more auspicious system without risk or chaos. America needs sincere and innovative men, poisoned as it is already by so much corruption. The Spanish colonies of the Americas need pure and honest men to purge themselves of despotism and bureaucratic vices through independence. And the world needs compassionate and visionary men who will heal the wounds that their axes must carve in the uncharted forest with the soothing balm of their love. The three sister nations—the three islands which must save themselves together or together must perish—have done well at Azúa to crown with flowers that wise and righteous rebel, that founding father, that American, Román Baldorioty de Castro.

Doc. 51
José Martí, "'¡*Vengo a darte patria!*': Puerto Rico and Cuba"
March 14, 1893 (#53)

A simple postcard, signed by two Puerto Ricans and one Cuban, invited chosen friends of Antillean independence "to exchange ideas around a fraternal table." Fifteen men gathered at Raymond's dining room table in a spirit of brotherly love to discuss their shared faith, the binding affection that grows every day between the two Antillean islands, the secured terrain left open for the task of emancipation by the miserable and anticipated outcome of the pointless observance of electoral reform. This reform might have served as another respite for timid Cubans and another deferment for Spanish domination, if—from the guajiro to the distinguished gentleman on the Island of Cuba and from the jíbaro to the powerful in Puerto Rico—the land were not incapacitated by one of those spontaneous uprisings which are, perhaps, all that is needed to shatter the convenient pretext of a concession that is actually a new offense and the legitimate discontent of a people who, from the hands of their despots, turn to those from whom they expected enough integrity and impetus to overthrow these despots. What matter the names of those who put their people—at the cost of some bloodshed—in such a state of truth and vigor? Make way for the emancipators, whether they come from Cuba or abroad! The vainglorious man looks for his name; the honorable man, to the patria. What is piteous and futile is voluntary submission to an incessant and ever-increasing state of misery and disgrace. What is reprehensible, in these decisive hours, is indecision. In times of crisis, the lawyer's pen dries up; children are kissed on their brows; and one proceeds—with the soul illuminated and a fortune greater than all the world's riches—to the sacrifice demanded by the client's threatened rights and whose defense we accept along with the respective fees and perils. A pueblo is not an endless banquet set out for our enjoyment, with fireworks as the first course. Rather, hope and suffering must first be combined with triumph over injustice and a virtue worthy of defense to make the daily bread, which must also include impassioned ignorance and enlightenment, as well as the strength of character to rescue and guide it. Men must be ministered and served, as the doctor serves the sick patient who bites his hand. To serve the patria, one stands naked; the wind strips away the flesh; and savage beasts suck out the marrow until there is nothing left of that voluntary immolation, except for the light that guides and incites its assassins. *La patria* is not a pretext that rings true or false as we wish; nor is the republic a new form to keep lazy and arrogant men in the lap of luxury and protected under the shield—men who, with depraved selfishness, believe themselves to be the natural charges and inevitable masters of their inferior people. *La Patria*, in both Cuba and Puerto Rico, is the valiant will of a people ready for the triumph of their emancipation—a triumph that is incontestable because of the unified and powerful attack that independence launches against the immoral soul and ruined fortune of its oppressors. The republic, in Puerto Rico as in Cuba, will not be the unjust dominance of one class of people over the rest; rather it is the open and sincere balance between all the country's genuine forces and the liberated hopes and ideals of all Cubans. We do not want to emancipate ourselves from one tyranny only to enter into another. We do not want to escape from one lie to fall for another. We love freedom because, in it, we see the truth. We are willing to die for true freedom, but not for the kind of freedom that functions as a pretext for maintaining some men in extravagant affluence and others in unnecessary suffering. We will die for the republic later, when the time comes, as we will first die for independence. From the very outset of the war for independence, which must be as sharp and direct as lightning, there will be those who die—let us say, from this day onward!—to reconcile the spirit behind our actions with the virtue of the republic. Once again, there will be men in Cuba and Puerto Rico who die with integrity—without the stain of self-interest—defending the rights of others. What is despicable is cowardice when we need courage, the crinoline when we need the cutlass. And although it may have erred at times and persisted in its error, the ultimate fulfillment would be to see by their side at the hour of sacrifice and worthy of their country those who—from habitual deferment, colonial custom, or fear and ignorance of the crude, hidden virtue of their people—sometimes work in such a way that makes them seem more like servants of the government, which rots them and their patria, than agents of the homeland; that country where, for at least ten years, men have succeeded in joining strength of character, which is mankind's masculine force, with intelligence, our feminine one! With that determined and devout spirit, those principles, and those words on their lips, they sat down to the humble menu of the day—those fifteen brothers—at Raymond's table; fifteen intimate friends who wanted to talk about their shared land, to proclaim—as did Club Lares y Yara in Key West, as did those two flags flown by the people to receive the Partido Revolucionario, and as did the Puerto Rican who, pledging his blood and his faith, embraced in Ocala yesterday the Cuban through whom the voice of his people speaks today—that in the times before us, those from Ponce and San Juan will fall in Yara and Guásimas, and those from Cuba will fall in Puerto Rico.

The very table—with the hero to the left and the financier to the right, the typesetter author across from the revolutionary lawyer, the tobacco laborer alongside the doctor with a title from Paris, next to the recently arrived criollo, the spirited recruit who saved his wages to buy his rifle, along with the master of weapons who is as sharp and steady as his own sword—was a living response to those who doubt our people's capacity to replace, with the least turmoil, the conditions of indifference and discord created in the colonies with the republican virtues of united action and respect for dignity. This may, perhaps, be easier and more enduring between us than with the nations that passion or friendly relations would have us use as models. Where in the North could a table be found like the one that bade Martí farewell before one of his last trips; a table free of caste or color, where wealth sits alongside a working wage, and the pen alongside the *chabeta*; a table of rare distinction, where opposing positions debated with the integrity and grace characteristic of the descendants of a people who only need this final provocation to become—through our extraordinary spirit—a true blessing and asset to the world? Where in the North, which is more glorified than understood, could a table be found crafted from all the universities of life—from the academy and the shop—than Raymond's table and those fifteen friends? Those who live off others and walk through the world on stilts—sustaining themselves through the life's hardships without bile or sweat—must not be admired; they distrust themselves and their people. Those who live self-sufficiently—who, in the course of righteous living, have graduated to men—recognize and believe in each other. They will defend independence first, the republic within independence, and independence within that republic! We are not unaware of the dangers we face: the dangers of arrogance and the ambitions of a people who until yesterday owned slaves; the dangers of baneful examples of self-glorification, which, in another era, cursed the first American republics. Our subsequent era contains other men and other political dimensions in which the rebel spirit of a more mature country clashes against all systems or people who—from an insufficient or impetuous understanding of other people's histories—would want to annihilate it. From the vantage of our experience and culture in both Puerto Rico and Cuba, we spoke of the inferior state of independence regarding America's colonies; the duties imposed on us by geography, the dreadful slums, and the hemispheric problems of the time; and the innovative, resolute, and honest methods required of us as these duties were born. We spoke of the transcendent, harmonious, and magnanimous spirit—that vigorous human compassion attributed today to the name of the Partido Revolucionario Cubano by its actions in the Antilles—which inspired and sustains, in rich and poor alike, the multitudes of poor and the few rich. We spoke of the heroism of our native land, of the valor and abnegation of our leaders. We spoke of the great feats that virtue can achieve in this world with scant resources; of the honor in loving that little patch of land where we learned of the world's beauty, along with the sorrow and love that bind us to it. And, we spoke of the artful trespass that corrupts that powerful and sacred love to the extreme of backing and participating in attempts against the patria and its freedom, because they too belong to our little patch of land. We spoke of all the noble principles that can rejuvenate an old man's soul, incite the youth, and meet our wary founders' demands for an edifice as complex and precarious as a nation. We spoke with devotion, and we spoke with candor at that meeting of unconditional revolutionaries who find in our patria's character—in its renowned and evident talents—the augers of its fate were it to aspire to an immoral independence based solely on the opprobrious pleasure of seeing a fantastical ideology prevail over a people without the conditions to maintain it in actuality. The foremost quality of patriotism is the relinquishing of one's self, the disappearance of personal passions and preferences before public life, and the need to accommodate its structures to the ideal of justice. And, around that fraternal table, there only sat men who were capable of relinquishing their selfhood; there sat souls pledging, once and for all, to break pernicious chains with edifying hands. We felt the flame, the ardor, the embrace, and the sudden silence that presaged—as the dawn does the sun—the eras when man, shaken to the depths of his unwavering heart, radiates only strength and light. Words that are merely artful and glib are contemptible and repulsive, like the paintings of a prostitute. On the eve of a people's uprising, prudent and loving words are swift and bright, like our master of arms' sword.

Thus were all the words spoken by the fifteen friends: incisive and vibrant; fully aware of the inherent risks; with no animosity toward any of those who today are mistaken; and without the patriotic pomp and circumstance that disgusts men of truth and sacrifice. Thus they expressed—more through the fire in their eyes than by their words themselves—deep devotion, heroic affection, and fervent unity in this sacred hour of renewal. It was spoken as a declaration of what is right, and with the abiding affection that joins the souls who breathe it in common—just as combat and death forever join those who have fought side by side on the fields of battle. They spoke of the unity between those two islands with different names that tomorrow will fight with the same heart, defend themselves with the same fist, and were founded on the same sentiment: the island of Puerto Rico, where the commissioners who asked Spain's Junta de Información to abolish slavery were born, and the island of Cuba, where the first act of white Cubans who gathered as a nation was to abolish the slavery of Blacks, Cubans, and Africans. Thus spoke the man who stands before you, as the sincere emissary of Borinquen's ideology in New York, as the spiritual son of Betances—who fourteen years ago in Paris rejected the proposal for a republic to accept, from the hands of the same Delegate here today, the position of representative in the war that would be reborn with Calixto García Iñiguez. Thus spoke the reelected chairman of the Puerto Rican club, the generous and brave Sotero Figueroa. Since his days on the Junta, he has recounted the fraternal history between Cubans and Puerto Ricans; he has reported on the conflicts in Lares, which were prior to those in Yara, and the passionate love and admiration in the heart of his land for those Cuban predecessors, albeit with the anguish of shackled hands. While he was previously an autonomist, he spoke of the sincere hope with which he, along with many of his homeland's free souls, demanded that Spain—through the open treatment of political life—recognize the peaceful emancipation of the daughter who has come of age. He described the suffering and indignation of his people—branded as indifferent only by those who do not know them—upon once again confronting the audacity and insolence of a possessive, despotic nation that is unwilling—at precisely the moment when the suffocated Antilles need it—to transform a nation established entirely, from its roof to its foundation, on official colonial exploitation and exclusive commerce into a hard-working and self-sufficient one. He indicated with due pride—a pride that, were we not Cuban revolutionaries, we would have been unable to share with him—for all the people of his island, who were only just released from the tortures of an inquisition, that the pittance of electoral reform ingloriously called for by the Partido Autonomista Cubano is valiantly rejected as the shameful offense that it is. And his reasoned address—based on his superior knowledge as a leading figure of autonomism—concluded with heated words that embraced truth and prescience, his love of mankind, the faith he has in his people with whom Cubans, arm in arm with the Puerto Rican people, enter into this inevitable war.

 Antonio Vélez Alvarado fervently expressed his allegiance to the cause he eagerly champions, and his affectionate words for Cuba drew intense words from Gonzalo de Quesada, whose presence there was like a speaking heart that—remembering a great man with the same last name who extinguished Puerto Rico's first attempt at independence—promised to wash away his ancestor's sin with the filial determination he has sworn to the liberation Puerto Rico, as he has to Cuba. From the grandeur of youth—and with the rectitude and harmony of passion stoked by reason—Quesada fervently remembered Felipe Goita, the Puerto Rican who was the first to fall wounded for Cuban independence at the feet of Narciso López; Baldorioty de Castro, who was reduced to the deliberate maturing of character that must precede revolutionary action; Eugenio María de Hostos, whose example was followed less than it should have been during the confusing times when—between a war in the interior that was poorly supported from abroad and the vacillating discussions that prevailed among exiled Cubans—the Cuban revolution went off course. And, upon finishing, Quesada justifiably remarked that—with the expertise gained since then and the renewed spirit Puerto Rico brings to the task—no distinction will be made, in this new era, between a Cuban and a Puerto Rican!

 Then, there occurred one of those rare moments of truth that guide man's life through the greed and injustice of this world, like signposts on a path. Memorable and resonant words arose from both reticent men and eloquent ones. Every sentence was a revelation. Every man contributed galvanizing and vital words. In a fiery discourse, Benjamín Guerra celebrated the natural and indestructible friendship between the Antillean islands that confront shared perils. All of Lares spoke—abounding with Cuba's spirit—through one of the valiant men of that glorious movement. Virgilio Zayas Bazán, pale with emotion, declared with brotherly passion that we are now at a time when we must either emulate or improve upon the heroic deeds of our fathers. Lorenzo García, the master of arms, said that he loves his work because it allows him to teach his brothers to be strong and courageous. Manuel Collazo said that he awaits—certain of victory—the redress of so much useless vanity and complacency; that is, redress by revolution. Modesto Tirado, who discerns the truth, recognized today's hopes in yesterday's veterans. Vicente Díaz Comas admired the task of assembling all our forces to combat an adversary whose only power lies in our inertia. José Agramonte, Manuel Vélez, and Regino González found just cause for the campaign's fervor in the palpable indignation felt on the islands—a campaign launched for the first time with collective force against an enemy whose only power lay in its tacit alliance with the country's government, and which periodically unleashed a wrath that now—in the final rejection of that ploy—will explode with all its concentrated power. And José Núñez—demonstrating exceptional command of the spoken word for one unaccustomed to exercising it—described the masked, hypocritical life of those who live affecting an unattainable contentment amidst the misery of a despondent people. He invoked the memory of his father—who brought him into this world without the fundamental freedom necessary to successfully and valiantly fulfill life's supreme duties—and he pledged to return to his homeland so that he could one day say, while kneeling before the grave of the man who gave him life, "I bring you in death what you were not able to bring me in life: *Vengo a darte Patria!*"

Only one voice was unaccounted for among those fifteen friends: the voice of the Partido Revolucionario Delegate who has managed to ignite so much fraternity and trust among our kindred islands. At that meeting of hearts and minds, he lifted his voice—sparkling like the first light of a decisive dawn and as grave as the palpable duty that now weighs upon all shoulders—to honor the reason that must precede—and forever accompany—a passion that can turn pernicious when not measured by the forces at its command and the opportunities to make use of them. He dismissed as unnecessary—as plain as the blood that runs hot in our veins and the sun that warms the earth—the fraternal declarations between our two lands, which exist as a single tragedy with a single heart. He emphasized the robust celebration of autonomist events by those sincere men which did not, incidentally, signal a defeat for our revolutionary plans. Rather, the celebration of the sad campaign that dispatched a small minority to a council in Spain—a minority which the council is not obliged to heed as it believes itself thrice superior in judgment—was an unequivocal victory for our principles without any direction from shrewd revolutionaries. He declared that the most heinous oversight of the elections—which enraged the people with its lies and audacity, and which could not predict the inevitable consequences of that rage—was to place an even greater burden on Cubans and Puerto Ricans who already shoulder the burden of answering the patria in the hour of war, the patria which has been abandoned to conflict by those who have failed to prepare her for it. Finally, he saluted impending independence of Cuba and Puerto Rico, now close at hand.

Doc. 52
José Martí, "March 22, 1873: The Abolition of Slavery in Puerto Rico"
April 1, 1893 (#55)

On April 10, 1869, during the initial moments of their declaration of independence, the Cubans united in Guáimaro declared all Cuban slaves free without reluctance or redress; and that declaration—the revolution's purest, most vital act of righteous glory—emancipated the black man once and for all from slavery, and Cuba from the violence and upheaval that freedmen, who were grateful rather than ashamed of their position, would never tolerate in the republic. When dawn broke, four years later, a peculiar excitement possessed the delegates in the bustling chamber at the *Cortes* in Madrid: an influential and elated group congratulated each other; a small faction fled the halls as if beaten; a brilliant orator spoke illuminated words that seemed unleashed from the heavens and let them fall upon the men gathered there; an elderly general gave a cheer for the republic; and the chairman—pale with emotion and as if tearing a scab from the maternal breast—declared, "Slavery is forever abolished on the island of Puerto Rico." Freedmen would be employed by their masters for three years; three administrators would supervise their contracts; the owners would be paid in "cash" through a government loan of 35,000,000 pesetas from the island's treasury or in government bonds issued from a public loan equal to the price of the slaves; a board comprising government officials and former slave owners would "distribute them;" and, after five years, freedmen would begin exercising their full political rights. In Cuba, masters freed their own slaves with their own hands, even eliminating "color" from the republic's constitution; and they sat former slaves by their side from the very first day of emancipation. In Madrid, four years later—before the other fifteen that would come to pass before the *Cortes* recognized the emancipation of slaves in Cuba—in the *congresos*, Labra and Vizcarrondo, Castelar and Gabriel Rodríguez, and Benot and Balart voted for the abolition of slavery in Puerto Rico; and it was signed by President Salmerón, the Spaniard who proclaimed before the delegates the right of the colonies to secede from the metropolis, "as those who come of age have the need and capacity to renounce parental custody." On the morning of March 22, 1873, slaves in Puerto Rico were emancipated.

The long-anticipated news arrived in San Juan by telegram, and the population received it before dawn. Just after the sun rose, a state of celebration was declared for all of San Juan. *La Gaceta* flew through the streets. Stores opened out onto the sidewalks.

Men left their houses in their Sunday best. Horses, decorated with braids and bows, paraded their riders through the streets. Young people organized the celebration, embracing and communing. There, in the Plaza de Armas, a house was shuttered as if in mourning. Such a livid fist threatened the heavens! But all of San Juan was a banner, draped in damask, and decorated in blue. A sassy young girl in a blue cloak wore a small white rose on one side and a red one on the other. By noon, the people—gossiping and acclaiming as if in a great outdoor church—had already lined up and poured into Plaza Santiago as an impressive whole. San Cristóbal fort looked on from the distance blankly, carved into the clouds in the background, and a ray of sun glinted off a guard's bayonet overhead against the barrack walls. Nobody noticed its old, bare-winged eaves, its puckered ramparts or its crumbling walls. Rather, they only saw the gate where the celebration was being organized—with orators and poets as chaperones—by the leaders of Puerto Rican emancipation: Julián Acosta—his voice tender and his eyes gleaming with a lover's intensity—led and listened to one and all. Ramón Abad, then as quick as his pen, pontificated to a circle of youths. Félix Padial—his blond head raised as in battle—assembled, organized, and showed black men the way, embracing them and kissing their children: "And whoever says that this glory has not been achieved—that these slaves have not entered emancipation without hate—I will tell him he lies!" Two youths of tantalizing beauty—whose gazes resembled the anticipated reward to be heroically won in battle—tossed plucked petals, which a campesino collected in his *yarey* hat from Julián Acosta's balcony. Finally, the procession of both slaves and masters left for the Plaza de Armas along Calle de la Fortaleza.

The music offered in tribute to this celebration played beloved melodies; and the people made their way through the cheering masses with handkerchiefs waving from doors and windows. Leading the way, arm in arm, as if they themselves were the freedmen, were all those who had fought to strike down slavery, whether by speech or pen, by pronouncement or action: lawyers and doctors; young and old; merchants and writers. Then, passed the slaves, with their children by the hand, the men in shirts and britches and the women in white tunics and madras headscarves; some passed naked; one guided a blind man—all marched in silence. A father bent down to kiss his child and continued with the child in his arms. Another, formidably built, held his wife's hand tightly. Others walked in single file—all young men and splendidly dressed. One poor old woman fell to her knees in the middle of the procession. Behind the slaves came the jíbaros, the campesinos who were passing through the city, shirts untucked and barefoot, their *yareys* high on their heads and machetes at their waist.

They did not have to reach the governor's palace because Governor Primo de Rivera awaited them on the balcony of the Palacio de la Intendencia. The Spaniards of the Círculo Hispano Ultramarino—that hostile, broken-down mansion—were crowded behind the railings above the plaza. According to the words spoken from the heart of the republic, Primo de Rivera was dressed as a fellow countryman. The day had arrived—the blessing, the dawn of new days, and the just law with which he would come to govern. He spoke to them candidly—as if addressing a country being born—and his magnificent stature appeared greater due to the virtue and sincerity expressed by his words. A whistle came from among Spaniards of the Círculo, and the crowd wanted to pull the man down over the railing. But the governor asked them to adorn that glorious moment with forgiveness. And, a stentorian cheer to a free Puerto Rico rose up, and—the music!—the people's choir broke out into "La Borinqueña."

The entire afternoon was jubilation. Later, the celebration spread throughout the city. But, no longer did anyone walk alone, because all of San Juan was like one family. Businesses forgot to sell; entire houses were all out on their balconies; and the impromptu dancing drew in any passer-by. A frenetic, deep drumming was heard throughout the slums, those hearts of Africa. Campesinos danced their merengues and *seises* in the purified *batey* to the sound of the tiple and bordonua, the penetrating marimba and the boisterous maraca. A raucous *trulla* sang *aguinaldos* of freedom at their neighbors' doors with the overseer's violin, asking for candy and dances. To a master who told his black slave "You're finally free!" the former slave responded, "I won't be free while my master lives!" One slave woman said, "No, my child, I'll stay with my mistress!" Yet another, seated in a doorway, wept with tears streaming down his face. He cried without knowing why, catching his sobs in the palms of his hands.

The night shone with so much light, and the sight of a darkened anti-abolitionist's house was so extraordinary during the city's revelry that, to the night, it appeared like a stoically perched owl amidst a blazing fire. And, the sentiment and beauty of the celebration—the passion and courage, the music and poetry, the gratitude and eloquence—so filled the cramped house of the Círculo Artístico y Literario that, as the day went on, it turned into a celebration honoring Primo de Rivera. The Círculo's façade was all light; it was so illuminated that its inscriptions shone in praise of that great day. Those inside passionately raised their glasses to the fathers of abolition: to Ruiz Belvis y Acosta and Quiñones, who had gone to Madrid in 1866 using deeply republican arguments to plead for immediate abolition before Spain's Junta de Información; to the Indian, Baldorioty, that steady and poised author of Borinquen's new soul and of what is most admirable and valuable about Moret's law of gradual abolition; to Betances, who escaped the violence of the anti-abolitionists—after the commissioners circumvented him—on the ship he sailed around the republics of the world in search of aid for his homeland—for the soil where he was born—and for Ruiz Belvis. This search consumed his fortune and, later, his contentment. The celebration sprung from an abounding spirit, more than from any agenda. The podium became a stage, where speeches commemorated the great journey of poverty and torment traveled by the enemies of slavery. Patriotic music rang out with new significance. Clotilde Tavares sang the valiant verses of the hymn written to celebrate emancipation. A young man with a fearless demeanor and indomitable gaze came forward—arm in arm with two beautiful women, and followed by the entire multitude—to offer Primo de Rivera the tortoiseshell staff, which the Círculo presented him with as a token of that great day: Sotero Figueroa was that young man, the Círculo's secretary. The Spaniard listened, his hand on his heart, and his eyes full of compassion; the Puerto Rican—that virtuous son of both bloodlines—spoke to him with modest assurance about Captain Correa, the *Arecibeño* who—with might and machete—fell, swimming against the British invaders; and of the brave Amézquita who—when the Dutchman, Boudewijn Hendricksz, challenged him to a singular duel at El Morro—struck down all of Holland. The Puerto Rican spoke to the Spaniard of his country's vigor and independent spirit from his own natural sense of freedom. Primo de Rivera responded honorably; he received the tortoiseshell staff from one pair of hands and a fan from another. On the fan, a woman's hand had artfully written the names of the abolitionist delegates before the Cortes, leaf by leaf. Many a house was still ablaze when, on March 22, the crowd at the Círculo returned to the homes that continued to brighten that hour of justice with a fleeting sense of gratification, for there is still many a slave—both white and black—in Puerto Rico!

Doc. 53
José Martí, "Poverty and *Patria*"
August 19, 1893 (#75)

A crisis has been developing for some time in the United States that, today, ripples across the rest of the world. Sustained in large part on credit, that country does not know how much money it will need to cover its debts or how much to charge its consumers for goods whose price depends on the import tariff currently being amended. Nor will it be able to manufacture profitably under the conditions created by the new tariff. The North does not know where to export the enormous quantity of products it manufactures; nor can it manufacture these products at the low prices and easy installments offered by other countries. It refuses to risk the money it does make to aid saturated industries whose production has no market. Credit is a future concession to compensate for the instability of currency values, the lack of information about the effects of this amended tariff, and the disastrous, oppressive impact of overproduction on a country's trade and commerce. The confusion and threat are such that faith in the new tariff has justifiably died. The anxious creditor demands advance payment from the debtor, who—in a distrustful market with unstable currencies—cannot find the means to pay it. The manufacturer cannot sell on credit; nor does the merchant dare buy with it. All industries—particularly, those related to the production of goods—are paralyzed. The tobacco industry, already crippled by overproduction and the high duties imposed on *capas*, has been among the first to suffer. And that suffering has already lasted a long time; and now the North has turned surly and sullen! Key West, the largest center of production, anticipates—at great expense—the imminent and inevitable hour when the consumption of current inventory will force buyers to make new orders. Tampa, which exists solely from tobacco, barely gets by on the little it produces. Whoever lives from tobacco, suffers. New York is closing its factories or reducing production by half. Beneficent hearts—whether they live among the tobacco leaves or away from them—bleed from what they are witnessing. Some become agitated and anxious; and others seek solace silently.

Certain benevolent Antilleans thought it fitting to call workers to a public meeting with the intent of ascertaining ways to avoid extreme poverty, and invited them to the upcoming meeting. However, *PATRIA* received a document for insertion today that honors both the compassion and patriotism of its subscribers. They are withdrawing the invitation because they do not want the vigilant enemy—who incites and exploits any indictment of a poverty that will never be permitted to reach its extreme unchecked—to use this judicious civic act as proof of the incompetence of the exile communities, to whom the faithful patria turns toward today in the well-founded hope that they will deliver independence. Because all can be forsaken or vanquished! However, the sacred war continues its path without those criminal hands grabbing its heels from the shadows and stopping it short. Cubans everywhere demand it; not just those living in one place. The task is everyone's; and the pledge, to all. The war comes from Key West and from Bolivia; from Cubans in workshops and those in law offices; from those already weary of the apprehensive North and those who live in the South, in kindred lands. The war effort does not languish, nor is it boastful. We are in dire straits, and up to our waists. And there is no impudent or spurious police force capable of diverting its firm, careful path toward this measured and intrepid war. No conflict exists between patriotism and poverty, although Spain—with its concentrated influence—incites and encourages one. No one insults the poor man. And, if some scoundrel were to tell a cigar maker that, by being poor, he has stopped loving freedom—that, by losing his position at the cigar factory, he has lost his brotherly love of man, his desire to find him a happy home in his own land, the pain of his oppressed compatriots' humiliation, and all that comprises the purity and dignity of human beings—that unemployed cigar maker would violently backhand him and anybody who believed that, by losing his job, he has lost his honor. Tabaqueros, outlaws: the Indian, Benito Juárez, cast an empire into the sea and fought poverty with honor, reclaiming and securing his land's independence!

The insertion by those noble Antilleans reads as follows:

TO CUBANS AND PUERTO RICANS
RESIDING IN NEW YORK

The undersigned, sharing the legitimate alarm of all the industries affected by the current panic in the United States, have felt obliged to convene a meeting with the Antilleans in New York as a precautionary measure in confronting the poverty that may fall upon our homes. But, a most profound analysis of the situation, the precautions already taken unbeknownst to us, and the advantage that the patria's shrewd enemies have attempted to gain from the meeting's mere announcement, force us to withdraw the invitation. Our poor will not be neglected. Nor shall the enemies of our freedom be able to benefit from a civic act—a simple act of compassion and foresight—by presenting it to the Patria during these days of uncertainty as proof of our inability to contribute to its independence.

The meeting announcement—born from the purest part of our heart—was enough for Spain's watchful government agencies to begin exploiting it in Cuba and Puerto Rico as proof of the chaos and desolation of the exile communities from whom they seek relief. We cannot lend ourselves to such cunning. We are poor—and we could be poorer—but we will find ways to bring relief to our homes without allowing this bitterness to steal the faith those oppressed peoples have in us. Never have we felt the Patria's poverty more than in these moments when we see how unstable foreign soil is under our feet.

We will never allow our actions to give the enemy the right to present the exile community as incapable of bringing salvation to our oppressed islands, especially when they have placed all their faith in us.

And our decision to suspend the meeting is based all the more on our certainty that, if misery enters our houses, the banished will not want for a roof over their heads, nor the destitute, for shelter. The Antilles shall be free and our poor brothers in New York shall be sustained by their brothers of all classes and colors.

New York, August 22, 1893

GABRIEL P. LÓPEZ. –F.G. MARÍN. –FEDERICO PACHECO. –F.J. PRIETO. –NARCISO GARCÍA. –SILVESTRE BRESSMAN. –S. PIVALÓ. –ISIDORO APOCADA. –ANTONIO MOLINA. –ROSENDO RODRÍGUEZ. –ARTURO SCHOMBURG.

Doc. 54
José Martí, "The Revolution in Puerto Rico"
January 6, 1894 (#93)

What must a people who find themselves expelled from their own land do? How must they feel? Where must true Cuban revolutionary sentiment draw from—besides its enduring roots—but from the task of properly setting all its cutlery on the table, of positioning all its seats in the workshop correctly, and gaining all the public and private benefits from the growing hoards of wretched and worthless Spaniards pouring out of Spain? Who is the blind man who does not see this? And, in this same spirit, Puerto Rico rises up. Just read what the valiant Luis Muñoz Rivera wrote in Ponce's *La Democracia*. He has certainly not been a garrulous and imprudent defender of his patria's rights; rather, until today, he has been both judicious and fearless. It reads as follows:

A new class of police, clerks, functionaries, and administrators has already been published in the official newspaper, according to government leaflets.

And now, not only are the names of corporals and sergeants appearing, but so are the names of soldiers in the Volunteer Corps, and even those of private citizens who are active in the military.

The system is brilliant, if backward.

The municipal juntas of 1840 had more authority than the ayuntamientos of 1893.

The governor is very polite and sociable, quite genteel. But he is forcing us to lose the ground we gained over half a century.

Palacio executed his inquisition on the country; first, Dabán crushed its spirit.

So it seems that in these American lands the arbitrary and anomalous should always be expected.

The general has no right by law to appoint municipal officials; but appoint them he does. And, silence in the ranks!

Enough of leaving the sons of our country with barren wastelands, the toil, and the dregs of that speculative banquet!

What more can spineless fools—who never knew how to take what was theirs—aspire to?

A Spanish author, Rosario de Acuña, wrote these masterful verses:

Freedom, freedom! Rome, is that what you crave?
That is not something you pray for; it is something you take!

But, if PATRIA recalls correctly, she is not Spanish: she is Cuban.

Doc. 55
José Martí, "The Third Year of the Partido Revolucionario Cubano: The Soul of the Revolution and Cuba's Duty in America"
April 17, 1894 (#108)

Through a direct vote by all members and elected officials, this venture in the Americas, because of its scope and spirit, enters a third year of action in systematically fomenting and aiding all its genuine elements through structures which insure that the full force of executive energies unite in achieving that singular aspiration—the Cuban and Puerto Rican revolutions for their absolute independence. How beautiful it is to see, in the chaotic aftermath of a long and hopeless exile, men of all conditions and degrees of fortune—from war and exile, from both far-away countries and from the North—unite under one deliberate, disciplined, and dynamic task and stand triumphant over the indifference and disillusionment that stems from the continuous company of Cuba's misery. And, with the free confirmation of the party for independence, all—from Jamaica to Chicago—defend their patria through the promise of readying her in exile for the redemption that she herself cannot prepare while mired in fear, despair, and the agony of her enslavement. How beautiful it is to see the union of a people's disparate factions—a pueblo whose own children sometimes unjustly doubt her, either from ignorance or pride—in the sacred exercise of their rights and raise proof, before the eyes of the downhearted, of the success of diligent work and the just treatment of souls, leaving parricidal tyranny anxious and spiteful. But this unquestionably glorious spectacle would be vain indulgence and pernicious debility if ordered by blind and fearsome devotion, if the sober knowledge of the patria's reality— its vices and virtues—were not the source of power for the revolutionary organism; if it were not rooted in a judicious willingness to adapt the structures of a budding pueblo to progressive phases and to the actual, local reality of a freedom

that strives and triumphs. How beautiful it is to see the efforts of the Partido Revolucionario Cubano united by the dignity—never tainted by intrigue, flattery, or entreaty—of its members and the officials who have led it; by the equity of their stated purpose, which does not find the country's success in the predominance of one class over another in the new state or the intentional humiliation and poison contained in the very concept of classes. Rather, success lies in the full individual fulfillment of the legitimate rights of the people, which can only be diminished by indolence or abuses by those who exercise them, and the nearly fleeting opportunity for the enslaved Antilles to rise up and take their place as a nation within the American world before the disproportionate expansion of the most powerful region of the Americas turns into a theater of universal greed those lands which may still become their neighbors' gardens and the world's moral compass.

Every public political party must tailor itself to its people, and politics is—or should be—nothing more than the art of guiding, with due sacrifice, the diverse and opposing factions within a country so that the various elements in the *patria* who have equal rights to representation and prosperity may live without conflict and without the unjust indulgence of the impatient few or the culpable denial of the need for social order; and, so they may live with the freedom to aspire or resist, which can only be safeguarded by abundant rights and the continuing peace of having those rights recognized. *Un pueblo* is not the will of a single man—regardless of how pure he may be—nor is it the childish attempt to capture within a human organization the naïve ideals of a celestial spirit, which would make him but a blind graduate of the unfettered university of the clouds. *Los pueblos* are made of hatred and love—and of more hatred than love—except that love, as the sun that it is, embraces and encompasses everything. It strikes down what greed and privilege have accumulated for centuries with one jolt from its army of souls, like the fury of one compassionate soul. Nations are built with these two forces—expansive love and repressive hate—whose civic embodiments are interest and privilege. Compassion toward the less fortunate, the ignorant, and the dispossessed should not go so far as to drive or encourage its aberration. The recognition of negligent and malignant forces in society, which—under the epithet of "order"—conceals the rising rage of those whom yesterday they had at their feet, should not go so far as to shake hands with impotent pride and incur the certain wrath of mighty freedom. *Un pueblo* is the configuration of diverse wills—vile and pure, sincere and inauspicious, hindered by timidity and hastened by ignorance. Much must be overthrown, much must be attacked, and much must be sacrificed—one must descend from fantasy, set foot on the ground in the *patria revuelta*, hang sinners by the neck, and dress the offense in rags or burlap; one must wring virtues from the deepest recesses without misjudging them because they come dressed in humble clothes or rejecting them because they come accompanied by riches and refinement. The danger to our society lies in conceding too much to the hardened colonial spirit, which will continue burrowing in the very roots of the republic, as if the nation's government were the natural property of those who sacrifice themselves to serve her with less, yet are closer to offering her up to the foreigner and compromising the independence of American nations with the surrender of Cuba to hostile and contemptuous interests. And, another danger could be lurking for Cuba: the cowardly exaltation of the resentment and turmoil latent in the wounded or needy, which the arrogant colony leaves in its wake; the elevation of the unspeakable influence of hatred and contempt for a nascent democratic society in those who—in the exercise of their sacred liberties—disarm or oppose it. Sever the hand from whoever undermines a human right, whether it be the domineering man who undermines it for the ignorant one or the ignorant man who undermines it for the domineering one. But these efforts will be less dangerous in Cuba due to the fusion of the country's opposing factions in a healing war, the dignity that the freedman gains through the friendships forged in death with yesterday's master, and the peculiar social leavening that, distinct from the inherent tasks of a nation, will make the masses of émigré campesinos and slaves rise up in the republic—hand in hand with doctors, the rich of times past, and the heroes of the revolution—after twenty-five years of toiling and reading, of speaking and listening to others speak, as if in a continuous and mindful exercise of the people's potential within the republic. And, while a reluctant and incompetent segment—the least efficient—of old Cuban gentry corrals itself vilely and unjustly against this new people of culture and virtue, of free minds and fertile hands, another segment of the Cuban gentry—much more powerful than the former—has lived among the turbulent masses. It recognizes and directs their potential. It has worked side by side with them; it has grown to love them and be loved by them. And today many a doltish charlatan roams the earth in a battle of wits, denying authority to many a child of this natural maternal soul, which has been forged by toil and character! In Cuba there is no clash between a toothless Neapolitan gentry and the nation, which is inherently as moderate as it is exceptional, and which joins the fieldworker, the slave, and the poor tradesman—now aware of their rights and the risk, in old Cuban society, of overextending all their creative value and compassionate energy—in mutual respect for the common effort and with the purest hope for commensurate freedom. The genuine desire to participate in a just life and occupy valuable labor in a land healed by its dead springs forth decisively from the Cuban soul—a land that is sheltered by the shadow of its heroes and watered by a mighty current of the tears it has shed. The hope for a righteous and dignified life today equally inspires yesterday's prudent gentry, who see the danger in undeserved privileges for worthless men, and Cubans from humble lineage, who, in the building of their own character, have discovered an invincible nobility. The Cuban people do not expect from the revolution what the revolution cannot offer. If it were to enter from the shadows bound to either the humble or the proud, the revolution would be a crime, and it would be an outrage to die for her. Sincere and attainable, the revolution today has the strength of all prescient men, the worthy gentry, and the cultivated masses: from generals to lawyers, from tabaqueros to guajiros, from doctors to businessmen, and from masters to freedmen. She will triumph with that spirit and, without it, she will perish. This hope—just and pure—is the soul of the revolution. With equity for all rights, with mercy for all wrongdoing, with vigilance against all subversion, and with loyalty to the hopeful rebel soul that inspires her, the revolution has no enemies because Spain has no power beyond what she is given—despite the doubts that they wish to instill in our hearts and the offensive, insolent adulation for concerns that suspect or humor our unbiased, admirable men—by those who, under the pretext of devotion to the independence of their country, abhor whoever fights for it. But when it seems inevitable, they make sure to crown their noxious and impotent heads with these sacrifices, which they neither respect nor share. To tread across a land, one must first know it well. We know the land on which we tread. We will be saved by our loyalty to the homeland—which has placed her hopes for liberty and order in us—and by a vigilant tolerance for those who have shown themselves to be incapable of offering force and structure to their country's rebellion. May this be our slogan: Freedom without fury. The majestic display of our union, the joining of free wills in the Partido Revolucionario Cubano, would be worthless if—understanding the country's internal conflicts, its wounds, and how to heal them—the party did not realize its greater mission in these crucial times and its place at this universal crossroads. But Cuba and Puerto Rico will achieve a very different kind of freedom in a very different era, and with much greater responsibilities than the rest of Latin American nations. It is necessary to embody the force of greatness and be worthy of fulfilling its duties. The world is full of friars who denied Columbus the prospect of defining a new course—full of them, indeed. What is important is to not sit with the friars, but to embark with Columbus on his ship. And we already know the story of the man who set out with a flag as a warning for men to fear the locomotive: the locomotive arrived and, if the man with the flag had stood in front of it, he would have been seen furiously panting alongside the tracks or smashed to a pulp. One must anticipate and march in step with the world. Glory is not for those with hindsight, but for those with foresight. We do not merely want to shed light on these two verdant islands, which still contain divergent elements. Rather, we want to save and serve them, so that the capable and brave factions present—less distant from each other than those in ruthless and ravenous European societies—may secure independence for the spirited archipelago facing the potential greed of a strong and more powerful neighbor; so that the archipelago which nature has placed at the world's crossroads, and which history will lead to freedom at the moment when they embrace on the open field of combat and the hemisphere is prepared for communion. The axis of balance of the Americas [*en el fiel de América*] resides in the Antilles, which shall be—if they remain slaves—the mere carcass of an imperial republic's war against what it sees as an envious and competitive world preparing to deny them power, or an insignificant Roman fort in the Americas. But, if they become free—and worthy of such status by the dictates of just and diligent freedom—the hemisphere will stand as the promise of equilibrium, of independence for a still-vulnerable Spanish America, and of honor for the great republic of the North. The expansion of its territory in a free hemisphere—unfortunately, already feudal and distributed among hostile factions—will find a more secure prominence than in the ignoble conquest of its less-powerful neighbors and the ruthless battle that their possession would incite against those world powers seeking global domination. The new life of the redeemed Antilles must not be fashioned hastily, but with an awareness of centuries past. This great responsibility to humanity must be assumed with august apprehension. The righteousness of the cause will take us far, or we will fall all the lower for having been unable to achieve it.

We are putting an entire world in balance, not merely liberating two islands. How petty is everything; how petty is small-town gossip, the sharp prick of womanly vanity, the hollow ruse of being accused of demagoguery, and the adulation of the masses before this project of hemispheric foresight! True greatness lies in securing friendship among the divergent segments of a continent through the vindication of men struggling for their pueblos' independence, and preventing unnecessary conflicts between a tyrannical America and a world allied against its ambitions through the free life of a prosperous Antilles! We know how to build a ladder to the heavens from squalor. With our sights set on high, we shall spill and mix our own blood—in good faith and with pure intent—to procure this spirit of nations forged from the glory of virtue; from the fury of rights which have fallen due to the abuses of just aspirations.

The mission will set the stage for the Cuban people to proclaim their independence without hatred and direct their force with moderation. A failure in Cuba is a fail-ure for the Americas, a failure for contemporary humanity. Whoever stands today with Cuba stands for all time. She, the sacred patria, demands singular attention and serving her in such a glorious and onerous hour fulfills her dignity and majesty. This venerable duty bolsters us with strength of spirit and guides us as a constant star. It serves as a beacon of perpetual vigilance that will shine forth from our graves. We must attack our far-reaching problems with singular reverence and an honor that extends as far as their reach. It is with this reverence that the Partido Revolucionario Cubano compassionate-ly and confidently enters its third year of life, convinced that the independence of Cuba and Puerto Rico is not only the sole means for securing decorous well-being of free citi-zens through the just task of the inhabitants on both islands. The necessary succession of historic events will also safeguard that independence from the threats against a free Antilles, protecting the vulnerable independence of the free Americas and the dignity of the North American republic. To the cowardly and weak: we demand respect. To our great men: March onward! This task is for the mighty.

Doc. 56
José Martí, "Old and New History: Salvador Brau's *Historia de Puerto Rico*"
January 26, 1895 (#75)

There is still much to learn about our America. And, everything that comes to light proves how abject—how crude and exposed, how abandoned and accidental—are the foundations of poor countries. So much so, that they must rise up from that carnage and incompetence. They must rise up against those harquebuses and escape from those Molossian hounds—from that rapacious greed and persecution—in fits and starts. They must rise up until they have books and machines, and the customs and respect that give order to the world. The Americanist, Salvador Brau, traveled to Spain in search of new material for his *Historia de Puerto Rico*—he already knows all there is about his Indi-ans—and he has written it in his authentic and sumptuous Spanish. Now, he examines the sources of colonial history, which has always been as it is today: dismal and inept.

Section 4

MARTÍ'S LEGACY

Doc. 57
Sotero Figueroa, "Immortal!"
June 25, 1895 (#167)

To Estrada, Guerra, Quesada, and Fraga:
    Did he die?
    "Yes!" says the implacable reality that sees no more than the hard truth.
    "No!" says the sovereign thought that hovers over that which is pitiable, makes us live in the past, and fortifies us for the future.
    Infamous persecution and treasonous bullets were able to wound the frail and fragile body of José Martí, but his indomitable spirit—his great, majestic soul propelled by concern for his enslaved Cuba, and which, for this reason, rebelled against all bondage by breaking the chains that confined him to his earthly prison—rose to the heights of immortality to live on in time and history. His lessons on patriotism became all the more irresistible, for they were sanctified by his exemplary evolution—not his death—and inspired zeal in this apostle so that he might rigorously fulfill the promise he made to "serve as the carpet" under the feet of the saviors of his patria, to offer himself in sacrifice to the Cuban republic.
    The mercenaries of implacable Spain, the illegitimate holder of that most beautiful portion of the Americas, did no more than grant the apotheosis of this martyr and offer a salvo of honor to his immortal soul when they fired their rifles from their beastly dens in the forests of Remanganaguas upon that virtuous man who passed them by smiling as he brought a triumphant message to his brothers in exile.
    To those of us, the forever faithful, who shared his hopes and concerns and suffered with him along his bitter path, Martí has not died; he lives on with ineffable life, and we feel him more than ever in our modest hearth. He is an exceptional friend who is but absent from us; yet wherever we go, our thoughts overflow with the immensity of his name, with the remnants of his benevolence, and with the splendors of his pen. From him they came and to him they shall go, these vehement affections that subordinate the head to the heart; these intimate letters that were not penned for indifferent readers, but for those select friends who admired the agitator, followed the activist, and supported the teacher. Here at my desk are so many of Martí's precious relics! So many invaluable letters in which he poured out the tenderness of a friend, the energy of a combatant, and the longing of a patriot! Scattered around the small room, there is the bust that calls to mind the young man in his prison garb, with shackles around his ankles, a pick in his hand, and the invincible stare of a tenacious warrior; the album in which his portrait occupies the most prominent position; the figurines of two Mexican peasants—man and woman—which he brought for our little ones after his last trip to Mexico, and which we treasure not for their

intrinsic value, but for the astonishing esteem he showed us. Even while elaborating such vast plans in his mind, he still found time to be gracious with his most modest assistants, raising them up to his stature. On the shelves of that low library stand the books that extol his liberalism and, in those first pages, confound us with the indulgence of his dedications; the books drafted in the throes of exile, and those which we will leaf through when wishing to converse with him, the books that will be forever faithful to our affections and will forever respond to our queries with an unflinching pronouncement, with that desperate originality that constitutes his inimitable style—fervid for Cuba and affectionate to the Americas, which he called *our own*. There, above the library in a conspicuous pyramid, is the complete collection of *PATRIA*, from that first twin issue that we sent him—signed by all those who were present as the press cast forth those first two copies of the newspaper that would come to raise the revolutionary flag—to the latest edition, which seems orphaned without his diligent labor, but which is still saturated with his spirit and will continue to be so as long as there is a Partido Revolucionario, which, better said, is until Cuba becomes independent.

Outside of our quarters, in our social relations, in the public square, with professors and department chairs, among the consuls and diplomats, at the speaker's podium where he achieved his greatest and most noteworthy triumphs, how can we not see Martí wherever we may look if his commendable deeds continue to reveal him to us? How can he be taken for dead, if his exploits as an activist and liberator are still afoot?

. . . .

This is not the appropriate time to chronicle his life in full detail, as it was a life full of both adversity and fortunate events; a life that continues today to spread his name throughout the Americas and has wrapped all Cuban homes in a shroud of mourning. Nor would the narrow columns of this newspaper be sufficient space to pass judgment on his patriotic, philanthropic, and intellectual work. Martí shall be examined and judged within the pages of history books or biographies; he strove to restore justice and pride in the Cuban republic and shall not be overlooked.

Restless, passionate, vehement in nature, he could never remain passive or indifferent when faced with any iniquity. A soul tempered for sacrifice and with a clear vision of human perfectibility, all nefarious plundering or any denial of rights would find in Martí a most formidable and decided adversary. This was how he was seen, from his early years, just as reason gave direction to his intelligence and provided him with two very powerful tools for combat: the pen and the word. When little more than a boy, he was ready to go head-to-head with the colonial despots and brand the all-powerful governor's brow with fiery words and valiantly champion the idea of Cuban sovereignty. He escaped death by going to jail. After proving himself as an orator to his executioners, and quite an eloquent one at that, he was able to persuade them that he was the exclusive compiler of that "criminal" publication, managing in this way to save his close friend, Valdés Domínguez, who was implicated along with Martí. During his time in prison and due to the consoling law of compensation, he learned more about the human heart than he could have from any book, and counseled that, in this implacable fight that entrenches the criminal against society, the latter is too often found guilty of the former's monstrosities.

"I have seen in prison," he would say during those enchanting conversations, irresistibly seducing all those who listened to him, "such disgruntled virtue, such hasty abnegation from a lack of learned temperance, that I could never count those days spent in chains among my darkest. As time advances, all around me I have encountered countless criminals, so sure of their impunity, whom I judge as much more fearsome than those in the Spanish prisons."

Such affirmations were accompanied by examples, so many admirable examples that they would not be possible to enumerate within these pages.

Later—we must now be extremely succinct—he wrote a pamphlet about the horrors of prison in Cuba. He went to Spain and graduated with a degree in Law. He advocated for Cuban independence, going so far as to proclaim it a republic. He opposed those Cubans in Madrid who opted for a federation and abandoned the idea of independence; and upon witnessing the initial suppression of public freedoms, he sought asylum in Mexico, where he became a playwright, journalist, and representative in a workers' congress.

From Mexico, he went to Guatemala, where his talent and prestige grew, holding positions as a professor of the History of Philosophy, First Principles, and Literature, also writing for newspapers and the theater and was the main attraction at all intellectual affairs.

He returned to Havana just as the Zanjón Pact was being signed, and the following year he was deported to Spain on charges of conspiracy. He escaped imprisonment and fled to New York; but his frank and vehement character, ready and longing for sacrifice, did not adapt well to that environment. He traveled to Venezuela, where his name was already known among the great figures of the Americas, and served as a university professor in Literature at the Colegio Villegas, created a school of rhetoric that produced excellent students, and founded the *Revista Venezolana*, which died as soon as it was launched, since it rightly exalted Cecilio Acosta upon his death, whom Guzmán Blanco had squeezed to the point of misery. He demanded, both through threat and flattery, that Martí give in to the politics of the conceited leader, but the response of the proud Cuban was to ask for a small loan from the wise Arístides Rojas, with which he bought passage to New York, and the following day he set sail.

Upon his return to the great metropolis, he further refined his noble and admirable talents. Just like Heredia, who knew how to sing of sublime concepts in writing, he became a professor with many distinctions at a young age, as well as a journalist, news correspondent, poet, translator, publicist, consul to many South American republics, Washington diplomat, benefactor, activist, man of vast erudition, and, above all, an orator. He was an orator so well-spoken and irresistible, of such fluid diction and fecund talent, that he would speak hour after hour without ever taxing the enthusiasm of his audience, or revealing any signs of weariness or fatigue.

. . . .

His most accomplished work, though—which continues to resonate in posterity and places him among the world's great liberators—is having stoked the Cuban protest to a potency even greater than that of the Spanish aggression and having preached through his word, restraint, and martyrdom this heroic awakening of the Cuban people to a life of independence. That indelible and sickly body was transformed on the podium and inspired even the most incredulous and disheartened to answer the call of duty. He united disparate and displaced elements in exile; he erased the animosity and distrust that had endured as an inevitable consequence of earlier unsuccessful attempts. Sparked by his prophetic and fervent speech, prestigious leaders once more contemplated victory; the troops of the Ten Years' War again filed into the ranks and impatiently awaited the voice of command; the sons of enterprise—those contributing laborers—shored up their faith, and, with more vigor than ever, they hunched over their work tables and divided their day's wages between family needs and the no-less-sacred demands of the homeland. Revolutionary clubs sprung up wherever there were groups of Cubans or Puerto Ricans, throughout the whole of the American republic, and the war, systematized around harmonious and substantive bases, did not appear as the dream of some overheated imagination or persistent neurosis, but as an easily remedied problem if the perseverance and intelligence of Cubans abroad were united with those on the island through a sense of common cause and magnanimity. The revolutionary treasury grew; clever and skillful communication was established with Cuba; on surprisingly swift and efficient trips, emissaries came and went, eluding all danger. Martí shared intelligence with leaders known to be scattered among friendly lands and returned from those trips more hopeful, but, oh! with evidence on his face of how he sacrificed great portions of his life for his country, which continued to grow more noble and more idolized.

To those who were still weary, to the impatient who believed that a dormant people or those ravaged by the opiate of speculative colonial government could rise up in revolution in a few short months, he would say without presumption or arrogance, "Can one do more than what one has done?" "If Cuba should will it, then war will come about, for the tree of freedom has the deep roots that are needed to grow lush and prosper."

Echoing Prada, the abstruse Peruvian writer, he was able to add:

We are fallen, but not pinned against a rock; mutilated but not impotent; bloody, but not dead. A few years of sanity, of storing up our strength, and we shall see ourselves ready to act effectively. Let us be a perennial threat, as it is we can be nothing more. With our indignation ever flaring and the austere attitude of our men, we will keep the enemy in a

state of constant anxiety, we will force them to spend their gold on massive stockpiles of armaments, and we will exhaust their mettle. One day of revolutionary progress in Cuba is a night of terror in Spain.

How to keep pace with him in this frenzied excitement, moment after moment, in that truceless battle that gave no repose to the pen, rest to the body, or calm to the spirit! There were occasions when three or four writers, with the delegation's secretary at the helm, were barely able to keep up with him as he dictated correspondence from his office.

As for public dissemination, it was *PATRIA*—the newspaper that was born along with the Partido Revolucionario Cubano—that served as his warrior *palenque*, his doctrinal pulpit, the prestigious flag that was unfurled, waving in the winds of righteousness at the zenith of true democracy. "Nothing of hate, nothing of caustic or personal controversy: respect to all honorable opinions, and disdain or indifference to Cuban sinners for their wickedness, arrogance, or lack of foresight." These were his exhortations to those who shared his work drafting compositions. How many sleepless nights, after days of rigorous labor! And what painstaking demands were made of others so this vehicle for his revolutionary ideas would equal the pace with which he produced his speeches and articles! Martí, who was of a sweet, serene nature, only turned severe when he believed that others did not pour into *PATRIA* all the effort that he himself demonstrated in decisive moments to ensure that the project did not falter. Thus, the soul of the agitator was poured into that publication, more objective than an encyclopedia, so that it could serve as a copious arsenal of deeds and details for the history of a free Cuba.

War finally broke out in the beloved patria—against the wishes of a minority of the island's obstructionists, who were encouraged by the dubious proceedings of the Spanish government—thanks to the tenacity and orderly preparation of the Partido Revolucionario Cubano. Those of us who admired and feared for Martí reminded him, through respectful intimations, of the advantage of staying in New York. "I would hold a sad image of myself if I were to remain here, when my brothers in Cuba are spilling their blood for the cause that I have preached. Those rash individuals, who slander so freely, will not be given occasion to say that I propelled my people to sacrifice while remaining beyond the range of the enemy's bullets." This is what he said, with a resolve that did not warrant a reply, and he kept his word, offering up his life for Cuban independence.

. . . .

In his social affairs, José Martí was irresistible. He coupled a beautiful heart with extreme affability, and all those who met him instantly became his friends. The poor, the lowly, and the unfortunate were always given support, warmth, and affection. In his ranks, there were neither categories nor hierarchies: Men were valued for their ability to captivate through diligence and aptitude, and there was no sign of affectations or pretenses about his abilities. The most astute observer had to surrender to that honorable relationship between his words and his actions. He was virtuous, with the simple kindness of one who had suffered greatly, and he knew that a helping hand at the right moment was the best strategy in any noble cause. For this he was venerated by his people, who followed him without hesitation wherever he wished to lead them, all the while receiving a tribute of admiration from those who were wise enough to appreciate him. The afflicted who sought out his presence left comforted. He often made contributions to his friend's coffers, and in his delicate way of performing such charitable deeds, he brought no shame to the indigent. Overwhelmed by work, restless, and feverish—yet always polite and friendly to whomever disturbed him—he could not refuse anything that was asked of him; thus, on many occasions, he was unable to do all he promised, but, even so, no one ever left unsatisfied. Those who suffered found Martí by their side, fully sharing in their grief. He would conduct himself at a stately table the same as he would at the table of the humble laborer who had invited him to a criollo meal. He could have been rich, but he scorned wealth by continuing to be the voice of Cuban independence. He corrected without insult; he was firm without arrogance; quick to praise, slow to censure, and an effective and benevolent teacher to his working-class brothers, as proven in his unforgettable lectures to *La Liga*'s estimable followers. Is it any wonder, then, that his name today is followed by a chorus of praise? This great figure was never free from fierce, incisive contempt! Moreover, what did it matter, if this would prove necessary to better assess his glory? An acclaimed author once said, "Give me envy as great as a mountain, and I will give you a reputation as enormous as the world."

History, just and impartial, begins where life ends.

For José Martí, the doors to eternity have been opened. He prevails today with inextinguishable life. He nourished the lands of a free Cuba with his blood, and his spirit is now infused into the army of liberators and guides them to victory.

Onward to a triumphant revolution! Immortality is our destiny!

Doc. 58
J.M. Terreforte, "Our Brother"
June 25, 1895 (#167)

He died... So they say... Yes, it's true, they killed him.

The enslaved Cuban lands have been watered and nourished by his generous blood.

There, in Santiago de Cuba, they have deposited his body in a deep vault of a cemetery.

The officials in Spain are rejoicing, and their assassins are handsomely rewarded.

"With the death of Martí, the death of the revolution," exclaim the wielders of those armies of human machines and hope to drown the people's aspirations in blood.

Foolish illusion!

The body that they have smitten is not José Martí's. That body is of organic material; it has been delivered to nature's laboratory for decomposition and submitted to the laws of physics and chemistry.

The saviors of nations, while they live, lend great service to their cause through the dedication of their physical and intellectual energies. Even in death, they continue serving, for their mind's content does not consist of degradable matter. If they are lowered into their tombs as martyrs, the grandeur of the gods is theirs, and the continuation of their work is like a religious calling to their people.

People of the Antilles, let us mourn José Martí!

It is natural to bereave our dead brother, even though he has bequeathed us an invaluable legacy.

Spaniards! Rejoice in his death, congratulate his murderers, and reward them.

It is fitting that you revel in this small remuneration, for soon you will see the gnashing and gnawing of teeth that await you, and you will feel to what good use we have put our brother's legacy.

Doc. 59
[Condolences Upon the Death of Martí]
The Clubs: Club Borinquen
June 25, 1895 (#167)

Office of the Secretary
Esteemed Editor of *PATRIA*
My Dear Sir,

I have the honor to inform you that during this club's meeting on June 19, in which we covered certain important points related to the patriotic work to which we are all so committed, it was proposed by our honorable chairman, Mr. Terreforte, and unanimously seconded by the assembly gathered there, to announce our club's condolences in this party's publication. We do so, as an entity, representing the proud Puerto Rican element of the Partido Revolucionario Cubano, upon the grievous death of our sublime hero, the indefatigable and brilliant apostle José Martí, who died on the battlefields of the Cuban revolution. He went to that noble island, on behalf of his brothers, in search of the patria that they lacked, overcoming the storms that obstructed his path to deliver it to them, after witnessing the culmination of this worthy endeavor as he dreamed it— happy and impervious to the wrath of fate feared by others after a sudden defeat—by virtue of the seed planted in her fertile fields by that illustrious gentleman, a seed that will not die along with his body, but which will come to bear fruit far and wide.

Still latent in our memory is his natural and persuasive language, in which we still hear the voice of his magnanimous deeds. Noble and enthused at the podium, he spoke with the great authority and faith of a prophet, and the ardor of his political convictions were tempered by his benevolence and the sweetness of his character. Wherever his steps led him, they left behind a blazing trail of brotherhood and affection. His face was rather pale and serene; a certain handsome youthfulness still remained on his half-bald brow, and, with his lively and altruistic imagination, he fashioned his demeanor through the grace of his smile and his hunger for sacrifice.

Our father has not died, though. His spirit will continue to serve as a guide for our people as they emerge from the shadows of subjugation and rise up, bathed in light and framed by the brilliant dawn of freedom. He will lead us safely to harbor without crashing our ship against any rocks, unlike the great ship capsized by man's perversity; he will govern our movements from his celestial mansion and shower upon us manna and honey from heaven; he will continue his self-sacrifice for the independence of the people whom he passionately loved like his own children. When he heard the rustle of insatiable tyranny in the thick of Cuba's forests and his people calling out to him for help with an anguished voice, he heeded their voice, and he will likewise continue to do so in the stormy hours of doubt and hesitation.

If Cuba, with the death of José Martí, has lost her prescient father, then Puerto Rico—a sister in slavery who also bears upon her white dress the stain of humiliation—has been deprived of her loyal and tender friend; a friend who believed, in his feverish love for the freedom of oppressed peoples, that all were under the protective wing of his benevolence.

Puerto Rico is in mourning. The Puerto Rican Martí has died. Venezuela laments the loss of her favorite son; they have just lowered the Venezuelan Martí into his tomb. Argentina is inconsolable over the premature death of one of her kin; the Argentine Martí. In a word, all of the Americas are grieving, because Martí did not just dedicate his entire life to the redemption of his patria, rather he employed it in the service of all the peoples of the Americas.

May you see fit, esteemed Editor, to publish this communication in your courageous newspaper as a genuine expression of affection from your fellow Puerto Rican revolutionaries whom this club represents.

Secretary,
D. Collazo

Doc. 60
Sotero Figueroa, "Inaugural Meeting"
July 20, 1895 (#171)

If it is true that from the great heights of splendid light the spirit of once-great redeemers—now free from the innate agony of this mortal coil—shines and revels radiantly in the triumph of their sacred work, then José Martí—the Creator, the Word, the august spirit who offered his body to the tyrannous Spaniards, the example of his civic duty to the patria he adored, and the resonant relegation of his name to the pages of history—must have enjoyed last Thursday night when the ineffable rapture of an Almighty God breathed a handful of magnanimous ideas into the minds of an enslaved people and how these ideas were then transformed into a devastating torrent against despotism. These ideas surged forward, with the irresistible push of heroic valor, creating a new republic in the heart of the Americas. He must have enjoyed a most lofty triumph since the revolution he predicted, organized, and nourished with his blood on the field of battle is still alive today, stronger than ever; a revolution that is impossible to wrest from Cuban soil without converting it into a mountain of rubble, enough to entomb the remains of all patriots-in-arms.

Who did not think of him on the eighteenth of this month, that memorable night in Hardman Hall, when we celebrated the inauguration of our new delegate? There, in that same room where his rapturous speech so often echoed—always inspired, always fervent, so full of love and harmony, even when addressing empty seats—he received the most coveted glory that any mortal, in the role of political reformer, could aspire to after his brief time on this earth. He was in the thoughts of all those present because of his ideals on patriotism and freedom, in the minds of all the orators because of his passionate and persuasive lessons on eloquence, and in the hearts of the most modest attendees because of his evangelic preaching, which never lacked solace and hope for all the unfortunate of the world. Is it any surprise that our eyes teared, our arms trembled, and our minds filled with an irrevocable determination for victory or death upon hearing his name resound numerous times within that site made holy by that purest of ideals—liberty?

There, within the realm of immortality, the lovers of glory—for whom sacrifice for one's country is the most sublime act of heroism—will see Martí at the heart of the world's greatest emancipators, presiding over that Areopagus with history's greatest titans, and he will be newly christened "the Selfless One." And, not because he individually shines brighter than all the rest, but because he embodies their most salient traits. Washington gave him the simplicity of his demeanor; Bolívar, the sagacity of his foresight; San Martín, his love for independence; Sucre, his passions free of rivalry; Hidalgo, his surrender to sacrifice; Juárez, his unassailable constancy and rectitude; Morazán, his warrior temperament; O'Higgins, his passion for glory; Toussaint, the humble—Toussaint, who rises up out of the despondency of slavery and defeats the great armies of Napoleonic France—his love for all those woefully subjugated and his magnanimity for all those conquered. Like Jesus, the great model of Christianity, Martí can present himself to posterity with unbloodied hands and a heart brimming over with good deeds. How then not to envy and exalt this Cuban Nazarene, who fell valiantly clutching his messianic cross and commanded admiration even from his implacable executioners. May that majestic spirit so named José Martí live on, hereafter, through the adoration of his people, in the apotheosis of his admirers, and in the impartiality of history.

As if enveloped by the aura of this man, the new delegate—the venerable Tomás Estrada Palma—appeared on the proscenium. He is a man who uproots his fellow citizens from their peaceful lives in Central Valley to serve their patria while in exile, and he accepts the people's mandate, fraught with responsibility, for he was never one to withhold his efficient and selfless assistance in girding Cuba against Spanish dominance. There is none other who has as many merits as the noble and conciliatory Estrada Palma to continue the work of Martí. A man far removed from passions, he most urgently sought the help of his compatriots to see this transcendent work, to which we are all committed, rise to its zenith. The rectitude of his life; his exemplary, steadfast patriotism; his simple and accessible concern for Cubans, without any class preferences; his charitable and uncompromising action throughout his years of exile; his kind character, which bore neither the smallest of grudges nor the greatest of exaltations; his revolutionary lineage, of which he was never ostentatious, even if his ten years in Cuba at the highest ranks of public office were well known; his impartial legislative statements, which did not favor any of the factions that destroyed the republic, nor did he fall prey to the shameless flattery of the Spanish authorities when he was taken prisoner and jailed in a Spanish fortress; and his duty and sincere devotion to the Cuban people—in which he acknowledged neither class nor color, only patriotic brothers in liberty—gave Estrada Palma an ascendency over the public, the likes of which have never been seen before. The main themes of the night's speeches were about Estrada and Martí, in beautiful conjunction, and they were both exalted with resounding accolades. The Ever-Living Father, glorified His late, illustrious son; and similarly covered the brow of this thoughtful delegate with an unfading halo—this commendable man now charged with continuing the work of independence.

What more could be related from that meeting in which the new delegate was appointed that would not pale before the flood of eloquence, sparks of genius, and patriotic declarations that have been previously mentioned? We will, henceforth, be brief.

The chairman of the New York Cuerpo de Consejo, Mr. Fraga, honorably presented to all those in attendance the new delegate, who with moving phrases recalled the exceptional, patriotic virtues of his predecessor. His good will was evident in his administrative plan, which was presented in broad brushstrokes to those in attendance. General Rafael de Quesada mourned the loss of the fallen hero, commended those still fighting, and announced his plan to lead the fourth expedition to liberate Cuba. Enrique Trujillo recalled and exalted the last battle of the Maceo brothers in which General Santoscilde died, praised the memory of Martí, and advocated union and harmony. Carlos Manuel de Céspedes, the younger, was the happy representative for the youth of 1895, who will be worthy of the official seal of the youth of 1868. Eduardo Yero declared that he had broken his pen and would abandon his role as orator until the right to be free has been won on the fields of battle. Ramón de Armas made a heartfelt display of Cuban patriotism and paid homage to Martí's memory. Dr. Fernández Ibarra recognized the righteousness of the Cuban revolution and proved, with statements from President Cleveland, that the current democratic government would not be hostile to our independence. Colonel Agramonte, with his peculiar speech, full of such characteristic and unexpected turns of phrase, condemned the loathsome Spaniards, whose war offends the modesty of our women, and who unleash convicts from their prisons upon the defenders of a nation. Gonzalo de Quesada, Martí's dear disciple, in a ninety minute speech, outlined what we might call the "Master's Bitter March", from when he left Santo Domingo until he fell, overtaken by the ferocity of his enemies; he hailed the heroic soldiers and made an ardent appeal to the patriots gathered there to support and contribute to the war, an appeal that quickly resulted in a substantial sum amassed upon the chairman's table.

The most thunderous applause of the evening, though, erupted upon the presentation of Mrs. Caridad Agüero de Pichardo, the heroine from Camagüey, who defied the brutality and savagery of the Spaniards by carrying from Havana to Puerto Principe the artillery with which Camagüey—ever insurmountable—used in its revolution. Upon her return to Havana, she was subjected to a most disgraceful search, which belied the proverbial and much exalted Spanish chivalry toward women. From Havana she recently arrived in New York, and upon being introduced to the exile community present at that solemn meeting, she asked the patriots, in return, to actively contribute to the expenses of the war, so Cuba may hasten her independence.

The radiant attendees were so numerous that it was necessary to turn away many families due to a lack of space in the room.

May the new delegate now have the glory of bringing to a majestic conclusion the many aspirations that spur him onward.

S. Figueroa

Doc. 61
Sotero Figueroa, *"Club Los Independientes to José Martí"*
July 20, 1895 (#171)

New York, July 18, 1895
Esteemed Editor of *PATRIA*,
We, the members of the Club Los Independientes, are compelled to pay tribute, in the name of our club, and offer our deepest regards and condolences to the memory of the great Cuban patriot, José Martí. We are confident that this eulogy will find a warm reception within the columns of your newspaper, in which he also fought for the triumph of Cuban independence.

S. Figueroa
Ramón de Armas

CLUB LOS INDEPENDIENTES
IN MEMORY OF JOSÉ MARTÍ

We gather the remains of his thoughts, as we cannot gather the remains of his bones.

To praise the great liberators, to pay an homage of gratitude and admiration to the champions of freedom, to manifest our inexpressible pain caused by his proud and majestic death, the writer with his quill loses his sure footing, and neither the lyre nor the chisel is enough to convey the profound emotion felt by those who follow in his footsteps and are energized by the resplendence of his magnanimous ideas.

There are pains that one hides in the most remote, unexplored crevasses of the soul, much like tears that never reach the eyes and slowly build up behind floodgates, brimming with indignation and overflowing with desperation. There is no community in the world that better embodies the vast history of bloody affairs like the already legendary community of ill-fated Cuba. If one wished to find the exact personification of this pain, it would be, without a doubt, in that bloodstained pilgrim who searched since time immemorial—carrying his people upon his back across foreign and inhospitable beaches—for an obscure corner fit to nourish his country's hopes and silently lament the ruin of her altars and the relentless massacre—which continues most wicked, inhumane, and unavenged—of the most precious flower of her noble and robust people.

Cubans have seen, like a modern-day Tantalus, the tree of civilization blossom, yet its ripened fruit lay beyond the reach of their timid hands, like the proverbial traveler who wanders the world with a bruised flower unable to unite the remains of his ruined lands. Their poets die of disenchantment in the misery of that strange world, if not already silenced by the nefarious blow of the vicious executioner; there is no light or environment in which their untouched, tropical lands may flourish; honest work does not find space to hone its noble faculties; nor can we, in the end, gather from our beloved lands the lost and entangled bones of our august martyrs, the saddest of condolences.

We have been quite accustomed to our pale companion—Misfortune—and we believe that our heart, without bursting, can still make room for the mournful memory of yet one more martyr.

Ah! but this man . . . this man sat at our table and shared our miseries, our anguishes, and our hopes; he lightened our sorrows, dressed our wounds, and livened our spirits; he relinquished the throne of his innate greatness to suffer and fight with the people; and he gave his hand to the fallen, vigor to the weak, and encouragement to those who wavered. He identified greatly with the sorrows and aspirations of this humble class for whom he has preserved, like none other, the glorious lamp of patriotism forever burning, and his death has brought these people to their knees—the souls of the workers who professed great love for him broken into pieces.

No longer in vain, this titan fills us with the immortal breath that has blocked the bullet of the traitorous despot. By pausing for a moment to pay tribute to the memory of José Martí, our gushing tears are not a symbol of weakness or faintness of heart, but a purifying ablution that obliges us to forever hold fresh in our minds that solemn vow to forgo any respite until we wrest his glorious remains from the loathsome tyrants and inter them in the pantheon of our heroes under the clear, serene sky of our free and independent homeland.

Martyr, poet, father, freedom fighter, you have not died in vain! Just as you spoke of those who proceeded you on this glorious path, we will gather your luminous spirit, even if we cannot presently gather the remains of your mutilated corpse; and we, *Club Los Independientes*, who had the glory of counting you among our members and receiving your inspiration, will not be the last to bathe in the light of your divine example and avail ourselves of your immortal teachings.

For *Los Independientes*,

Ramón de Armas
Sotero Figueroa

Section 5
PUERTO RICANS

Doc. 62
José Martí, "The Poet Marín"
April 23, 1892 (#7)

One cannot speak lightly of the poet Marín because he infuses in his easy and elegant—albeit at times flowery—style the pains and contradictions of his agitated existence with fire and artistic modesty. In Puerto Rico, he loved freedom; in his ongoing exile, he continues incorrigibly to love romance. With one blow, any of us could be toppled like a house of cards for the grievous sins of our burning youth. But what this blow does not create in us is such elegant and swift style, such strong and firm verse, and such personal and natural treatment of the subjects in his dramatic poetry. He is enamored of compassion, through which all pain is consumed; compassion, the aristocracy of the soul.

Doc. 63
José Martí, "Ana Otero"
August 20, 1892 (#24)

How is it that *PATRIA*, in its love for sincerity and delicacy, does not adorn its desks, normally draped with death and anguish, with roses to honor that person who as both an artist and a woman—an art form in itself—is, above all, sincere and delicate? Is she not the extraordinary protégée who would greet a greatly moved Marmontel in the triumphant Parisian concert halls; is she not the pianist of refined taste, equal in bravura and lightness to those within the ranks of the great artists of *L'Événement* in Paris; is she not the interpreter of such remarkable range, who mesmerized Barcelona with the majesty of her Liszt, the nuance of her Saint-Saëns, and the richness and mystery of her Schumann? She is the loyal *Borinqueña* whom we acclaim, who draws neither haughtiness from her exquisite music with which to disdain her fellow patriots nor dry and vulgar drudgery with which to dull and devour the most beautiful aspects of art, but carries her people with her, those who raised her, sent her to Paris, and generously opened the door to the world for her. Thus, the piano has never acquiesced to her so tenderly as when—without the pomp of the salons or the incentive of profit—she sits at the piano surrounded by her friends and countrymen, and also by the sunsets, serene nights, lovely hills, and her early dreams from Humacao. Her hand wanders at times, as if hovering over an orange blossom; and at times, as if remembering what can never be forgotten, indignantly punishes the piano.

   She received from her beloved father—along with written music—romance and passion like a lunar tempest—common in fervid and tender souls, where music, like a silver ray of light, first chills and then softens the soul, making the silent body forget its confines.

She does not seek the prosaic or theatrical from countries whose art does not rival the craft and refinement of her native school, but from the city that tunes and corrects universal genius, whose elegance our American genius has cultivated, by her innate restraint and refinement.

She has not taken theatrics or jealousy from her profession, or the mercenary desire that consumes the wings of music; rather, she beautifully adorns herself with simplicity, without letting the art which gives her life—much like a chosen soul— freeze, from pure servitude, the poetry that spills out from an innocent heart and that goes through the world wrapped in a white veil. She is faithful to the truth, to friendship, and to her homeland.

From this—as well as from her pious and sincere soul— comes the gift of understanding and interpreting the most varied and sought-after composers, just as music is born of real emotion or the desire to extract a painting from nature. She extracts the grievous love of the shepherd, of the withered flower, and of the butterfly; or penetrates the immense night, where the German musician rides, smitten by his lovers. Her range does not rise out of indifference, but from her ability, rare in illustrious musicians and poets, of finding beauty—whether clog or patent leather—wherever man—cheerful or sinister—has felt a flash of light in his eyes or a surge of blood in his heart. They say that the generous hand that wrote her country's heroic *danza* for *PATRIA* —the danza that moves the Puerto Rican, like an order from his conscience, to battle and honor—weaves subtle lace upon the keys, and through whose threads emerge sparks of starlight, heroic cavalcades, and glimmers of dawn.

In the next issue of *PATRIA,* we will indeed publish that heroic danza, "La Borinqueña," a work that stirs her Puerto Rican compatriots and whose expressive lyrics enrapture the heart, along with a few of the notes about the noble Spaniard, which she wrote upon that majestic staff of solemnity.

Doc. 64
Betances, "The Voice of a Patriot"
October 8, 1892 (#31)

In these moments when hearts overflow with declarations of divine faith in the redemptive cause, and the tenacious and hardworking soldiers of the past war show themselves disposed to continue the fight for independence so as to make amends to the spirits of the fallen heroes who blessed the homeland by sacrificing their lives; in these moments of vigorous emulation, when the youth with poorly suppressed impatience await the solemn occasion to prove themselves worthy sons of the beautiful Antilles, who will no longer be slaves and who will find their call to duty in the expressive eyes and loving lips of amorous women; in these moments, lacking is he who, yearning to flee an insupportable dominion, tries to cast the opinion of the Antilles as that of the path of annexation to a foreign nation, as if man's will or desire could make what is different by nature somehow similar or harmonious; in these moments, it is beautiful to hear the consoling voice of he who combines the merits of an immaculate name, made great by his virtue and knowledge—like a patriotic consequence never refuted—and reaffirming the most sacred dogma of independence without punctiliousness or reservation. It is beautiful to hear he who places himself resolutely on the side of the Partido Revolucionario Cubano, to such a point that together they will be able to revitalize the most hardworking, the most indomitably tenacious, or those of a heart most accustomed to setbacks; but not allowing the dignified protest to get the better of him by refusing to accept any half measures, he says inflexibly to those who are wavering and timorous: *To be or not to be.*

We are referring to Dr. Betances, the illustrious advocate for Antillean independence, whom neither the weight of years nor the ingratitude of his native country—which is listlessly awakening to its sense of duty—can subdue. He addresses a Puerto Rican friend—a staunch defender of independence—in a letter so fraught with patriotism and resolution that we can only extract a few paragraphs. Although we risk violating the private nature of the letter, we dare to assume this responsibility because we know that these excerpts have been chosen with predilection for the readers of *PATRIA*, and we are protected by the belief that men like Dr. Betances do not have private matters that cannot be divulged.

I have here the eloquent paragraphs that we have obtained:

"I have read your letter with intense excitement, and it has been of great comfort to me, for within it shines sovereign faith, more powerful than all despotism, and it alone is capable of securing the triumph of our sacred cause. I already have my reward, friend; and so too will our fallen: Ruiz, Basora, Lacroix, Dávila, Brugman, Broavín, Parrilla, Díaz, my unforgettable companions, and so many others. As they gave their lives for their nation, they were able to see—as do I—that the seed has not perished and that the lush tree of liberty lives on.

"They too will find it in the eloquent manifestations of the Cuban and Puerto Rican colonies, in those who, with sadness, turned their gaze back toward their country, exasperated to find it hypnotized as always by tyranny; in those like the incorruptible and unbreakable Hostos; the gallant Rojas; the venerable elder Andrés Vizcarrondo, who was the first of his precursors; and Terreforte, who lived and was silenced there amidst all of you, and who was, among the revolutionaries of Lares, as loyal as he was valiant and as constant as he was discrete. There are no eulogies that ought not to be showered upon that humble patriot.

....

"You are those patriots who are dedicated to that cause, which surely will not be pursued in vain, but which demands the greatest valor in committing oneself to a life of sacrifice, suffering, anguish, and disappointment, and which is capable of seducing burning hearts, as only the deep northern snows can, and stirring up, as only a mother's love does, the most desperate feelings of generosity.

"This tremendous battle that irreversibly penetrates great souls, like that of Martí, is worthy of all of you, with Martí as your leader; and glorious victory will be yours, all yours, because you come—after our forefathers who appeared no more than simple, imprudent dreamers—to establish a reign of justice among the Cuban and Puerto Rican peoples and replace the shameful humiliation of slavery with the rights and dignity of free men. Tell Martí to take full advantage of my name, if he so wishes, for the country's benefit, and, *if necessary, to expose my name to the infamy of posterity to help save our patria. To such extremes would I go!*

....

"With my most heartfelt interest, I continue to follow your efforts and wish you the most beautiful compensation possible for this most sacred of duties: revolution and, in turn, the glory of a free and independent patria.

"With an indivisible union between Cubans and Puerto Ricans, triumph is ours! The Puerto Rican proclaims, "¡Viva Cuba!" The Cuban exclaims, "¡Viva Borinquen!" Both sing out together, "¡Vivan las Antillas!" By your deeds a glorious patria awaits you, one that is free, happy, and independent!"

....

When these concepts are read—so potent and enthusiastic that they appear to have blossomed in the heat of spirited youth and with such profound intention that it gives flesh to both idea and word—we are proud to count in our numbers such an invaluable compatriot, and we believe our efforts grow nourished by the words of this pure apostle and model of Antillean freedom.

Doc. 65
José Martí, "Ana Otero, February 3"
January 21, 1893 (#46)

For her modesty, her goodness, and her generosity; because she loves the truth, her people, and her art; and because she always colors one love with the accents of the other, *PATRIA* has a special fondness for Ana Otero, the acclaimed Puerto Rican pianist, none other than she who was praised as never before by the severe Marmontel. How could one forget her music—soothing while vibrant—after hearing her during the Colombian night of the Sociedad Literaria Hispano Americana, her finest moment of triumph? She shone like a sister to all men, and the laurels at her feet resembled violets.

On February 3, the general public will finally hear her, and there is no doubt that, for us, the event will be unforgettable. She will receive applause from many people from many countries, which is befitting all artists who so honor their art; but how can our dear sister not recognize above all the rest the fiery and proud applause of her fellow Puerto Ricans and Cubans?

Doc. 66
José Martí, "Ana Otero's Concert"
January 28, 1893 (#47)

It is not just to a renowned artist, all truth and fire, who our American family in New York prepares to show boisterous proof of our affection on the night when she first regales this Northern audience with her talents. It is to Ana Otero, the generous pianist, who is found wherever charity prevails, and whose performance is nothing less than noble. It is to our dear Puerto Rican sister. In truth, such a genuine admiration, such an affectionate curiosity, and such an uplifting program have rarely taken place within our celebrations. Who other than an artist of great courage and with such a remarkable heart would offer to accompany Maestro Emilio Agramonte, who is as sincere in his art as he is in his life?

Doc. 67
Betances, "With the Revolution"
September 23, 1893 (#79)

From his prestigious Parisian retreat and with his patriotic fervor never dampened by the snows of his many years or the disappointments he has suffered, the venerable Dr. Betances addressed this noble letter to our hardworking compatriot from Key West, Francisco María González.

Steadfast Cubans or confident revolutionaries never need encouragement to continue carrying out their duties at all times, but it has undeniably fortified their enthusiasm and revived their faith in their dream of Antillean independence to see hoary combatants—those who in their best years volunteered their efforts, intelligence, and fortunes to their patria—stand together at this solemn time to steel up their reserve and avow their courageous support once again to the rallying cry of the people who truly yearn to be free: REVOLUTION.

Here is the letter:

Paris, [sic] 20, 1893
Mr. Francisco María González
Key West

My dear compatriot,

I had the pleasure of receiving your letter dated July 2 and the issues of your interesting newspaper, *La Revolución*, which you brought to my attention.

I extend my gratitude to you for all these items.

In spite of the years and in spite of my sufferings—such as the grave illness I have recently endured, which unfortunately leaves me without the necessary strength to complete all the work to which I am committed—I always enthusiastically read the ardent writings from the pen of those brilliant, young Cubans and Puerto Ricans, who are determined to bring forth what your newspaper announces every day: *La Revolución*.

There is no other road to salvation for our country. After being exiled from Puerto Rico in 1867, Ruiz Belvis and I, along with Basora, would say to our compatriots, "Spain cannot give what it does not have." Today, after twenty-six years of expatriation, battles, disappointments, and all manner of pain, and without my companions who have nobly fallen, I can repeat while invoking their memory: No, a thousand times no! Spain cannot give what it does not have, and there is nothing for Cuba and Puerto Rico, save one true and unique opportunity for salvation: *REVOLUTION*.

In Chile, there roams another great Antillean patriot—Eugenio María de Hostos—and I am sure of his consent if, in this affirmation, you unite his patriotic voice with ours.

Onward forever! And if the youth live to see our patria free, we, the elders, can die with the hope of such a happy future for those who continue fighting and believing that the blood of Céspedes and Parrilla, of Agramonte and Bouvín, of Goicuría and Brugman was not spilt in vain for the independence of the Antilles.

Onward!

Cordially Yours,
BETANCES

Doc. 68
"José de Celis Aguilera"
January 16, 1894 (#94)

One of Puerto Rico's noble freedom fighters has just fallen, never to rise again.

He was persecuted and condemned, and he never wavered when called to make sacrifices for the rights of his native land. As part of that admirable group of valiant Puerto Ricans, those who are framed by blessed halos, such as Baldorioty, Acosta, Quiñones, Blanco, Padial, Morales, Goico, Alonso, Corchado, Géigel, Sancerrit, Martorell, and the many others not honored at this time, Celis was the most frank, active, selfless, and generous. Small in stature, with dark features and a kind character, quick to respond, and sure in his attack, he was always positioned at the forefront of the harsh battles that were waged against the colonial power by the Partido Reformista, whose flag heralded the abolition of slavery together with the recognition of the individual rights of free men. During these times of savage government beasts, he suffered most from the severity of this power, he who lost so much time in the vicissitudes of a public life rife with ingratitudes and setbacks. Never did he hesitate to sacrifice his substantial fortune for the cause of Antillean reparation.

When his candidacy for Diputado to the Spanish Cortes was first announced, his enemies who did not wish to see him vested with such responsibility, knowing he would work arduously against all colonial iniquity, burned down his sugar refinery in the town of Ceiba. At that moment, he was in the island's capital, and, upon hearing of the catastrophe, far from removing himself from the battlefield where his presence was so necessary, he said with patriotic conviction, "It does not matter: I can rebuild it." And the campaign continued unperturbed, and he did not allow the smoke from his precious, burned property to blur his singular focus on contributing to and executing the action with which he was charged.

At the Spanish *Cortes* in 1873, he acted in line with his own reformist history. In the September 18 session of that year, referencing a comment made by the Puerto Rican Diputados, above all, to abolish slavery in Cuba, and after having already declared in his strident, yet sympathetic voice that all those who pertained to the Partido Liberal Reformista would defend abolition, he concluded his response in the following manner:

I believe that one of the glorious commendations of this republic's government is having decreed the abolition of slavery in Puerto Rico, having reached a part of this glory under the previous reign of King Amadeo, when this proposal was first presented; as it is, I believe that this republican chamber has committed a great error, one which it will probably regret, and it is the error of not having either raised or discussed the proposal of the abolition of slavery in Cuba.

The entrenched reaction in the metropolis to Pavía's *coup d'état* ruined Puerto Rico's Partido Liberal Reformista, and he had to withdraw indefinitely—much like the current Autonomist party. An agreement between Conservatives and Liberals brought back these reserve factions to an active conflict; Celis, along with Corchado, Acosta, Ferrer, and Alonso, showed himself a supporter of assimilation into the metropolis, acknowledging equal political rights and administrative decentralization as a foundation, slightly less than what the modern Autonomists call for. He was the prestigious leader of the current liberal evolution. In the municipalities, in the Diputación Provincial, in the press, and in public forum, wherever his support was needed, he lent it, with as much competence as compassion, not skimping on the new liberal campaign the little that remained of his fortune after the fire destroyed his property in Ceiba.

Ungratefulness came to hurt him when he had retired to private life, not wanting to follow his party in this newly evolved Autonomist form. In reaction to the attacks that his unwarranted challengers fired at him in the press, he returned to defend his political honor and, in a pamphlet teeming with numerous irrefutable facts, he stated:

I have chronicled my history so that certain acts remain recorded, and sensible men may judge by my conduct if I came to the Partido Liberal seeking glory, profit, honor, or popularity. This history was earned, as few other men in my district can say, from more than thirty years of sowing good deeds, and of rectitude and honesty, not due to politics. My name was used as a banner—I can say this with pride—to form the Partido Liberal Reformista, because many important men, who in 1869 were either on the side of the conservatives or retired, joined the ranks of the Liberal party when they received word of my candidacy for the Diputado Provincial. I came to work for my country in good faith, and I have made as many sacrifices for her as I could. I did not come to live off of politics, because I have never been a member of a party, nor could I become one for political utilitarianism.

If I have not invested in the scientific approach to politics which others have so readily adopted, I have worked unparalleled in the service of the party and have made more sacrifices than anyone.

The Partido Liberal Reformista has accomplished nothing wherein the presence of my contribution is not evident. In this province's abolition of slavery and in the creation of the Instituto Provincial, I have given preferential service to no one, except to my distinguished friends José Julián Acosta, Francisco Mariano Quiñones, and, concerning the former, the fallen Segundo Ruiz Belvis. Forever an abolitionist, I have felt no shame after reading the reports of the Junta de Información, as neither my signature nor that of my friends from Fajardo is to be found within those protests, which were written in such a way as to have been the cause for the persecutions that we in the opposition suffered shortly thereafter.

These affirmations remain ever alive and present because they are true; and the name José de Celis Aguilera will always be remembered as one of the great friends of Puerto Rican freedom.

He never joined the Antillean independence camp, like Ruiz Belvis, Betances, and Hostos, but what should that matter? He led Puerto Ricans as they took their first steps toward freedom, and he was one of the many who cleared our path, fraught with thorns and thistles. We march onward, and if we advance more and more resolutely, it is because we have traversed the most fatiguing part of the journey upon the shoulders of our forefathers.

Doc. 69
José Martí, "Farewell to a Sister"
March 2, 1894 (#101)

With heartfelt modesty, surrounded by brotherly respect, cherished as one of their own even by those who did not know her intimately, devoid of any impropriety, and present in times of misfortune, Demetria Betances, the sister of that magnanimous Puerto Rican, lived in New York for some years. Only goodness knew the way to her doorstep. She, who was unacquainted with pompous ways, knew all too well where unhappiness dwelled. She did not want to live in her enslaved land, or in any land of suffering, even if it masquerades under the name of liberty. She embroidered our flag—procuring its gold trim through her own toil—placed her own bouquet of flowers on the orator's podium and on the hero's tomb, and encouraged those who looked exhausted or bewildered with her principled counsel and her passion for freedom. Work was her pleasure; her trade, mercy; her honored brother, her idol; Borinquen, her heart. Fire consumed her because in life she was a pure flame that no storm could cause to tremble or extinguish, and she wished to die like that flame. The crematorium received her body, but Cuba and Puerto Rico now hold her legacy. Three offerings were placed in the conflagration: the crown of Faithful John, evergreens with a white ribbon; the gift of friendship from Dr. Henna, who said, "From your patria, Borinquen;" and an arrangement of Cuban flowers from Club Cuerpo de Ingenieros.

Doc. 70
"Puerto Rican Revolutionaries"
August 25, 1894 (#126)

Within the pages of *PATRIA*, in the not-too-distant future, a series of biographical articles will be presented on the Antillean revolutionaries from Puerto Rico who would not resign themselves to live under the yoke of Spanish domination and who, with acts of proven courage and exceptional selflessness, inscribed their names in the eternal book of martyrs who died for the cause of Antillean independence.

In this period of reflection and preparation, of emulation and distributive justice, the names of those who gave special meaning to the redemption of their enslaved island—Cuba's sister in pains and aspirations—must not remain among the forgotten. They should rise to their glorious plenitude, basking in the admiration of foreigners and the gratitude of the nation for which they sacrificed everything. In this historic evocation, we take note of a comforting fact, one to which our Cuba, in her glorious decade, has already borne witness: distinguished champions from all the free Americas fighting so extraordinarily on behalf of Puerto Rican independence that it earns them a place among the free-dom fighters of the highest echelon.

In this work of justice and reparation, there is one who has helped us greatly with his example and competence, one who currently has earned the greatest acco-lades along with the veneration and gratitude of all Puerto Ricans. He is none other than the indomitable Betances, whose life of love and sacrifice for Antillean inde-pendence is but poetry, and whose revolutionary energy was never overwhelmed by numerous setbacks and misfortunes.

He states, in an admirable letter:

Those who judge our revolution in Lares with disdain do not know of the dangers that stemmed from that uprising, all that it accomplished; the results it achieved; the pains, the suffering, the deaths, and the vigils that were held; nor are they at all aware of what the exiles themselves suffered or the recognition they deserve. For the world is plagued by ungratefulness, and the arrogant forget that this revolutionary act is nothing less than the greatest demonstration of dignity that Puerto Rico has achieved in four centuries of egregious slavery, stamping the abolition of slavery and independence for the island into her very flag.

The gallery of Puerto Rican revolutionaries shall eternally showcase the venerable patriarch Andrés Vizcarrondo; the ironclad Rojas; the resolute Millán; the generous Ezequiel Díaz; the intrepid Brugman; the valiant Braoín; the brave Padilla, who inspired such great respect that even his enemy (the lieutenant who ordered the bullet that killed him) carried the hero's bloodstained handkerchief as a sacred relic; and many others who should not be forgotten—Ponce's Lacroix, as cheerful in the face of adversity as in his hilarious verses; Terreforte, a rebel by all accounts; Derieux, with his bellicose character; and the discrete and Herculean Sandalio Delgado from Cabo Rojo, whom no Spanish regiment could have withstood if only arms had arrived in time; that is to say, if only the patriots had not had to precipitate their role in the plot. Sandalio died in a foreign land; Dávila—the scourge of tyrants—ended his days far from his beloved Borinquen in New York; like Basora, the ardent and faithful activist; like Ruiz Belvis, who was dignity made man, the eloquent mouthpiece of the exiles from Lares living in Valparaíso; and Hostos, the talented architect and fiery orator, who makes a pilgrimage through the republics of America, apportioning glorious days to his homeland.

After invoking such revered names and offering his invaluable cooperation in the task that we now undertake with such enthusiasm, the noble Betances, exiled to Paris, exclaimed with melancholy bitterness:

Ah, do not make me remember such pain and toil merely because there are those who claim not to know about this great, redeeming work. This was the virtue of the nation, the virtue of the entire Puerto Rican people, all of whom were conspirators and suffered for today's freedom. Come, oh sacred day of revolution in the Spanish Antilles, and I will die content!

Regarding my biography, I have decided for some time now to refrain from writing it until I myself am able to present my defense—if I am to have such an occasion—and if not and I am forgotten, so be it.

No, one cannot forget that name which was bestowed with so many noble titles and so commemorated by his countrymen: Betances must never be omitted—even if his modesty would deem it unworthy—from the honored portrait of Puerto Rican revolutionaries. What of the immortality of history if in its pages the most prestigious, outstanding defenders of an oppressed people are overlooked? Justice must be made complete if we truly profess the ennobling veneration of memories, and *PATRIA* is called to do just that at every opportunity.

We honor those who are deserving of honor.

Doc. 71
José Martí, "The Figueroa Press"
September 8, 1894 (#128)

We should not speak well of those of our own stock, or those whom we love and consider dear to us—regarding the merit that their assiduous work affords such honored talent, because righteousness is taken for flattery according to the world's shameless perspective. The award-winning biographer and energetic Puerto Rican poet, Sotero Figueroa, our brother in hope and in toil, is so highly esteemed for the order and innate quality of his reasoning, for his elegant and concise speech, and for his active and edifying patriotism. We will speak no more of him or his excellent publishing house than what was printed in the latest installment of Figueredo's Venezuelan periodical, *El Americano,* in an issue full of contemporary variety and interest and which is quite dear to us:

The fact that we were waiting for the opinion of the public on this matter—which has now become manifest as justified and unanimous—is why we have not previously called attention to the acumen, clarity, and integrity evident in El Americano. This is due to Sotero Figueroa, who, as owner of Imprenta América—which publishes El Americano—and as the expert typographer he is known to be, employs all his skill to present our newspaper as the best of its class. The greatest recommendation for Imprenta América is to review the pages of El Americano. These words are nothing less than a tribute to our friend Figueroa in the form of a public ovation.

Doc. 72
Betances, "To Puerto Ricans"
May 4, 1895 (#160)

Betances—the Puerto Rican revolutionary and untiring activist for Antillean independence, whose spirit has not been broken by the many winters he has known—has seen Puerto Rico begin to stir from the stupor that overcame her since the valiant revolt in Lares. He now stands unyielding in the French capital and directs these words of spirited encouragement to his Puerto Rican compatriots:

Onward! In Puerto Rico, and in Cuba as well, the very spirit of the people has been infused with revolution. There are no Puerto Ricans, from *Puerto Rico* herself, who are not revolutionaries at their very core. Furthermore, there exists no illustrious Spaniard of good faith who does not concede our legitimacy.

Onward! Is Puerto Rico small? What of it? Corsica is even smaller and she produced Paoli; even smaller is Margarita—just a fourth of the size of Puerto Rico—and she produced Arismendi, and even her women surrendered their jewels to take up arms in active combat, and this new Sparta tossed the Spanish army into the sea.

Onward! Onward! What are you waiting for? I am at a loss. I feel compelled to repeat this to everyone I meet: sacred Liberty never descends from heaven like a virgin of peace, and she does indeed demand that all those worthy of her be willing to spill their blood for their homeland.

And what do they ask of Spain? For almost thirty years, the unforgettable patriots Ruiz and Basora—and later Hostos and Rius, along with many others—have joined my voice in proclaiming the defense for the Antillean revolution—'Spain cannot give what it does not have'—and today's Spain is the same Spain that has always been, where a military uprising of cadets is squelched by the government and journalists are dragged before war counsels.

Alas, here we are at the end of the nineteenth century!

Let us remember the free men who were slain on honorable fields for their patria: the heroic Parrilla, Braoín, Brugman; and those who died in exile, which is yet another field of honor: Basora, Ruiz, Lacroix, Dávila, and so many others.

While Cuba gains glory and obliges foreign nations to admit that 'in her bloody fields she has reached the most sublime manifestations of human heroism,' what are you waiting for?

It is time! Raise funds, amass arms!

Onward! Onward! Onward!

¡Viva la Revolución!
Fraternally yours,
BETANCES

Doc. 73
"The Forrest Incident"
August 3, 1895 (#173)

We reprint the following article from Caracas' *El Republicano*. This article is worthy of our reader's attention for the noble principles of hemispheric solidarity it espouses. We are pleased to announce that our hardworking friend, Mr. Forrest, is free of all Spanish persecution and machinations, and it is likely that we will have the pleasure of welcoming him here shortly:

Mr. Gerardo Forrest continues to be confined at Villa de Cura, punished for his sympathies for the Cuban cause. They have yet to prove any action that may in some way be considered an attack or hostile aggression toward Spain and, if he did indeed confirm his separatist inclinations in his statements, he asserts that nothing he formally declared could effectively be used to serve Spain's interests.

Thus, they punish him for harboring the same sentiments found in all the peoples of the Americas; for considering the mandate—sanctioned by Spain itself—a righteous one; for the mandate—now a right—of Latin American independence, now the basis of our international doctrine. They punish him for what ought to have immunity—his thoughts—which roam free within us so long as they do not proceed down the path of action, and which exists and develops despite and against our will. They exist and toil despite and against our will, and we are left without the power to contain their incessant and spontaneous activity. And yet another of our civil rights is violated, for this confinement is a severe punishment that goes against public interest, and one cannot be punished in Venezuela without first being tried and found guilty.

If Venezuela would share a border with Cuba, Mr. Forrest's internment may have been demanded after presenting proof of his hostility toward Spain; but La Guaira is more than six hundred miles from the closest point on the island, whose coasts are guarded by a fleet of warships and in whose territory martial law has been declared. This provides the government with exceptional means for rescinding not just the various forms of aid received from men on distant shores, but also those who aspire to unite the island's considerable population, who were at the point of joining the revolutionaries.

The reciprocal obligations between friendly nations impose on us a neutrality of facts, but they do not extend so far as to inhibit our ability to think, or as to make us declare ourselves bastards and denounce our own ancestry, which is exactly what inspires the Cubans to raise their emerging republic. Either the Cubans are right, or we continue to be insurgent rebels.

On the other hand, whereas Spain has not been able to punish even a single man from the United States—a strong nation full of men who have openly supported the revolution on the island of Cuba—it is indecent, to say the least, that they punish peaceful citizens in Venezuela.

Doc. 74
"Cuba in Paris"
March 21, 1896 (#232)
Our latest correspondence from Paris provides a detailed account of the banquet held in that city by our compatriots to celebrate the revolution's first anniversary. We translate the following lines from *L'Intransigeant*, a noble and courageous friend to a free Cuba:

Last night a banquet was held at the restaurant Marguery, organized by the Cuban community in Paris, to celebrate the first anniversary of the revolution, which has continued to decimate the forces of the Spanish monarchy, day after day, for the better part of a year.

Never has the world witnessed a more courteous and animated gathering, replete with enthusiastic freedom fighters. As dessert arrived, our friend Dr. Betances, the patriarch of this event, gave the floor to our collaborator Cosmo, who expressed L´Intransigeant editorial staff's concern for the brave Cubans who fight not to win posts, but liberty; and he read the following letter:

Letter from Henri Rochefort
My Dear Friend,

You know how seldom I go out and that my work, which I find impossible to abandon, chains me to this newspaper and shackles me to my articles, but I will not allow this great day, February 24—the anniversary of both the French and Cuban revolutions—to pass without expressing, on behalf of myself and all the world's republican emancipators, how far I would go to follow the heroic efforts of our friends from that great island with all my heart and all my soul.

After my escape from New Caledonia in 1874, I was keen to meet the various leaders of the admirable revolution of 1868, now in New York. So long as there has been time, pen, and paper, I have not stopped proclaiming to the nations of Europe:

"Think of the Cubans."

Thus, I have followed with great elation that brilliant movement that dates back one year and brings our friends closer each day to final and inevitable triumph.

We hail with enthusiastic and victorious cheers the proclamation of their independence, along with the energy, perseverance, and bravery that so distinguishes them.

Let them know, conclusively, that we will never abandon them, and give my warmest regards to my friend, the brave and loyal Dr. Betances, on my behalf and on behalf of all of us.

Long live the Cuban Republic!
Henri Rochefort

Vibrant discourses were delivered by Dr. Domenici; by Mr. Alfonso Preciado, who, on behalf of the Cubans, expressed his gratitude to our editor-in-chief; and by Messrs. Isaac and Gerville-Réache. Afterwards, our friend Ernest Roche eloquently coupled the date of the French revolution, February 24, 1848, with that of the Cuban revolution, February 24, 1895.

As they did to us,' he said, 'they brand them with the epithet "insurrectionist." For that, we ought to feel proud, since we find ourselves in good company. Spartacus was a rebel against slavery; Galileo a rebel against science; Blanqui and Proudhon were rebels, too.

Amilcare Cipriani applauded the small Antillean island that gave the world such a model of heroism.

Dr. Betances, after thanking the friends of Cuban independence for their cooperation, gave a speech full of audacity and eloquence. He said, among other things:

First, let me tell you how the Spanish newspapers will cover our banquet: After having looted the restaurant Marguery, two hundred insurgents took refuge in a few outposts, which they soon fled after being pursued by three heroic gendarmes. To escape, they divided up into various bands, and the main group, headed by Henri Rochefort, proceeded to 144 Montmartre.

Equally as stirring was a speech that described a Cuban martyr in the midst of battle who heroically exclaimed with no hostility:

Let us forgive, then we triumph!

Given their humanitarian sentiments, as well as their fortitude, the children of the great island are indeed worthy of victory.

Doc. 75
Francisco Gonzalo Marín, "Wenceslao Tomás Marín"
June 13, 1896 (#256)

He was born in Arecibo, Puerto Rico, of mixed heritage: his grandfathers were an Italian and an Englishman; his grandmothers were a *mulata* from Curaçao and a black African. His parents were two Puerto Ricans—no Spanish blood coursed through his veins.

His Italian grandfather never learned how to write. Since then, we have called ourselves Marín, but our real name is Marini.

As a young boy, he received a severe head injury, and his cognitive aptitude deteriorated. His professor lamented, "This unfortunate boy will never recover his full mental faculties."

I am our family's first child, and he is the second. After finishing elementary school and lacking the means for universities or institutes, our family sent him to a blacksmith and me to a print shop.

Thus, I became a journalist. The first time that he saw me in jail—sentenced for defending freedom—he returned home crying and recounted everything to our mother. Another time, he saw me arrive home sick, pale, and in shackles for the same reason. Many of our neighbors had been bought off by my tyrants, so I gestured to him that he should be stoic, but he did not heed me and wept once again.

My brother has died. He died defending those ideals that I planted in his heart; he died without ever turning his back on his patria, offering her all the wages he earned in his final months in New York; he died never doubting the future of Cuba and Puerto Rico; Oh! maybe even cherishing in his heart that far-off day when he would return to his enslaved country as a famous warrior to offer his own mother— my mother as well—a patria worthy of our grandparents' honor. He died confronting the enemy I taught him to hate with my articles and my verses; he died at the very forefront of the fight, where the brave battled; in the end, he died elevated from blacksmith to patriot, from man to hero, from fighter to martyr.

One day while I was managing a newspaper in New York with the fleeting halo of celebrity and fame encircling my brow, I had to visit many of the city's tobacco manufacturers in search of support for our cause. In one of these establishments, I found my brother priming tobacco, work taken up on sunless days by countless men of prominence from every corner of Latin America!

Upon arriving and seeing him, I greeted and embraced him. He was disconcerted. Some of the others there began to interrogate him:

"Marín, why have you renounced this man as your brother?"

He lowered his gaze and then, with a sad, sweet tone, said:

"You, a journalist; me, a tobacco primer. How are we equal?"

These are the humble biographical facts of my brother, WENCESLAO TOMÁS MARÍN. Did I say brother? Then I have lied. My father is his father, my mother is his mother, but in the same modest way that he once renounced me from his tobacco primer's workbench, I too renounce him, standing here today on this miserable tier within the human hierarchy; for I cannot—woe is me!—aspire to call myself his brother while I do not give myself up in sacrifice to his executioners or fail to avenge his death by contributing to the salvation of these two wretched islands.

The early years of our adolescence were spent in a blacksmith's shop and a printing press: he forged iron and I pressed lead.

Today I will shed no tears in his memory. What good are tears?

The only offerings that I believe to be worthy of him are those of iron and lead.

Doc. 76
"Rius Rivera"
April 3, 1897 (#340)

Just as everything seemed to be going our way after hearing the auspicious news that two brave expeditions had arrived on Cuban soil, the terrible news that the intrepid Rius Rivera had been taken prisoner arrived, poisoning our happiness and dampening our spirits.

As prepared as we were to bear, with a serene spirit, the blows of random fortune and for events we find ourselves rationalizing as the whims of war, the contrast was too painful and the news too sudden to not leave behind a profound and tragic impression.

Since then the feeling that has seized us is purely personal as a result of the misfortune that has befallen this illustrious leader. He, nonetheless, continues to be a model of dignity and integrity, worthy by his own merits and the important services he rendered to our cause, and deserving of the love of all Cubans and the good fortune that always smiled upon him.

Since the death of the heroic MACEO, a heavy burden had fallen upon Rius' shoulders. He handled this arduous responsibility with imperturbable stability and commendable modesty, and without yielding an inch or losing any ground in a province teeming with enemy soldiers. From the beginning, he demonstrated that he was worthy of the rank and confidence granted him by that shrewd leader, who was ever appreciative of his compatriot's military strengths.

General Rius Rivera has fully lived up to the demands of the extremely difficult position in which he found himself. His expertise, bravery, and leadership qualities have been clearly displayed after four months of unquestionable trials. What is more, his unrelenting support for our independence was clearly evident when the enemy tested his resolve with offerings of peace and reforms.

An unfortunate accident has allowed our sovereign leader to fall into the hands of the Spaniards. Three wounds made it impossible for him to continue in combat, and his soldiers—a handful of men—were forced to surrender to the enemy's greater numbers. In true form, he fell bathed in his own blood, surrounded and cornered by numerous enemies. Though he lost his freedom, his honor remains unblemished.

The deep remorse with which we describe this painful event should not, however, impair our judgment. Our feelings of brotherhood and admiration for that renowned patriot have been bruised, but the cause that he defended—Cuba's noble cause—has not lost any of its vigor since that sad day. This is certainly not because the merits of this general-turned-prisoner have lost their importance, but because the strength of the revolution is not bound to any one of its members—they will be the first to remember and proclaim this as true. The strength of this great movement, which has reeled our beloved land from one extreme to the other, is in the spirit of her people. That is why MARTÍ fell, and the revolution, inspired by the great ideas that sprung forth from his brilliant mind, has not ceased. That is why ANTONIO MACEO fell, whose very arm seemed to hold the might of the revolution, and yet the revolution continues its triumphant march. As they fell, these great men left the heart of their people enflamed, and thousands of minds and bodies have continued the struggle that they began, striving to complete it in their honor.

Rius Rivera, upon seeing himself in the hands of the enemy, asked only that they treat him as a soldier. This entreaty—noble, yet severe—will serve as an example to his brothers remaining in the field. A soldier must always stand up for his flag, even in the face of danger. It is certain that Maceo and Rius Rivera's soldiers need no other saint or model to perform their duty. Their flag is that of *patria y libertad*; these men are all well acquainted with danger. Very soon, the Spanish will come to understand—the entire world, in fact—that the patriots from Pinar del Río carry on in the trenches, ever faithful to the lessons that they learned from their heroic leaders.

Doc. 77
Eusebio Blasco, "Betances"*
September 28, 1898 (#495)

Dr. Betances is dead.

The mocking fist of fate or the just hand of providence has wrested the life from this fanatic for Puerto Rican independence just as the doctor's native island fell under United States control—not Spain's or her own.

He did not forfeit his friendship with those Spaniards living in France—not even after proclaiming himself firmly against our possession of the Antillean island—until the moment that war was declared. We all knew him and spent much time in his company. Ruiz Zorrilla, a dear friend greatly admired by the doctor, had introduced us. Betances was our family physician, and he saved the life of my Sofía, who had been diagnosed as terminally ill by French practitioners. Such acts are seldom forgotten.

Before the onset of the war, when Betances took up the role of political filibus-ter in France, we had an intimate friendship; but later, we both admitted that such a bond was untenable and prompted rumors, so we parted ways. For seven or eight years, we saw each other frequently, not only in private, but in various French circles, international banquets, and parties for the Exposition Universelle. Betances worked extensively in Paris, where he was well-known and well-loved, initially as a journalist and later as a first class doctor. The government of the French Republic honored him with the Legion of Honor cross, a distinction that typically eludes most foreigners.

He was a man of handsome features: tall, dressed in black with a white tie. He cut an artist's profile like few others—white, naturally curly hair in abundance as well as a full, white beard at an age when other men, who had yet to know true work or suffering, still wore theirs black.

He resembled an apostle with his sweet appearance and tender eyes. He always spoke in soft tones and was never seen upset. Anger never furrowed his brow. Ev-erything about him was evangelical and distinguished. His integrity was never ques-tioned. He made a career and a name for himself in Paris as he worked and waited for his ideals to become a reality. He resembled a dreamer, a tenacious sectarian who never, at any moment, stopped conspiring to win independence for Puerto Rico.

At a young age, he made his first attempt at insurrection, that first one, which produced little more than a flicker, yet sparked future misfortunes. Condemned to death, he managed to escape and fled to Haiti to join his wife. From there, he entered the United States and then traveled on to France.

Shortly after arriving in Paris, he met Edmundo About—a benefactor and friend. He began to work as an editor—as he was already fluent in French—in *Le XIX Siècle*, which was run by that great man.

About put him in contact with Gambetta, Favre, Spuller, Jules Simon, Berthe-lot, and Humbert—all men of the Revolution of September 4 and the Commune. Be-tances, a foreigner with the air of a man who had wagered his life for his nationalist vision, was in constant communication with these gentlemen. These relationships procured him patients, and he made a living—and quite a good one—as a doctor due to his medical expertise. When he stopped calling upon my house, my good friend Max Nourdau started caring for my family and would say:

"It is nonsense to cut ties with a man who has committed no greater offense than to work for something so essentially human. Your grandparents fought against Napoleon, and you live in Paris. Those men who are Betances' filibusters today will be called **American brothers** by your children tomorrow."

As the war began, Dr. Betances was the leader, director, and representative of these filibustering organizations in Paris. All eyes followed him, including those of the embassy and its futile surveillance. This did not change his demeanor, life, or habits. He never raised his voice over a level pitch, and he directed everything without anyone perceiving it. "He would slip in like a shadow," Hebrard said, "but that shadow dealt out orders to everyone."

The last I saw of him was in the spring of 1890, when I received a serious head wound as a result of an overturned carriage. They published the incident in the newspapers, and the following day the doctor appeared in my room, sweet and smiling. "I have come to help you; we shall call a truce for eight days." He then treated me, said, "*Adiós*" in a low voice, grasped my hand, and left. I never saw him again.

His private life was a paradigm of intimacy and love. He had a close, loving relationship with his wife, who adored him. The goodness in his heart was recognized by all. During Ruiz Zorrilla's illness, he spent night after night watching over him until sending him off on a train: always sweet, always calm in speech—a slave to his friendship with that Spanish revolutionary he so admired.

All fanaticism is respectable. When one sees fanatics who fight for their country's independence and are shackled and subdued by enemies—as much theirs as our own—it compels one to bless Providence, which lifts up from this wretched Earth those that patriotism bids us not to love, and our hearts—common to all countries and devoid of borders—are tugged with pangs of pity for this ill-fated doctor, so good, so sincere, and, due to circumstances in Spain, so detested.

* (Editor's Note [from *Patria*]): "The purely Spanish sentiments that stand out in this article do not besmirch, but extol the brilliant figure of the illustrious doctor whose profile was traced by the steady hand of the famous Eusebio Blasco. For this reason, this beautiful article is presented here in its entirety. It clearly shows the recalcitrant Spaniard bowing down before this irrepressible man from the Antilles.")

Doc. 78
Lola Rodríguez de Tió, "October 10!"
October 12, 1898 (#499)

I found myself in the heady, early days of youth; in the blissful age of ineffable love, when my hopes were high and my happiness fluttered about like a small, mottled butterfly in the land of pure imagination.

Hardly had my feminine sensibility begun to flourish, when in my ear resounded—echoed by voices of feverish enthusiasm in my heart—the cry of war that a few resolute patriots sounded in Yara. They were led by the heroic and unforgettable leader Carlos Manuel de Céspedes.

From that glorious day, my life has been but an offering to the exquisite ideals of our patria!

My only thought was to see our patria rescued from her ominous yoke and united with Cuba by unbreakable bonds of love—for our pains are one and the same, as is the cause of our sorrows! Tenaciously, I fought is a society—incensed by a multitude of injustices and morally decimated by the horrors of oppression—against the obstructionists who opposed the redemptive ideas that nourished that most intimate part of my soul with faith!

Exiles, disappointments, and misfortunes due to expatriation...nothing was enough to dampen the zeal for freedom that blazed in my heart with the brilliance of a sun!

Time has passed slowly, but under the heaviness of its wheel, there persists a fervid devotion to the glorious memory of the heroes who began this sublime epic, which those of us today with greater fortune may see crowned with Victory!

Overwhelmed by my infinite sadness, I see the splendor of glory glisten on the brow of the victorious, those who have known how to fight for the most sacred of causes—Independence! I yearn for the broken wing of that lost ideal, and, among the shadows of an eternal nostalgia, I hear that still-fervent echo: Forever! Forever!

Lola R. de Tió

Doc. 79
"In Honor of General Rius Rivera"
December 31, 1898 (#522)

A large portion of the Cuban-Puerto Rican exile community (which surely included the most learned, courageous, and diligent of its men and women) were invited by the Figueroas to gather in their home to give a warm welcome and congratulations to the famous compatriot General Rius Rivera, who is passing through the city on his way to British Honduras to attend to personal affairs. He hopes to return very shortly to a free Cuba, where he will play an important role in the difficult task of reconstruction.

The reception, not for being impromptu, could never do justice to the figures assembled there. The employees of the delegation—including Messrs. Benjamin Giberga, Manuel Ros, Gustavo Escoto, and Manuel Moré (M. Remo), editor and executive of *PATRIA*—convened there along with our distinguished delegate, Mr. Estrada Palma. Messrs. Emilio Agramonte, our foremost pianist and maestro, and Martín Aróstegui, the representative of Havana's youth contingency, were also present, beaming with their own innate brilliance.

An illustrious group of individuals were gathered for this commemoration alongside the eminent intellectual, Eugenio María de Hostos, establishing a veritable court of honor: Dr. Manuel Zeno Gandía and Eduardo Lugo Viña, who are commissioned as envoys to Washington to report on the aspirations of the Puerto Rican people; Antonio Molina, the sociologist and publicist; Francisco Barnés, representing Ponce's business interests; Ulises del Valle, renowned for his entrepreneurial and enthusiastic spirit; and Lola, the unparalleled Lola Rodríguez de Tió, that eminent poet in the classic tradition, who sparkled and left all entranced by the refinement of Puerto Rican women; and with her Patria—sweet Patria—her admired and admirable daughter, who stands as proof of an inspired genealogy, despite her modesty, which cannot diminish the greatness of such inspiration.

The Antillean working classes was represented by Messrs. Crespo, Rodríguez, Schomburg, Agostini, Méndez, Carigord, etc.

Finally, rounding out the picture and framing such grandeur with great dignity, the associates of the Club Hermanas de Rius Rivera and other women and young ladies...

Section 6

THE WAR

Doc. 80
"Puerto Rico"
April 10, 1897 (#342)

According to telegrams published in the city's newspapers, an uprising has occurred on the island of Puerto Rico, our sister in slavery and suffering.

The insurrection took place between Yauco and Adjuntas, in the southwestern part of the island.

It seems strange that until now the American press, privy to news the world over, is not aware of it, even though the movement began on March 24.

Oh Spanish power, you appreciate nothing, neither the cable nor anything else you may invent during this century of marvels!

If a conspicuous event such as this goes unnoticed, what else may be occurring in Cuba—yet unbeknownst to the world—where the great assassin of our era, the deplorable Weyley, is hoping to accomplish what he proposed upon leaving his homeland, the Moorish Spain?

"I will leave Cuba in such a state," he proclaimed, "that it would not dare to dream of rebelling for the next fifty years to come."

As we await news, we salute our Puerto Rican brothers, whom we see are resolved to shake off the infamous Spanish yoke.

Doc. 81
"The Yauco Rebellion"
April 14, 1897 (#343)

Great confusion still reigns after hearing the latest news from Puerto Rico. The Spaniards, adhering closely to their tired credo of concealment at all costs, have managed to bury stories of the insurrection at Yauco and Adjuntas, which began more than fifteen days ago. During this time, the world has been left blind to the harrowing events that have transpired on this enslaved island in the midst of the Antilles, populous and rich with important commercial and business interests that affect the principal markets in Europe and America.

In the end, this is all that the influence of Spanish politics has achieved, which has always had faith in its ability to obscure facts and obstruct the dissemination of information. Today the whole world knows, beyond the shadow of a doubt, that the powder keg of discontent that has been lodged within the native Puerto Rican population has been ignited. On March 24, the rebellion in Yauco erupted. Although Spanish newspapers circulating in New York claim that it was quashed on March 29, it is through them that we know that some patriots remain armed, and marching against them is a battalion of Spanish troops, and we now hear of numerous prisoners being held in Yauco and nearby regions.

For those who are familiar with Spanish protocol, no more proof is needed to understand what is occurring in Puerto Rico. And yet there is a plethora of such stories and precedents, further illustrating the true importance of these events, regardless of their immediate outcome.

No, the sister island bears her yoke with more patience than we Cubans have borne ours. She wishes to shake loose of it; and, until now, only her topography has impeded her from sounding the decisive call to arms to secure freedom. Her discontent has very deep roots, much like our own—Spanish dominion has been no more lenient, prudent, or just for her inhabitants than ours. Spain exploits them just as she has us and distrusts them just as equally. When those in the Treasury have sapped the precious island of her bounty and filled their coffers, they have no plans to make her more productive or redevelop her natural resources. Instead, they intend to increase the invading army and make even more impregnable those fortifications upon which flutters their conquistador's flag. Spain has ruled this industrious, intelligent, and genteel people with an unyielding scepter. Spain has made no attempt to win the affection of these people, preferring instead to have them cower. One reaps what one has sown. Puerto Rico yearns for freedom and has worked toward this goal for many years. As Spain has not shown a path to freedom through decentralizing laws, sooner or later violence and war will find the means to that end.

Spaniards are obstinate and blind. By now they may have stifled the rebellion in Yauco—as they claim—much in the way they suppressed the rebellion in Lares in that golden era. In doing so, they would also have one believe that they have stifled the spirit of freedom. They will not remember Cuba or the sea of blood their stubborn arrogance and wicked dealings with us have cost them, nor will they consider the Philippines, which has collapsed on top of them and places their empire in Oceania at imminent risk, now when what remains of their American empire is all but toppled. They will insist that there are no insurrections in Puerto Rico, that peace reigns, and that they have no fear of upheaval; they will fill their jails and prisons with suspects and convicts; and they will continue onward, without realizing that all things comes to an end.

However, it is our duty to tell them once more that their arrogance is baseless, as they insist on ignoring reality and denying the inevitable. If Spain persists in withholding justice from Cuba and Puerto Rico, negotiating their eventual independence separately, and denying liberty to the Philippines, she should not expect peace, not even within her own land. Cuba must press on to the end, and Puerto Rico will follow suit, sooner or later. Now is the moment to bring the facts to the fore, demand compensation, and secure domestic tranquility. Tomorrow will be too late. [Illegible text in the original]... witnessing and we must bear witness. Yauco is the spark, tomorrow the blaze.

Doc. 82
"In Puerto Rico"
September 18, 1897 (#388)

On September 16th, *The Sun* published a report—taken from a letter that arrived from Puerto Rico—detailing the current state of alarm on the island.

The government fears a serious uprising. It is securing strongholds in various sites between Aibonito and Cayey, between Cayey and Caguas, between Adjuntas and Lares, between Comerío and Bayamón, and another in Luquillo.

Many merchants from Camuy, Vega Baja, Sabana Grande, and Yauco have been imprisoned. The jails are full of prisoners, subject to all manner of torture and abuse.

It has been recently reported that General Marín resigned from his post.

This interesting report, which we make reference to but are unable to reprint in its entirety, shows that Spanish control has become insufferable on the sister island, as everywhere else.

What will be, will be.

Doc. 83
"The Only Solution"
October 13, 1897 (#395)

The death of Cánovas was the deciding factor in the multi-faction division that had been threatening the party ever since he was their leader and inspiration. General Azcárraga's provisional rule has only served to precipitate the fall of the conservatives and to make their party's dissolution more ridiculous due to the ineptitudes of the general, who, upon taking up Cánovas' methods, lacked the skill and authority to wield them. The Queen Regent, restraining her proclivity toward the men of that party, finds herself obliged to entrust Mr. Práxedes M. Sagasta with the task of forming an organization composed of what the Spanish deem a liberal party. It is not befitting of this article to point out the unending contradictions, which these gentlemen have committed, denigrating the title that they themselves have bestowed on one another. Backing one agenda when they are in power and another when they are not, Sagasta's liberals have shown themselves to be masters in the art of balancing acts, which they employ to tailor themselves to their situation, much like their leader. In their hunger to stay in power, they sacrifice many of the policies and democratic principles that they proposed in their campaign speeches, which they invoked with such authoritative tones.

Irrefutable proof of this assertion is their flagrant apostasy with regard to their colonies. Without enough influence or sufficient authority to bring about reforms that would check the privileges enjoyed by those who rule the colonies by the eternal right of conquest, their administration has been in no way advantageous for Spanish overseas territories. These lands, which remain unchanged under either a conservative or liberal regime—whether Cánovas or Sagasta or any other distinguished politician who hails from the Iberian Peninsula—have been conquered solely for wealth and exploitation, not for the sons of the conquerors, but for all the upstarts who arrive in these far-off lands, armed with their noble titles in Catalan or Andalusian, in Galician or Asturian, readily assuming the airs, superiority, and privileges of the master and head of a foreign household.

To Spain, the colonies have been, are, and—so long as any remain—will continue to be their property, whose progeny—divested of all political status and considered only as simple, socially inferior laborers—must maintain it in a constant state of production for the exclusive, direct or indirect, benefit of the distant metropolis. Such is the colonial system embodied in the Spanish people, from distinguished leaders down to uncouth farmhands. This regime reflects the very nature of that nation; asking them to reform their system is like trying to squeeze blood from a stone. First, begin by transforming their character; that is to say, to de-Spanify them. Is that even possible? Look at their own history. Neither the cruelest blows nor the bitterest lessons have been able to change them. Blinded by avarice and innate cruelty, Spain lost what it possessed in Europe, lost almost an entire continent in the Americas, has all but lost Cuba, and, possibly, is about to suffer a similar fate in respect to the Philippines.

Why, then, should it matter to us that the conservatives in Madrid fall and the liberals rise to power? Cuba is no longer a colony; she is, in fact, an independent nation because she possesses those rights that validate her sovereignty. She has a political constitution, passes laws, elects leaders, imposes and collects taxes, and organizes and maintains an army. Meanwhile, Spain suffers disappointment after disappointment in her mad endeavor to reconquer the lost colony; her two most famous generals—according to their own criteria—have fallen into disgrace, one after the other, as a result of the outright failures of their campaigns; her formidable army of more than two hundred thousand men lies broken; the national Treasury is bankrupt; her credit is exhausted; and her people, upon opening their eyes to reality, resolutely oppose any further sacrifice of men or money, for they know quite well that such sacrifices will be just as fruitless as they were in the past.

In short, this is Spain's miserable situation. However, if we were to compare this to Cuba's advantages and observe the decidedly favorable chance for the definitive triumph of our forces in this fight, would we not be correct in judging as quixotic pretension the promise of granting lesser freedoms, through the grace and mercy of the cowardly Queen Regent—at such a late hour—to those people who are already in full possession of their rights as men and as a nation? These men exercise their rights with ease and broad vision after having conquered them with the lead of their rifles and the steel of their machetes. Learning their lesson from this experience and proceeding with understandable fearfulness, it would be more logical, prudent, and prescient of these gentlemen serving the current Spanish government (in the crown city of Madrid) to oblige themselves to implement an autonomous regime in Puerto Rico before it is too late; a regime that the sister island has been seeking for a great number of years through all the peaceful measures within her reach, as Cuba did, but to no avail.

Puerto Rico is Spain's only colonial possession that still holds onto peace; her grievances and complaints against the metropolis are the same that provoked the wars for freedom in Spain's other colonies. Why, then, does Mr. Sagasta not begin to show his liberal stripes and statesmanship and work toward justice, which this loyal land so deserves? Or is it that Spaniards are condemned by a divine curse to waste oats on a dead donkey? At least this is what Sagasta's government platform is attempting—to persuade Cuba, who has resolved the problem on her own by breaking her Iberian yoke, by saying, "Get me out of the well, and I will spare your life." With regard to government proposals, Spain does not even deem Puerto Rico worthy of honorific mention and turns a blind eye to her, she who patiently awaits an encouraging promise of fulfillment and justice.

Even if the countless other examples did not exist, this fact alone would be proof enough of bad faith by these incorrigible Spanish politicians. Whatever it may be, their character does not wholly concern us. For us, it is enough that they know once and for all that the time they spend blotting paper with winsome legislative projects for Cuba is in vain. Let it be known, so as not to call it deception, that the people who rose up in arms on February 24, 1895—resolute in claiming their absolute independence—continue onward; noble, triumphant, and proud of the work accomplished thus far and determined to fight with tireless valor in defense of those liberties and rights gallantly won through blood and fire. Those who fight on the battlefields, those who lend their support in the surrounding towns, and those who, not living on the island, deprive their children of bread and deny themselves all manner of comforts so to ensure that there is no shortage of the money needed to buy and send rifles and munitions, dynamite and artillery, and medicine and clothes to their heroic brothers—all united together for a single cause, who have sworn on the altar of their homeland to never cease in their efforts, to bear hardships of all stripes, and to never forego any sacrifice, however bloody it may be, until peace has been secured under the solitary star of their glorious flag.

Ponder this, Mr. Sagasta and your colleagues in the liberal party: Is it possible to defeat men of similar mettle through armed force or hollow promises, regardless of what they may consist of? Reflect and rest assured that Cubans, who harbor no hatred toward the Spanish people in general, are ready to suspend all hostilities—inspired by a generous spirit of conciliation—and enter into talks that would put an end to the war, provided that the first stipulation be Spain's acknowledgment of a sovereign and independent Cuban republic.

Doc. 84
Betances, "From Paris"
January 8, 1898 (#420)

December 23, 1897
Editor of *PATRIA*
New York

My Esteemed Compatriot,

Allow me to recommend the following paragraph from the front page of *El Heraldo de Madrid* dated December 17, 1897.

Following the report of surrender in the Philippines, which has caused so much panic in Spain, a journalist callously drafted the following article upon witnessing flags unfurled and balconies adorned with banners, and hearing throughout the streets music, songs, and bells tolling.

We have already conceded too many honors to *ragged* and *ignorant* Indians, who we were unable to prevent from organizing a *powerful* insurrection, only to later enter into treaties with them so that they would surrender. Are we also to prematurely forfeit the tribute of our happiness to them? Would it not be more dignified to restrain some of this merriment, rather than dragging it before the feet of such a *despicable* people? It is painful to think that—given how Aguinaldo and Llanera were unable to achieve more than they might have, and how our countrymen achieved even less—we express our humiliation by celebrating in the streets and decorating the façades of our houses. And, although we have said that the spirit of the people celebrates peace and nothing more than peace—even if the means employed to arrive at such a point remain unexamined—it does not appear justified to completely ignore the kind of enemy we have thus inherited.

What an important lesson for both the clever and the humble! Now see here, Autonomists and discontented Puerto Ricans, this is the arrogance and great disdain with which these **illustrious** Spanish journalists treat those who surrender. Would it not be far better to bear the brunt of these barbarians' furious boasts?

* * *

"In truth, those journalists are beasts!" states Bonafoux in El Progreso on December 17, that same day.

And yet, he goes on to say in his article, when speaking of my meeting with Mr.

Canalejas, "In that meeting, **which was not pursued by either of the parties involved in the dispute,** rather by the natural result of a mutual desire for expansion that has long been suppressed, etc."

This statement may sit well with Messrs. Canalejas and Méndez, but I am with nothing less than the exact truth. For this reason, I beseech you to make known in the pages of *PATRIA* that "the conference was requested by Canalejas and Méndez, and that in spite of representatives **from all** parties having passed through my office—and I repeat **from all** parties, one even being an ambassador—I have never had the slightest inclination to see either Canalejas or Méndez, or any of those other gentlemen.

Let this stand as a correction.

Your friend and compatriot,
Betances

Doc. 85
"The Situation in Puerto Rico"
June 29, 1898 (#469)

According to ministerial reports, Puerto Rico is filled with great anti-American sentiment, comparable to Santiago de Cuba, and hopes to see the **Yankees** defeated; it is true that not everything is a bed of roses.

A Madrid newspaper writes, attempting to console and prepare the people for the imminent and glorious disaster:

Hunger has begun to set in due to the paralysis of businesses all over the island; the people ask for arms, but there are none. With regard to the Puerto Ricans, always loyal to Spain, we should not think that they would brandish these weapons against us. We have learned from some official letters, in which the government's carelessness is censured, that in Puerto Rico—as in all places—Spanish life and honor is at the mercy of divine Providence, without remembering that, as penance for our sins, Providence usually protects the wicked, when they are none other than the righteous.

Not a single cannon or soldier has touched Puerto Rican soil after our last glorious tour.

There is a colonel, a commander, and four cavalrymen in the capital. A sufficient number to head up an expedition, if one were to arrive on the island!

The Minister of War will shrug his shoulders, laying the blame upon General Macías when disaster strikes without a second thought. We comply with our duty by publishing this warning: General Correa listens to us the same way that one listens to the rain, and this only confirms his negligence.

Doc. 86
"The News"
July 23, 1898 (#476)
The Herald, July 20.

Santiago de Cuba:
—Before the week is through, Spanish prisoners will embark for Spain.
—Vice Admiral Sampson has entered the bay, on the **Vixen,** and held a meeting with General Shafter about the embargo on Spanish troops.
— General Shafter believes that those troops will have left the island by next Sunday.
— Refugees have begun returning to the city from the outskirts of Santiago.
— The number of torpedoes that were blockading the port has been diminished.
— Sylvester Scovel, the well-known American correspondent, has been arrested and will be brought to the United States where he will be prosecuted.
— Scovel was arrested for having attacked and punched General Shafter.
— It is reported that Cuban troops are angry for continuing to be barred from entering Santiago de Cuba.
— Cases of yellow fever, although not yet in alarming numbers, continue to be found among the Americans.
— A troubling situation has emerged between Vice Admiral Sampson and General Shafter. The Vice Admiral claims that the merchant ships that are docked in the bay are to be considered prisoners of the Navy and not, as the American general contends, of the Army.

Washington, D.C.:
— Due to the inaccurate interpretation of a cablegram, the departure of General Miles for Puerto Rico was delayed.
— His first order of business will be to establish a base of operations in an advantageous location on the island. Next, he will mount an attack by both land and sea on the capital.
— Fourteen thousand men are now headed to Puerto Rico, which may bring the entire invading army to thirty thousand.
— As soon as San Juan is taken, a National Bank will be established in the city.
— It is reported that the German admiral in the Philippines has received payment without authorization from his government.

Cádiz:
—Southern ports on the peninsula are making great defense preparations.

Madrid:
— The Council of Ministers has discussed the loss of Santiago de Cuba. It has asked General Blanco for details of the event and, upon reviewing them, will decide whether General Toral should or should not be summoned before a war council, after having agreed to surrender all forces under his control in the province.
— There is talk of retaking lost territory.

The Herald, July 21.

Santiago de Cuba:
— Order has been completely reestablished. No loud celebrations of victory have been permitted. Until last night, cafés were closed, and the authorities are now worried that the positive public impression regarding the change of regimes may in some way be sullied.
— Spanish and American troops are on friendly terms. All are rejoicing.
— Stores remain open and the problem of food shortages has been resolved, thanks to a recent shipment of supplies.
— American and Spanish officers are gathering in the cafés, drinking together, and exchanging swords to commemorate their campaigns.
— Many claim that they feel no shame in having surrendered to the Americans.
— The Spaniards say, "You are generous enemies. We do not consider ourselves disgraced by being your prisoners, but would have preferred to die fighting than surrender to the Cubans."
— American sentiment falls more favorably on the Spanish than on the Cubans. (This is according to the *Herald*.)
— In compliance with the conditions that General Wheeler offered to General Toral, the Cubans have not yet been permitted to enter the city.

Washington, D.C.:
— General Miles has left Guantánamo for Puerto Rico.
— As of now, the total number of available armed forces is fourteen thousand men; a number that shortly will be increased to nearly thirty thousand.
— Vice Admiral Sampson's fleet will protect the arrival of the troops.
— United States policy toward Puerto Rico will be to annex the island.
— Well-informed sources state that the number of soldiers who surrendered along with General Toral did not exceed twelve thousand.
— The deployment of the Asiatic Squadron to Europe is not intended to intimidate the Spaniards, but to show the nations of the Old World the power of the United States Navy.

Charleston, S.C.:

— Three transport ships have left carrying troops to Puerto Rico.

— Arriving from Santiago de Cuba, the *SS Seneca* has arrived in port in New York, carrying sick and wounded Americans.

— The ship was not equipped to handle the number of patients it carried, and both medical attention and supplies provided on board left much to be desired.

Havana:

— The situation worsens each day, and food continues to be in short supply. Prices are constantly rising, and people will soon lack the basic goods needed to survive.

Kingston, Jamaica:

— A rumor has circulated that General García has died, but this news has not been given much credibility.

Madrid:

— *El Imparcial* begins to advocate in favor of peace.

— The newspaper praises the conduct of the Americans toward their Spanish prisoners.

— It is believed that General Polavieja may rise to power.

— The warrior spirit still prevails.

London:

— Carlists appear increasingly active and enlivened with regard to Spain's situation.

Vancouver, B.C.:

— The city of Manila can hardly sustain itself, and the Spanish flag will be lowered only under threat of attack.

The Herald, July 22.

Santiago de Cuba:

— General Calixto García, leader of the Cuban troops stationed there, has discussed with General Shafter to cease giving orders to his troops.

— General García, it appears, has decided to mount operations against Spanish troops in the interior of the island.

— General Leonard Wood, former commander of the Rough Riders, has been appointed military governor of the city of Santiago de Cuba.

Washington, D.C.:

— Accompanied by a powerful fleet, General Miles and his troops have left Guantánamo for Puerto Rico.

— The formation of that fleet has been the cause of serious friction between General

Miles and Vice Admiral Sampson.

— The substandard care that wounded American soldiers received during their recent passage on the *Seneca* will be subject to an investigation.

— Some ships from the Spanish Line will take Spanish soldiers, now prisoners in Santiago de Cuba, back to Spain.

— Commodore Watson's fleet will not return to Spain so long as Puerto Rico is not under American power.

Cavite, Philippines:

— The second expedition of American troops has arrived.

— Manila will be attacked within the next few days.

Madrid:

— Given the conditions that one presumes the United States will most likely demand of Spain, it is impossible for Spain to make peace.

London:

— In Barcelona it is said that the formation of a cabinet presided over by Wayler is expected, with Polavieja as Minister of War...

Doc. 87
"The News"
July 30, 1898 (#478)

The Herald, July 27.

Washington, D.C.:

— Spain seeks peace. This delicate matter has been entrusted to the French ambassador, Mr. Cambon, who presented a telegram from Spain to President McKinley at the White House yesterday at three o'clock in the afternoon.

— He was accompanied by his embassy's First Secretary, Mr. Thiebaut.

— In the telegram, after stating that the reason that the United States had entered the war was to intimidate Spain into abandoning Cuba, Spain admits defeat, with the war having caused considerable suffering. Believing that the moment to make peace has arrived, the French ambassador inquires about the terms that the United States will demand to reach a peace settlement.

— President McKinley told the ambassador that he wished to consult his cabinet before responding.

— Spain, it appears, hopes to save the Philippines. They would also prefer that the United States take possession of Cuba, rather than allowing the island to remain in the hands of the Cubans.

— The peace terms that the United States is expected to demand are:

* Full Cuban independence, under protection of the United States

* The absolute cession of Puerto Rico and the Marianas Islands

A coaling station in the Philippines

— The major concessions that Spain is believed to make are:

* The cession of Puerto Rico

* The cession of Cuba to the United States, which they would prefer to the independence of the island

— The government will not modify any of their operations in Puerto Rico, in spite of the telegram from Spain seeking peace, which was just recently presented by the French ambassador.

— The attack on the island will continue without interruption.

— After taking San Juan in Puerto Rico, military operations will focus on Cienfuegos and Bahía Honda in Cuba.

— The government was surprised when it received official news that spoke of a deployment of American troops in Guánica, Puerto Rico, as they believed the deployment of troops would occur in Fajardo...

The Herald, July 28

— Cuban independence and the cession of Puerto Rico remain completely beyond debate.

— The most controversial point will surely be that of the Philippines.

— The so-called "Cuban debt" will be another area of contention, as it is the opinion of the administration that Spain should assume this debt, as it was created by Spain.

— Meanwhile, military operations will continue without interruption.

— European powers are anxious to learn the terms that the United States will offer in order to secure a peace agreement, and they are trying to find out the position of the American government regarding the Philippines.

— Watson's fleet will be sent to European waters, in a show of force by the United States to bolster support for the reasonable terms that the government demands.

— General Shafter reports from Santiago de Cuba that the total number of cases of yellow fever there is 2,924.

— There have been 639 new cases; 538 men have recuperated and returned to service.

— The deployment of troops to Puerto Rico continues...

Doc. 88

"The News"

August 3, 1898 (#479)

The Herald, July 30.

Washington, D.C.:

— This afternoon President McKinley will deliver his government's response to the telegram that Spain sent in reference to a peace treaty. The French ambassador, who recently delivered the telegram, will receive the response.

— The resolute and categorical response presents the terms that the United States will demand to end hostilities and begin negotiations over the Philippines.

— The fundamental tenets of the peace treaty, as approved by the Cabinet during a session held yesterday, are the following:

* Absolute cession of Puerto Rico to the United States

* Cuban independence

* Cession of the island of Guam, as a coaling station, to the United States

* Another coaling station in the Philippines

— All terms regarding the Philippines will be discussed after Spain has accepted the aforementioned conditions.

— An immediate peace would follow Spain's acceptance of these terms. If Spain refuses, the war will continue with greater intensity, and, as a result, Spain will pay indemnities and lose the Philippines.

— In order to enter into peace talks, the United States demands that Spain immediately abandon Cuba and Puerto Rico.

— Troops continue to leave for Puerto Rico from Southern ports.

Ponce, Puerto Rico:

— On Wednesday afternoon, the city of Ponce surrendered to Commander Davis of the *Dixie*.

— Not a single shot was fired.

— General Miles and a number of his troops arrived at the city on Thursday morning.

— It was a day of great celebration. The American flag was hoisted above many of the city's main buildings, and the invading army was greeted with music and enthusiastic cheers.

— Twelve hundred Spanish soldiers from the garrison joined in the festivities.

— In his proclamation, General Miles issued a proclamation in which he declared that the war is not against the people living on the island, but against Spanish domination.

— The Americans have become enchanted with the island.

....

The Herald, July 31.

Washington, D.C.:

— Peace with Spain appears all but certain, and an end to hostilities may be reached within a matter of days.

— At two o'clock in the afternoon on Saturday, the French ambassador, Mr. Cambon, was called to the White House to attend a meeting with President McKinley and the Secretary of State, Mr. Day. Mr. Thiebaut, the French ambassador's First Secretary, was also present to witness the act, which lasted until almost five o'clock.
— The response to Spain's telegram was delivered to Mr. Cambon.
— The peace terms presented by the American government are the following:
* Spain must abandon the island of Cuba, ending their domination over the island and withdrawing their armed forces, leaving the island under United States control until a stable government is established there.
* Spain must withdraw, likewise, from the island of Puerto Rico and cede the island to the United States.
* Spain must also cede the island of Guam in the Marianas to the United States.
* The United States will occupy Manila and all conquered territory, including Cavite, until the future of the archipelago is decided and a final agreement is ratified by both nations.
* Spain must assume the so-called "Cuban debt," and rightly so.

....

The Herald, August 1.

Washington, D.C.:
— Both President McKinley and the French ambassador hope that Spain acquiesces and accepts the terms of the peace treaty as presented by the United States government.
— General Miles sent a telegram in which he states that U.S. Customs in Ponce has already collected $14,000.

San Juan, Puerto Rico:
— The situation in the island's capital has changed greatly since the Americans landed and took control of Ponce.
— The excitement produced by this chain of events has been enormous.
— The Spaniards are preparing their defenses and claim that they would rather die before surrendering.
— This we shall wait and see.

Ponce, Puerto Rico, U.S.A.:
— Spanish troops have committed great atrocities as they retreated from the capital.
— In their withdrawal, they have burned down towns and haciendas, giving into pillaging and murdering women and children.

....

Doc. 89
"Lesson from Puerto Rico"
August 6, 1898 (#480)

One of the most memorable events from this extraordinary land is the occupation of the populous city of Ponce, on the island of Puerto Rico, by the invading army from the North in hopes of completing the work of Hidalgo, San Martín, and Bolívar. It was not a significant act of war, as not a single shot was fired, nor was it the result of adept strategic planning, as the invaders, up until the present, have seen only the backs of their fleeing enemies. It seems that the Americans carry the magical trumpets of Jericho, whose blasts alone brought down its fabled walls.

It is worthy to note the cordial reception that the entire populace of this prosperous city prepared for the invading army. Amid cheers and enthusiastic acclamations, the army made its triumphant entrance, and the people celebrated its presence with impromptu parties lasting well into the night.

"Everything is pure merriment today in the great city of Ponce," her people appeared to proclaim, using nearly the same words as the author of *La Raquel*. And we must confess that they were not without reason. Instead of the fearsome specter of war, which hovered over their heads, they saw the sudden arrival of shining freedom.

We can understand the astonishment of our spirited neighbors, and we can easily understand the now famous proclamation of the mayor of Yauco, who is well versed in the technicalities of bureaucratic language and gives life to an *ever-American* Puerto Rico, which only yesterday was proclaimed an *ever-Spanish* Puerto Rico. Without an act of Congress or more formalities than a stroke of his pen, he declared his municipality annexed to the Union, signing his effusive proclamation, "Yauco, Puerto Rico, U.S.A."

From now on, only the superficial layer of this interesting matter will be remembered, that being the comical aspect of Mayor Mejía's hastiness. It is not our desire to seek out the celebratory nature that can almost always be found in all human activity, even the gravest of moments. We have only paused on this incident to punctuate the profound lesson that can be learned from it, much like the lesson learned from the vigorous rejoicing of the people as America's liberating army arrived in Ponce, a lesson that is infinitely more important.

Spain occupied Puerto Rico for nearly four centuries; during this considerable amount of time, her domination has never been seriously challenged. The sunny island has not experienced the tremendous convulsions that have twice unhinged Cuban society. However, the Americans have hardly planted their feet on Borinquen soil and the colonial infrastructure has begun to tremble—shaken to its very core—and will collapse on its own. These people, who in the eyes of the disillusioned Spanish ought to take up arms to repel the invaders, instead raise their arms to applaud and bless them. The same lips that cheer those foreigners who bring liberty now curse the Spaniards and the tyranny that flees with them.

It would not be possible to find, or even imagine, a more absolute demonstration of ineptitude than in Spain's handling of her colonies; likewise, it is not possible to imagine a more perfect punishment for her pride and transgressions. France was expelled from Canada, but the Canadians heroically defended her flag, and the descendants of the brave soldiers who fell alongside Montcalm, there on the plains of Abraham, have faithfully conserved the tongue of their forefathers and the rich memory of the French homeland. At the hour of definitive expulsion from the Americas, Spain finds Cuban fists raised up against her own and Puerto Rican backs turning against her flag. Spain will flee Cuba, leaving behind a sea of steaming blood and heaps of emaciated corpses. Spain will flee Puerto Rico, leaving only the indelible footprints of her shameful corruption and ferocious cruelty.

It is not possible to assert that the people went suddenly from feelings of love to those of hate; or that they painlessly broke the bonds of blood, language, beliefs, and customs in one day. Spain was not loved, but abhorred in Cuba. Spain was not loved, but feared in Puerto Rico. Spain herself had broken the ties that bind together those first communities and the façade of institutions, bestowing greater privileges on a handful of merchants, bureaucrats, and soldiers to better exploit, humiliate, and corrupt the Cuban and Puerto Rican colonies.

To the honor of both nations, the tremendous pressure of Spanish tyranny was not able to quash their sense of dignity and their aspirations for a life with natural rights. Conspiracies, Cuba's wars, and Puerto Rico's muffled revolt are proof that they are not resigned to wallow in abject depravity. They wanted, nay, they demanded civic dignity and liberty. Cuba has sought these qualities along the path of martyrdom. Puerto Rico—whose circumstances in the struggle were very different—received them from a powerful hand, and reacted with shouts of elation. A common cause—Spain's criminal despotism—sparked these natural outcomes.

Doc. 90
"A Little Bit of Everything" (Dissolution of the *SPR*)
August 6, 1898 (#480)

The Sección Puerto Rico of the Partido Revolucionario Cubano was dissolved last Tuesday night. In its absence, the Sociedad de Patriotas Puertorriqueños has been established. In light of the new circumstances created by the U.S. invasion of the island, its objective is to obtain greater benefits within the context of modern constitutional law, beginning with promoting Puerto Rican nationhood to better develop its regional interests. The following board of directors was named in the enabling session held on the night of August 4:

    Mr. Eugenio M. Hostos
    Mr. Cecilio Delgado

Mr. J.J. Henna

Mr. Pedro Salazar

Mr. F.J. Amy

* * *

Doc. 91

Eugenio María de Hostos

"Liga de Patriotas Puertorriqueños"

September 10, 1898 (#490)

The meeting held last Wednesday night by this group of compatriots was quite memorable, as they bid farewell to their honorable chairman, Eugenio María de Hostos. He departs for Puerto Rico, his homeland, to lay the foundations of its new government and to begin his political life, which will undoubtedly be quite influential in the new regime created by U.S. intervention on the island.

After a brilliant speech confirming the Liga's importance and significance, in which Hostos demonstrated his talents as a poised speaker and a robust thinker, there was pleasant and fruitful conversation, which resulted in valuable lessons on the exercise of both individual and collective rights.

The Liga has two principle objectives; first, to work in Puerto Rico and the United States to petition Congress to grant Puerto Ricans the right to vote by plebiscite to determine if they desire annexation to this great republic; and second, to educate the Puerto Rican people and raise awareness of the opportunities that their new legal rights afford them in the exercise of civil liberties and in the active expression of natural rights, so suppressed by the colonial government of these former Spanish colonies.

These two objectives are listed in the Liga's statutes, which Hostos presented in a previous meeting and which were approved after a short discussion and some amendments. All agreed on the publication and wide circulation of these objectives throughout Puerto Rico, the United States, and South America, along with a manifesto, the drafting of which has been naturally entrusted to the Liga's founder, and which gives Puerto Ricans a sense of the *Liga's* proposals.

PATRIA, upon wishing farewell to an invaluable activist, hopes that his noble ideas will bear fruit in terrain now primed for freedom by the heroic strength of the Cubans, the American intervention, and the persistent, yet muted, refusal by Puerto Ricans to conform to Spanish despotism.

A nation that produces such sons like Betances and Hostos cannot be a nation of slaves. Here is Hostos' brilliant manifesto:

TO THE PEOPLE OF PUERTO RICO

Dear Compatriots,

The Liga de Patriotas Puertorriqueños, in whose name I speak to you, has been constituted with two purposes: first and foremost, to prepare our mother island to receive her lawful rights; and second, to implement the necessary measures to educate our people in the exercise of freedoms, which will improve their lives: private and public, individual and collective, economic and political, moral and material.

Readying Puerto Rico to receive her lawful rights seems to be a difficult task, when to all appearances nothing more has transpired than a change from a de facto government run by Spain to another one run by the United States. This is not the case: the Constitution of the United States and the traditions, customs, and solid foundation of justice, impartiality, and liberty which form the foundation of this potent American federation grant us the opportunity to exercise our natural right to advocate for justice and the good of our land; we are endowed with all manner of substantial rights that will be essential and useful resources during the life of this society.

Granting Puerto Rico the opportunity to educate herself in the ways of a healthy and dignified life is to work toward a better future, and that future will decide if we were as able and willing to rise to the occasion as we were able to dream and imagine.

In order to leave this de facto situation and begin a new life based on rights, it is necessary to follow this obvious path: the only path of rights established by law.

In order to leave behind an Iberian past and begin a new American future, here, too, there is only one path—no other path leads to healing; this is the only cure. In terms of honor, there is none other than that of duty fulfilled.

The resources of written law will allow us to put an end to martial law and enter into a civil one. The very powerful resources that are available to us are the ability to petition the United States Congress to recognize our potential statehood in the Union or to develop our capacity to gloriously serve the future of America, without having to obsequiously submit ourselves to the brutal consequences of a war that we did not declare nor was declared against us. In the intrigues of the federation, the people's initiative is equally important to better their own situation and to work together for the common good.

The means that these initiatives offer societies represented by a legally recognized State are as all-encompassing as that of human activity in general; and, similarly, they facilitate the structuring of work, government, public education, private beliefs, and popular strength. This new order has placed these means in our hands, and we must learn how to employ them.

We will go to the plebiscite and exercise our natural right as human beings, who cannot be treated like objects; our rights as accidental citizens in the American Union who cannot be compelled against their will to be or not to be what they do not want or aspire to be. In the United States, there is no authority, force, power, or will that is capable of imposing on any people the shame of an annexation achieved through armed violence or of conspiring against that most developed civilization currently in existence among men, resorting to the ignominy of conquest in order to subdue spirits.

By engaging in those activities that generally comprise a civilization—which is the sum of human activity—Puerto Rican society will become resolute in testing the effectiveness of liberty in the education of her peoples.

Our history now imposes on us many duties: To seek out a plebiscite to determine whether we wish to be or not to be American citizens; to continue or end our status as citizens of our geographic and historic patria; and to seek and follow the example of the American people so we may cease to be representatives of the past by becoming men of a current and a future society. The *LIGA* has been founded to ensure that these objectives are realized; in order to accomplish them effectively, I thereby return to my patria.

Eugenio María de Hostos

NOTES

Chapter 1

[1] On Martí and the CRP, see: Aguirre (1982), Azcuy (1930), Estrade (1983), Hidalgo Paz (1981), Ibarra (1981, ch. 3), Llanos (1975), Poyo (1983, ch. 8), Torres-Cuevas, Mencía and Benítez (1984), Aguirre (1982).

[2] For different summaries of José Martí's thoughts in all of his facets, see the references in footnote 1; also, Armas (1990).

[3] On the idea to create an Antillean Confederation, see González (1986), Mathews (1955), Reyes and Ruscalleda (1973).

[4] "Cuba," article first published in Revista Latino-Americana (Paris, 1874, and republished in Betances (1983, 145).

[5] Letter from Hostos to Francisco Sellén, July 12, 1896. Hostos's Caribbeanist and Americanist ideals are discussed in the following: Comisión Pro Celebración del Centenario del Natalicio de Hostos (1954), Hostos (1980); Pedreira (1932); Roig de Leuchsenring (1939). On the ideologial and historical links between Martí and Hostos, see Ferrer Canales (2001) and Maldonado Denis (1985).

[6] For more information on Martí's anti-imperialist thought, see Centro de Estudios Martianos 1984, 1989) and Roig de Leuchsenring (1983).

[7] Puerto Rico's presence in the Cuban wars is discussed in Freire (1966), Figueroa (1985) and Piedra (1945, appendix 2). Notable Puerto Ricans linked to the CRP—such as Rius Rivera, Sotero Figueroa, and Lola Rodríguez de Tió—are discussed in Ojeda Reyes (1992). See also Dávila (2002) and Toledo (2002).

[8] This opinion was clearly stated by Mr. L.E. Hatton, representative of the CRP in the Dominican Republic, in a letter to Estrada Palma on July 19, 1896: "My opinion is that we can have a large part of the island (Puerto Rico) under revolt. The uprising's endurance and success depends on so many things that no one can form an opinion, but, expecting the worse, we should have two results: the seed shall have been planted, and the Spaniards shall ignite the revolutionary fire, which is still dormant. Cuba will still in many ways win. You will take advantage of the army's distraction, and they will be distracted by the many ships you say will be going to Puerto Rico, but you will command them to go to Cuba. They will receive the final blow to the little reputation they have left in Europe." In Partido Revolucionario Cubano 1932–1937 vol: 5, 156–7.

[9] On the reformist autonomist movement led by the Creole elite of the XIX century, see: Barbosa (1974), Cubano Iguina (1990), Mattos Cintrón (1980, ch. 1), Negrón Portillo (1981), Quintero-Rivera (1976), Tirado Merced (1981).

[10] Betances, who from France remained as the patriarch of Puerto Rican separatism and continuously tried to join all sectors of the movement, recognized their lack of strength to launch a revolt on the island. Given this situation, Betances (in a letter addressed to José Julio Henna dated October 9, 1895) advised to fuse the Puerto Rican cause to the Cuban, and Puerto

Ricans to join the CPR: "Mr. Estrada, Delegate for the Cuban and 'Puerto Rican' Revolutionary Party, has been presented with a very good Commission (of Puerto Ricans). This is how I will address him, as does the patriot Javier Cisneros, as I have advised him. I believe it is of great importance that the name of Puerto Rico always appears besides Cuba's. This way, if Spain consents tomorrow in receiving indemnity for withdrawing from Cuba, Puerto Rico would have to be in this agreement even if not a single sugarcane leaf had been snapped there. It is convenient for both Cubans and Puerto Ricans. This would be the only way that Bolívar's plan could be carried out" (Guzmán Rodríguez 1943, 27). The notion that there was no possibility for an uprising in Puerto Rico before a US invasion and that the cause of the island's independence had to be linked to the Cuban war and its solution was a constant in Betances's correspondence with other Puerto Ricans during this period. See Betances (2013, 303–5, 479–80, 487–8, 507–9, 511–3, 523–5).

The development of the Puerto Rican separatist movement in the nineteenth century is discussed in the following: Delgado Pasapera (1984), Jiménez de Wagenheim (1985), Lidin (1981).

[11] In a letter to the Cuban José González Lanuza on July 8, 1898, Betances says of Henna: "I know that Henna is an annexationist, as he confesses, but I also know that he does not engage in annexationist politics, because he does not have the right. Henna is a good citizen, and I have his word. I am sure he acts with the utmost correctness" (PRC 1943 vol: III, 145–6). Betances states the same opinion about Henna in a June 9, 1898 letter to his Puerto Rican friend Manuel Guzmán Rodríguez (Betances 2013 vol: 5, 511–3). Betances constantly warned Henna against the dangers of an annexation of Puerto Rico by the United States (Betances 2013, vol: 5, 503–4). In a letter to Hostos on June 7, 1898, weeks before the US invasion of Puerto Rico, Betances complained that "Henna is too much of a yankee" and that "Henna only worries about pulling away [arrancar] the island from the hands of Spaniards, even though it might fall later in those of the Americans as a territory" (Betances 2013 vol: 5, 507–9).

Always attentive to political strategy, in a letter to Henna weeks before the creation of the PRS, Betances recommends that Puerto Rican rebels in New York should appoint Estrada Palma, CRP delegate, as "Delegate of the Puerto Rican Revolutionary Party." He assumed that, by linking the fate of both islands in the Cuban struggle, Cuban rebels would have no other option than to negotiate Puerto Rico's independence when negotiating for Cuba's. See letter to Henna, November 14, 1895 (Betances 2013, vol 5:, 311–3).

On Puerto Rican annexationism in the nineteenth century, see: Meléndez (1993, ch. 2), Ramos (1987, 12–5), Rosario Natal (1985).

[12] The social class divisions were linked to political differences on Puerto Rico's destiny: "While the tobacco workers and others wanted nothing less than absolute Independence for the island, the professional and commercial sectors favored annexationism by the United States" (Ortiz 1986, 34).

[13] Aware of the conflicts between Estrada Palma and Henna, Betances warned Puerto Ricans not to break away from the Cuban party and the war effort there. Supporting Estrada Palma's position regarding Puerto Rico, Betances emphasized the need to marshal all resources to the Cuban war front as the priority for Cuban and Puerto Rican rebels. See letters to Henna in Betances (2013, 479–80, 487–8).

[14] According to Todd, the PRS Executive Committee sought US intervention because "we understood that once the situation in Cuba would be resolved, the United States could not have Puerto Rico in consideration since the inhabitants of this Island did not mobilize in a revolutionary and practical sense against Spain. Our organization had not achieved in its three years of propaganda to interest the Island in a war. The Executive Committee of this Section immediately agreed in personally contacting authorities in Washington..." (Todd 1938, 7).

[15] From France, Betances saw with sadness the conflicts between the CRP and the PRS and among Puerto Rican separatists as well. In a letter to Henna on July 22, 1898, days before the US invasion of Puerto Rico, Betances tells Henna to stop fighting with the Cuban leadership in New York and that he should ask Terreforte and Figueroa to join the PRS once again in the effort to win independence for Puerto Rico, claiming that all Puerto Ricans should be joining hands for this common goal. He ended his letter claiming "union, union, union!" (Betances 2013 vol: 5, 523-5).

Chapter 2

[1] In another article, the authors present the issue in the following manner: "These (the colonies), as once mentioned by one of the most eloquent Spanish orators, are not extensions of our country, but embryonic nationalities under tutelage as long as the conditions are not viable. But once these are obtained, and the inhabitants demonstrate through their culture that they are not inferior to the dominating nation; once the metropolis has given everything it could to the colony and by the influence of the agitation in which it finds itself immerged wants to be the owner of its destiny in order to set off and awaken its progress, it is reasonable to yield, and do so in time, if they do not want to face extreme resolutions that justice will eventually resolve—if unfortunately there is no other option—by reason of force" (Figueroa, Vélez Alvarado and Marín 1892e).

[2] Admiration for Betances is evident in the letter of appointment sent to him by the Club Borinquen as "honorary Chairman of our organization, which thus recognizes your indisputable eminence and the sacrifices you have made fully and completely to, first, educate our people in the pursuit of a free and independent life and, then, to struggle vigorously to establish it as a sovereign nation, and which, if unable to triumph in this most noble undertaking, has nonetheless kept alive the regionalist idea that today flourishes mightily again. We are pleased to raise this glorious banner around which all those who seek to achieve a free patria gather—without hatred or condemnation—on the path toward justice and dignity" (Club Patriótico Borinquen 1892).

The life and work of Betances is described in the following texts from Puerto Rico: Betances (1978), González Vales (1978), Guzmán Rodríguez (1943), Ojeda Reyes (n.d.), Suárez (1968, 1984), Rama (1980), Ramos Mattei (1987). Betances's writings are collected in Betances (2013 vol: 5).

[3] In "El Club Borinquen y Betances", Martí (1892k) describes Betances as "the son of wealth and culture—whose natural talents lifted him to the elegance and comforts of life. Those things he put aside when he saw that they must be acquired through sheer cunning and at the cost of his

honor. Rather than toil in the public service, allowing an ideology that debases humanity and obstructs the path to happiness to persist in his homeland—America—, he preferred always to work toward a political ideology that would lift the human condition and firmly establish its enduring happiness. With his feet rooted in history and his eyes fixed toward the future, he saw the independence of his homeland in the opportune combination of concession and resolve, and in the honest treatment of all the country's principled and constructive elements, rather than—foolishly and small-heartedly—in the cruel and indifferent treatment of its various elements. Noble is the man who is obstinate in rational virtue, devout in his heart, and tightly bound to good judgment. Noble is the man who has devoted his life—a somber shadow voluntarily cast over it—to rescuing the homeland through the united efforts of both the great and the humble." Further on, he adds: "stamping impatiently before injustice, activist in the colony, stoic in exile, compassionate in his bitterness... that man who, from the solace of his work, neither small-heartedly recalls the wealth he invested in the seeds of liberty for his patria's future prosperity, nor cowardly vacillates, but courageously stands up at the appointed time alongside the brave men who are forging the future, his fine compatriots in whom dignity takes refuge."

[4] The diplomatic correspondence of the CRP compiled by the Cuban National Archives reflects the importance of Betances's work for the party and the Antillean cause, as well as his relations with various factions of Cuban separatism. The book's introduction states that "one of the most active agents with whom the revolution counted on abroad was Dr. Betances" (PRC 1943–1946 vol: 1, IX). The third volume, dedicated to France, reflects "the efficiency and patriotism of the man that despite not being a fellow countryman, served the Cuban cause with valor and loving consideration" ((PRC 1943–1946 vol: III, V).

[5] The response of Betances to Henna reads the following: "Confidential: I must let you know that I have the following four: I am old, poor, sick, and ugly, and I must look handsome, strong, rich, and young. My incurable illness (albuminurea) is what unfortunately bothers me the most because of the pain. Also, Simplicia is sick (uterine fibrosis). With so many calamities, it is impossible for me to leave. I would have already been in New York if possible. Your question has been answered. Despite everything, Go Forward!" (Betances 1983, 270).

[6] For more on the Puerto Rican general, see Piedra (1945) and Ojeda Reyes (2007).

[7] In another writing, Martí elaborates further on this topic: "The patria is not meant to profit from the land, nor should one live off of it, like the worm off the tree. Rather, we are meant to give everything over to it, as parents give themselves to their children. The patria is not vengeance, forever excluding those who have sinned, nor a village where there is no room for those who live outside its borders. Rather, it is a heart with room for all" (1892b). On Puerto Rico's presence in the thought of Martí, see Armas (1985), Delgado Pasapera (1972), Ferrer Canales (1955).

[8] For a biography on Figueroa, see Toledo (1985).

[9] In a letter to Figueroa dated September 30, 1894, Martí advised his dear friend on a forthcoming issue of Patria, showing how much he trusted the Puerto Rican with his most treasured means of propaganda. "My absence and the delay with Patria will give you an idea of my work. Try to love me, follow me with good eyes, wherever I have to go..." He tells his friend to keep the newspaper "amiable, with a leading article of a public and popular soul, of revolutionary respect for the realities of the country"; like a doctor who cares for the sick "without

ever showing anger and without losing sight of philosophy..., and enhanced by the effort of combat and culture: something that puts the truth in the spirit, and leans, without saying, to October 10... And something of Puerto Rico?... Ah! Figueroa; How you are going to talk this October 10th! What a word and what a harangue! Make good for the two of us.... Without brothers, what would your... José Martí do?" (1975 vol: 3, 279–80).

[10] A similar appreciation is mentioned in the article "Hombres del día: Sotero Figueroa" (1901); a reprinted article from *La Vida* newspaper, Havana, Cuba. "Mr. Sotero Figueroa, whom today acts as the Secretary of the Provincial Government, has the glory of being one of the few who, beside the apostle Martí, has been present since the Father of our Nation began his glorious revolutionary campaign in the United States. Since that time, and in the *Patria* newspaper, established by José Martí, where Mr. Sotero Figueroa begins his proselytizing since its very its first issue. A highly educated writer, skillful and hardworking journalist, and making brilliant use of the language of Cervantes, his revolutionary soul dictated emotions and beautiful deeds that, along with the very few men that closely collaborated with Martí, laid the foundations of, let's put it this way, the independence of Cuba..."

[11] Originally published in La Igualdad, Havana, 1892.

[12] The relationship between Puerto Ricans and Martí is discussed in Ferrer Canales (1955), Roig de Leuchsenring (1974), Santiago Santovenia (1930) and Solá (1974).

[13] María Mercedes Solá comments: "Who would say by reading this that Martí was never in San Juan! Where did such extensive detail come from? Where did such an account come from? Towards the end, Martí tells us his source of information that is the culminating moment of the party 'a young man, fearless, with an indomitable gaze,' a Puerto Rican man, 'a virtuous son of both bloods' who talks to the Captain General with 'simple pride': Sotero Figueroa. How delightful it must have been for Figueroa to meticulously tell Martí this story from his youth! Or was it Martí, whose desire to visualize the story before writing it, who bothered him with questions on every detail?" (1974, 96).

[14] See also the following essays on Martí written by Puerto Ricans: Figueroa (1896) and the May 19, 1897 issue of the newspaper *Cuba y Puerto Rico* (edited by Puerto Rican Gerardo Forrest) dedicated to the memory of Martí, with articles by Forrest, Vélez Alvarado, and other Puerto Ricans. Another tribute to Martí comes from Marín (1900—reprinted).

[15] For more on La Doctrina de Martí, see: Deschamps Chapeaux (1975), González Veranes (1943) and Toledo (1985, 82–95).

[16] Betances's link to Puerto Rican independentistas in New York was through his longtime friend Henna. In his correspondence with Henna during this period, Betances warned the PRS leader against allowing the United States to annex Puerto Rico. Before the war began, Betances believed that public opinion in the United States and elsewhere would prevent the US government from openly annexing the island. He also sustained that if war erupted, Puerto Ricans should support the US war effort on the island against the Spanish regime. Once the war started, Betances encouraged Henna and others to engage in diplomatic negotiations with the US government to support Puerto Rican independence in exchange for close diplomatic and economic relations with the future Puerto Rican republic. At the same time, Betances was engaged in talks with Spanish representatives in France trying to convince the Spanish government that giving

the island its independence would be the only alternative to prevent Puerto Rico's annexation by the United States. Betances also urged Henna and others on the necessity of Puerto Ricans to rise up in armed rebellion against the Spanish regime before the United States invaded the island in order to prevent its annexation to the northern metropolis. See the following correspondence from Betances in Betances (2013 vol: 5): letters to José Julio Henna (pp. 499–500, 503–4, 531–2), to Eugenio María de Hostos (pp. 507–9) and to Manuel Guzmán Rodríguez (pp. 511–3).

[17] In a letter to Juan Gualberto Gómez dated May 27, 1898, Betances says: "And Puerto Rico?: It is with sadness that I observe the Cubans' indifference to this matter; and I will finish by establishing this relationship: Cuba: Puerto Rico: South America: Cuba... Ah, brotherhood! To be honest, I have only found two patriots among the Cubans that have expressed a positive interest in Borinquen: Javier Cisneros and you. Go and see how light-heartedly *El Porvenir* talks about the annexing of Puerto Rico compared to the independence of Cuba, as if by placing your left foot on the smallest Big Antille, the Yankees would not have their right heel lifted crossing over the Dominican Republic to step on Cuba's neck...Cubans and Puerto Ricans must dare to demand absolute independence of the Antilles from the American people. I would like to believe that if they are truly generous, they will not decide to use force to annex us. It is necessary that our islands abstain themselves from giving their entire body and soul to the American Union and that they be friendly not only to them but to all civilized nations; this will only be obtained with our absolute independence. Please work towards this, my friend, as I am sure Martí would if he were here" (Betances 1985, 416–7). The newspaper Betances is referring to, *El Porvenir*, was edited by Enrique Trujillo, who rejoined the party after Martí's death. See also, on the need to link Puerto Rico to the Cuban cause and war effort, Betances' correspondence in Betances 2013 vol: 5: to José Julio Henna (pp. 479–80, 487–8)); to Eugenio María de Hostos (pp. 507–9); to Manuel Guzmán Rodríguez (pp. 511–3).

[18] In January 1899, a Puerto Rican commision met with President McKinley in Washington to discuss the status of Puerto Rico in US plans. The Commission was formed by Hostos, Henna, and the autonomist Manuel Zeno Gandía. Among the issues discussed was the request to allow Puerto Ricans to decide their political future in a plebiscite that would include the options of statehood to the United States or independence (Delgado Cintrón 2006). Before the war began, Betances had suggested to Henna, Hostos and others the creation of a Puerto Rican commission to negotiate the island's future with US officials, including the possibility of holding a status plebiscite after the US takeover. See Betances' correspondence in Betances (2013 vol: 5): letter to José Julio Henna (pp. 523–5); letter to Eugenio María de Hostos (507–9); letter to Manuel Guzmán Rodríguez (511–3).

Chapter 3

[1] On how and why New York City became an economic, financial, and manufacturing center in the United States and its central links with Latin America and the Caribbean, see Glasser (2005).

[2] On the war of 1898 and the Sugar Trust, see Ayala (1999) and Sparrow (2006). On Puerto Rican tobacco industry during the last three decades of the nineteenth century, see Baldrich (2005)—with economic data in p. 160.

[3] There is no clear idea of how many Puerto Ricans were living in New York City during the nineteenth century. One answer to the very low numbers in the 1900 census might be that many Puerto Ricans left New York after 1898, either going back to Puerto Rico or to Cuba, like so many revolutionaries did. Carlos Vargas provides another explanation, saying that many might have been identified as Spaniards or Latin Americans by census takers or even by Puerto Ricans themselves.

[4] This translation is from Shnookal and Muñiz (2001, 172–6). On the turmoil of Cuban and Puerto Rican exiles living in the United States, struggling to make ends meet while at the same time devoting their lives to their homeland's freedom, living in a society marked by class struggles and racial hatreds, see Martí's "A la raíz" (1983e).

[5] Some of the extensive literature on these two leaders is cited in chapter 1 of this book.

[6] For a limited and definitely one-sided biography of his conservative and pro-annexationist PRS partner, see Todd (1930).

[7] On the Puerto Rican autonomist movement in the nineteenth century, see Barbosa de Rosario (1974), Cubano (1990) and Negrón Portillo (1983). Compontes refers to the different forms of bodily tortures and techniques used by the Spanish government against autonomists and those acused of separatism in 1887.

[8] Lidín recounts that, as told by Martí, when the Cuban leader first met the Puerto Rican poet he asked him if he was a fellow cubano, to which Marín replied: "Sí, señor, from the province of Puerto Rico" (1981, 124).

[9] Vélez Alvarado (1892—document 45) discusses how the anthem came into existance.

[10] The cigar incident is also referenced by Burrows and Wallace (1999, 1212). *Patria* published many instances of the financial support given by tabaqueros to the independence cause. One such example is related to the celebration of the October 10th commemoration in 1894 by a group of tobacco workers from Key West: "Cuban workers unanimously agree to work on OC-TOBER TEN, dedicating product to Revolutionary Treasure. We invite the exile community (*las emigraciones*) to solemnize in the same way" (*Patria*, October 10, 1894).

[11] The same number is quoted by Burrows and Wallace (1999, 1212).

[12] On the tobacco industry during this period, see Baldrich (2005). On the labor movement and struggles in the nineteenth and early-twentieth centuries, see García and Quintero Rivera (1991, chs. 1-4).

[13] Website of the Archives of the Cigar Makers' International Union, Special Collections, University of Maryland Libraries; http://hdl.handle.net/1903.1/1229. Accessed 2 July 2015.

Chapter 4

[1] "One of the strangest ads in the pages of Patria for a long time was for Carne líquida: extracto líquido de carne peptógeno y peptonizado, which might be translated as "Liquid meat: peptone and peptogenized liquid meat extract." It was invented by Dr. Valdés García from Montevideo, Uruguay, and was advertised as winning gold medals in fairs in Barcelona and Paris. It was described as "the healthiest and most effective extract of all food tonics known to this day."

REFERENCES

Agitación en Puerto Rico. 1894. *Patria* 8 December.

Aguirre, Sergio. 1982. Martí y el partido de la revolución. In *El partido revolucionario de José Martí*, eds. José Martí and others. 37–59. La Habana: Editorial Política.

Algo de todo. 1898. *Patria* 6 August.

Armas, Ramón de. 1975. La revolución pospuesta. La Habana: Editorial de Ciencias Sociales.

_____. 1985. Apuntes acerca de la estrategia continental de José Martí: el papel de Cuba y Puerto Rico. *Islas* 80(January-April), 9–34.

_____. 1990. José Martí: su república de mayoría popular. Revista de Ciencias Sociales 29(1-2), 139–56.

Ayala, César J. 1999. *American Sugar Kingdom: The Plantation Economy of the Spanish Caribbean, 1898-1934*. Chapel Hill: University of North Carolina Press.

Azcuy, Fanny. 1930. *El Partido Revolucionario y la independencia de Cuba*. La Habana: Molina.

Baldrich, Juan José. 2005. From Handcrafted Tobacco Rolls to Machine-made Cigarettes: The Transformation and Americanization of Puerto Rican Tobacco, 1847-1903. *CENTRO: Journal of the Center for Puerto Rican Studies* 17(2), 145–69.

Barbosa de Rosario, Pilar. 1974. *De Baldorioty a Barbosa: historia del autonomismo puertorriqueño*. San Juan: La Obra de José Celso Barbosa.

Bases del Partido Revolucionario Cubano. 1892. *Patria* 14 March.

Betances, Ramón Emeterio. 1892. La voz de un patriota. *Patria* 8 October.

_____. 1893. Con la revolución. *Patria* 23 September.

_____. 1895. A los puertorriqueños. *Patria* 4 May.

_____. 1978. *Obras del doctor Ramón Emeterio Betances II: Epistolario año 1895*. Edited and with an introduction by Ada Suárez. Río Piedras, PR: Ediciones Huracán.

_____. 1983. *Ramón Emeterio Betances*. Edited by Haroldo Dilla and Emilio Godínez. La Habana: Casa de las Américas.

_____. 1985. *Cuba en Betances*. Edited by Emilio Godínez Sosa, La Habana: Editorial de Ciencias Sociales.

_____. 2013. *Ramón Emeterio Betances: obras completas*. Edited by Félix Ojeda Reyes and Paul Estrade. San Juan: Ediciones Puerto.

Blasco, Eusebio. 1898. Betances. *Patria* 28 September.

Bonafoux, Luis. 1987. *Betances*. San Juan: Instituto de Cultura Puertorriqueña.

Borinquen: Club Político Antillano. 1892. *Patria* 1 October.

Burrrows, Edwin G. and Mike Wallace. 1999. *Gotham: A History of New York City to 1898*. New York: Oxford University Press.

Carroll, Henry K. 1975 [1899]. *Report on the Island of Porto Rico*. New York: Arno Press.

Casasus, Juan J. E. 1953. *La emigración cubana y la independencia de la patria*. La Habana: Editorial Lex.

Centro de Estudios Martianos. 1984. *José Martí, antimperialista*. La Habana: Editorial de Ciencias Sociales.

_____. 1989. Simposio Internacional: Pensamiento Político y Antimperialismo en José

Martí. La Habana: Editorial de Ciencias Sociales.

Citación del Club Borinquen. 1895. *Patria* 4 March.

Club Borinquen. 1892. Al pueblo puertorriqueño. *Patria* 14 March.

Club Borinquen. 1894. *Patria* 15 December.

Club Mercedes Varona. 1896. *Patria* 25 January.

Club Patriótico Borinquen. 1892. *Patria* 10 April.

Colón, E. D. 1930. *Datos sobre la agricultura de Puerto Rico antes de 1898*. San Juan: Tipografía Cantero, Fernández & Co.

Comisión Pro Celebración del Centenario del Natalicio de Hostos. 1954. *Hostos, peregrino del ideal*. Paris: Ediciones Literarias y Artísticas.

Cubano Iguina, Astrid. 1990. *El hilo en el laberinto: claves de la lucha política en Puerto Rico (siglo XIX)*. Río Piedras, PR: Ediciones Huracán.

Dávila, Ovidio. 2002. *Antonio Vélez Alvarado: amigo y colaborador de Martí y Betances*. San Juan: Instituto de Cultura Puertorriqueña.

de la Luz León, José. 1947. *La diplomacia de la manigua: Betances*. La Habana: Editorial Lex.

Delgado Cintrón, Carmelo. 2006. El pensamiento de Hostos frente a la invasión y anexión de Puerto Rico. *Focus* 5(2), 59–77.

Delgado Pasapera, Germán. 1972. Puerto Rico en el pensamiento de José Martí. *Atenea* 9(1-2), 89–96.

_____. 1984. *Puerto Rico: sus luchas emancipadoras*. Río Piedras, PR: Editorial Cultural.

Deschamps Chapeaux, Pedro.1975. *Rafael Serra y Montalvo: Obrero incansable de nuestra independencia*. La Habana: Unión de Escritores y Artistas de Cuba.

Diez de octubre en Chickering Hall. 1895. *Patria* 12 October.

El 10 de octubre. 1892. *Patria* 15 October.

El banquete. 1892. *Patria* 1 November.

El meeting. 1895. *Patria* 24 February.

El meeting de Hardman Hall.1893. *Patria* 8 May.

El movimiento de Yauco. 1897a. *Patria* 14 April.

El periódico. 1893. *Patria* 17 June.

El Postillón, por Francisco Gonzalo Marín. 1892. *Patria* 22 October.

En Puerto Rico. 1887a. *Patria* 18 September.

En honor del general Rius Rivera.1898. *Patria* 31 December.

Estrade, Paul. 1983. *José Martí: militante y estratega*. La Habana: Editorial de Ciencias Sociales.

_____. 1984. *La colonia cubana de París, 1895-1898*. La Habana: Editorial de Ciencias Sociales.

Fair Cigar Fabricators: Women Far Superior to Men in Their Delicacy of Touch and Dexterity. 1887. *St. Paul Daily Globe* 14 November, 2. Accessed 2 July 2015.   < http://www. nationalcigarmuseum.com/Site/NCM_HOME.html/>.

Ferrer Canales, José. 1955. Martí y Puerto Rico. *Cuadernos americanos* 14(2), 141–69.

_____. 2001. *Martí y Hostos*. San Juan: Instituto de Estudios Hostosianos and Centro de Estudios Avanzados de Puerto Rico y el Caribe.

Figueroa, Loida. 1985. Los combatientes puertorriqueños en las guerras de independencia de

Cuba. *Revista de Historia* 1(2), 131–48.

Figueroa, Sotero. 1892a. La verdad de la historia I. *Patria* 19 March.

_____. 1892b. En la ratificación. *Patria* 19 March.

_____. 1892c. La verdad de la historia II. *Patria* 3 April.

_____. 1892d. La verdad de la historia III. *Patria* 16 April.

_____. 1892e. Discurso en la confirmación de la proclamación del Partido Revolucionario Cubano. *Patria* 23 April.

_____. 1892f. La verdad de la historia IV. *Patria* 21 May.

_____. 1892g. La verdad de la historia V. *Patria* 11 June.

_____. 1892h. La verdad de la historia VI. *Patria* 2 July.

_____. 1893a. Sr. Sotero Figueroa [Discurso]. *Patria* 4 February.

_____. 1893b. Sr. Sotero Figueroa [Discurso]. *Patria* 14 October.

_____. 1895a. ¡INMORTAL! *Patria* 25 June.

_____. 1895b. Meeting de proclamación. *Patria* 20 July.

_____. 1896. José Martí: Apóstol. *La Doctrina de Martí* 10 October.

_____. 1977. *Sotero Figueroa, La verdad de la historia*. Edited by Carlos Ripoll. San Juan: Instituto de Cultura Puertorriqueña.

Figueroa, Sotero, Antonio Vélez Alvarado and Francisco Gonzalo Marín 1892a. Al pueblo puertorriqueño. *Patria*. 14 March.

_____. 1892b. La dominación y la independencia I. *Patria* 16 July.

_____. 1892c. La dominación y la independencia II. *Patria* 6 August.

_____. 1892d. La dominación y la independencia III. *Patria* 20 August.

_____. 1892e. La dominación y la independencia IV. *Patria* 17 September.

_____. 1892f. La dominación y la independencia V. *Patria* 24 September.

Foner, Philip S. 1963. *A History of Cuba and Its Relations with the United States, vol. II [1848-1895]*. New York: International Publishers.

Fraga, Juan and Sotero Figueroa. 1893. Comunicaciones oficiales: El diez de octubre en Hardman Hall. *Patria* 6 October.

Freire, Joaquín. 1966. *Presencia de Puerto Rico en la historia de Cuba*. San Juan: Instituto de Cultura Puertorriqueña.

García, Gervasio and A. G. Quintero-Rivera. 1991. *Desafío y solidaridad: breve historia del movimiento obrero puertorriqueño*. Río Piedras, PR: Ediciones Huracán.

Glasser, Edward L. 2005. Urban Colossus: Why Is New York America's Largest City. *FRBNY Economic Policy Review* 11(December), 7–24.

González, José Emilio. 1986. Hostos y la Confederación de las Antillas. *Revista Jurídica de la Universidad de Puerto Rico* 55, 175–84.

González Vales, Luis. 1978. *Betances en París: historia de una misión diplomática*. San Juan: Colegio de Abogados.

González Veranes, Pedro N. 1943. *La personalidad de Rafael Serra y sus relaciones con Martí*. La Habana: Imprenta La Verónica.

Guzmán Rodríguez, Manuel. 1943. *Epistolario del Dr. Betances*. Mayagüez, PR: Tipografía Comercial.

Haslip-Viera, Gabriel. 2010. The Evolution of the Latino Community in New York City: Early Nineteenth Century to the 1990s. In *Hispanic New York: A Sourcebook*, ed Claudio Iván Remeseira. 33–53. New York: Columbia University Press.

Hermanas de Betances. 1895. *Patria* 23 October.

Hermanas de Rius Rivera. 1897. *Patria* 13 February.

Hidalgo Paz, Ibrahím. 1981. Reseña de los clubs fundadores del Partido Revolucionario Cubano. *Anuario del Centro de Estudios Martianos* 4, 208–30.

_____. 1989. *Incursiones en la obra de José Martí*. La Habana: Editorial de Ciencias Sociales.

Hombres del día: Sotero Figueroa. 1901. *Puerto Rico Ilustrado* 11 November.

Hostos, Eugenio María de. 1898. La Liga de Patriotas. *Patria* 10 September.

_____. 1980. *América: la lucha por la libertad*. Edited by Manuel Maldonado Denis. Mexico, DF: Siglo XIX Editores.

Ibarra, Jorge. 1981. *José Martí: Dirigente político e ideólogo revolucionario*. Mexico, DF: Editorial Nuestro Tiempo.

Jiménez de Wagenheim, Olga. 1985. *El Grito de Lares*. Río Piedras, PR: Ediciones Huracán.

José de Celis Aguilera. 1894. *Patria* 16 January.

La espontaneidad del patriotismo. 1893. *Patria* 10 April.

La fraternidad antillana. 1893. *Patria* 19 December.

La grandeza de un pueblo. 1894. *Patria* 8 July.

La única solución. 1897. *Patria* 17 October.

Las noticias. 1898a. *Patria* 23 July.

Las noticias. 1898b. *Patria* 30 July.

Las noticias. 1898c. *Patria* 3 August.

La reunión de los clubes. 1892. *Patria* 1 November.

La reunión pública. 1893. *Patria* 4 February.

La Sociedad Literaria. 1892. *Patria* 1 November.

Lección de Puerto Rico. *Patria* 6 August.

Lidín, Harold J. 1981. *History of the Puerto Rican Independence Movement Vol. I (19th century)*. San Juan: Master Typesetting.

Llanos, Marcos. 1975. Creación e intención del Partido Revolucionario Cubano. *Santiago* 20, 203–36.

Los Clubs: Club Borinquen [Condolences for the death of Martí]. 1895. *Patria* 25 June.

Lunes en la Liga. 1892. *Patria* 14 May.

Maldonado Denis, Manuel. 1985. Martí y Hostos: paralelismos en la lucha de ambos por la independencia de las Antillas en el siglo XIX. *La Revista del Centro de Estudios Avanzados de Puerto Rico y el Caribe* 1(July-December), 105–14.

Marín, Francisco Gonzalo "Pachín". 1896. Wenceslao Tomás Marín. *Patria* 13 June.

_____. 1900. Martí. *Cuba y América* 20 August, 11.

Martí, José. 1892a. Nuestras ideas. *Patria* 14 March.

_____. 1892b. Patria. *Patria* 14 March.

_____. 1892c. A nuestra prensa. *Patria* 14 March.

_____. 1892d. El convite a Puerto Rico. *Patria* 14 March.

_____. 1892e. La acción unánime. *Patria* 14 March.

_____. 1892f. La sesión del Club Borinquen *Patria* 14 March.

_____. 1892g. La proclamación. *Patria* 16 April.

_____. 1892h. Palabra generosa. *Patria* 10 April.

_____. 1892i. El poeta Marín. *Patria* 20 April.

_____. 1892j. Las Antillas y Baldorioty de Castro. *Patria* 14 May.

_____. 1892k. El Club Borinquen y Betances. *Patria* 4 June.

_____. 1892l. Nuestros periódicos. *Patria* 11 June.

_____. 1892m. Ana Otero. *Patria* 20 August.

_____. 1892n. El delegado en Nueva York: El Club Mercedes Varona. *Patria* 1 November.

_____. 1892o. El delegado en Nueva York; En La Liga. *Patria* 1 November.

_____. 1893a. ¡Vengo a darte patria!: Puerto Rico y Cuba. *Patria* 14 March.

_____. 1893b. El 22 de marzo del 1873: La abolición de la esclavitud en Puerto Rico. *Patria* 1 April.

_____. 1893c. El domingo, para la patria; los tabaqueros de la casa de O'Halloran. *Patria* 10 April.

_____. 1893d. Pobreza y patria. *Patria* 19 August.

_____. 1893e. A la raíz. *Patria* 26 August.

_____. 1893f. Banquete patrio del club 'Las Dos Antillas'. *Patria* 21 November.

_____. 1894a. Adiós a una hermana. *Patria* 2 March.

_____. 1894b. La verdad sobre Estados Unidos. *Patria* 23 March.

_____. 1894c. El tercer año del Partido Revolucionario Cubano: el alma de la revolución y el deber de Cuba en América. *Patria* 17 April.

_____. 1894d. Club Borinquen. *Patria* 10 April.

_____. 1894e. Nuestro adiós al General. *Patria* 21 April.

_____. 1894f. El adiós del general. *Patria* 21 April.

_____. 1894g. La imprenta Figueroa. *Patria* 8 September.

_____. 1895a. En casa. *Patria* 19 January.

_____. 1895b. Historia vieja y nueva: La Historia de Puerto Rico de Salvador Brau. *Patria* 26 January.

_____. 1970. *Martí y Puerto Rico*. Edited by Carlos A. Montaner. Río Piedras, PR: Editorial San Juan.

_____. 1975. *José Martí: Obras completas*. La Habana: Editorial de Ciencias Sociales.

_____. 1978. *El Partido Revolucionario y la guerra*. La Habana: Editorial de Ciencias Sociales.

_____. 1999. *José Martí Reader: Writings on the Americas*. Edited by Deborah Shnookal and Mirta Muñiz. Melbourne: Ocean Press.

Mathews, Thomas. 1955. The Project for a Confederation of the Greater Antilles. *Historia* 5(2), 183–231.

Mattos Cintrón, Wilfredo. 1980. *La política y lo político en Puerto Rico*. Mexico, DF: Ediciones Era.

Meléndez, Edgardo. 1988. *Puerto Rico's Statehood Movement*. Westport, CT: Greenwood Press.

_____. 1993. *Movimiento anexionista en Puerto Rico*. Río Piedras: Editorial de la Universidad de Puerto Rico.

Negrón Portillo, Mariano, 1981. *El autonomismo puertorriqueño*. Río Piedras, PR: Editorial Huracán.

Notas de los clubes puertorriqueños. 1895. *Patria* 17 June.

Nuestras mujeres. 1892. *Patria* 27 August.

Ojeda Reyes, Félix. 1992. *Peregrinos de la libertad*. Río Piedras: Editorial de la Universidad de Puerto Rico.

_____. 2007. *General Juan Rius Rivera: Héroe militar de Cuba, poderoso banquero y empresario de Honduras*. San Juan: Ediciones Puerto.

_____. n.d. La Manigua en París: Correspondencia diplomática de Betances. San Juan: Centro de Estudios Avanzados de Puerto Rico y el Caribe and Centro de Estudios Puertorriqueños.

Ortiz, Victoria. 1986. *The Legacy of Arthur A. Schomburg: A Celebration of the Past, A Vision for the Future*. New York: The Schomburg Center for Research in Black Culture.

Otra vez en Hardman Hall. 1893. *Patria* 27 May.

Partido Revolucionario Cubano [PRC]. 1932–1937. *La revolución del 95 según la correspondencia de la Delegación Cubana en Nueva York, Vol. V*. La Habana: Editorial Habanera.

_____. 1943–1946. *Correspondencia diplomática de la delegación cubana en Nueva York durante la guerra de independencia de 1895 a 1898*. La Habana: Publicaciones del Archivo Nacional de Cuba.

Partido Revolucionario Cubano—Sección Puerto Rico [PRC-SPR]. 1898. Memoria de los trabajos realizados por la Sección Puerto Rico del Partido Revolucionario Cubano de 1895 a 1898. New York: A. W. Howes.

Pedreira, Antonio S. 1932. *Hostos, ciudadano de América*. Madrid: Espasa-Calpe.

Pérez, Lisandro. 2010. Cubans in Nineteenth Century New York: A Story of Sugar, War and Revolution. In *Nueva York 1613-1945*, ed. Edward J. Sullivan. 97–103. New York: The New York Historical Society and Scala Publishers.

Pérez, Louis A, Jr. 1978. Cubans in Tampa; from Exiles to Immigrants, 1892-1901. *Florida Historical Quarterly* 57(October), 129–40.

_____. 1983. *Cuba Between Empires, 1878-1902*. Pittsburgh: University of Pittsburgh Press.

Perloff, Harvey S. 1975. *Puerto Rico's Economic Future*. Chicago: University of Chicago Press.

Piedra, Manuel. 1945. *Juan Rius Rivera y la independencia de Cuba*. La Habana: Imprenta El Siglo XX.

Por Puerto Rico. 1894a. *Patria* 23 June.

Por Puerto Rico. 1894b. *Patria* 28 July.

Poyo, Gerald E. 1983. Cuban Émigré Communities in the United States and the Independence of Their Homeland, 1852-1895. Ph.D. dissertation, University of Florida.

_____. 1989. *With All, and for the Good of All": The Emergence of Popular Nationalism in the Cuban Communities of the United States, 1848-1898*. Durham, NC: Duke University Press.

Preece, Carol A. 1976. Insurgent Guests: The Cuban Revolutionary Party and Its Activities in the United States, 1892-1898. Ph.D. dissertation, Georgetown University.

Puerto Rico. 1895. *Patria* 18 March.

Quesada, Gonzalo de. 1982. Labor del Partido Revolucionario Cubano. In *El Partido Revolucionario de José Martí*, eds. José Martí and others. 8–22. La Habana: Editorial Política.

Quintero-Rivera, A.G. 1976. *Conflictos de clase y política en Puerto Rico*. Río Piedras, PR: Editorial Huracán.

Rama, Carlos M. 1980. *La independencia de las Antillas y Ramón Emeterio Betances*. San Juan: Instituto de Cultura Puertorriqueña.

Ramos, Aarón G. 1987. *Las ideas anexionistas en Puerto Rico bajo la dominación norteamericana*. Río Piedras, PR: Ediciones Huracán.

Ramos Mattei, Andrés. 1981. *La hacienda azucarera: su crecimiento y crisis en Puerto Rico (siglo XIX)*. San Juan: CEREP.

_____. 1987. *Betances en el ciclo revolucionario Antillano: 1867-1875*. San Juan: Instituto de Cultura Puertorriqueña.

Revolucionarios puertorriqueños. 1894. *Patria* 25 August.

Reyes, América and Jorge M. Ruscalleda. 1973. El ideal de la Confederación de las grandes Antillas españolas en Eugenio María de Hostos y José Martí. *Revista del Instituto de Cultura Puertorriqueña* 16(58), 39–55.

Rius Rivera. 1897. *Patria* 3 April.

Rodríguez de Tió, Lola. 1898. 10 de octubre. *Patria* 12 October.

Roig de Leuchsenring, Emilio. 1939. *Hostos, apóstol de la independencia de Cuba y Puerto Rico*. La Habana: Municipio de la Habana.

_____. 1974. *Hostos y Cuba*. La Habana: Editorial de Ciencias Sociales.

_____. 1983. *Tres estudios Martianos*. La Habana: Centro de Estudios Martianos.

Rosario Natal, Carmelo. 1970. *El debate sobre el origen de la actual bandera puertorriqueña: un análisis crítico*. Río Piedras: Editorial Universidad de Puerto Rico.

_____. 1985. Betances y los anexionistas, 1850-1870: Apuntes sobre un problema. *Revista de Historia* 1(2), 113–30.

Sánchez Korrol, Virginia. 2010. Puerto Ricans in 'Olde' *Nueva York*: Migrant Colonias of the Nineteenth and Twentieth Centuries. In *Nueva York 1613*-1945, ed. Edward J. Sullivan. 110–20. New York: The New York Historical Society and Scala Publishers.

Santiago Santovenia, Emeterio. 1930. Hostos, precursor de Martí. *Revista Bimestre Cubana* 21(26), 249–53.

Serra, Rafael. 1897. El periódico Patria. *La Doctrina de Martí* 15 January.

Solá, María Mercedes. 1974. Presencia de Puerto Rico y los puertorriqueños en Martí (Un aspecto del desarrollo de su pensamiento antillano). In *Estudios Martianos*. 87–97. Río Piedras: Editorial Universitaria.

Sparrow, Bartholomew H. 2006. *The Insular Cases and the Emergence of American Empire*. Kansas City: University Press of Kansas.

Suárez, Ada. 1968. *El Dr. Ramón Emeterio Betances: su vida y su obra*. San Juan: Ateneo Puertorriqueño.

_____. 1984. *El doctor Ramón Emeterio Betances y la abolición de la esclavitud*. San Juan: Instituto de Cultura Puertorriqueña.

Terreforte, J. M. 1895. Nuestro hermano. *Patria* 25 June.

The Makers of Cigars. 1887. *The New York Sun* 28 October. Accessed 2 July 2015. < http://www.nationalcigarmuseum.com/Site/NCM_HOME.html/>.

Tirado Merced, Dulce M. 1981. Las raíces sociales del liberalismo criollo: el Partido Liberal Reformista (1870-1875). Master's Thesis, University of Puerto Rico.

Todd, Roberto H. 1930. *José Julio Henna, 1848-1924*. San Juan: Cantero-Fernández, Co.

_____. 1938. *La invasión americana: cómo surgió la idea de traer la guerra a Puerto Rico*. San Juan: Cantero Fernández, Co.

Toledo, Josefina. 1985. *Sotero Figueroa: Editor de Patria*. La Habana: Editorial Letras Cubanas.

_____. 2002. *Lola Rodríguez de Tió; contribución para un estudio integral*. San Juan: Editorial LEA-Ateneo Puertorriqueño.

Torres-Cuevas, Eduardo, Mario Mencía and Augusto E. Benítez. 1984. *El alma visible de Cuba: José Martí y el Partido Revolucionario Cubano*. La Habana: Editorial de Ciencias Sociales.

True, Marshall M. 1965. Revolutionaries in Exile: The Cuban Revolutionary Party, 1891-1898. Ph.D. dissertation, University of Virginia.

Vega, Bernardo. 1977. Memorias de Bernardo Vega. Edited by César Andreu Iglesias. Río Piedras, PR: Ediciones Huracán.

Vélez Alvarado, Antonio. 1892. El himno borincano. *Patria* 3 September.

Wallace, Mike. 2010. *Nueva York*: The Back Story; New York City and the Spanish-Speaking World from Dutch Days to the Second World War. In *Nueva York 1613-1945*, ed. Edward J. Sullivan. 25–30. New York: The New York Historical Society and Scala Publishers.

APPENDIX

Documents listed in chronological order according to publication date.

1. "Platform of the *Partido Revolucionario Cubano*," #1, March 14 1892
2. *Club Borinquen*, "To the People of Puerto Rico" (ibidem)
3. José Martí, "*Club Borinquen* Session," (ibidem)
4. Sotero Figueroa, "At the Ratification" #2, March 19, 1892
5. Sotero Figueroa, "The Truth about History, I," #2, March 19, 1892
6. Francisco Gonzalo Marín, "A Slap in the Face," #3, March 26, 1892
7. Sotero Figueroa, "The Truth about History, II," #4, April 3, 1892
8. José Martí, "*Borinquen to PATRIA*," (Ibidem)
9. José Martí, "Facts and Ideas" (ibidem)
10. "Patriotic *Club Borinquen*," #6, April 16, 1892
11. José Martí, "Benevolent Words," (ibidem)
12. Sotero Figueroa, "The Truth about History, III" (ibidem)
13. José Martí, "The Proclamation," (ibidem)
14. José Martí, "The Poet Marín," #7, April 23, 1892
15. Sotero Figueroa, "Speeches at the Confirmation of the Proclamation of the *Partido Revolucionario Cubano*" (ibidem)
16. Sotero Figueroa, Antonio Vélez Alvarado, Francisco Gonzalo Marín, "Let Us Have a Discussion (To the Puerto Rican Press)," #9, May 7, 1892
17. José Martí, "The Antilles and Baldorioty Castro," #10, May 14, 1892
18. Sotero Figueroa, "The Truth about History, IV," #11, May 21, 1892
19. José Martí, "*Club Borinquen* and Betances," #13, June 4, 1892
20. Sotero Figueroa, "The Truth about History, V," #14, June 11, 1892
21. José Martí, "Our Newspapers" (ibidem)
22. Sotero Figueroa, "The Truth about History, VI," #17, July 2, 1892
23. Sotero Figueroa, Antonio Vélez Alvarado, Francisco Gonzalo Marín, "Domination and Independence, I," #19, July 16, 1892
24. Sotero Figueroa, Antonio Vélez Alvarado, Francisco Gonzalo Marín, "Domination and Independence, II," #22, August 6, 1892
25. Sotero Figueroa, Antonio Vélez Alvarado, Francisco Gonzalo Marín, "Domination and Independence, III," #24, August 20, 1892
26. José Martí, "Ana Otero" (ibidem)
27. Antonio Vélez Alvarado, "The Puerto Rican Anthem," #26, September 3, 1892
28. Sotero Figueroa, Antonio Vélez Alvarado, Francisco Gonzalo Marín, "Domination and Independence, IV," #28, September 17, 1892
29. Sotero Figueroa, Antonio Vélez Alvarado, Francisco Gonzalo Marín, "Domination and Independence, V," #29, September 24, 1892
30. "*Borinquen*: Antillean Political Club," #30, October 1, 1892
31. Betances, "The Voice of a Patriot," #31, October 8, 1892
32. José Martí, "Club Mercedes *Varona*," #34, November 4, 1892
33. José Martí, "Ana Otero, February 3," #46, January 21, 1893

34. José Martí, "Ana Otero's Concert," #47, January 28, 1893

35. "Sotero Figueroa" (Speech), #48, February 4, 1893

36. José Martí, "¡*Vengo a darte patria!*': Puerto Rico and Cuba," #53, March 14, 1893

37. José Martí, "March 22, 1873: The Abolition of Slavery in Puerto Rico," #55, April 1, 1893

38. "Communication from Sotero Figueroa to José Martí," #57, April 16, 1893

39. "Sotero Figueroa" (Speech), #60, April 29, 1893

40. José Martí, "Poverty and *Patria*," #75, August 19, 1893

41. Betances, "With the Revolution," #79, September 23, 1893

42. "The Honorable Sotero Figueroa" (Speech), #82, October 14, 1893

43. José Martí, "Patriotic Banquet of *Club Las Dos Antillas*," #87, November 21, 1893

44. José Martí, "The Revolution in Puerto Rico," #93, January 6, 1894

45. "José de Celis Aguilera," #94, January 16, 1894

46. José Martí, "Farewell to a Sister," #101, March 2, 1894

47. José Martí, "*Club Borinquen*," #108, April 17, 1894

48. José Martí, "The Third Year of the *Partido Revolucionario Cubano*: The Soul of the Revolution and Cuba's Duty in the Americas" (ibidem)

49. "For Puerto Rico," #117, June 23, 1894

50. Sotero Figueroa, "Declarations," #118, June 30, 1894

51."For Puerto Rico," #122, July 28, 1894

52. "Puerto Rican Revolutionaries," #126, August 25, 1894

53. José Martí, "The Figueroa Press," #128, September 8, 1894

54. "Agitation in Puerto Rico," #140, December 8, 1894

55. "*Club Borinquen*," #141, December 15, 1894

56. José Martí, "Old and New History: Salvador Brau's *Historia de Puerto Rico*," #75, January 26, 1895

57. "Meeting Announcement from *Club Borinquen*," #151, March 4, 1895

58. "Puerto Rico," #153, March 18, 1895

59. Betances, "To Puerto Ricans," #160, May 4, 1895

60. "For Puerto Rico" (ibidem)

61. "Notes from the Clubs of Puerto Rico," #166, June 17, 1895

62. Sotero Figueroa, "Immortal!" #167, June 25, 1895

63. J.M. Terreforte, "Our Brother" (ibidem)

64. "The Clubs: *Club Borinquen*" (ibidem)

65. Sotero Figueroa, "Inaugural Meeting," #171, July 20, 1895

66. Sotero Figueroa, "*Club Los Independientes to José Martí*" (ibidem)

67. "The Forrest Incident," #173, August 3, 1895

68. "*Hermanas de Betances*," #189, October 23, 1895

69. Gumersindo Rivas, "Speech by Mr. Rivas," #191, October 30, 1895

70. "In Paris," #215, January 22, 1896

71. "*Club Mercedes Varona*," #216, January 25, 1896

72. "Cuba in Paris," #232, March 21, 1896

73. Francisco Gonzalo Marín, "Wenceslao Tomás Marín," #256, June 13, 1896

74. *"Hermanas de Rius Rivera,"* #326, February 13, 1897

75. "Rius Rivera," #340, April 3, 1897

76. "Puerto Rico," #342, April 10, 1897

77. "The Yauco Rebellion," #343, April 14, 1897

78. "In Puerto Rico," #388, September 18, 1897

79. "The Only Solution," #395, October 13, 1897

80. Betances, "From Paris," #420, January 8, 1898

81. "New Newspaper," #428, February 5, 1898

82. "The Situation in Puerto Rico," #469, June 29, 1898

83. "The News," #476, July 23, 1898

84. "The News," #478, July 30, 1898

85. "The News," #479, August 3, 1898

86. "Lesson from Puerto Rico," #480, August 6, 1898

87. "A Little Bit of Everything," (Dissolution of the SPR), #480, August 6, 1898

88. Eugenio María de Hostos, *"Liga de Patriotas Puertorriqueños,"* #490, September 10, 1898

89. Eusebio Blasco, "Betances," #495, September 28, 1898

90. Lola Rodríguez de Tió, "October 10!" #499, October 12, 1898

91. "In Honor of General Rius Rivera," #522, December 31, 1898

ABOUT THE AUTHOR

Edgardo Meléndez is Professor in the Department of Africana and Puerto Rican/ Latino Studies at Hunter College. He also taught for many years in the Department of Political Science at the University of Puerto Rico-Río Piedras. Among his publications are: *Sponsored Migration: The State and Postwar Puerto Rican Migration to the United States* (The Ohio State University Press, 2017); *Puerto Rican Government and Politics: A Comprehensive Bibliography* (Lynne Rienner Publishers, 2000), awarded the 2000 Outstanding Academic Title by *Choice*; *Partidos, política pública y status en Puerto Rico* (Ediciones Nueva Aurora, 1998); *Puerto Rico en "Patria"* (Editorial Edil, 1996); *Movimiento anexionista en Puerto Rico* (University of Puerto Rico Press, 1993); and *Puerto Rico's Statehood Movement* (Greenwood Press, 1988). He is coeditor with Edwin Meléndez of *Colonial Dilemma: Critical Perspectives on Contemporary Puerto Rico* (South End Press, 1993); and coeditor with Charles Venator-Santiago of the Special issue of *Centro Journal* "U.S. Citizenship in Puerto Rico: One Hundred Years After the Jones Act" (Spring 2017). He has also published in several academic journals, including *CENTRO Journal, Revista de ftlineCiencias Sociales* (Puerto Rico), *Homines* (Puerto Rico), *Revista de Administración Pública* (Puerto Rico), and *Radical America*, among others. He is currently working on issues related to Puerto Rican migration, political incorporation, and citizenship. His forthcoming book is tentatively titled "The Puerto Rican Problem in New York City, 1945-1960: Migration and Incorporation from the Periphery of the American Empire."

Made in the USA
Middletown, DE
22 January 2021